Open Source Intelligence in a Networked World

Open Source Intelligence in a Networked World

ANTHONY OLCOTT

continuum

The Continuum International Publishing Group

The Tower Building	80 Maiden Lane
11 York Road	Suite 704
London	New York
SE1 7NX	NY 10038

www.continuumbooks.com

ISBN: 9781441166081

Typeset by Fakenham Prepress Solutions, Fakenham, Norfolk NR21 8NN, UK
Printed in the United States of America

CONTENTS

FOREWORD

My first book-length manuscript was a PhD thesis. I began the research in 1973 and submitted the completed manuscript in 1976. The manuscript was about 300 pages long – laboriously typed, if I remember correctly, by me, then photocopied (at a nickel a page, meaning two copies cost about two weeks of my first-year professorial take-home pay). I presume that the dissertation even now sits in its red library cover somewhere in the bowels of Stanford's Memorial Library, visited only by the occasional spider.

This book is the nineteenth book-length manuscript I have completed since that time – the fourteenth to be published, plus the PhD dissertation, plus three novels that were still-born. Only one other of these books was an academic study, with footnotes and the other professional apparatuses – my maculate career has also included five book-length translations, several edited volumes (including at least one which I had to rewrite completely in order to give the various authors a consistent voice), and five published novels.

I tell you this not to boast, or to assure you that what follows may at least be literately composed, but rather because the experience of writing this book was fundamentally different from anything I had written before. Those differences are, in short, what this book is about.

That was then

Other than the QWERTY keyboard, my earlier composition experiences had basically nothing in common with what I experienced with this one. Research, for example – both for the PhD thesis in the mid-1970s and for a book of literary criticism written in the late 1990s and published in 2001 – the research method was the same. I had to seek out, track down, and physically acquire the materials on which I would base my studies. In both cases I had to travel to Russia, in the first instance to get access to old newspapers and out-of-print books held in a handful of libraries scattered across the USSR (which would have been tough to access even without the obstructionist bureaucracy of Soviet libraries, archives, and universities), and in the second to buy the pulp fiction and weekly news magazines I needed for my study of Russian detective fiction. In the first case, of course, there was nothing like the internet – research consisted of chasing footnotes through the card catalog (dingy limp slices of grey cardboard, many with handwritten entries), then hand-copying the desired bits onto other 3x5 cards or sheets of paper (using really leaky Soviet ballpoint pens). Since there was no way of being quite sure what you might need when you actually started writing, you tended to over-copy (I remember hand-copying at least three short books in their entirety) – and *still* when it came to actual composing, often enough a dimly remembered phrase would spring to mind, not copied down, and still in a volume on a shelf somewhere deep in Lenin Library, the other side of the ocean, and of the Iron Curtain. My wife and I used to joke that we should source all of those half-remembered phrases to *Dalekii Narynets*, a made-up newspaper which, if had existed, would have been published in the most remote city (Naryn) of the most remote Soviet republic (Kyrgyz SSR) – because who could possibly check the accuracy of our quotations?

Life was far better by the second volume – I could compose on a (7 pound) laptop, which made both the various drafts and the production of the final text much easier (though I still had to go to a print shop to get a laser version of the text, since my dot-matrix printer and its tear-apart holed paper were insufficiently elegant) and I could also type up my notes in electronic form, making them easier to store, sort, and move around in the text (I recently had to explain to my son-in-law that what for him was an electronic process of "cut&paste" for me had meant physically cutting out bits of manuscripts and pasting them elsewhere, transitions marked by barely legible hand-written text). Some of the journals I needed were just beginning to appear online, a few classics of Soviet-era *detektivy* were beginning to appear on the internet (findable, sometimes, with early versions of search engines such as A-Port, AltaVista, Northern Lights, and, around 2000, Google), and there were early experiments with "e-commerce" that I *could* have used to purchase the books I needed. If I hadn't feared that my credit card would also be used for … uh … other purposes? And if there had been a way for the budding e-commerce enterprises to send me the books from Russia, which there wasn't.

I could exchange emails with some colleagues (though not yet all, and the more senior ones still seemed to require physical letters, which felt more respectful and deferential), and, had I been working on a topic that had broader appeal, I could have joined listservs and chat rooms (some measure of the scope of my topic, and the democratizing effects of subject matter even on the early web, is that I was able to find, and join, such groups devoted to another interest of mine at the time, exotic Caucasian and Central Asian flock-guarding dogs).

Still, for all the greater ease of manuscript production – at least three of my earlier manuscripts I composed by hand (making them *true* "manuscripts"), then typed myself, then cut&pasted, then re-typed, and then paid a typist to produce a clean "submission copy" – the processes I used to write the 2000 book were not substantially different than those I had followed a quarter century earlier, and indeed that I might have followed a full century earlier had I been writing then. The information that I needed was still mostly stored in printed form, in physical repositories that I had to visit in person. True, it became easier and cheaper to photocopy – but only if the journals were not too tightly bound, or had not been rendered on microfiche or microfilm. Even if I could photocopy though, I had still to read everything, underlining or hand-copying out what I wanted.

This was also hierarchical information, credentialed in ways that I think none of us then noticed or understood – journal X was more "important" than journal Y, scholar A was "more reputable" than scholar B. The information delivered to me by the internet was also strangely ahistorical – texts produced from the mid-1990s on had ever-greater chances of being found in electronic form, but anything before that had to be searched out in physical form, just as had been the case in 1975. Although at the time there seemed to be reams of information through which I had to plow, the confines of the subject, and of the larger field in which my book-to-be sat, were relatively defined. I had to "cover the literature" in order to credential my contribution, making clear to any potential readers the books that had come before mine, and the context into which I was now fitting my own.

This is now

Life took a detour in 2000, when I left academia and went into the intelligence community. In retrospect, it was a lucky time to join the Foreign Broadcast Information Service (FBIS), because the migration to digital information was just beginning, and the frenetic horrors of 9/11 were still about 18 months away. This meant that I had time to master the traditional business model (which is explained in the first chapters of this book), but also to begin to understand how that model was going to become ever more inadequate as the amount, and type, of available information grew with the internet. Thus when the "system shock" of 9/11 hit, coinciding with what author Clay Shirky called "a massive positive supply-side shock to the cost and availability of information,"[1] I was reasonably well positioned to help the intelligence community (IC)'s effort to re-conceptualize just what "open source intelligence" could mean. Thrust into a series of "change" positions, organizations, and exercises, I had the chance to meet and to work with a great many intelligent, imaginative, and serious individuals, both from within government and from outside (some of them far outside – some of my activities let me work with colleagues from other countries, which particularly stretched my thinking). Throughout the decade I continued to write – indeed, more often and in greater volume than I had in academia – turning out, first, traditional analytic pieces (though often not on traditional topics), then some experimental efforts with web-based and film-based analysis, in curriculum design, and then, from about 2005 on, as an internal blogger, where at one point I was maintaining blogs on three different platforms, and mirroring one of them on a fourth (I confess I may sometimes have repeated myself).

What I did not have the opportunity to do, however, was to step back, to summarize and systematize my thoughts. That changed in 2009, when the Open Source Center (what FBIS had become at the stroke of midnight on Halloween 2005) agreed that I could apply to become an Officer in Residence, part of a long-standing IC outreach effort. I had the great good fortune not only to be selected, but also to be named as an Associate at Georgetown University's Institute for the Study of Diplomacy, a think-tank-like body attached to the Walsh School for Foreign Service. The past two years of study, teaching, and elbow-rubbing with my fellow Associates and other Georgetown faculty has given me the time and – as I quickly learned is even more important – the *resources* to pull my thoughts together, the results of which can be found in several articles and now also this book.

Some of these resources I had perhaps known about, but not fully used. Google had become dramatically more powerful, not only enlarging its primary cache to mind-boggling proportions (as I explain in the text which follows), but also creating Google Scholar, which proved to be an extraordinarily useful search tool. Google Books has proven a boon as well – for many books (though far from all), either Google itself has a searchable, digitized version which I may read at my computer, or it will find me the version which someone else has digitized. Unlike 2000, when the "circle of history" on the internet only extended back to about 1995, I found in writing this book that I had Edward Bernays, Walter Lippman, Guy LeBon, Arthur Ponsonby and many others (the need for whom is all explained within) immediately at hand. Nor was that all – the Church Committee report (which in my Vietnam-era graduate school years I had tried to read in Government Printing Office green-bound "word bricks") exists in two fully searchable versions, and of course the Aspin-Brown Report, the 9/11 Commission Report and the WMD Commission report are all equally available, searchable and at hand. The Freedom of Information Act (FOIA) has resulted in the digitizing and indexing of thousands, if not hundreds of thousands, of documents from the early days of the IC, making it possible to see the assumptions, compromises, and pressures which shaped the modern security establishment.

Newspapers, magazines, and all kinds of ephemera which a decade ago could have been found only on microfiche (or not at all) were instantly available, letting me see, for example, wartime stories about FBIS in *Popular*

Science and *The Saturday Evening Post.* This allowed me not only to see the summaries that others had made of early budget battles, but also to read the newspaper accounts from the time, and so get a feel for what the early days of open source intelligence had been like (reflections of which I hope will be evident in this book). The search engines also are far more catholic than any library taxonomy, so that, for example, searches on intelligence issues will turn up citations from law review articles or business journals, sources that I otherwise would never have suspected to exist for this topic.

Of course, many articles were findable through Google Scholar, but required library access actually to read. Here I owe an enormous thanks to Georgetown's Lauinger Library and its online catalog George – using my "off-campus log-in" I could (and did) access, from anywhere I chanced to be, thousands upon thousands of journals, newspapers, including even the digitized, searchable versions of the FBIS materials that in my old home office exist only on paper, bound and stored in hallway closets. The databases to which Georgetown subscribes are expensive, but the convenience and intellectual riches they offered me were extraordinary – in just a few hours I was able to work my way through dozens of articles of possible value to whatever I was writing, as opposed to the days I might once have spent deep in the library stacks.

Google of course has not digitized every book, so here too Lauinger and George came to the rescue, with its online catalog, and the ability to request that a book be brought to the front desk, even if (as happened) I might be requesting it from Michigan, France, or Greece. On the fairly rare occasions when Lauinger did not have a book I wanted, I could use George to search Chesapeake Information and Research Library Alliance (CIRLA) and the Washington Research Library Consortium (WRLC); if that too failed (and no equally usable substitute came to light), there was always inter-library loan, which Lauinger also did cheerfully and well.

It was not just in locating sources, however, that digitization proved to be magic. Anyone who has written a long argument based on supporting materials will know how a half-forgotten phrase or barely-noticed example will suddenly, in the course of composition, be precisely the thing that is needed to firm up an argument or provide the proper illustration. In the old days of, say, five years ago, that half-remembered phrase could force you to spend hours, even days, flipping back through books or articles, trying to recall exactly where that dimly remembered bit might be found. With books, of course, you still have to do this, but with anything that has been digitized a couple of quick queries will find the passage – and then allow you to copy and paste the found passage into the text. It was precisely because of this searchability that I increasingly turned to electronic books as I wrote – whatever its clunks and kinks may still be, Kindle has an excellent text search feature (which has prompted the interesting bibliographic issue of how such passages should be footnoted). It was also a great plus to be able to carry around the equivalent of a working library in a device that weighs less than a standard paperback, and to purchase from, say, a beach while on vacation, a book that suddenly seems as if it might prove useful.

It took me some time to get accustomed to this feature, but digitization also made it much easier to store and transport materials. Within the IC, of course, I had access to share drives, but there was no way to transfer information if I wanted to work in more than one location, or to work at home or in someplace "beyond the firewall." Once at Georgetown I experimented with USB sticks – basically updated versions of the floppies I had schlepped around in the 1990s, but (as I explain in the text below) forbidden on corporate computers. Then I discovered "the cloud" –Dropbox, Google Docs, and other virtual storage facilities. The cloud allowed me always to have my materials where I was, and also allowed me to feel secure that I had multiple backups of work, "just in case" (I still remember the lobotomized sense of having accidentally, and unrecoverably, scrambled a 40-page draft of an article on our first home computer, a DEC the size of a large suitcase, which had one floppy for the operating system and a second for data storage).

To be sure, there were downsides to digitization. Most of these I explore more fully in the book that follows, but suffice it here to say that the volume of materials that *might* be used is Sisyphean, and so variegate that it sometimes was hard to know where to start – and, more important perhaps, where to stop. A search on a given topic might turn up relevant materials in:

- library books;
- books to be purchased;
- digitized old books;
- new books downloadable as PDFs through the Creative Commons license;
- established journals (either available through George or library only);
- new online-only journals;
- newspapers (old and digitalized, or new and online only);
- expert-community-of-interest blogs;
- commercial blogs;
- qualified and intelligent amateur blogs (domestic and foreign);
- the comment fields of any of those blogs, or indeed of the journals and newspaper articles;
- shared Powerpoint slide decks;
- amateur and professional data visualization websites;

- MA, PhD, and even Senior Honors theses;

- government reports (from *lots* of different governments);

- NGO and commercial reports (again from everywhere);

- Facebook;

- Twitter;

- and – in some ways the hardest of all to deal with – a huge array of podcasts and videos (a person could probably spend an entire lifetime watching nothing but TED and Google talks).

As I explain more fully in the book which follows, this hyper-abundance of information makes the story far richer – but it also makes quite clear that this is *a* story, not *the* story. One of the changes which governments and government organs (including the IC) have difficulty adjusting to is that the notion that there is one single story, a single truth, is proving to be an artifact of a time when information was expensive to create and disseminate, so that there wasn't so much of it, and those who did send it (or whose content was sent through its systems) appeared to have possession of "the truth."

No more. Another person who looked at the questions I examine in this book might well offer different answers. In a sense to say this is a version of the traditional *mea culpa* of book forewords, that "any mistakes made here are mine." That is true – but what is even truer is that the *choices* I have made in this book are mine. Even if I understood and used the sources I did correctly, the sheer abundance of materials means that I omitted others, and no doubt failed to find even more. Still, I think that I have been able to capture some important features of a moment in time, and to suggest, if not the direction that events are moving, then at least the pressures and potentials that are building, and how those "information systems" might roil in the future.

Although the book is primarily about "open source intelligence," and thus may be read as one answer to the question "How do you do OSINT?" (OSINT = "open source intelligence," one of several so-called "INTs," or information sources for intelligence. See Chapter Five). I intend the book to draw a wider circle, proposing some ways to think about the emerging information environment, and how it might inform anyone who has to make a decision.

My thanks to . . .

If there are any victories to be found in this volume, they easily have a thousand fathers. I am grateful to the Open Source Center and its senior management for allowing me this two years away, and I am equally grateful to the Institute for the Study of Diplomacy, and Georgetown as a whole, for letting me spend the two years with them. The Center for the Study of Intelligence selected me for the Officer in Residence (OIR) program, and gave me timely backup and resources. As for more personal thanks, one of the cultural traditions of the IC is that no one has a last name. I have decided to extend that to everyone who helped me, inspired me, challenged me, drove me crazy enough that I pushed harder to make my argument, or otherwise moved life along to help me reach this point, and this book. So, semi-anonymous thanks to: Aaron, Aaron, Arash, Barbara, Barbara, Bev, Carmen, Carole, Charlie, Chris, Courtney, Craig, Darren, David, Denny, Donn, Doug, Doug, Doug, Doug, Elsie, Emma, Ethan, Eugene, HanTeng, Helene, Jan, Janet, Jean-Louis, Jeff, Jim, Joan, John, John, Josh, Joyce, Karen, Katie, Kay, Kelly, Ken, Kirsten, Krypto, Laura, Laurie, Lois, Marcela, Martin, Melissa, Michael, Mike, Mike, Mike, Millie, Nahid, Nancy, Pat, Paula, Roger, Sabra, Sandra, Scott, Scott, Snezhana, Steve, Sue, Susie, Tim, Tim, Tony, Warren, and Yasmine. Please forgive me if I have forgotten anyone. I would also like to thank the members of my two Georgetown classes (MSFS635: Open Source Analysis, and CCT 630: Propaganda, Old Methods and New Tools) and my editor, Marie-Claire Antoine, for taking this book on, and for helping me shape it into what now lies in your hands. I must also remind you that whatever you read here is my opinion only, expressed entirely in my private capacities, and does not represent the views or positions of any government entity.

My biggest thanks, as ever, goes to my family and, especially, to my wife Martha – who 37 years later remains the most amazing person I have ever met.

Notes

1 From a 31 March 2011 appearance at the Council on Foreign Relations, the transcript of which is at: http://www.cfr.org/health-science-and-technology/digital-power-social-media-political-change/p24576, accessed 30 May 2011.

The Official Definitions of "Open Source Information" and "Open Source Intelligence"

INTELLIGENCE COMMUNITY DIRECTIVE

NUMBER 301

NATIONAL OPEN SOURCE ENTERPRISE
(EFFECTIVE: JULY 11, 2006)

F. DEFINITIONS

1. **Open Source Acquisition:** The act of gaining possession of, or access to, open source information synonymous with "open source collection." The preferred term is acquisition because by definition, open sources are collected and disseminated by others open source exploiters acquire previously collected and publicly available information second-hand.

2. **Open Source Collection:** See "Open Source Acquisition."

3. **Open Source Information:** Publicly available information that anyone can lawfully obtain by request, purchase, or observation.

4. **Open Source Intelligence:** Produced from publicly available information that is collected, exploited, and disseminated in a timely manner to an appropriate audience for the purpose of addressing a specific intelligence requirement.[1]

G. EFFECTIVE DATE: This ICD becomes effective on the date of signature.

_____   7/11/06
Director of National Intelligence   Date

ACRONYMS

ACH	Alternative Competing Hypotheses
BBC	British Broadcasting Corporation
BBCM	BBC Monitoring
BWN	Bored at Work Network
CBI	Cumulative Book Index
CCTV	Closed circuit TV
CIA	Central Intelligence Agency
CIG	Central Intelligence Group
CNN	Cable News Network
COE	Contemporary Operating Environment
COIN ISR	Counterinsurgency intelligence, survey, and reconnaissance
CPI	Committee on Public Information
CPSU	Communist Party of the Soviet Union
CSIS	Center for Strategic and International Studies
CTR	click-through rate
D&D	denial and deception
DARPA	Defense Advanced Research Projects Agency
DDOS	Distributed Denial of Service (attack)
DI	Directorate of Intelligence (CIA division)
DIA	Defense Intelligence Agency
DIY	do it yourself
DNI	Director of National Intelligence (*also* Directorate of National Intelligence)
DNS	Domain Name System (Internet address protocol)

DoD	Department of Defense
DPRK	Democratic People's Republic of Korea (North Korea)
DS&T	Directorate of Science and Technology (CIA division)
DVC	Democracy Video Challenge (State Department program)
FARC	Revolutionary Armed Forces of Colombia
FAS	Federation of American Scientists
FBIS	Foreign Broadcast Information Service (*also* Foreign Broadcast Intelligence Service)
FBMS	Foreign Broadcast Monitoring Service
FCC	Federal Communications Commission
FDAD	Foreign Demographic Analysis Division
FDD	Foreign Documents Division
HUMINT	intelligence based on covert collection of secrets provided by humans
IC	Intelligence Community
ICD	Intelligence Community Directive
IDC	International Department for the Acquisition of Foreign Publications
IG	Inspector General
INR	Office of Intelligence and Research (State Department office)
IR	Information Retrieval
JPRS	Joint Publication Research Service
KIT	Key Intelligence Topics
LBC	Lebanon Broadcasting Company
MASINT	intelligence based on "measurement and signature"
MBC	Middle East Broadcasting Center
MSRP	Mission Strategic and Resource Plan
NDP	National Democratic Party (of Egypt)
NFAC	National Foreign Assessment Center
NGA	National Geospatial-Intelligence Agency

NGO	non-governmental organization
NIE	National Intelligence Estimate
NIMA	National Imagery and Mapping Agency
NIPF	National Intelligence Priorities Framework
NOSE	National Open Source Enterprise
NPIC	National Photo Interpretation Center
NRO	National Reconnaissance Office
NSA	National Security Agency
NSC	National Security Council
NSCID	National Security Council Intelligence Directive
NORA	Non-Obvious Relationship Awareness
OMB	Office of Management and Budget
OSC	Open Source Center
OSD	Open Source Directorate
OSINT	Open Source Intelligence
OSS	Office of Strategic Services
OWI	Office of War Information
PDB	President's Daily Brief
R&A	Research and Analysis (Branch of OSS)
R&D	Research and Development
RFQ	Request for quotation
RIAA	Recording Industry Association of America
ROI	Return on investment
RRU	Rapid Response Unit (office in the Department of State)
RTLM	Radio Télévision Libre des Mille Collines (Rwanda)
SCIP	Strategic and Competitive Intelligence Professionals
SEC	Securities and Exchange Commission
SEO	Search Engine Optimization
SID	Strategic Intelligence Digest

SIGINT	Signals intelligence
SVI	Shared Values Initiative (State Department program)
UAV	Unmanned aerial vehicle
UCLA	University of California, Los Angeles
UCSD	University of California, San Diego
U&G	Uses and gratifications theory of communication
URL	Uniform Resource locator
USB	Universal Serial Bus
USSR	Union of Soviet Socialist Republics
VIRAT	Visual Image Retrieval and Analysis Tool
WMD	Weapons of Mass Destruction

PART ONE

When "information retrieval system" meant the memory of the oldest employee

CHAPTER ONE

The screwballs of K Street and the bad-eyes brigade

Intelligence of words and intelligence of things

David Kahn, author and historian of intelligence, has argued[1] that there are two basic types of intelligence information, physical and verbal. The first, which has predominated throughout human history (indeed, Kahn goes even further back than the dawn of humans, to argue that "even a protozoan" must have a means of determining whether the elements in its environment are noxious or beneficial), is information received by observation. It was to get this kind of information that generals situated their camps on high ground, and that rulers sent spies into enemy encampments, to count the number of soldiers, see their armaments, and divine their deployment.

The second kind of intelligence, the verbal, "acquires information from a written or oral source, such as a stolen plan, a report on troop morale, an overheard order, even a computerized strength report." To Kahn, this kind of intelligence was comparatively unimportant for most of the history of humankind, since battles were generally decided by physical superiority. It was not until the middle of the nineteenth century that things began to change, as technological innovation introduced ever greater numbers of ways in which humans could leverage their own physical capacities. Some of this technology – observation balloons, airplanes, cameras – greatly increased the volume and the range of physical intelligence that could be obtained. Even greater advances, however, occurred in the realm of verbal intelligence. Direct communications via telegraph, radio, and telephone became ever more widely used, with the consequence that these could be tapped and taken advantage of. Sometimes these messages were in the clear (as in the Battle of Tannenberg, when the Russians didn't bother to encode their radio commands, and thus obligingly told the Germans everything they were doing). More often they were encoded – but codes could be broken, as they frequently were.

Perhaps even more importantly, though, technology increasingly made it possible for leaders to become aware not only of military preparedness, but also of enemy intentions – daily newspapers now could capture parliamentary debate or statements of the rulers, in a gauge of public sentiment. Leaders and the military commanders who served them could now understand not only what antagonists were doing, but also could see why – and, moreover, they now had the opportunity to try to influence those foreign populations themselves, whether through manipulation of their leaders or directly, by appealing around the leaders to address the populace themselves.

According to Kahn, World War I was generally the "tipping point" which elevated verbal intelligence past physical intelligence – in his account, the role played by the Zimmermann telegram (an intercepted and decoded telegram from German Foreign Minister Arthur Zimmermann to the Mexican leadership promising the return of Mexico's "lost territories" if Mexico would enter the war on Germany's side) in bringing the US into the war signaled a new role for verbal intelligence, the transformation which, in his words, "crowned the ascent of intelligence from its humble biological origins as a mere instrument of survival to its supreme capability: helping a nation win a war."[2]

"A shocking deficiency" of information

The vast new possibilities of both physical and verbal intelligence which had helped America to win World War I so startled, even traumatized, the American public and policymakers that the apparatus which had been built up to fight the first war was almost immediately dismantled as soon as the war was over. As Kahn detailed in his biography of cryptographer Herbert Yardley,[3] the Black Chamber, a message intercept and decoding effort, was shut down and its efforts repudiated (as captured in Secretary of State Henry Stimson's famous rebuke of Yardley, that "gentlemen do not read each other's mail"). More importantly, even as a new war began to brew in Europe, much of the US remained isolationist and aloof, with the consequence that capabilities for the collection of both verbal intelligence and physical intelligence atrophied back to what they had been in the previous century. As Harvard historian Harry Ransom put it in his 1959 book, *Central Intelligence and National Security*, "On the eve of World War II, the United States intelligence system was highly compartmented, largely uncoordinated, and almost starved for funds." Ransom quotes then-General Eisenhower to the same effect, that there was "a shocking deficiency [of information] that impeded all constructive planning" because there was no "far-flung organization of fact-finders."[4] Various military units collected the information that they required for the execution of their immediate duties, but did not share their findings. State Department officials gathered what they considered to be necessary for their work, often storing it in what author G. J. A. O'Toole called "State's intelligence retrieval system: the memory of the oldest employee in the Department."[5] In any event, there were no more than a dozen or so State employees who performed intelligence-like functions,[6] because, as Dean Acheson later testified before Congress, State's manner of gathering information "differed only by reason of the typewriter and telegraph from the techniques which John Quincy Adams was using in St. Petersburg and Benjamin Franklin was using in Paris."[7]

This degree of disarray was not the product of incompetence or inattention, but rather was the consequence of a series of deliberate choices made by the government, politicians, and the American public. Although the country has a historical pattern of assembling martial capacities in times of war and then rapidly dispersing them when conflict has passed, the experience of World War I was different, in scale, but even more in the revelation of what information, and information control, might mean in the new industrial age. As early as 1854 the age-old practice of building morale by informing the public of how many soldiers and how much materiel a government was sending into battle had been obviated by the invention of the telegraph, which allowed the Russian government to know how many ships Britain was sending to Crimea almost before the ships cleared their harbor.[8] The sinking of the *Titanic*, in 1912, had a similar effect on the development of radio, a device which the Navy had initially resisted, but which became widely accepted as a military and civilian necessity after it became clear that all of the doomed passengers could have been saved had either of the near-by ships had their wireless radios turned on and manned.[9] Telephone too had become a feature of the world's landscape, although differently distributed. By the turn of the century, telephone penetration varied from 1 per 1216 people in France to 1 per 115 in Sweden (with the US at 1 per 208),[10] concentrated most heavily among the elites and in the cities, but nevertheless this instrument had become a fact of modern life even before the war began.

What astonished – and frightened – many people as the "Great War" began were not the new tools of communication themselves, but rather the new phenomena that they presented in combination. As Edward Bernays, father of modern PR and one of the first students of the new information world (as well as being the nephew of Sigmund Freud), exulted, "With the printing press and the newspaper, the railroad, the telephone, telegraph, radio, and airplanes, ideas can be spread rapidly and even instantaneously over the whole of America," and of course, by extension, the world.[11] For the first time huge masses of population – indeed, the notion of "the masses" itself was a product of these times[12] – could be shown film or press illustrations of what their opponents were said to be doing, thus inflaming passions and drawing populations into the fray via "public opinion" – yet another invention of the era. Importantly, this information was far from being data – rather the Great War offered the first massive effusion of modern propaganda, on a scale never previously seen. Indeed, "propaganda" itself, in the modern sense of the term, was another invention of the war. As British journalist Arthur Ponsonby documented in his 1928 book, *Falsehoods in Wartime*, all of the parties in the war had conducted massive propaganda campaigns, not scrupling even at outright fabrication if the result was deemed to serve the larger purpose of victory. By Ponsonby's reckoning, "there must have been more deliberate lying ... from 1914 to 1918 than in any other period of the world's history."[13] The result, argued Walter Lippmann, another of the social-science pioneers of the inter-war era, was "plebiscite autocracy or government by newspapers."[14] It was for this reason, Lippmann argued in another book, that "every democrat feels in his bones that dangerous crises are incompatible with democracy, because the inertia of the masses is such that a very few must act quickly and the rest follow rather blindly."[15]

In America, perhaps, "the masses" might follow the natural elite whom Bernays celebrated, the "invisible government which is the true ruling power of our government,"[16] but Europe was already beginning just a few years after the war to show what might happen if other "invisible governments" began to seize control of the masses. Both Bernays and Lippmann (and many of the newly-minted advertisers who were beginning to colonize Madison Avenue[17]) were veterans of America's first – and, to date, still most complete – experiment in total information control.

The Committee of Public Information (CPI), which was also known as the Creel Committee, after its founder and main inspiration, journalist George Creel, managed during its brief existence to impose an extraordinary harnessing of American information output. In its 28 months of activity, the CPI seized near-total control of the country's press, commandeered a good portion of the fledgling film industry, and – what frightened Creel's opponents most – imposed an ideological conformity on the country that rivaled that of any of the European powers. An ardent supporter of US entry into the war, Creel convinced President Wilson that his CPI was vitally necessary to wage "the fight for the *minds* of men, for the 'conquest of their convictions.'"[18] To that end, the CPI poured out an extraordinary flood of pamphlets, films, speech texts, press releases, and other materials,[19] all designed to create a tight unanimity of opinion at home, and a clear picture elsewhere in the world of the high ideals for which the US was claiming to fight. Among the most remarkable of the CPI's inventions were the so-called "Four-Minute Men," several thousand volunteers who would stand unbidden at all kinds of public gatherings to give patriotic speeches of precisely that eponymous length, using texts supplied by the CPI. This was not propaganda, Creel wrote, a word that "in German hands had come to be associated with deceit and corruption," but rather his efforts relied upon "the simple, straightforward presentation of the facts."[20]

Like all good rhetoricians, Creel was of course disingenuous – his "facts" were disputed by others, especially after the war, when even people who had supported the war during its course later came to the conclusion that they had been duped into fighting for interests that were not theirs.[21] Even those who generally shared the values that Creel and his Four-Minute Men had been advancing were disconcerted by the power of concentrated propaganda, which created what one historian has called "a vigilante climate."[22] The question of whether the government should be involved in the active shaping of public opinion was fought throughout the interwar period,[23] with educators like John Dewey and Everett Dean Martin arguing that propaganda was detrimental to traditional American values, and "scientific liberals" like Lippmann, Bernays, Harold Lasswell, Paul Lazersfeld, and a host of other names who were soon to play significant roles in the transformation of American communications, arguing that, in Lippmann's words, "the ancient dogma of democracy, that the knowledge needed for the management of human affairs comes up spontaneously from the human heart" was no longer true, requiring now that a "machinery of knowledge" be created to provide "organized intelligence."[24]

This battle was far from theoretical, because it had profound implications for the information landscape that was emerging across America. The movie industry was already a powerful economic engine, churning out thousands of movies, and bringing with it the tangled issues of censorship, free speech, and economic interests. Radio was even more problematic, because the physics of the electro-magnetic spectrum required that some entity – the government being the obvious choice – intercede to regulate wavelength allocation, an act which of necessity brought with it the questions of who should get the wavelengths, how strong their transmitters might be, and – very importantly – whether the contents broadcast were to be informational and educational, as was generally the decision made in Europe, or was to be advertiser-supported commercial entertainment, as became the case in the US.[25] In general, the government tended to take a relatively hands-off approach to domestically produced information, while coping with the potential threats posed by "alien information" through such legislation as the Foreign Agents Registration Act (1938) and the Voorhis Act (1940), which required that those wishing to "spread doctrines alien to our democratic form of government, or propaganda for the purpose of influencing American public opinion on a political question"[26] be required to register their affiliations, purposes, and activities.

The Screwballs Division

That approach, of course, assumed that those wishing to spread alien doctrines, or at least the materials that contained them, had to be physically present in the US – which is precisely why in May 1941, with Europe already deep in war but the US officially neutral, Federal Communications Commission (FCC) official Harold N. Graves Jr. published *War on the Short Wave*,[27] a short pamphlet designed to inform the American public about a powerful new "instrument of war" – the shortwave radio. A Columbia-trained journalist, Graves had until a few months before been Director of the Short Wave Listening Center at Princeton University, which had been established with Rockefeller Foundation support[28] to monitor and analyze the growing flood of broadcasts emanating from Europe's main capitals.

Graves noted that a journalist had dubbed radio a "fourth front" of warfare, a new field of conflict which had come to join the age-old fields of economic, diplomatic, and military warfare. Strictly speaking, Graves argued, the fourth front was propaganda, which had always existed as an element of war. Different now, however, were the long reach of this new medium, and the volume of propaganda that radio permitted. The discovery in the 1920s that short-frequency radio waves could be bounced off earth's ionosphere, and so reach almost halfway around the globe, suddenly allowed competing powers to circumvent the sovereign gatekeepers of traditional information, and now appeal directly to populations who might be literally on the other side of the planet. As Graves wrote, "Italian broadcasters have suggested that English workers sabotage British war industry, Englishmen have urged Germans and Italians to get rid of Hitler and Mussolini, and Germans have told Britons they should remove ... Churchill from office" – all attempts at direct persuasion of distant populations that had not been possible before. Even more impressive than the reach though was the volume – the BBC, Graves pointed out, was transmitting 200,000 words per day, in two dozen languages, meaning that in just five days the British were transmitting "as many words as there are in the Bible, or as many words as there are in all the works of Shakespeare." Nor was it just the British – Graves outlines a theoretical "listening day" during the course of which a listener in the US might have breakfast with "a German station broadcasting news in Spanish" and "Japan broadcasting to Australia in

English, Germany in German and Afrikaans to South Africa and in English to England; Britain in English to her Empire, in French to France and Belgium" and then end the day with "news in English from the Soviet Union … [and also] Tokyo, Ankara, Budapest, and Bucharest."[29]

When Graves wrote, international radio broadcasting was approximately as new as the internet is for us today. Commercial broadcasting had not begun in the US until 1920,[30] and state-supported international broadcasting was even newer, begun by the French in 1931, with the BBC's Empire Service joining the ranks of international broadcasters the following year. Just as the internet has startled us by the rapidity of its uptake, so did radio blossom throughout the world – in the US, for example, only about 400,000 households had radios in 1922, while by 1940 the number had grown to 51 million,[31] or more than 80 percent of US households, in addition to being found in a growing number of automobiles.[32] As Graves warned, this ubiquity now allowed "leaders to address the whole world in person." Potentially even more dangerous was that radio transmits the human voice, which Graves characterized as "still the most subtle, the most used, and probably the most persuasive of all communications." Furthermore, "radio, better than print and the platform speaker, and better even than the stage or the motion picture, can create an illusion of reality [through which] listeners may be tricked into accepting the false or the ridiculous."[33] Indeed, the power of radio to command public attention and force specific behaviors had been spectacularly illustrated just a few years before, when Orson Well's dramatization of *War of the Worlds* had convinced great swathes of the US that Martians were attacking Earth. Unlike that commercial experiment, however, radio was now harnessed to the nightmare that Alfred Ponsonby had predicted just a decade before, that "in future wars we have now to look forward to a new and far more efficient instrument of propaganda – the Government control of broadcasting."[34]

Despite the apparent power of shortwave radio, the US government was ignoring it entirely, leaving only a few commercial entities to try to make sense of the new medium. In 1939 three New York daily newspapers (the *Times*, *Herald-Tribune*, and *News*) and the National and Columbia Broadcasting companies began regular digests of the English-language messages being beamed from Europe, but quickly it was realized that the media were essentially relaying Nazi and fascist propaganda.[35] At about the same time, first Princeton University and then, somewhat later, Stanford University, began more sophisticated efforts to collect the propaganda broadcasts, with the goal of making sense of what the hostile powers were trying to achieve. The results of such efforts were evident already in Graves' pamphlet, in which he was able to demonstrate that Nazi propaganda beamed at the US had changed once the Germans had invaded Netherlands and Belgium. Before the invasion only 20 percent of airtime had been devoted to criticism of US support for England, and 21.5 percent had been in praise of US isolationism; after the invasion, though, Graves showed that the praise quotient had shrunk to 18 percent, while criticism had swelled to 43 percent of all broadcast time, much of that anti-Semitic claims intended, Graves argued, "to cause dissension in the United States, which, it was hoped, would choke the stream of aid to Britain."[36]

This was precisely the kind of information that Assistant Secretary of State Breckinridge Long hoped to gain, which is why he had tasked FCC head James Fly to expand its purview over domestic radio, now to include foreign broadcasting.[37] The result was the Foreign Broadcasting Monitoring Service (FBMS),[38] which received the $150,000 allocated by President Roosevelt for that purpose from his special funds on 26 February 1941.[39] The first task, of course, was to begin staffing the new enterprise, which proved to be far more difficult than had been the case for its civilian predecessors. For one thing, FBMS was attempting monitoring on a far larger scale than had been the case at Princeton or Stanford, so considerable energy (and money) was expended in trying to establish listening posts in Maryland (for broadcasts aimed at the US from Europe), Puerto Rico (for those aimed at South America), Texas (also for South America), and the West Coast (for those from Japan). There also was no clear business model, for what quickly proved to be a unique effort. After a summer of experimenting with various formats and delivery methods,[40] the growing team hit on a formula of daily digests which conveyed through a combination of summaries and full translations what had been broadcast the previous day. The team also experimented with products that moved beyond simple synopsizing, trying to draw analytic conclusions about what they were hearing every day on the radio. Early attempts at daily analysis did not fare well, so the team hit on a formula of weekly analysis – it is a point of corporate pride that the first such "Weekly Review" appeared on 6 December 1941 (the day before Pearl Harbor), warning that Japanese radio had "dropped its tone of caution and was assuming a belligerent attitude."[41]

The corporate histories are silent about the impact of that particular product, but in general the FBMS pioneers also faced the task of creating a market for their product. By dint of sending special reports directly to President Roosevelt and selected principals in State, the new service managed to acquire 87 subscribers by November 1941 – a figure which jumped to more than 460 just two months later. From that point forward the FBMS corporate history seems a typical bureaucratic success story, with increasing demand for output causing a scramble for resources which, when secured, only increase demand further. The staff doubled in size in less than a year, and as a result had to move to new offices. Within a year of setting up, the new organization was monitoring close to a million words a day in its four bureaus, and also had access to a similar volume being monitored by their counterparts at the BBC.[42] Another, less positive, sign of bureaucratic success was that FBMS (now FBIS[43]) began to develop a rival, in the

Office of War Information (OWI), a somewhat restrained simulacrum of the Creel Committee which was put in charge of US propaganda and information efforts. Since some of the most popular FBIS products were the full texts of speeches by enemy leaders, OWI argued that this fell under their responsibility for public relations, and so fought on and off with FBIS for resources and position.[44]

There were two other challenges however that were more substantive, and also were harbingers of problems that would continue to bedevil US open source intelligence efforts for many decades. The first of these was the conundrum that the ability to monitor scratchy, faint, foreign radio broadcasts, especially those aimed at the enemies' domestic audiences (one of FBIS's most closely guarded secrets in wartime was that the West Coast monitors could hear domestic Japanese broadcasts as well as those aimed internationally, and so offered one of the US's few sources about the state of Japan's home front[45]) or those that used precise military, economic, or political terms, required superb mastery of what in essence were enemy languages. Many applicants who were qualified because of their language had to be turned away because they were not US citizens or, in the case of those who were Japanese, even if they were.[46] The second challenge was that of where FBIS should "sit" and how it should be paid for. Although locating the service within the FCC made a certain bureaucratic sense, it made FBIS a potential victim in other battles. Representative Martin Dies, founder of the House Committee on Un-American Activities, and his supporters in Congress squeezed FBIS hard, charging that FBIS employees were "communists" and using both riders to funding bills and direct subpoenas as tools to try to force the FCC to fire FBIS employees who were thought to hold "socialistic views."[47]

Ultimately Dies and his supporters demanded that the FCC fire two suspect FBIS employees – which FCC head James Fly refused to do. This set off a protracted bureaucratic battle which in 1945 resulted in Congress cutting the FCC's funding by 25 percent, in what ex-FBIS head Robert Leigh characterized in a magazine article about the affair as "not a *fiscal* cut [but] a *punitive* cut."[48] Although the underlying reason for the continued battle was a licensing dispute between FCC head Fly and Rules Committee head Eugene Cox, who owned a radio station in rural Georgia that Fly contended had been fraudulently obtained,[49] the dispute highlighted what would prove to be a persistent problem for FBIS, as to what should be its administrative home.

The success of propaganda analysis

FBIS was originally placed in the FCC because of the medium it was supposed to monitor, not the content. The fact that the FCC was a regulatory body, not a military or intelligence one, combined with the fact that most of what FBIS was monitoring was openly available to anyone with the proper radio equipment and linguistic skills, presented persistent problems. Newspapers and wire services wanted access to the various daily reports, which, more often than not, they received, save for the periods when budget crunches prompted the service to try to prune its distribution lists. A different problem arose in 1942, when first the Japanese, and then the Germans, began to broadcast the names of soldiers who had been taken captive, sometimes accompanied by what purported to be their statements in support of their captors' war aims. FBIS began sending the information to the office of the Provost Marshal General, which then undertook official notification of the prisoners' families. However, amateur monitors were also picking up the same information, sometimes notifying the families out of good-heartedness, sometimes trying to extort payment for confirming that a missing loved one was a prisoner, not dead. Although various remedies were tried, the problem persisted through the end of the war, at times requiring that the chronically fund-strapped organization spend as much as $60,000 to send telegrams to next-of-kin.[50]

In a somewhat larger sense, the two problems pointed up a persistent puzzle of open source intelligence, which is what precisely is the value it offers. Users tended to be effusive in their praise for access that FBIS gave them to foreign sources, but at the same time to undervalue the product, because, in comparison to information obtained by more derring-do methods, it seems relatively easy to obtain. Moreover, the skills required to obtain and use the information made the staff of FBIS stick out in a generally spit-and-polish military crowd, one reason why a journalist of the day insisted that FBIS was known in Washington as the "Screwball Division."[51] Perhaps it was precisely to assert a unique value for FBIS that a small group of analysts within the organization pioneered the effort to extract not just informative value, but also analytic insights from the millions of words of propaganda which they processed every day.

The methodology that was developed was grounded in work done in the late 1930s by a group of scholars funded by the Rockefeller Foundation, who generally followed the communication theories laid down by Harold Lasswell.[52] As explained by Alexander George, a very junior member of the FBIS analytic staff during World War II who later became a distinguished political scientist, "when the FCC [FBIS] began its operations, there existed no blueprint of procedures for drawing inferences about the intentions and calculations of a propagandist from his communications."[53] Working from the double principle that propaganda was an instrument of state policy, and thus closely controlled, and that the analysts of FBIS would monitor *all* of it, so as to see the entire corpus and its possible changes over time, the analysts groped their way toward a methodology which gradually allowed them to make inferences in which they had some confidence. Because they realized that official propaganda is forced to respond to known public events, even when the hostile government would prefer to remain silent, the FBIS analysts began to calibrate what was said – or not said – against what was known, thus gaining a sense of what was more or less important to the Nazi leadership at a given time. Crucial to the analysts' assumptions was the idea that Nazi ideology would be stable over extended periods of time, allowing the analysts to infer situational causes behind changes in the content, tone, or focus of the propaganda with which they became increasingly familiar. As George explained, "the propaganda analyst shares with the [medical] clinician an interest in evaluating the significance of small segments of behavior in the larger context in which they occur. In attempting to make precise explanations of the individual case, both train themselves to notice what is *unusual* about the case at hand."[54]

Using this method, which they elaborated, refined, and – George charged – sometimes ignored, the FBIS analysts began to disseminate not just translations of the content of foreign propaganda, but also speculation about the political, economic, social, or military situations which might lie behind what was being translated. As they progressed, the analysts were trying both to provide good insight into the actions, intentions, and views of the Nazi elite, and to document and substantiate their evolving methodology as sound. Thus analysts noted not only their suppositions, but recorded as completely as they could the reasoning by which they had reached their conclusions.

It was of course impossible during the war to get more than a general sense of the value of their methodology, which is why George later took advantage of the huge amount of German archives and other material that was captured when the war ended to go back and compare the inferences he and his fellows had made against what the historical record now showed. Based on an exhaustive study of a sample two-month period (March–April 1943) and spot checks of a two-year period (June 1942–June 1944), George reached the conclusion that about 80 percent of the inferences made by the FBIS Analysis Division had been essentially correct.[55] As he noted, this level of accuracy was about the same whether the inferences had been about Nazi propaganda goals, Nazi elite behavior, or objective situations – an astonishing record of accuracy, which seemed more than to justify FBIS's continued reliance on the methodology long after FBIS had been passed from the FCC to the War Department, and then, in 1947, to the new-born CIA.[56]

The Bad-Eyes Brigade

FBMS was much less-heralded than was America's other war-time experiment in open source intelligence, the Research and Analysis (R&A) branch of Col. William "Wild Bill" Donovan's Office of Strategic Services (OSS). A hero of World War I who cultivated a swashbuckling, charismatic air, Donovan parlayed his friendship with President Roosevelt to create what is generally recognized as the prototype for today's intelligence community. Although OSS and Donovan are usually associated with the cloak and dagger images of clandestine espionage, in fact the first activities that Roosevelt permitted Donovan were "the collection, analysis, correlation, and dissemination of data on national security."[57]

It is difficult in this data-drenched age to understand how completely ignorant the US was about basic information necessary to begin strategic, or even tactical, preparation for the war. As the Japanese attack on Pearl Harbor had made painfully clear, the US had little understanding of enemy capacities and intentions, while the enemy knew a great deal – including that US sailors usually got shore leave on weekends, meaning that ships would be particularly vulnerable on a Sunday morning.[58] As Donovan and Librarian of Congress Archibald McLeish had agreed even before Pearl Harbor, however, it was not that the information did not exist – everything the country needed, and more, was available, in the country's libraries. What was required, therefore, was an army of experts who best knew how to handle "the most powerful weapon in the OSS arsenal: the three-by-five index card."[59]

Thus was born R&A, the self-described "bad-eyes brigade"[60] (derided by more spit-and-polish types as the "Chairborne Division"[61]), which quickly blossomed into an astonishing enterprise, staffed by an army of scholars, young and old, most of them drawn from the best of America's universities – almost 2,000 of them by war's end.[62] From their ranks emerged at least seven future presidents of the American Historical Association, as well as a host of names later to become famous: Ralph Bunche, Perry Miller, Walt Rostow. Even more remarkable were the names to be added later, including 47 foreigners, among their number more than a dozen who as refugees from occupied Europe were technically "enemy aliens" – these included such luminaries as Herbert Marcuse, Theodor Adorno, Franz Neumann, and other adherents of the Marxist-influenced "Frankfurt School."[63]

Headed by young Harvard historian Sherman Kent, the Europe-Africa branch gave R&A what Donovan called the new unit's "first victory" when Kent and his small team pulled a government version of an "all-nighter," in just 50 hours turning out an encyclopedic report on Morocco in support of the projected US invasion of North Africa. Over the next two weeks, at a pace only slightly less intense, the group produced similar reports on Algeria and Tunisia, astonishing the military with both the richness of their content, and the speed with which they were able to produce the reports.[64] Although a later division chief was to complain that his motley crew of professors, graduate students, and Marxist Europeans found it easier to "get out a 250-page epitome of what Europe will be like in 1986, to be delivered tomorrow morning at 8:30" than it was to have them produce a "2-page summary of what you most want to know about the job you're doing,"[65] the various R&A teams turned out a staggering volume of information, all of it based on openly available sources.

Although most of the "2,000 R&A Reports"[66] turned out over the four years of the group's existence apparently remain in storage, their range, variety, and depth are suggested by descriptions in scholarly accounts:

> the condition of rail transports on the Russian front, the relation between aggression and business structure during the Weimar Republic, attitude of the Roman Catholic Church in Hungary, the political ideas of Charles DeGaulle, the looting and damage of artworks, the location of concentration camps in central Europe … the Communist Party of India and the puppet regime in Nanking, inflation in Burma and guerillas in the Philippines, trade routes in the Congo basin and rival cliques in the Japanese army …[67]

This production was supported by a sophisticated information retrieval system that proved capable of indexing and cross-indexing the more than 200,000 documents that R&A had already amassed, making it possible for R&A "on a day's notice [to] compile a list of important targets in Germany in order of their importance." The system depended upon those same 3x5 cards, which eventually grew in number to more than a million, all set up in such a way that R&A staffers could endlessly reproduce the "miracle" they had performed when they instantly had given the answer to the first question put them – which was what type of electrical current was used in Surinam. By the account of one scholar, this system appears to have remained in use in the CIA well into the 1970s.[68]

Like the FBIS analysts, although using different methodologies, R&A's analysts also showed remarkable ingenuity in deriving meaning from available data. They used the serial numbers on captured German truck tires and engines to extrapolate where war materials were being produced, and in what quantity. R&A economists could figure out production bottlenecks – ball bearings, for example – and so direct bombers more efficiently. One economist used the obituaries in German newspapers, purchased through intermediaries in Sweden and Turkey, to extrapolate both the disposition of German forces and their relative rates of attrition. In fact, so much information was obtained from German newspapers that the Germans themselves began to notice how frequently Allied propaganda cited the Berlin financial newspaper and so stopped allowing its sale abroad.[69]

Feeding all that analysis, of course, required raw material, which was provided by another of OSS's creatures, the Interdepartmental Committee for the Acquisition of Foreign Publications, or IDC. Working through intermediaries, the IDC very quickly began to drown the analysts in material

– within a year they were receiving 8,000 pages of European newspapers and another 3,000 pages of economic, political, and scientific periodicals *every week*, a figure that further doubled the next year, to 20,000 pages per week, and then doubled again, to 45,000 pages. R&A also tried to set up a photo repository, which eventually had more than 300,000 photos indexed so that they could be easily accessed. Indeed, at war's end, R&A had more than three million index cards, 300,000 photos, 350,000 serial publications, 50,000 books, more than a million maps, and 300,000 classified intelligence documents.[70]

So what?

It is not clear, however, how many of those R&A reports were ever read, and, if they were, what effect they had. This is not to say that they had no value, but rather that their nature, and their claims, were such that there was no easy or convenient way of verifying their accuracy, as Alexander George had been able to do for the FBIS analyses. Such checking as was done – of the results of the Strategic Bombing Survey, for example – suggested that targeting work at least had been good, but not superb. The economic analysis too had problems. In the words at least of one participant, George Pettee, who had the chance to check the economic impact of the bombing, "The Japanese underestimated us and most seriously underestimated our economy. The Germans underestimated our economy. They underestimated the Russian economy, and we know very well, also, that the Germans underestimated their own economy. We underestimated the Germans, the Japanese, and the Russians. The British underestimated the Germans, the Japanese, and the Russians,"[71] leading him to conclude that "we won the war in spite of, and not because of ... our intelligence system."[72]

Although historians have written far more about the performance of R&A and its contribution to the development of open source intelligence than they have about that of FBIS, it was FBIS that survived the end of the war (albeit with stress), while R&A was disbanded. To be sure, some of R&A's function were absorbed into the State Department, first as the Office of Research and Intelligence, which later became INR ("Intelligence and Research" – the meaning of the "N" is a mystery), while some of the personnel, including most prominently Sherman Kent (after a brief hiatus back in academia during which he wrote his most famous and influential book, *Strategic Intelligence for American World Policy*), and a great deal of the ethos of R&A were incorporated into the CIA, becoming what is now the Directorate of Intelligence.

In a larger sense, though, the open source intelligence function that R&A pioneered largely dissipated once the war ended. To be sure, some historians have argued that the R&A experience did not so much disappear as become instead the skeleton for American academia, or at least its social-science departments, for the rest of the twentieth century. This was in part because of the personalities who had cut their teeth in R&A and then went back to teaching and research, and also in part because the immediate necessity to deal somehow with the USSR quickly shaped research funding priorities, thus creating virtually overnight the various disciplines of Soviet studies.[73] In that sense at least, the thousands of scholars who have gone on to amass the vast corpus of American knowledge may be said to spring – in some part at least – from the R&A experiment.

In many important ways, however, that body of knowledge was lost to the intelligence community, which became increasingly obsessed with secrets. As Robin Winks points out,[74] Nazi Germany was totalitarian but not physically isolated, making it possible for conventional research to yield results. The Soviet Union, by contrast, was both totalitarian *and* remote, especially as the Cold War began in earnest.

One of the most commonly bruited figures about open source information is that 80 percent[75] of intelligence is based on openly available material, although some raise that figure to 90 percent,[76] or even 95 percent.[77] For at least the next decade after the end of World War II, however, open source information – or at least information which analysts were willing to believe was reliable, and not deliberate deception – came virtually to be non-existent. In such an atmosphere the wide-ranging research efforts of an organization like an R&A seemed to offer little of value in understanding the new adversary, while the very much more narrow methodology of propaganda analysis was moving into what would prove to be its glory years.

Notes

1 David Kahn, "An Historical Theory of Intelligence," *Intelligence and National Security,* vol. 16, Autumn 2001, pp. 79–92. Quoted from his website, http://david-kahn.com/articles-historical-theory-intelligence.htm, which is unpaginated.

2 Kahn, "An Historical Theory of Intelligence."

3 David Kahn, *The Reader of Gentlemen's Mail* (New Haven, CT: Yale University Press, 2004).

4 Harry Howe Ransom, *Central Intelligence and National Security* (Cambridge, MA: Harvard University Press, 1959), pp. 45, 51.

5 George J. A. O'Toole, *Honorable Treachery: A History of U.S. Intelligence, Espionage, and Covert Action from the American Revolution to the CIA* (New York: Atlantic Monthly Press, 1991), caption, unpaginated photo.

6 Ransom, p. 53.

7 As quoted in George S. Pettee, *The Future of American Secret Intelligence* (Washington DC: Infantry Journal Press, 1946), pp. 36–37.

8 Tom Standage, *The Victorian Internet* (New York: Walker & Co., 1998), pp. 155–57.

9 Paul Starr, *The Creation of the Media* (New York: Basic Books, 2004), pp. 218–19.

10 Starr, p. 200.

11 Edward Bernays, *Propaganda* (New York: H. Liveright, 1928), p. 12.

12 The notion of "the crowd" or the "the masses" as a separate political entity is said to date from 1895, when French sociologist Gustave Le Bon published his book *Psychologie des Foules*, translated as *The Crowd: A Study of the Popular Mind* (NY: Macmillan, 1896). See Stuart Ewen, "Reflections on Visual Persuasion," *New York Law School Law Review*, vol. 43, 1999.

13 Arthur Ponsonby, *Falsehood in Wartime* (New York: Allen & Unwin, 1928), p. 19.

14 Walter Lippmann, *Liberty and the News* (New York: Harcourt, Brace, and Howe, 1920), p. 61.

15 Walter Lippmann, *Public Opinion* (New York: Harcourt, Brace, and Co., 1922), p. 272.

16 Bernays, p. 20.

17 Roland Marchand, *Advertising the American Dream* (Berkeley, CA: University of California Press, 1985), p. 8.

18 George Creel, *How We Advertised America* (New York: Harper and Brothers, 1920), p. 1, original emphasis.

19 Creel, pp. 6–9, 119–29. Creel claims in his book that "30 odd" booklets "covering every phase of America's ideals" were written and translated, "75 million" copies of which were distributed in the US and "many millions" elsewhere; "75,000 speakers" in "5,200 communities" gave "755,190 speeches, every one having the carry of shrapnel"; artists donated "1,438 drawings" which were reproduced and distributed; as were "over 200,000" photographs and "stereopticon slides;" and scores of motion pictures.

20 Creel, pp. 3, 4.

21 Timothy Glander, *Origins of Mass Communications Research During the American Cold War* (Mahwah, NJ: Lawrence Erlbaum Associates, 2000), p. 11.

22 Brett Gary, *Nervous Liberals* (New York: Columbia University Press, 1999), p. 22.

23 This period is examined extensively by Timothy Glander, and also by Brett Gary.

24 Lippmann, *Public Opinion*, pp. 249, 379.

25 These issues are explored in detail by Paul Starr.

26 As quoted in Gary, p. 195.

27 Harold N. Graves Jr, *War on the Short Wave* (New York: Headline Books, Foreign Policy Association, 1941).

28 See description at Mudd Manuscript Library, Princeton University Library, permanent URL at: http://arks.princeton.edu/ark:/88435/0v838057k.

29 Graves, pp. 10–11.

30 Pittsburgh station KDKA is generally accepted to have been the first commercial station to do regular broadcasts, starting in November 1920. Stan J. Liebowitz, "The Elusive Symbiosis: The Impact of Radio on the Record Industry," *Review of Economic Research on Copyright Issues*, vol. 1(1), 2004, pp. 93–118.

31 Glander, p. 1.

32 Starr, p. 379.

33 Graves, p. 61.

34 Ponsonby, pp. 19, 27.

35 Joseph E. Roop, *Foreign Broadcast Information Service: History Part I: 1941–1947*, CIA internal document, April 1969, p. 5. Available at: https://www.cia.gov/library/center-for-the-study-of-intelligence/csi-publications/books-and-monographs/foreign-broadcast-information-service/index.html accessed 13 July 2010.

36 Graves, pp. 36–37.

37 Stephen C. Mercado, "FBIS Against the Axis, 1941–1945," *Studies in Intelligence*, Fall–Winter 2001, unpaginated PDF, at: https://www.cia.gov/library/center-for-the-study-of-intelligence/kent-csi/vol45no5/html/v45i5a04p.htm

38 The organization was renamed the Foreign Broadcast Intelligence Service in 1942 and the Foreign Broadcast Information Service (FBIS) in 1967. It remained FBIS until 2005, when it became the Open Source Center.

39 Roop, p. 7.

40 In those pre-electronic days, not only did the texts have to be typed manually, but the publications were initially distributed in mimeograph form. Even more time-consuming at first was that the broadcasts were monitored and recorded in Laurel, MD, then transported (by station wagon) to the FBMS office in Washington. Within a year, however, telephone lines were run from the new monitoring station, in Silver Hill, MD, directly to FBMS (Roop, pp. 18–19). The broadcasts themselves were captured on wax cylinders via Dictaphone machines. See Edwin Teale, "America Listens In," *Popular Science Monthly*, June 1941.

41 Roop, p. 23.

42 Roop, p. 52.

43 Depending on the date, the initials could stand for either Foreign Broadcast Intelligence Service or Foreign Broadcast Information Service.

44 Roop, pp. 52 ff.

45 Roop, p. 45.

46 Roop, pp. 16–18.

47 Roop, pp. 189 ff.

48 Robert D. Leigh, "Politicians vs. Bureaucrats," *Harper's Magazine,* vol. 190, n. 1136, January 1945, p. 105.

49 Leigh, p. 99.

50 Roop, pp. 105–115.

51 Mercado, unpaginated.

52 Both Glander and Gary, op. cit., have thorough explanations of this group, and Lasswell's contributions to it.

53 Alexander L. George, *Propaganda Analysis* (Evanston, IL: Row, Peterson, & Co., 1959), p. x.

54 George, p. 65 n., original emphasis.

55 George, pp. 260 ff.

56 Roop, pp. 299 ff.

57 Thomas F. Troy, *Donovan and the CIA* (Frederick, MD: Aletheia Books, 1981), p. 84.

58 Ransom, p. 56.

59 Robin Winks, *Cloak and Gown* (New Haven, CT: Yale University Press, 1996), p. 63.

60 Jack Davis, "Sherman Kent and the Profession of Intelligence Analysis," *The Sherman Kent Center for Intelligence Analysis, Occasional Papers,* vol. 1, no. 5, November 2002, unpaginated, at: https://www.cia.gov/library/kent-center-occasional-papers/vol1no5.htm, accessed 14 July 2010.

61 Barry M. Katz, *Foreign Intelligence* (Cambridge, MA: Harvard University Press, 1989), p. xii.

62 Winks, p. 113.

63 Winks, pp. xii, 29 ff.

64 Winks, pp. 84–85.

65 Katz, p. 4.

66 Katz, p. 18.

67 Katz, p. 18.

68 Winks, p. 100.

69 Winks, pp. 87, 103.

70 Winks, pp. 101–111.

71 George S. Pettee, "Economic Intelligence," lecture to the Industrial College of the Armed Forces, 24 February 1950, at: https://digitalndulibrary.ndu.edu/cdm4/document.php?CISOROOT=/icafarchive&CISOPTR=17222&REC=20, accessed 31 May 2011.

72 Pettee, *American Secret Intelligence*, p. 2.

73 Katz argues this most directly, but other scholars too have made similar arguments. For an overview see the review essay by David Engerman, "Rethinking Cold War Universities: Some Recent Histories," *Journal of Cold War Studies*, vol. 5, no. 3, summer 2003.

74 Winks, p. 62.

75 For example see Ransom, p. 19.

76 Richard A. Best Jr and Alfred Cumming, "CRS Report for Congress: Open Source Intelligence (OSINT): Issues for Congress," RL34270, 5 December 2007, p. 4.

77 Winks, p. 475.

CHAPTER TWO

Intelligence analysis and open sources – the early days

When World War II ended, the US began to repeat the process that had marked the close of World War I, dismantling the information gathering and analytic components that had been so hastily slapped together just a few years before. The impulses behind the dismantling were much as they had been 27 years earlier, captured in newspaper headlines charging that Donovan and others arguing for a centralized intelligence organization were intent on creating "an American Gestapo."[1] This time, however, the forces seeking to continue, and even expand, the intelligence functions were far stronger than were those opposing it. Part of the reason, of course, was that the new enemy – the Soviet Union – was already seen by many to be looming on the horizon. Perhaps even more important, if the argument made by author Garry Wills in a recent book is correct, was that the creation of the atomic bomb had fundamentally changed the nature of the US presidency and, along with that, the defense and intelligence functions that supported it.[2]

Certainly Wills' position is borne out by the bureaucratic donnybrook which followed President Truman's dismantling of the OSS. The details of the battle leading up to the creation of the CIA (in 1947) are byzantine – in part because the various working groups grappling with the problem frequently changed their names, and thus their acronyms – but the basic outlines of the conflict had two central issues: the first, whether "intelligence" was to be primarily analytic and informational in nature, or if it was to include (or indeed be limited only to) covert cloak-and-dagger "operations"; and, the second, to whom those responsible for intelligence should answer – the State Department, the military (which at the time was divided into separate departments, War and Navy), or the President.[3]

While not central to that battle, what information is understood to be, and the uses to which it can (or should) be put in the policymaking process underlay to a great degree the process which ultimately resulted in the formation of the CIA. Although the "bad-eyes brigade" had begun the war with almost no information, by the end of it the collection process that had been set in motion pulled in so much material that intelligence units were drowning in it. Two *tons* of German maps, for example, were captured, as were the 2 million volumes of the Prussian State Library, found stuffed into a German mine without apparent order or plan.[4] Specially created teams had to be set up to try to translate and process the huge troves of captured documents. The fact that this information had been captured, however, and therefore was owned mostly by the military, tended to reinforce at least two perceptions about it: that its primary value was for the data that it contained – "the facts" – and that the collection of this sort of data required or was similar to clandestine collection,[5] which was precisely the kind of activity which made large parts of post-war Washington nervous about continuing the so-called "Donovan Plan" for centralized intelligence.

Because it was part of Donovan's OSS, R&A was quickly dismantled. The State Department had begun making plans even before the end of the war to absorb R&A, which it accomplished in a formal sense with President Truman's disbanding of OSS, dating officially to the funding cut-off of 13 September 1945. Much of the R&A staff, however, had already begun drifting away, either returning to academia or beginning to spiral into the gravity well that became a unitary, centralized intelligence organization. R&A alumni in general resisted the transfer to the Department of State because the Department's plan – encouraged by the Office of Management and Budget (OMB), which was concerned about the costs attendant on a larger intelligence community – was to distribute the 1,000 or so analysts who had been on the R&A staff among the various policy units of State, which as an organization would retain overall responsibility for intelligence.[6]

Both the Army and the Navy objected to this plan, arguing that the State Department did not or could not collect the operational and tactical information they required. In addition, neither military branch would cede intelligence primacy to the other, so that all three entities could complain with some justice that the others were refusing to share information. President Truman meanwhile suspected that his own information needs were not being met – one measure of which is that for a time he was receiving two competing morning briefing summaries, one from the State Department and one from the Central Intelligence Group (importantly, both promised to offer only "factual statements" devoid of "information … interpreted to advise the President").[7]

Perhaps the most pressing problem confronting the defense and policy-making establishments – and therefore the nascent intelligence community – was just how little the US knew about the emerging enemy, the USSR. Even during the war, when the US and the USSR had ostensibly been allies, the Soviets had been supplying virtually no information to the R&A teams – in June and July 1943, for example, the Soviets gave the OSS just 40 mimeographed pages of information, while important periodicals like *Pravda* (the Party newspaper) and *Izvestiya* (the government newspaper) took up to two months to arrive, and other periodicals (e.g., *Under the Banner of Marxism*) never came at all.[8] As the Cold War began, even that dribble disappeared, turning the Soviet Union essentially into a "black box." Thus the firm directive of Admiral Sidney W. Souers, first Director of the Central Intelligence Group (CIG, formed in January 1946), which ordered the still-scattered elements of the various intelligence functions to address "the urgent need to develop the highest possible intelligence of the USSR in the shortest possible time."[9]

This was precisely the same need which had confronted the US when World War II began, overcome almost immediately by the "all-nighters" performed by Sherman Kent and the rest of the R&A teams. In the case of the USSR, the first proposed solution was similar, to pull together research teams from across the three departments (State, War, and Navy) to create an encyclopedia of "all types of <u>factual</u> strategic intelligence on the USSR [underlining in original]."[10] This three-volume *Strategic Intelligence Digest* (SID), for circulation only at the highest levels of government, was to be produced by the combined efforts of units from State, the War Department (both Army and the Air Force, which did not become a separate service until 1947), and the Navy. Though it would of necessity make heavy use of openly available information, the SID was to be classified TOP SECRET, and, as the memorandum imposing the classification warned, "The greatest care will be taken to maintain the security of the operation."[11]

The attempt to create that encyclopedia – which had been scheduled to come out within a year but was not completed until 1949[12] – reproduces in miniature many of the problems and paradoxes which shaped the use of openly available information in the early years of the CIA, and indeed continues to condition it even today. One measure of how little information was available to anyone in those years, for example, was the fact that among the subjects that the emerging CIG had to parcel out in a proposed directive coordinating collection activities (i.e., who was responsible for information about what) was meteorology – in that memo assigned to "Army Air Force."[13] Difficult as it may be to remember (or imagine) today, one of the major, and most important, activities of clandestine "agents in place" during those early years of the IC was simply to keep track of, and, when possible, report on weather conditions in the far-flung places where the US had interests. Another indicator of the way that information was conceptualized in those days is that the SID was originally intended to be a static document, an encyclopedia which would – once and forever – provide the answers about any questions the policymakers might have about the USSR. Although it was evident even before the SID's appearance that the USSR, however static it might seem, was in fact a changing, evolving enemy, the point became overwhelmingly obvious a few months after the SID's appearance, when the Soviet Union exploded an atomic bomb of its own.

Perversely enough, however, as their needs for information grew, IC analysts were also increasingly distrustful of any information that could be freely or openly obtained. The general belief about information emanating from the USSR was summed up in an article in a 1954 article in *Commentary* magazine, in which author Franz Borkenau claimed:

> never has so large an area of the inhabited earth been so tightly sealed off from the rest of humanity – not even the China of the Manchus, or the Japan of the Shoguns: at least, these countries did not lie so consistently and systematically about what went on inside them [as does the USSR] ... Soviet Russia, having been founded by force in the name of a utopian ideal, and being maintained by force in a way that goes directly counter to that ideal, must persuade the world that its inner reality is the opposite of what it actually is. Thus the largest part of Soviet publicistic and intellectual life ... is devoted to falsification on a scale without precedent in history.[14]

The conviction that, as one compendium of Soviet information efforts put it, "From the earliest days of Marxism down to the present, propaganda has played a leading role in Communist strategy,"[15] meant that many analysts increasingly placed their trust only in data which they, or their collectors, managed to acquire independently of the Soviet "propaganda machine." At the same time, however, there was another group of analysts who argued strenuously that that "propaganda machine" itself could be a significant source of useful information – provided one knew how to read it.

Knowing what we didn't know

How little the US knew about the USSR is underscored by the volume, variety, and sheer granularity of the products that were turned out in the early years of the Cold War. Large quantities of that analysis have been declassified, allowing us to see that topics ranged from basic political history ("ORE 55-49: Theory and Practice of Communist Subversion"[16]) to industry-specific studies ("The Coke-Chemical Industry in the USSR"; "The Ethyl Alcohol Industry in the USSR"[17]) to a whole series of leadership studies which were grouped together under the rubric CAESAR.[18] Indeed, such titles as "Analysis of Traffic Density Between Omsk and Novosibirsk" (6 October 1953) and "Machine Analysis of Aeroflot Scheduled Operations 1964 Summer Timetable" (15 December 1964)[19] convey well how deeply the IC analysts dug in their efforts to learn whatever they might about the enigmatic, secretive enemy.

It is also useful to note the various sources of the information for these reports, and the processes by which they were written. To judge by their contents, most of the reports were almost certainly responses to direct taskings,[20] or to specific collection requirements. Although it took some time for the process to be fully regularized, what was emerging even early on in the formation of the intelligence community was something similar to Henry Ford's assembly line – probably not surprising, given that it was precisely that industrial model which was widely credited with having helped win the recent war. Indeed, CIA's analytic "founding father," Sherman Kent, had argued in his seminal *Strategic Intelligence for American World Policy* that intelligence analysis should share the best qualities of "the large university faculty," "our greatest metropolitan newspapers," and "a good business organization ... engaged in the manufacture of a product (knowledge) out of raw materials (all manner of data)."[21]

What that meant in this case was that policymakers, or their staff, marked out the topics about which they wished, or needed, to know more. Those became "collection requirements," or information categories which particular "collectors" then set out to fill. As was delineated even in the first CIG memos,[22] certain types of information were to be collected by certain types of institutions and their processes. Some of those built large-scale technical solutions, some used the kind of covert operations that have become synonymous in the public mind with "intelligence," and some, like FBIS, accessed publicly available information. All of this, however, was grouped under the rubric "collection," which was understood to be the value-neutral acquisition of data.

Once the data was collected, it was "processed." The term had various meanings, depending upon the way in which the information had been gathered – processed information taken from human sources had to be disguised in order to protect the providers; electronic intercepts or, as they became possible, overhead photographs, had to be made intelligible to non-adepts, and foreign publications had to be translated into English – all activities which not only slowed down transmission of information, but also changed it as it moved along the "production belt." The penultimate step in the production process was "analysis" (the last step being delivery of a "finished intelligence product" to "the consumers" – what they did with it will be explored in the next chapter). What precisely was meant by "analysis" has been a consistent point of contention within the IC, down even to the present, and is a subject to which this book will return. For now, it is enough to note that analysis was understood to be an activity distinct from the information itself. Not necessarily evident from the formulation, but a fact, was that analysis was also regarded as a higher and more important activity than was collection, which inevitably led to turf battles, "stovepiping" of information, and other problems.

The steps of this "intelligence cycle," and the divisions in what people kept imagining should be a common discipline, led repeatedly to conflict. Even in the darkest of the Stalinist days, collectors and analysts interested in certain kinds of problems – most particularly, how well Soviet hard science was performing – were able to get at least some information from open sources, even if that "information" was that there was no information. This was shown, for example, by a study from 1949, which demonstrated that the number of Soviet publications in chemical research offered in the standard discipline abstracts had dropped by about two-thirds between 1941 and 1949, thus allowing analysts to conclude that important sub-fields of chemical research were probably now top-secret military priorities.[23] Other analysts, however, tended to discount information received through published sources, arguing that such information was either deliberately deceptive, incomplete, or incompetently assembled, and so could only be used to the extent that it could be checked against information received through clandestine means. That skepticism is clearly reflected in, for example, a study of household consumption in the USSR from 1956, which attempts a dispassionate measure of "the probable extent of dissatisfaction among Soviet consumers." As a prefatory reference note explains,

the estimates ... in this report were obtained almost entirely from overt source material, including Soviet newspapers, periodicals, trade journals, and monographs. Although no attempt at deliberate falsification has been discovered, it was found that data from these sources must be interpreted with extreme caution because of what amounts to deliberate Soviet casualness with definitions... For information on Soviet consumer prices since 1948, official price data were utilized where available, but of necessity primary reliance was placed on the State Department reporting, and on covert sources.[24]

FDD and FBIS

The tensions between the two views of information were exacerbated by the fact that, when CIG was created, it took control of two legacy open source providers, each of which had quite different histories but very similar functions – which only grew more similar as time went on and technologies changed. After its near-death by politics in the FCC (explained in Chapter 1), and a budget scare near the end of 1945 (countered with some adroit public relations work[25]), FBIS by the war's end was universally recognized as a "service of common concern" and so passed fairly smoothly from the FCC to the War Department, which was understood to be a temporary accommodation while Washington sorted out the future of intelligence. FBIS's presumed future home was the State Department, but the Department proved unwilling or unable to assume financial and other responsibility for the approximately 300 people still working in FBIS.[26] Efforts were made to pass the organization to CIG, but that body had no statutory right to sign contracts or disburse funds, so FBIS remained in the War Department until 1947, when the Central Intelligence Agency was formed. A brief battle ensued over the question of where FBIS ought to be housed in that organization, in the emergent "operations" side (the name of which changed frequently, but the purpose of which was always covert collection of information) or the analytic side – with always the caveat that too much "analysis" might interfere with what Admiral Hillenkoetter called the chief value of the group, "the rapidity of its service."[27]

Which of course raised the issue of what precisely was the service provided by FBIS. The original funding from President Roosevelt had been for "recording, translating, transcribing, and analyzing certain radio programs broadcast from foreign transmitters."[28] One of the first memos sent by Harold Graves made clear that he expected analysis would be a fundamental part of the new organization's activities: "An Analysis section will conduct scientific studies of content, primarily from a psychological point of view, with a purpose of clearly delineating the purposes and objectives of foreign efforts to influence the attitudes of various national publics toward the United States and toward war efforts generally."[29] Within a year, however, FBIS analytic efforts came under fire from analysts in the OSS, with the eventual resolution that the Office of War Information (OWI) agreed to stop duplicating the monitoring of radio broadcasts, while FBIS agreed to pass responsibility for analysis (and many of its analysts) to OWI. As the head of the FBIS analytic unit wrote, "many offices felt that they would be better served if they got the raw materials from FBIS and controlled the full process of the analysis."[30] Although FBIS continued to supply both translations (summaries and full texts) and analysis, that same tension continued, with FBIS fighting to keep an analytic capability and other components showing higher regard for the translations.[31]

It must be remembered that FBIS was, as its name implied, responsible only for information transmitted by radio, which at the time played a role more like that of the internet today – it was faster, and often carried more localized, specific information than did the large daily newspapers, especially those put out in the Soviet Union. Some sense of the information that FBIS could deliver is conveyed by a 1947 report in the *Washington Post* which described how FBIS monitors had used a French broadcast from Dakar which in turn was based on a dispatch from Shanghai to corroborate a report by a Swiss monitoring service that the Soviets had begun large-scale maneuvers near the Bering Straits.[32]

Printed matter – newspapers, books, journal articles, and anything else that was not electronic – was the responsibility of another division, the Foreign Documents Branch (later apparently made a Division, and thus usually known as FDD). Unlike FBIS, FDD was a new entity, formed from the war-time Washington Documents Center (WDC), which had primarily translated captured Japanese materials, and the Army's German Military Documents Center.[33] Some sense of both the volume and the nature of the work the FDD's military antecedents had done is apparent in the reminiscences of a WDC "alumnus," who describes how he and his group "plowed through 40 mail sacks of classified Japanese military patents."[34] After the war, FDD appears to have switched its attention to Soviet materials. The scale of their activities is evident in an account which states that in 1956 FDD had examined "15,179 Soviet newspapers, periodicals, and books," searching for "intelligence based on requirements submitted by various agencies" – one reason why "roughly 75 to 90 percent of our economic, scientific, and geographic knowledge of the Soviet Bloc comes from analysis of open source material."[35] That same article suggests that FDD was also involved in what we now would call "data mining" when the group "transliterated, codified, consolidated, and punched ... into IBM machine cards" the contents of a 1951 Moscow phone book (followed later by one from Leningrad) in order to try to gain insight into the personnel of the Soviet scientific establishment.[36]

Although there are suggestions that FDD and FBIS worked together at least to a certain degree – for example by co-producing analysis on China (details given below) – there is also evidence in the available materials that there was a great deal of friction and overlap, as the distinctions between print and radio began to fray. Even before the end of the war, for example, technology made it possible for news services to transmit their copy by radio, meaning that "newspaper stories" were accessible to radio monitors before they reached the actual papers. A complication of another sort is evident in a 1946 newspaper article on Soviet intentions in Iran, which mentions in passing a report by the "War Department's foreign broadcast intelligence service" (capitalization as in the original) which had noted that "Moscow radio [recently] broadcast for Russian listeners an article from *Pravda Ukrainy*"[37] on the subject – thus implying not only that both FDD and FBIS might claim "ownership" of the broadcast, but also that FBIS would probably have received the article before FDD did. A clear indicator that there was conflict between the two is the number of National Security Council Intelligence Directives (known as NSCIDs) which were intended to clarify relations. Most of the NSCIDs seem still to be classified, but there is a declassified list of the titles,[38] which show that at least four – NSCID 6, "Foreign Wireless and Radio Monitoring" (issued 12 December 1947),

NSCID 10, "Collection of Foreign Scientific and Technological Data" (issued 18 January 1949), NSCID 15, "Coordination and Production of Foreign Economic Intelligence" (issued in two parts, 13 and 22 June 1951), and NSCD 16, "Foreign Language Publications" (issued 7 March 1953) – were issued to untangle responsibilities disputed among the various collectors. Available resources don't explain how or why, but FDD was folded into FBIS in 1967, when (according to promotional materials), the "service mission" of the one-time radio monitoring service "was officially expanded to include all relevant foreign mass media, including radio, television, newspapers and magazines."[39] Although the name seems no longer to have been used, the Church Report wrote that "FDD remains in FBIS to this day [1976]."[40]

The published accounts suggest that FDD was primarily a translation service, which meant that it must have been constantly challenged by the volume of information that customers demanded it produce, particularly as the Soviets began to publish more after Stalin's death – increasing the number of scientific journals, for example, from 1,408 in 1950 to 2,026 in 1955. Even more daunting, the Library of Congress had received 8,250 items from the Soviet Union in 1953, compared to 19,000 in 1956.[41] By October 1957, when the Soviets launched the first artificial earth satellite, the US scientific community declared the translation of Soviet scientific journals to be scandalously inadequate, charging that "thousands of Soviet scientific reports are collecting dust on Library of Congress shelves for lack of a program to translate them."[42] Presumably in response, FDD seems to have transformed a small covert operation called Transworld Language Services – which is described in a participant memoir as a "cover-blown CIA proprietary [that was] doing stuff for FDD using unclearable foreign nationals"[43] – into the US Joint Publication Research Service (JPRS).[44] Described as "the largest English-language translator in the world," JPRS is credited with having produced "more than 80,000 reports" since its founding in 1957.[45] Although newspaper reports from 1957 do not mention JPRS by name (as one library source description delicately puts it, "Between 1957 and 1962 JPRS reports were distributed to government agencies only; documents were unavailable to the general public"[46]), urgency about the need to cope with the rising flood of Soviet scientific publications is clear – one account from 1957 suggests that one "Government measure" being explored was to create "electronic 'brains' that can translate foreign languages, abstract and catalogue the information, and then retrieve it at the push of a button."[47]

Data … but what does it mean?

The histories of FDD, FBIS, and, for that matter, R&A, OWI, and the other OSS-era antecedents all show that there were three fundamental ways of understanding – and therefore solving – the information needs of the intelligence community. One focused on information capture and retrieval, so that, for example, FBIS engineers argued among themselves and with counterparts elsewhere about what kinds of antennae, receivers, and transcribers were best for bringing in and recording the signals coming over the ether – regardless of what was being transmitted within those signals. While the people who filled this information need were of course vital – for without their intercession the work of the other two groups would have been impossible – they also constantly posed the danger of inundating the intelligence and policymaking communities with more information than they could cope with. That is reflected in the newspaper accounts from 1957, which show that the *collection* of Soviet scientific literature was proceeding well, but the *processing* of it was not. The *New York Times*, for example, lamented that only 30 of the 1,200 journals received by the Library of Congress were being regularly translated, and further complained that details of the impending Sputnik launch had been published – unnoticed – in a Soviet journal for amateur radio enthusiasts three months before the satellite's lift-off.[48] The same problem shows in the complaint by a senior FBIS official during the war, that a listening post in Texas that was devoted to Latin American broadcasting should be closed, because after 16 months of operation, the output of the sources had proven to be "the worst drivel imaginable."[49]

A second way of understanding information was that of FDD and, to a somewhat lesser extent, FBIS, as reflected in the recurrent emphasis that these services were interested only in "factual information," or the contents of broadcasts and publications. As has already been noted above, there was persistent pressure within the IC about how best to handle the information that the Soviets were providing openly. FDD in particular struggled simply to translate the ever-swelling volume, apparently partly in response to standing requirements, and partly in response to requests from other government bodies. Not surprisingly, that approach led inevitably to charges and complaints that other "important documents" had been missed. In 1966, for example, an internal CIA study into reasons why the agency had underestimated the by-then obvious Sino-Soviet split was that "CIA's sinologists were so immersed in the large volume of daily FBIS and other source reports on Communist China in the early 1960s that they failed to consider adequately the broader question of the slowly developing Sino-Soviet dispute."[50]

Most of the information supplied by FDD, just like that of most of the rest of the CIA, was overwhelmingly tactical, as the US tried to understand Soviet capabilities and capacities. As important as knowing what a country *could* do, however, was trying to know what it *would* do, or at least *might* do – or, to put the question another way, the Soviets had the Bomb, but would they *use* it? Given a closed, impenetrable society like that of the

USSR, where gaining access to the innermost circle of leadership was for all practical purposes impossible, how could the intentions and purposes of the Soviet leaders be divined? It was precisely here that the third way of using information flourished, growing out of the propaganda analysis methodology that FBIS had forged (or fumbled its way toward) in attempting to discern Nazi intentions during the war.

Propaganda analysis was based on communications theories which had been explored in the late 1930s by the Rockefeller Group on Mass Communications Research. By stressing that communicative acts were deliberate, analysts were able to use text as evidence of thought. The choice of media, for example, could be assumed to be significant – publication in one venue, it was assumed, could have a different meaning than it might if published elsewhere, even if the words of a given publication were identical. This was true in part because different media reached different audiences, so that a publication in one newspaper might be assumed to be addressed in part at least to "insiders," while publication in another might signal that the intended audience was society as a whole.

To be sure, the contents of the communications were still considered to be important indicators, but not so much for whether or not they were factually accurate, as much as for the degree to which they continued past usage, or deviated from it. The science of exploiting such information was *content analysis*, which in turn was devoted to *propaganda analysis*. Just as Harold Graves before the war had counted, and characterized, the number of minutes of Nazi radio broadcasts devoted to particular topics (thus demonstrating, as was shown in Chapter One, that the Nazis were shifting from wooing the US to begin to make threats), so did propaganda analysts begin to track how many times particular phrases were used, as contrasted with other usages.

It is not easy to find unclassified examples of FBIS analytic products, particularly from the early days of the Cold War, in part because analytic and interpretive findings seem often to have been incorporated into classified documents. The leadership studies grouped under the TOP SECRET "CAESAR" rubric,[51] for example, rely heavily on newspaper and journal accounts to offer explanations for the reasons behind Byzantine-seeming events like "the Doctors' Plot," the reaction to Stalin's death, the subsequent removal of secret police head Lavrentii Beria, and other "mysteries of the Kremlin."

Fortunately, examples exist of content analysis that was performed outside of the CIA. One of the first illustrations of the method was provided by Franz Borkenau, in an article published in *Commentary* magazine in April 1954.[52] As an editorial note which accompanies the article explains, Borkenau was an Austrian communist who had left the party in 1929 and then had been further disillusioned by the Spanish Civil War. A theorist of totalitarianism, Borkenau was the author of a number of influential books and articles about Nazism and, when the war ended, communism. He reached a high point of sorts in January 1953, when he announced in a German weekly that Stalin must be on the verge of death – a prediction which seven weeks later proved correct.

Borkenau's *Commentary* article explained in detail how he had arrived at his conclusion. While acknowledging that content analysis has serious limitations, Borkenau argued that the method was valid because of "the structural peculiarities of the Soviet regime and Soviet society." Rather than being monolithic, as most people presumed, Soviet society was riven with internal conflict – a fact which gives the researcher "his entering wedge." The vehicle for understanding Soviet politics is the Soviet press, which, Borkenau noted, is "filled mostly with quotations, direct and indirect." Far from being "boring and depressing," this style is the key to unlocking Soviet politics in process. "Little is printed in the Communist press that does not depend, in wording even more than in meaning, on the text of some party decision, some leader's speech, or some doctrine as laid down by the founding fathers of Communism." As he noted: "different machines, factions, and political groupings inside the Soviet regime usually quote correspondingly different people and different texts." As Borkenau acknowledges, following this train of battling quotations requires that "the investigator must know the history and content of numberless party controversies in the past as thoroughly as a learned theologian would the countless disputes that marked the course of Christian dogma."[53]

Having laid out his methodology, Borkenau ends his article with a quick sketch of the evidence trail which had led him to his prediction – in the run-up to the Doctors' Plot, the East German communist party passed a resolution "on the teachings of the Slansky case" (Rudolf Slansky having been General Secretary of the Czechoslovak communist party until his arrest as a "Titoist" in November 1951, for which crime he was executed in December 1952). The resolution, Borkenau writes, "attracted much attention," in part because of its pronounced anti-Semitic character, and also because it suggested that a resolution was impending for an internal German power struggle. What Borkenau noticed that others did not, however (or at least no one whose writing is now available) is that the German accounts of the Slansky resolution quoted Malenkov and German leader Ulbricht, "who by adding his own yelp to the anti-Semitic chorus … proclaimed himself a Malenkov client." What most struck Borkenau in the resolution itself was that "Stalin *was quoted with a mere half-sentence dating from 1910* [cursive in the original]." Borkenau then reasoned that "such a deliberate affront could have been offered only by people sure of that tyrant's approaching downfall or else out of the reach of his retribution. Otherwise it was sure suicide. It was primarily on the strength of the evidence found in this resolution that I then predicted, in print, Stalin's imminent death – which, sure enough, came seven weeks later."[54]

Borkenau's most important point, however, was not that he had been correct, but rather that the method he espoused was actually more reliable in the communist context than would have been "direct 'inside' information from the Soviet world." He acknowledged that observers in Moscow in early January had noted that "something strange was going on," and there was also "no lack of straws in the wind to show that Stalin was in a political as well as physical decline." However, Borkenau cautioned, such indicators were not grounds for anything more than guesswork, while "direct information from behind the Iron Curtain" would have been even more suspect, since "much of it is 'planted' by Communist agents." In contrast, "the mere counting of the words devoted to Malenkov and Stalin ... in a satellite resolution gave an unambiguous answer to the question whether any faction at the Communist top intended Stalin's overthrow."[55]

"The Talmudists" – mastering "esoteric communication"

The kind of open source analysis that Borkenau described became a robust industry within the intelligence community (although the vagaries of the declassification process make it hard to judge how great a part it was of the overall analytic effort). Despite the criticisms implied by the 1966 study of CIA analytic failures cited above, finding the Sino-Soviet split is generally described as the single largest success of the propaganda analysis methodology. It was not, however, the only one. Donald Zagoria, a China expert who worked at FBIS before moving on to a distinguished academic career, sketched in the methodological outline that prefaced his 1962 book, *The Sino-Soviet Conflict*, the "major political problems of the Communist world in the post-Stalin era" which, in his words, "protruded above the surface like icebergs."[56] These included: the Stalin succession crisis; the Soviet-Yugoslav controversy; the fissures in the Communist world wrought by Khrushchev's "secret speech"; Soviet-Polish tensions in 1956–57; and the Sino-Soviet tensions which had been growing since at least 1956. All of these were, by implication, issues which skilled open source analysts might have caught – or did catch – using content analysis, propaganda analysis, and – a new term that appeared in the analytic lexicon toward the end of the 1950s – the study of "esoteric communication."

Another FBIS alumnus, Myron Rush, who wrote about Khrushchev's rise to power, characterized this esoteric communication as "hidden messages, which enable factional leaders to communicate quickly, safely, and decisively with the sub-elites whose support they solicit."[57] The search for those hidden messages, Rush wrote, led other analysts to characterize him and his fellow adherents of this style of open source political analysis as "Talmudists" – "as though," he expostulates, "[the analysts] rather than some Soviet politician or publicist had devised these variations." Rush concedes that it may be hard for those not adept at esoteric communication to accept that "piddling with stereotyped formulas can be an important mode of political behavior for powerful leaders," but asserts nevertheless that "these minutiae – no less than purges and policy debates – are the very stuff of Soviet politics."[58]

Zagoria provided an even fuller defense of studying esoteric communications[59] – the communist world was too large and too disparate, he asserted, to permit its rulers to rely only on closed, person-to-person communications. This was particularly true following the death of Stalin, when "Communist communication" became a two-way flow. Absent other means, public media must be used for this conversation, which allows outside analysts access to them. However, Communist protocol forbids the open airing of differences, so battles must be waged precisely through obscure "doctrinal exegesis," the language of which would-be analysts must master. Zagoria characterizes this esoteric communication as "the third outermost layer of communication in the Communist world." The second layer of "secret Party documents, diplomatic correspondence and similar sources" is rarely glimpsed by westerners, but when it is, Zagoria asserted, the terms of dispute remain doctrinal; in his words, "Ideology and reality have become so interconnected in the Communist mind ... that discussions about reality are never free from ideological assumptions and terminology."[60] That being the case, the study of the third layer allows insight into the next deeper layer, and indeed perhaps even into the innermost layer, what leaders say directly to one another.

As Zagoria's explication of the method shows, propaganda analysis was labor-intensive, and required a particular kind of mind to do it well. One sign of growing Soviet-Chinese tension, for example, was that the official list of slogans issued by the CPSU (Communist Party of the Soviet Union) in celebration of the October 1958 commemoration of the Bolshevik revolution characterized China as "building socialism." When analysts compared this to analogous previous Octobers, and also May Day celebrations, they found that the previous formula had been that China, alone among the other presumed satellite states, had been called "a builder of socialism." Since propaganda analysis requires the assumption that no deviations from past norms are accidental, the analysts tried to find an explanation. Because the Soviets had in another setting described themselves as "builders of communism," the propaganda analysts surmised that it is more auspicious to be "builders of ..." than it is to be "building ...," leading to the analytic conclusion that the Soviets in 1958 were now subtly disputing Chinese claims to have found a road to socialism different from that which Moscow had laid down, and in general Moscow was trying to show Beijing obscure disrespect.

Rush offered an example that hinged on even smaller deviations from past norms. On 3 November 1955 *Pravda* reprinted a congratulatory telegram to Khrushchev – at the time still just one among three supposedly equal successors to Stalin – from someone in New Zealand, who incorrectly addressed Khrushchev as "general secretary" – one of Stalin's titles, which had fallen in abeyance even before Stalin's death. Rush and his fellow analysts of esoterica followed a paper trail through years' worth of newspapers and reference materials in order to establish that the title had not been printed for more than three years but was now apparently being rehabilitated, presumably for use by Khrushchev in his attempt to elevate himself to first-among-equals in the succession struggle. It was because of this research that analysts came to understand why Khrushchev's proper title – "first secretary" – had recently begun to be capitalized – "First secretary" – to make a subtle distinction which nevertheless confirmed that Khrushchev was out-maneuvering his rivals in the battle for power.

Open source analysis and its competitors

Although the propaganda analysts have been embraced in retrospect, particularly for their work on the Sino-Soviet split, available records suggest that their arguments, and also their methods, were met with considerable skepticism. A history of CIA's analysis of the Sino-Soviet split by veteran analyst Harold Ford, for example, notes that the first product to highlight at least potential points of conflict between Moscow and Beijing was an FDD-FBIS joint effort, "Propaganda Evidence Concerning Sino-Soviet Relations," released 30 April 1952.[61] FDD published a study of its own the following year, after which FBIS took up the subject in earnest, first using the noun "conflict" in 1954, with a steady stream of products continuing to flow up to the early 1960s.

According to Ford's history, however, even after what he terms a "windfall of clandestine reporting ... in the 1960s" generally confirmed what the propaganda analysts were arguing, their views were still stoutly resisted, both by other analysts, and – more importantly – by policymakers. The reasons for that resistance are worth detailing, because they point to recurrent issues and challenges in the relationship between information and intelligence. According to Ford, the analysts who were persuaded by arguments that there was a growing conflict tended to be history buffs who were either proficient in at least one of the two languages, or were steady readers of the FBIS translations. Arrayed against them were political theorists and students of Marxism, who held that the specifics of national histories were irrelevant in the context of Marxist theory.

Among those analysts whom Ford dubbed "Sino-Soviet heretics" (by which he seems to mean that they accepted there was a split) was Richard Shryock, who published a tongue-in-cheek account[62] of what those internal analytic battles must have been like. Shryock takes as his jumping-off point Rush's "first vs. First" clue to Khrushchev's rise. While conceding that the study of esoteric communications can be "an occasionally useful tool," Shryock warns that the approach "raises more questions than it can answer, and so its practitioners are prone to discover messages and then forget about their possible implications."[63] As an example, he offers the recent discovery that *Pravda* and other authoritative newspapers had printed a list with the name of one prominent CPSU Presidium member in incorrect alphabetical order. The problem, however, was that no one could come up with a plausible explanation for the anomaly – except perhaps that offered by what he called "the waggish school," who argued this was evidence of "a plot by the Soviet typesetters' union."

Shryock is only slightly more generous to the IC's political scientists, who "think that all politics – indeed, all life – can be diagrammed according to a set of political rules derived from the assumption that the political behavior of mankind is essentially a struggle for pure power (no matter what the Freudians say)." He also lacerates the "biographic school" of analysis, the adherents of which "spend anxious hours scanning the backgrounds and careers of Soviet officials [because] a common element in the lives of two functionaries – a coincidence of birthplace or congruence of careers – somehow creates a political alliance in perpetuity." A related sub-group of that school is the "provincial faction group, which resolves all politics by place of birth and subsequent service." Shryock further lampoons "a few lesser but well-known Washington schools … the economic determinists and their brethren the scientific determinists [to whom] all politics is but a reflection of economics (or science) and can be studied only in the light of this great truth" and "finally there is the clandestine school, for which everything is subordinated to the greater mission of espionage, clandestine sources, and secret data" (of this last group Shryock writes archly: " it would be improper, really, to think of [the clandestine school] as a school of Soviet studies; rather it is an approach which transcends the purely Soviet and all studies, including its own substantive results: it is a way of life").[64]

Also required for propaganda analysis

The analytic methods described by Borkenau, Rush, Zagoria, and other proponents of propaganda analysis, and the findings which they achieved with them, are undoubtedly ingenious. It is another question, however, whether these findings were helpful or useful, or indeed whether they had any impact at all on the course of US politics. As the next chapter will show, the answers to that question are ambiguous, depending a great deal upon how success is defined. For present purposes, it is sufficient to note that propaganda analysis, and the open source collection which supported it, was judged sufficiently useful that FBIS remained an integral part of the CIA, collecting and translating enormous quantities of material drawn from newspapers, radio, and – once it became technically possible – television. The service also translated larger works such as books or important articles, gisted the contents of major journals, and generally provided the grist for hundreds of IC analysts and then, once it became possible for libraries and individuals to subscribe to at least the unclassified version of the service, for additional thousands of academics, students, and researchers.

Because FBIS played such a central role in the development of Soviet studies and China studies – and, through them, area studies in general – it is worth making explicit some of the consequences of the propaganda analysis approach that Borkenau, Zagoria, and Rush left implicit, or may not have noticed at all, since most of the conditions in which they worked then were shared by all researchers. All three of the propaganda analysts cited above refer in one way or another to the huge volumes of material that a conscientious analyst had to digest every day. This of course was in keeping with the dictum laid down in World War II, and made explicit in Alexander George's book about the method, that good propaganda analysis required that *all* of the pertinent material be studied, in order to establish the base line against which significant deviation would show.

Given the ease with which information may be created, transmitted, and stored today, it is worth remembering the enormous effort that was necessary to achieve the abundance which the propaganda analysis method required. Radio intercepts (which could, and increasingly did, include newspaper content being sent by wire services) had to be recorded and transcribed. Newspapers and other periodicals had to be physically transported to Washington, where they were read by language-proficient monitors[65] who made decisions about what to send for translation, what to summarize, and what to ignore. Although those choices were based on "collection requirements," in fact most selection was idiosyncratic, depending upon the experience, judgment, and – it must be admitted – prejudices of the selectors. Those articles had then to be translated, the English texts typed out onto stencils, and the results printed (at first by mimeograph, later by industrial printers), bound, and then physically distributed – all activities which required time, meaning that in the best of circumstances the analysis of propaganda lagged well behind its dissemination in the Soviet Union, China, and elsewhere.[66]

Getting the bound booklets to the users ended the collectors' task, but created a whole new set of challenges for the analysts – most pressing of which was how to digest and store the information these booklets contained. Although the CIA and other intelligence units began to experiment very early with automation (as the next chapter explains), FBIS and JPRS products were paper-only until 1993. Perhaps even more importantly, the flood of daily translations had no indexes until the mid-1970s, when there began to appear *quarterly* lists of the articles that had been translated. Not only was there nothing remotely like the word-search capabilities that makes it possible today to search almost instantaneously through thousands (or millions) of documents, but articles did not even have topic indicators. The only taxonomic aids provided were regional, indicating where something had been published (even if the topic of the article was about another region of interest).

All this required that analysts develop their own methods of cataloging and storing this flow of daily information. Indeed, until photocopiers became common (the proliferation of which was lamented in a 1966 internal report[67]), it was not possible even to tear out and file pages, because one might find articles of value on both sides of a printed sheet. Most analysts thus developed some version of the card catalogs that the R&A staff had made during World War II – and often enough, when they left or retired, their cards, and the knowledge they contained, went with them. Even with their cards, however, analysts had to have capacious memories, and an eye for deviations in minute details. As has already been noted, the deviations were judged *a priori* to be significant, even if the significance was not immediately apparent. At least two consequences flowed from this: analysts tended to have pre-existing convictions about what was important and what was not, which encouraged them to compete against each other for "scoops," so that – the second consequence – information hoarding was encouraged, and analysts became heavily invested in their own positions. Shryock's sardonic account of this process tells how in 1955 the Soviets' willingness to sign the peace treaty establishing the existence of Austria "caught just about everyone by surprise" because the "esoteric communication" analysts were "looking under rocks for invisible writing on slugs and whatever else was uncovered, [but] were not looking under the headlines in their morning papers," while the intelligence community political scientists, "who normally speak only to one another, were concentrating on those very headlines but were ignorant of the factional duel in the Kremlin [that the propaganda analysts were watching]." The author notes that not only could "neither [of those two analytic groups] add the two and two together" but other analytic "tribes" were also distracted in the pursuit of their own pet theories: "the researchers at this point were still playing games with the removal of Beria, the Stalinists were looking for evidence of an increase in troop strength in the Soviet zone in Austria, and the economic determinists were racking up the statistics concerning the shipment of Austrian POL [petroleum, oil, & lubricants] to the Soviet Union."[68] Harold Ford's descriptions sound even nastier, with one side of the Sino-Soviet debate accusing the other of having "19th century minds," and the other riposting that "that's better than having 13th century minds!"[69]

Unspoken here, and probably even unrecognized by the analysts themselves, were also important assumptions about the nature of reality, and the relation that bore to information. Zagoria made the linear, predictable linkage of the past, present, and future fully explicit in a study he wrote for the Rand Corporation, "Talmudism and Communist Communications." In order to give the essence of the esoteric communication methodology, Zagoria opens the paper with what he describes as one of Freud's favorite anecdotes, about an old East European Jew who notices a well-dressed young man traveling with him in the same train car. The old man goes through an elaborate process of deciding who this young man must be – a potential groom sent for from the big city by the rich pretentious family in the old man's village – and so in the end astonishes his fellow traveler by offering him a ride to his bride's house, should they fail to meet him at the station. Astonished, the young man asked how this total stranger had known who he was. The punchline, and the essence of Zagoria's argument, was "it stands to reason!"

What Zagoria did not address in that paper was that the world upon which Freud's anecdote depended – the closely confined, ethnically homogeneous, and largely parochial world of the East European *shtetl* – no longer existed, but rather had vanished into history. It is logical enough, then, that Zagoria did not also explore the possibility that the same thing could happen – indeed was happening – to the world which he was trying to explain through propaganda analysis.

Notes

1   "Donovan Upheld on Peace Spy Plan," *New York Times,* 13 February 1945; "Donovan's Plan," *Washington Post,* 16 February 1945.

2   See Garry Wills, *Bomb Power: The Modern Presidency and the National Security State* (New York: Penguin, 2010).

3   The FBI advanced claims as well, while the Office of Management and Budget (OMB) was also voicing opinions. See Department of State, *Foreign Relations of the United States: 1945–1950: Emergence of the Intelligence Establishment,* introduction, at: http://webdoc.sub.gwdg.de/ebook/p/2005/dep_of_state/www. state.gov/www/about_state/history/intel/intro.html, accessed 25 July 2010.

4   Winks, p. 113.

5   Arthur Darling, *The Central Intelligence Agency: An Instrument of Government, to 1950* (University Park, PA: Pennsylvania State University Press, 1990), pp. 108–115.

6   This was known as the Russell Plan, after Donald S. Russell, who served as

Dean Acheson's Assistant Secretary of State for Administration. Largely driven by OMB concerns about the cost of intelligence, the Russell Plan "died on the vine," as one of Donovan's biographers put it. See Troy, p. 320.

7   Darling, pp. 82, 81.

8   Katz, p. 145.

9   CIG Directive No. 9, "Development of Intelligence on USSR," 9 May 1946, paragraph 1, p. 1. Available at: http://www.foia.cia.gov/cgi/1946/05%20 -%20May%201946/CIG_Directive_No_9_Development_of_Intelligence_on_ USSR_9_May_1946.PDF

10 Ibid., Paragraph 4 (b), p. 2.

11 Ibid., memorandum of amendment, 28 August 1947.

12 Darling, p. 87.

13 CIG Directive No. 18/1, "Proposed Agreement to Coordinate Intelligence Activities of the State, War, and Navy Departments," 28 October 1946, paragraph 2(g). Available at: http://www.foia.cia.gov/cgi/1946/12%20 -%20December%201946/CIG_Directive_No_18-3_Coordination_of_ Collection_16_Dec_1946.PDF

14 Franz Borkenau, "Getting at the Facts Behind the Soviet Façade," *Commentary*, April 1954, p. 393. Presumably Arthur Ponsonby, quoted in the previous chapter, would have agreed.

15 USIA IRI Intelligence Summary, "Worldwide Communist Propaganda Activities in 1954," 15 February 1955, pg. II-2.

16 28 February 1950. Readable version at: http://www.foia.cia.gov/docs/ DOC_0000042667/DOC_0000042667.pdf, accessed 31 May 2011.

17 Both listed on "Declassified Intelligence Analyses on the Former Soviet Union Produced by CIA's Directorate of Intelligence, 1950–1993," at: http://www.fas. org/irp/cia/product/net_sov.htm, accessed 25 July 2010. The first report was disseminated 10 September 1951, the second 17 February 1953. These two are representative – the website lists hundreds of declassified documents.

18 See http://www.foia.cia.gov/cpe.asp

19 From http://www.fas.org/irp/cia/product/net_sov.htm

20 James Noren, "CIA's Analysis of the Soviet Economy," in Gerald K. Haines and Robert E. Leggett (eds), *Watching the Bear: Essays on CIA's Analysis of the Soviet Union* (Washington DC: Center for the Study of Intelligence, 2001), p. 21. Noren writes that that, as of 2001, the CIA had declassified 215 reports on civil industry, 152 on agriculture, 219 on transportation and communications, and 155 on energy.

21 Sherman Kent, *Strategic Intelligence for American World Policy* (Princeton, NJ: Princeton University Press, 1949), pp. 74–75.

22 See CIG Directive 18-3, op. cit.

23 See "Abstracting Services as an Intelligence Tool for Assessing Soviet Chemical Research," OSI-4/49, 19 December 1949, p. vi, which notes that abstracts of articles in technical journals are a "valuable intelligence tool" which, in the

"sensitive case of the USSR" seem to indicate that "foreign circulation of certain publications is being curtailed and ... quite likely much of the research of the country is not being published." Available as a dynamic document at http://www.foia.cia.gov, accessed 26 July 2010. That report was originally classified as CONFIDENTIAL and was to be either retained in a secure location or burned.

24 Office of Research and Reports, Provisional Intelligence Report, "Indexes of Household Consumption in the USSR 1928–1955," 13 November 1956, pp. iii, 57.

25 "An uninformed America is an endangered America" declared an article in the *Washington Post* (12 October 1945, p. 8). "Here is ... the most puissant power of the age deliberately stuffing its ears to international broadcasting." Nine days later another article in the same newspaper warned "The Senate now affords the one hope" that FBIS can be saved. "Careless dissipation of the equipment, organization and know-how of this agency would be a grave and senseless loss" (*Washington Post*, 21 October 1945, p. B4). Clearly FBIS had mastered the lesson on how to conduct a publicity campaign which had been laid out in Robert Leigh's article in *Harper's*.

26 There appear also to have been some concerns about the unusual types of people who had come to work in FBIS. In 1946 the CIG was "embarrassed" by questions about "security, loyalty, alcoholism, and homosexuality" among FBIS staff, according to Donovan's biographer Thomas Troy. See Troy, p. 394. In addition there was political dissension within FBIS, as "AFL's right-wing American Federation of Government Employees had been feuding with CIO's left-wing United Public Workers" ("The Federal Diary," *Washington Post*, 23 October 1947). Things got so bad in 1948 that the former head of FBIS sued the former head of the Daily Reports section for defamation of character, based on an article that the latter had written for *Argosy* magazine charging that the former was a "Red" who had "sabotaged the State Department" (*Washington Post*, 24 December 1948).

27 Darling, p. 331.

28 "Remarks by J. Niles Riddel, Deputy Director Foreign Broadcast Information Service," Open Source Solutions Conference, 2 December 1992, at: http://www.fas.org/irp/fbis/riddel.html, accessed 4 August 2010.

29 Roop, p. 14.

30 Roop, p. 121.

31 See Roop, p. 23, and also p. 275, which reports that, when asked, most customers reported that if they were forced to choose between the Daily Report (summaries and translations) and the analytic products, they would take the Daily Reports.

32 "Red Army Drill in Russia is Reported," *Washington Post*, 5 May 1947, p. 3.

33 Available sources make this history murky. According to the *Quarterly Journal of the Library of Congress*, no. 5-7, 1947, p. 31, FDD "was formerly known as" the Washington Document Center (WDC), which had been set up by the Navy to handle all the captured Japanese documents (see Library of Congress, "The Foreign Affairs Oral History Collection of the Association for

Diplomatic Studies and Training," interview of Walter Nichols by G. Lewis Schmidt, published 1 February 2006; the document may be found by searching via the "Frontline Diplomacy" oral history home page, at: http://memory. loc.gov/ammem/collections/diplomacy/). However, according to Lyman Kirkpatrick, "Origin, Missions, and Structure of CIA," *Studies in Intelligence*, vol. 2, no. 1, 1958, p. 5, the FDD was a combination of the WDC and the Army's German Military Documents Center. A letter from General Vanderberg, dated 1 October 1946, in which the CIG offers to take over the WDC, describes it as being "operated jointly by the War and Navy Departments" – see http://www.foia.cia.gov/cgi/1946/10%20-%20October%201946/ Washington_Document_Center_1_Oct_1946.PDF, accessed 29 July 2010. One account suggests that FDD remained in the clandestine side of the CIA while FBIS became its overt arm. See Joseph Becker, "Comparative Survey of US and Soviet Access to Published Information," *Studies in Intelligence*, vol. 1, no. 4, 1957, p. 45. The description of FDD in the Church Committee Report also places FDD in operations from 1947 until 1952, at which point it was moved to the Intelligence Directorate. In 1964 it was moved to the Office of Central Reference and then in 1967 "became part of FBIS." See Church Committee Report, *Foreign and Military Intelligence: Book 1: Final Report of the Select Committee to Study Governmental Operations with Respect to Intelligence Activities, United States Senate*, 26 April 1976, p. 264.

34 Letter from Bryan Battey, *The Interpreter: US Navy Japanese/Oriental Language School Archival Project*, University of Colorado at Boulder Libraries, 16 December 2006, p. 2, at: http://ucblibraries.colorado.edu/ archives/collections/jlsp/interpreter106a.pdf, accessed 31 May 2011.

35 Becker, pp. 40, 37.

36 Becker, p. 45.

37 Paul W. Ward, "Security and Oil Believed Not Real Soviet Aims in Iran," *Baltimore Sun*, 19 March 1946, p. 1.

38 Available at: http://clinton2.nara.gov/WH/EOP/NSC/html/historical/NSCID_ LIST.pdf.

39 John Hounsell, "The World News Connection: Keeping Americans Informed about their World," White Paper, World News Connection, at: http://wnc. fedworld.gov/WNCwhitepaper.pdf, accessed 7 August 2010.

40 Church Committee Report, p. 264.

41 Becker, pp. 37, 39.

42 John W. Finney, "US Fails to Heed Russian Journals," *New York Times*, 25 November 1957, p. 1.

43 Battey, *The Interpreter*.

44 Battey, *The Interpreter*.

45 See: http://libguides.emporia.edu/content.php?pid=195343&sid=1636413 and also: http://guides.lib.ku.edu/content.php?pid=78520&sid=1606350, both accessed 26 September 2011.

46 http://www.lib.umd.edu/MICROFORMS/uspub_research.html. Subsequently

JPRS was publicly acknowledged as a CIA body. See for example: http://gethelp.library.upenn.edu/guides/govdocs/jprs.html.

47 Finney, *NYT*, p. 1.

48 Finney, *NYT*, p. 1.

49 Roop, p. 230.

50 Church Committee Report, p. 273.

51 See CIA Freedom of Information Act (FOIA) Collection, "The CAESAR, POLO, and ESAU Papers," at http://www.foia.cia.gov/cpe.asp, accessed 29 July 2010.

52 Borkenau, pp. 393–400. Borkenau was not formally part of the CIA, but he was (in 1950) a founding member of the Congress for Cultural Freedom, which in 1967 was revealed to have been a CIA-funded organization.

53 Borkenau, pp. 394, 397, 398.

54 Borkenau, p. 400.

55 Borkenau, p. 400.

56 Donald S. Zagoria, *The Sino-Soviet Conflict: 1959–1961* (Princeton NJ: Princeton University Press, 1962), pp. 27–28.

57 Myron Rush, "Esoteric Communication in Soviet Politics," *World Politics*, vol. 11, no. 4, July 1959, p. 614.

58 Rush, p. 615.

59 See "A Note on Methodology," in Zagoria, pp. 24–35.

60 Zagoria, p. 28.

61 Harold P. Ford, "The CIA and Double Demonology: Calling the Sino-Soviet Split," *Studies in Intelligence*, vol. 42, no. 5, 1988–1989.

62 Richard Shryock, "For an Eclectic Sovietology," *Studies in Intelligence,* vol. 8, no. 1, winter 1964.

63 Shryock, p. 58.

64 Shryock, pp. 59, 61.

65 The lack of language-proficient analysts and other staff is a persistent lament in the IC, although the languages in short supply change with time.

66 One little-remarked, but potentially important, physical constraint of this process was that efficiency (or cost-effectiveness) demanded that text be printed in 32-page printer's signatures. Editorial decisions about whether or not a given text was worthy of translation and dissemination could rely not just on the text's intrinsic worth, but also on whether or not it would "fit" into a given printing.

67 As quoted in CIA, "An Historical Review of Studies of the Intelligence Community for the Commission on the Organization of the Government for the Conduct of Foreign Policy," December 1974, at: http://www.gwu.edu/~nsarchiv/NSAEBB/NSAEBB144/document%208.pdf, accessed 15 August 2010.

68 Shryock, p. 63.

69 Ford, p. 65.

CHAPTER THREE

"Not indigestion but gluttony"

FBIS and JPRS were not the only collectors and processors of open source information about the USSR. Other government units also monitored, collected, and processed freely available Soviet sources. Volume of output figures are difficult to find in US sources, but a Soviet book published in 1973 claimed that the US Embassy in Moscow was subscribing to 900 Soviet journals and magazines, as well as to another 130 publications from "socialist countries."[1] Most of these publications may have subsequently found their way to FBIS, but they were probably also being used on site. A top-secret CAESAR report on the Doctors' Plot from 1953 notes, for example, that the American Embassy had commented on the unusual allocation of quotations in the January 1953 editorials in *Izvestiya*,[2] thus making clear that at least some analysis was being done within the embassy. That same Soviet book also speaks of: "more than 100 Russia specialists" in the State Department (and another 30 in regional departments); separate open source operations in the Army, Navy, and Air Force; the Atomic Energy Commission; the United States Information Agency (USIA); the various "Russian Institutes" at America's universities; and corporate centers engaged in scientific research. There was even, this book claims, a "Buck Rogers Bureau" (institutional home unspecified) which read foreign science fiction for clues about possible scientific breakthroughs in Russia and elsewhere.[3]

Less far-fetched, although the results he achieved were perhaps even more fantastic, was the open-source data mining "shop" maintained by Murray Feshbach[4] at the Foreign Demographic Analysis Division (FDAD) of the US Census Bureau. Between 1957, when he first came to FDAD, and 1981, when he moved to Georgetown University's Center for Population Research (where he continued to work until a second retirement, in 2000), Feshbach and his small team of analysts dredged through mountains of Soviet population statistics, to come to alarming conclusions about the health, longevity, and reproductive capacities of the Soviet population.[5]

Also active was BBC Monitoring (BBCM),[6] part of the British Broadcasting Corporation, with which FBIS (then called the FBMS) had begun cooperating in August 1941, even before the US entered the war.[7] Although BBCM operated under tighter budgetary restrictions than did FBIS, so that it translated and processed much less than did its partner, the organization nevertheless was described as early as 1945 as monitoring 1.25 million words, in 30 languages *every day*.[8] The two services split coverage, taking advantage of places where the opposite partner might not have access, and generally trying to reduce duplication to a minimum. Despite differences in customers and in some editorial practices, the two services have managed to work in tandem for nearly 70 years.

Still, all of this is a pale reflection of the output of FBIS/JPRS. As noted in the previous chapter, the responsibilities of the organization grew steadily through the last part of the twentieth century. In addition to getting claim to printed materials when it took over FDD in 1967, FBIS also took responsibility for TV broadcasting, which became an increasingly important portion of its work.[9] Statistics for that output are difficult to find, but what is available suggests a staggering amount of monitoring and translation – for example, one-time National Security Agency (NSA) head Admiral William Studeman in a talk given in 1992 spoke of FBIS monitoring "3,500 publications in 55 foreign languages," collecting 1.5 million words daily only from print sources, with another 790 hours of TV per week, in 29 languages, from 50 countries (this latter presumably refers to monitoring, not translating or transcribing – the practice was generally to list broadcast topics and gist some segments, with only the most important bits turned back into verbatim text).[10] Even that figure, however, is minute compared to what the Soviets claimed FBIS was doing – "the monitoring service of the CIA" is described as processing "6 million words in 60 languages" every day.[11]

Hard as it is to find figures about how much open source information was being captured and processed by the various entities of the intelligence community, it is even harder to find figures about the volumes that more covert sources were generating. Admiral Studeman gives a glimpse of what those figures may have been like when he says that "one intelligence collection system alone" (no further details provided) can generate "a million inputs *per half hour* [emphasis in original]" (out of these, he goes on to say, "filters" discard all but about 6500, of which only about 1,000 "meet forwarding criteria." Analysts "normally choose 10 inputs," which results in 1 report).[12]

"The information explosion"

As was mentioned in the previous chapter, the CIA began experimenting with mechanical means to cope with information volume very early on. In early 1954, the CIA began funding a machine translation project, following the seemingly successful demonstration of a pilot project run by IBM and Georgetown University that translated sentences from a Russian chemistry text, and also rendered some common political slogans into English. Although the demonstration generated a great deal of enthusiastic press coverage, as well as more than $1.5 million in CIA funding, results were consistently disappointing, according to both contemporary accounts and more recent appraisals. At least one reason for the disappointing results was that the sentences to be translated all had to be transliterated into English characters and then punched onto data cards, meaning that processing was as slow – if not slower – than would have been the case with human translation.[13]

At least as pressing was the issue of how to store all the incoming information in such a way that it could be retrieved. The "3 million index cards" of which R&A had boasted (see Chapter 1) were clearly inadequate by the start of the 1960s, when a new science appeared in the lexicon. Called "information retrieval," or IR, the nascent field prospered alongside all the other new technologies that the post-Sputnik, Kennedy-era "science race" was spawning. First out of the gate with a document storage and retrieval system was IBM, which produced a system called WALNUT – described in contemporary newspaper reports as "100 washtub-sized cabinets" that could process a request for any of the CIA's "99 million-odd reports, newspapers, books, maps, and other documents ... in about a minute flat."[14] Unlike the punch-card controlled translation machines, WALNUT was a photo-based system which used a dry-process film to reproduce documents, so that any document requested would emerge from the machine as a postage-stamp size version of the original (which could, if necessary, be enlarged).

According to an article published in 1966 in *Studies in Intelligence*,[15] the CIA went so far as to establish its own Intelligence Sciences Laboratory, to explore the problems of information storage and retrieval. The particular pride of that article was Project Chive, which, it was hoped, would in the course of the decade to come provide search and retrieval capabilities – and yet, the author concluded, results were likely to come only half as fast as desired, and at twice the cost, because, experience shows, "the people using the machines are way behind the technology. They are not capable of utilizing the machines' capability."

Certainly the attempts to automate the propaganda analysis methodology suggest that results were not encouraging. RAND studies by Alexander

George, the "father" of propaganda analysis, in the mid-1950s had come to the conclusion that most content analysis was what George termed "pre-scientific,"[16] because interpretation depended upon the degree to which the analyst-readers could penetrate the nuances of each utterance under study. That made most pronouncements and media statements *sui generis*, so that there could not be the kind of one-to-one relation between phenomenon and result that characterizes analyses in the physical sciences. The only exception, or partial exception, was frequency analysis, which George was willing to accept could be more scientific, although he also had some hesitation about how useful the results might be for determining elite intentions.

It was perhaps for that reason that the experiments in automated propaganda analysis focused not on intentions but on attitudes – the kind of material which in another political climate might be obtained through opinion polling. In the 1970s DCI William Colby tasked the CIA analytic staff to experiment with unconventional methodologies,[17] in partial response to which a content analysis team tried to use computers to "test empirically the validity and reliability of four factors that are, or might be, used by Kremlinologists to judge the nature of a leader's attitude toward the general secretary of the Communist Party of the Soviet Union."[18] Presumably the same directive was the impetus for a more ambitious study undertaken by a contractor, CACI Inc., the purpose of which was to test the utility of four kinds of quantitative analytic methods: thematic content analysis; event data analysis; integrative analysis; and bureaucratic analysis.[19] The test material for the first of the studies above was quite limited – statements by republic leaders and other lesser officials at three large Party gatherings in early 1976 – while that for the second was massive – 10 years worth of FBIS reporting (from 1964 to 1974, stored on what is described as "a tape").

Despite the "gee-whiz!" tone of most of the newspaper accounts of these mechanized systems, the problems always out-paced possible solutions. Some of these were inherent in the system itself – WALNUT, for example, depended upon Kalvar, a UV-sensitive vesicular film that proved to have a nasty quality of degrading in such a way that it gave off hydrochloric acid, which "ate its way through microfilm boxes, metal storage cabinets, and other microfilms."[20] Even more important, however, were the human bottle-necks that seemed inevitably to arise. WALNUT, for example, required that each document receive a unique identifier – very much as the machine translation system in the end depended upon human punch coders. Human coding was also required for the content analysis experiments, to say nothing of the press scanning, selection, and translation which had to precede even that stage of supposed "automation."

The most persistent and insurmountable problem, however, was simply the ever-growing volume of information itself. The term "information explosion" seems to have appeared at about the start of the Kennedy Administration, when it first was used to describe the burgeoning number of articles being churned out by scientists around the world. Already by January 1966 *Newsweek* had produced a cover story, tied to the publication of a book by Marshall McLuhan, entitled "Good-by to Gutenberg,"[21] predicting the end of the information world as it had been. Tied as most things in the era were to competition with the Soviets, the fear of a science gap extended even into fields as arcane as zoology – the *Los Angeles Times* reported a talk by a researcher who complained that in his area of specialization, "the growth rate of turtles," there had recently been "more than 500 articles" published, symptomatic of the "avalanche of information" that was "smothering progress of the scientific revolution" and creating a widening "information gap."[22] Most of the proposed solutions involved some combination of new technology – a 1964 *Time* article writes for example of the "Ampex Videofile system" which could capture "250,000 document pages on a 14-inch reel," at a cost of "$200,000 to $1,000,000"[23] – and large-scale government programs, such as those proposed in a 1969 white paper by the National Academy of Sciences and the National Academy of Engineering, which recommended that "departments and agencies of the federal government fund the literature-access services that are needed for the effective utilization of the knowledge resulting from the research and technical activities that they sponsor,"[24] perhaps with something like the "National Information System for Physics" that the American Society for Physics proposed, to "digest virtually the world's physics literature," at a cost of $3.6 million, to be borne by the National Science Foundation.[25]

Although the amounts spent by the intelligence community on automated information storage and retrieval systems remain generally undisclosed, it can safely be presumed that the sums being spent for intelligence functions were probably higher – even significantly higher. The problem, however, as politicians and intelligence officials alike began to understand, was that it was far from clear whether the funds spent on information management were producing anything like the value which might be expected in return for massive outlays. Although there is no public record of whether or not the WALNUT system was useful, the translation experiment was roundly criticized for its limited scale, and the way that the "test" had been massaged to produce positive results. There is also no public record of the internal response to the content analysis experiments, but it is difficult to believe that their findings – one that omitting "Comrade" *and* using Brezhnev's name and patronymic in speeches is a good indicator of apparent support,[26] the other that the Soviet military leaders are more often quoted in the press about ideological and "benign" military issues than they are about hostile ones[27] – would have generated much excitement in either the analytic or the policymaking community.

"More is better"

The biggest driver for attempts to automate the processing and analytic steps of the intelligence cycle was that mechanization of collection was successful beyond anyone's wildest dreams. The advent of aerial photography, followed by satellite technologies, and increased capabilities in signal capture, meant that the IC was generating incomprehensible quantities of data. It was never clear, however, whether there was any relationship between the quantity of information accumulated and improved analytic support to policymakers, or even reduction of surprise. A study performed in 1971 under the direction of Deputy Director of OMB James Schlesinger (who became DCI in 1973), stated flatly that, with the exception of satellite photography, which had led to "greatly improved knowledge about the military capabilities of potential enemies," expanded collection efforts and capabilities had not "brought about a similar reduction in our uncertainty about the intentions, doctrines, and political processes of foreign powers." Instead, Schlesinger charged, "the growth in raw intelligence – and here satellite photography must be included – has come to serve as a proxy for improved analysis, inference, and estimation." As a result, not only had "the community's activities ... become exceedingly expensive," but "it is not at all clear that our hypotheses about foreign intentions, capabilities, and activities have improved commensurately in scope and quality" with the "richness of the data made available by modern methods of collection, and the rising costs of their acquisition." [28]

The disconnect between collection and results was a subject of concern even before the Schlesinger Report. An internal CIA study in 1966, the Cunningham Report, had flagged what it called "More Is Better" attitudes. "We were hypnotized by statistics and bits of information, particularly in the military and academia," the Cunningham Report complained. "Once we developed a collection capability we used it and it acquired a momentum of its own, controlling us, rather than vice versa." The result, that report charged, was that "analysts were becoming superficial because of the piles of papers in their in-boxes, and analysis in depth was out of the question." [29] The Church Committee Report of 1975 repeated the same criticism, quoting the Cunningham and Schlesinger Reports, then charged that "the intelligence establishment remains structured in such a way that collection guides production, rather than vice-versa; available data and 'the impetus of technology' tend to govern what is produced." [30]

The Cunningham Report provides the fullest description of the problems caused by indiscriminate collection. "Failing to get important information," the report wrote, collectors were "flooding the system with secondary material," which was "degrading production, making the recognition of significant material more difficult in the mass of the trivial." Collectors tended "to get what was easy to get, regardless of the priority or lack of it." The system could not even begin "to distinguish between what is essential in information and what is merely nice to know." Responsibility for the situation, however, must also be shared with the analysts, who do a poor job of telling collectors what they need, or evaluating what they have received. Even when asked by the collectors for feedback on the information supplied, the Cunningham Report said, analysts tend "to praise the collector and ask for 'more of the same,' regardless of actual or potential need," because they feared cutting off "a potential source of data."[31] The Church Committee added a third party to this list of causes, noting that policymakers and other end-users tended to regard intelligence products as "a free good" so that "instead of articulating priorities, they demand information about everything," making analysts feel "they *have* to cover every possible topic" out of fear of being "accused of an 'intelligence failure'."[32] In short, as the Cunningham Report summed up the IC's information problem, "the community's disease was not indigestion but gluttony."[33]

Close reading of the various reports shows that the IC was actually being accused of contradictory shortcomings. On the one hand, the community was seen to be chasing "current intelligence," trying to satisfy consumers' desires for instant information on all manner of things, so that (in the words of the Church Committee) "the demand exceeds the supply." On the other hand, because collection drove production, analytic tasks became increasingly self-defined, so that the cycle of task-collect-process-analyze became ever more closed, as a result of which (in the words of the Cunningham Report) "more and more the community was talking to itself." The Church Committee Report made a similar point, noting that the proliferation of intelligence community products, and the nuances of the different conclusions they sometimes reached, are only "clear to a sophisticated intelligence analyst."

These criticisms highlight a central problem in the structure of the IC, which is that "there was no definition of what the Government really needed from intelligence."[34] The basic purpose of the IC had been to "prevent surprise," yet, as these nearly annual reports and studies attest, surprise seemed a permanent feature of the political landscape. More instructive in many ways, though, is what happened when the IC attempted to warn of impending surprise. There were undoubtedly many such instances, but the Sino-Soviet split, discussed in the previous chapter, is particularly well documented. As described by Harold Ford, who was a participant in the process, 17 years elapsed between the first indicators of potential problems between China and the USSR and the irrefutable proof provided by armed border conflicts between the two sides (with talk even of pre-emptive nuclear strikes from the Soviet side).

There were a number of reasons why this "warning" took so long to be heard or heeded, and all are instructive about the epistemological problems that lie at the heart of the intelligence function. As both Ford and Shryock pointed out, one of the important early impediments was that the analytic *method* by which the potential for conflict had been identified was arcane, complex, and, importantly, required the acceptance of assumptions that were unfamiliar to those who were not versed in propaganda analysis. Myron Rush had acknowledged as much, when he conceded that American politicians might find it hard to believe that their Soviet counterparts would live their political lives through "piddling with stereotyped formulas." Implied here is another problem which surfaces again and again in discussions of the relationship between analysts and policymakers – analytic products must be short and pithy, because policymakers are extremely busy, which in effect makes it impossible to make analytic claims which rely upon lengthy explanations.[35]

Viewed through a somewhat different lens, the insistence that products be short and give "only the facts" provided a strong incentive for some analysts, and even more so, those who managed them, to tone predictions down, making them more anodyne and more dependent upon "common sense." As Ford noted, this affected particularly the National Intelligence Estimates (NIEs), created for the highest level consumers, which tended to "lag behind" the convictions of those analysts who believed there was a widening split, as intermediary managers not intimately involved with the analytic process itself tempered the claims and arguments put forward by the analysts. As a result, there was a tendency for the delivered analysis to confirm what the recipients already believed.

As myriad recent studies of psychology have shown, all humans are deeply susceptible to this so-called "confirmation bias" – or the tendency to accept evidence which confirms what we already believe while making us simply not even hear evidence that challenges our beliefs. Not surprisingly, powerful successful people tend to be even more convinced of the correctness of their judgments – meaning that the senior policymakers whom the "Sino-Soviet heretics" were trying to convince were even less likely to be swayed by arguments based on "invisible writing on slugs" (Shryock's sardonic phrase) than would have been less alpha personalities. This was even more true because, as Ford notes, counterpart members of the elites in other countries were contradicting the analysts' arguments. President Eisenhower, for example, more readily accepted the assurance of Taiwan's president Chiang Kai-Shek that "it was impossible for the Chinese Communists to split from the Soviet Communists" than he did the "say-so of midlevel officers from across the Potomac."[36]

The relationship between information and understanding

Some of the friction between the analysts and those whom they are trying to warn is inherent in the resource imbalance between the two groups.

As Sherman Kent noted in his last presentation before retirement, the "warners" have every incentive to "overwarn," because it costs them little to do so, while the costs of *not* warning are high, in reputation if not in loss of life and property. It may be a bit irritating to be accused, as some IC elements have been, of having "predicted 14 of the last three coups," but that is nothing compared to be accused of responsibility for "intelligence failures" or "not having connected the dots." The "warnees," on the other hand, or those who must take action on warnings, incur cost whenever they go into action, even if that cost is merely the time and attention required to call a meeting. Thus, Kent admonished in his valediction, "Warning is not complete until: (1) the Warner warns; and (2) the Warnee hears, believes, and acts."[37]

Kent's point is powerful, because it permits examination of why the intelligence community has been chastising itself (and being chastised by others) for almost five decades that it is (in the words of the Cunningham Report) "talking to itself." Philosopher Denis Hilton has made the same point in a slightly different fashion, one which makes even clearer what Kent was arguing. There is a "strong distinction," Hilton writes, between "causal attribution and causal explanation." The first act, of deciding what has caused something to happen, is an analytic process, but it is also a personal one. The second act, explaining to someone else what has caused something to happen (or warning them that something *will* or *is likely to* happen) is an act of communication, and as such is dependent upon what Hilton calls "the rules of conversation." This means that a good explanation "must be probably true, informative given an interlocutor's state of knowledge, relevant to her interests, and expressed clearly." As Hilton writes, "attributing the 9/11 attacks to someone is not the same as explaining them to him."[38]

Put more simply, this two-step schema makes it clear why the analysts who foresaw the Sino-Soviet split had so much difficulty making their case with those whom they were trying to serve – their methodologies were sufficient to convince themselves that they understood causality correctly, but they were not able to make that case to people who did not share their chain of causal attribution. Those who did not share, or who did not know, the propaganda analysis methodology, and the many assumptions on which it was built, would not be able to accept the conclusions produced by the methodology, unless of course they happened already to share the same conclusion, but reached by a different method or route.

Both Shryock and Ford in their articles touched on this same issue, that (in Shryock's terms) the "esoteric communications" analysts would never agree with the "political scientists," neither of whom ever agreed with "economic determinists," and so on. The reason for these disagreements is that none of the adherents of these schools recognize the hypotheses of the others as genuinely causal – that is, as linking phenomena together in a way that satisfactorily explains why X caused Y and therefore may cause Z. What does not seem to have been widely explored, however, was that virtually everyone in both the IC and the policy community appears to have believed that there exists one single reality. That reality may or may not be knowable – indeed, the purpose of the IC was precisely to make "reality known" – but, very importantly, the reason why it was not known was almost always perceived to be absence of data. As the Schlesinger Report had charged, and the Church Committee Report reiterated, "it has become commonplace to translate product criticism into demands for enlarged collection efforts."[39]

The metaphor of the jigsaw puzzle is important for understanding the complex relationship between the IC, the policymaking community, and information. A jigsaw puzzle has one – and only one – correct solution, which, when found, will give the "whole picture." The challenge then is to search for missing pieces – which, when we find them, can fit into only one place. That world view is explicit in the Schlesinger Report, which wrote that "In a world of perfect information, there would be no doubt about the present and future intentions, capabilities, and activities of foreign powers."[40] Collection and analysis are required precisely because that "world of perfect information" does not exist – but, by implication, the closer we come to it, the clearer the "present and future intentions, capabilities, and activities of foreign powers" should become.

This is precisely the same world view that informs Sherman Kent's approach to analysis. In his book, *Strategic Intelligence for American World Policy*, Kent writes that the purpose of analysis is to give policymakers the "objective situation" – by which he means, he explains in a footnote, "the situation as it exists in the understanding of some hypothetical omniscient Being ... the situation stripped of the subjective characteristics with which a prejudiced human observer is almost certain to endow it." Channeling Lippmann, who was one of a handful of authors whom Kent quoted in his book, Kent argued that analysts must always keep themselves at arm's length from policymakers precisely because it is the analysts' job to get as close to that Platonic ideal as possible, and not be seduced by policymakers anxious to "capture" their analysis.

Whether based on all-source or open source, the analysis performed from the 1950s through the 1980s tended to reflect the assumptions about the nature of reality that are evident in the remarks of both Kent and Schlesinger. Analysts seem not much to have thought about the implications of the many-stage process through which information came to them – in the case of propaganda analysis, for example, from the totality of the universe a tiny portion was reflected in Soviet and Chinese media, from which were further chosen portions for translation or summarization, out of which snippets were further selected, subjected to analytic manipulation, and then used as evidence to substantiate a hypothetic whole. As Rush had argued in his article, this whole did not necessarily change even over time – noticing "something odd" might suggest something about the future, but it was equally likely to lead analysts into re-examination of the past, using the new clue as a way to test their hypotheses against the *past* performance of the media in relation to known phenomena. While no doubt defensible as a means to strengthen and test the methodology, this impulse to look to the past as a way not only to explain the present but also, by implication, to predict the future helped reinforce a general analytic presumption that events progress in a linear fashion. It was that assurance which led Shryock to conclude his satire about competing schools of Soviet analysis with the plea that the various analytic schools had to work better together because of the inevitable need to analyze "the succession struggle sure to follow the death of Khrushchev." That statement suggests confidence that the only way in which a Soviet leader might relinquish power was through death – an assumption which, ironically enough, had already been proven wrong even before the article actually was published, because the "succession crisis" overtook Khrushchev well before his physical demise, when he was pushed from power into "non-person" obscurity by Leonid Brezhnev and his coterie – yet another "Kremlin surprise" which analysts had not foreseen.[41]

The many theories that analysts used to order the data which they were selecting differed each from the others, but they all had in common that analysts assumed there was some kind of overarching "law" which – if deciphered – would make Soviet behavior translucent and predictable. It was even argued – most prominently by Kent[42] – that "intelligence" might be or could become a distinct social science in its own right. Another intelligence analyst, R. A. Random,[43] disagreed that "intelligence" could be a distinct social science or, as he called it, "policy science," but argued strenuously that "the only way to effect any fundamental improvement in professional intelligence service" was to "build up within the intelligence community a knowledge of scientific method and the techniques and principles of the policy sciences" because "since World War II a great deal of progress has been made in finding practical applications [elsewhere than in the IC] for improved social science methodology and techniques, progress comparable in quality ... to contemporary technical advances in the physical sciences." It is worth noting that one "policy science" which Random specifically cited as worthy of emulation was "operations research," the statistics-based management tool that had been pioneered by, among others, Robert McNamara, who brought it first to running the Ford Motor company, and then the Pentagon during the war in Vietnam.[44]

Confidence that there exist what Random called "general truths and ... general laws" of social and political behavior was a fundamental part of intelligence analysis. The analysts' job, Random implied, was to help policymakers to move from "intuitive guesses and unanalyzed conjectures" towards more "scientific" decision making, because "when the situation is complicated and the actor is confronted with multiple choices of action, reliance on non-principled behavior [that is, behavior not guided by 'scientific principles'] introduces an unacceptably high level of probable error." Sherman Kent was absolutely unequivocal in his belief that societies – all societies – are governed by the same immutable laws, which it is the job of the analyst to discover and the policymaker to obey. Even before coming to work in the OSS, Kent had posited in his first book, *Writing History*, that:

> Systematic study ... is one of the foremost products of rationalism... The rationalists are the people who hold that the mind, when playing in the channels of right logic, can solve any problem it can set itself; and since many of the most compelling problems which beset the rationalist are problems of society – how to do away with poverty, disease, and war; how to promote happiness, health, and peace – he is likely to become a liberal. For the liberal believes that the mind, when turned upon social dilemmas, is capable of performing a positive and helpful social function. Now, although not all rationalists are liberals, all liberals must at least be rationalists. And the result is that the intellectual milieu of our society is heavily laden with a respect for reason and an optimistic faith in social conscience if it be led by the dictates of the mind. Our bill of rights and our liberal democratic tradition make free and systematic inquiry as typical of the American way as succotash and ham and eggs.[45]

The analytic community's faith in "the channels of right logic" and the "dictates of the mind" contributed to the near-disaster of the Cuban Missile Crisis. Special National Intelligence Estimate 85-3-62, entitled "The Military Buildup in Cuba," released as the official view of the United States Intelligence Board on 19 September 1962, had hedged on a number of important issues – after all, as Kent had said, "estimating is what you do when you don't know"[46] – but had stated unequivocally that the Soviets would not try to put "offensive strategic weapons" – meaning nuclear weapons – on Cuba. After the world had flirted for a few days with Armageddon, the crisis passed, and Kent returned to that NIE, trying to understand where he and his team had gone wrong. In his article about this re-examination he explores a number of factors which contributed to his analysts' error, but asserts that one of the biggest of these was his team proved to have understood the rules of "rational leadership behavior" better than had Khrushchev. In Kent's words:

> As long as all the discernible constants in the equation are operative the estimator can be fairly confident of making a sound judgment. It is when these constants do not rule that the real trouble begins. It is when the other man zigs violently out of the track of "normal" behavior that you are likely to lose him. If you lack hard evidence of the prospective erratic

tack and the zig is so far out of line as to seem to you to be suicidal, you will probably misestimate him every time. No estimating process can be expected to divine exactly when the enemy is about to make a dramatically wrong decision. We were not brought up to *under*estimate our enemies.

We missed the Soviet decision to put the missiles into Cuba because we could not believe that Khrushchev could make a mistake.[47]

As the rich literature on "intelligence failures" which has emerged in the past decade makes clear, this was not the last time that analysts would argue, in essence, that their analysis had been correct, but the outcomes had been wrong because the subjects of the analysis were too backwards, stupid, or irrational to follow the rules of "rational behavior."

The surprise of Iran

Kent speculates in that same *post mortem* that another reason the Soviets may have made their "suicidal misestimate" in attempting to put nuclear warheads on Cuba was that they had disregarded easily available open sources like "press, radio and TV, and the *Congressional Record*" because "the conspiratorial mind in the Kremlin, when faced with a choice of inter-pretations, will ... lean heavily to that which comes via the covert apparatus." Over-reliance on information obtained "via the covert apparatus" was also a recurrent sin in the American foreign policy and intelligence communities, but it arguably was not until 1978–1979 that the US committed an "open source blunder" on a similar scale, in the community's inability to perceive the onset of the Iranian revolution, and the fall of the Shah.

All accounts of the events of the end of 1978 and the beginning of 1979 agree that the fall of the Shah and the coming to power of the Ayatollah Khomeini caught the intelligence community and the policymakers by surprise. Robert Jervis, in his recently published *Why Intelligence Fails*,[48] has released the text of a classified study he had done of the performance of the CIA's National Foreign Assessment Center (NFAC) between mid-1977 and November 1978, an end-date chosen because that was when, Jervis writes, "the US government became alarmed" about what was going on in Iran. Written in spring 1979, and delivered to the sponsors in July 1979, the report has the advantage of hindsight, since it was fully clear by then just how alarmed the US government ought to have been (even though the seizure of the Embassy and the start of the hostage crisis was still months away). Jervis's focus is on the overall performance of the NFAC (which both before that time and after it has been known as the Directorate of Intelligence, or DI), thus highlighting primarily problems of analysis, or how information was understood, rather than upon the collection of information itself, so he does not much mention open source collection *per se*, although he does stress that whatever covert collection was being done was focused exclusively upon the activities of the Iranian Communist Party (the Tudeh Party) and on intercepts of Soviet communications and missile telemetry.

Jervis cites four "major errors" in NFAC's performance. Two were analytic misinterpretations – analysts assumed that the Shah was strong and decisive, and so would do what was necessary to retain power; and thus, the second assumption, the fact that he was doing nothing must mean that the situation was not grave. The third error, which was a failure to understand the power of nationalism (and its co-dependent, anti-Americanism), might be called one of ignorance, although it was also a product of the kind of assumptions that Kent and Random had made, about what constitutes "rationalism" and "principled decision-making."

The fourth error – the complete inability to understand Ayatollah Khomeini and the role of religion – was also in part caused by ignorance and assumptions (in Jervis's words, analysts found it "inconceivable that anything as retrograde as religion, especially fundamentalist religion, could be crucial"), but it also has the further dimension that the evidence of Khomeini's intentions and power was freely available everywhere in Iran – literally being broadcast from every mosque. Authors Annabelle Srebreny-Mohammadi and Ali Mohammadi have argued that there is no study which "specifically examines" the role played by "communications in the revolutionary process [in Iran], especially the role of small media" which "attempts to explain how and why the small media were effective,"[49] but they acknowledge nonetheless that the major conduit for Khomeini's message was cassette tapes, recordings of his sermons made in France, where he was in exile, and smuggled back into Iran. The tapes were widely duplicated and sold quite freely in the bazaars, and were also broadcast over loudspeakers from the mosques themselves.

By Jervis's account, there are a number of reasons why this information was ignored. Certainly almost no one in either the intelligence community or in the State Department had good enough Farsi to understand them, and it is highly unlikely that, even if they had, they would also have been able to understand the nuances of Khomeini's theological references. Jervis writes that only one tape was ever obtained, but speculates this meant either that no one knew where to obtain them or, more likely, did not think they were significant. Probably even more important was that no one was *asked* to obtain them – thus setting up the inevitable loop of collection failure: analysts ask collectors to get more of what they already consider to be important, and thus there is no mechanism for alerting them to the possibility that something previously *unknown* might be important.

What the Iranian revolution illustrated most clearly, for open source intelligence at least, was the fallacy of depending upon official media to provide information about threats to the regime itself. Geared to analyzing the behavior of official media and what they told their populaces, open source collectors simply did not notice – or at least did not bring to the attention of those for whom they were collecting – information drawn from sources other than the official ones. The *FBIS Daily Reports*,[50] the primary vehicle for transmitting material from the local sources, show clearly how peripheral Iran was to the intelligence community. In 1978 there were 2,838 articles which mentioned Iran, about twice the volume of the year before. However, only about 15 percent of those came from domestic Iranian sources, and those were PARS, the official news agency, and the Teheran domestic service, the official radio. Volume for most months runs in the 120–180 articles range, until November, when – as Jervis noted – the US suddenly got worried, and the volume doubled. The only exception before that was January, which had heavy reporting on President Carter's visit to Teheran (which took place on New Year's Eve, 1977). Although heavier than reporting of visits by dignitaries from other states, the coverage of the Carter trip was representative of much of what FBIS collectors and translators offered through the turmoil of the Shah's last year – accounts of official visits to and from Teheran. In addition to Carter these included: Jordan's King Husayn; Pakistan's Zial Khaq; Somalia's Siad Barre; UN General Secretary Kurt Waldheim; Nigeria's Shehu Musa Yar'adua; Japan's Foreign Minister Sunao Sonoda; Egypt's Hosni Mubarak (at the time the Vice President); and Belgium's Foreign Minister Henri Simonet. The *Daily Report* also provided articles on the Shah's own trip to Egypt and that of his son to Thailand – and that was only January!

This is not to suggest that FBIS failed to relay reports of more destabilizing events – between January and September approximately 50 articles about the country's demonstrations and riots were offered to FBIS readers. Especially in the beginning of the year, however, these tended to be gathered from such sources as the Tirana Domestic Service and the ATA news service (both Albanian) or the Voice of the Revolutionary Party for Reunification (VRPR), a pro-DPRK radio station operating clandestinely in South Korea, all of which were reprinted for their accounts of the anti-Carter demonstrations. This was important in two ways – not only would the nature of these sources probably have inclined analysts to discount the information, but the reports themselves would have been printed in *Daily Report* booklets that Iranian analysts – who in the CIA numbered four, according to Jervis,[51] – would not have had a reason to read (the Albanian articles were in the Eastern Europe book and the VRPR ones in the Asia-Pacific book).[52]

By the end of March FBIS was relaying information directly from Iranian sources, but always official ones. This meant that, for example, the 30 March 1978 *Daily Report* ascribed the demonstrations to "saboteurs and hooligans," "saboteurs," and "antinational" elements, thus downplaying the significance of the disturbances – despite the fact that similar, and quite violent, demonstrations had taken place in five different cities that day (Yazd, Benbahan, Qazvin, Khorramabad, and Mashad). Tellingly, the Iranian sources relayed by FBIS did not begin reporting on the religious opposition until the summer – the word "shi'ite" first appears in mid-May (in the account of a seminarian arrested for "urging the crowd to commit acts of sedition and agitation" after a religious funeral in Abadan); "ayatollah" is used at about the same time (in accounts of "antinational elements" who fled to the home of a religious leader after riots in Qom); and the crucial name "Khomeini" (which could appear in any of three different transliterations) does not come in an official Iranian news item until October.[53]

This is not to say that the clerics' challenge to the Shah was totally ignored. Beginning in mid-May the Middle East and North Africa *Daily Report*, the one which Iran analysts would have gotten, carried several reports about and even interviews with Khomeini, but all of these were from French newspapers (*Le Monde* and *Le Figaro*) or were from the French news agency AFP. In September the *Daily Report* also began carrying material about Ayatollah Shariatmadari, who by that time had turned against the Shah – a point which in retrospect was of crucial importance, since the more moderate Shariatmadari and the firebrand Khomeini were long-time rivals (indeed, according to Jervis, the only appearance of the word "hate" in all of the NFAC reporting is used to describe the relationship between the two ayatollahs[54]). However, once again, most of the reporting being carried by the *Daily Report* was from French sources, not Iranian ones.

To be fair ...

Hindsight bias is terribly misleading – the kind of critique of FBIS offered above inevitably makes the collectors and analysts seem, at best, a bit dim, because they missed what that critique implies was obvious. That implication is unfair, for several reasons. One is that the rise of the ayatollahs only seems important because they succeeded later in taking power – had the communist Tudeh Party managed to win instead (as essentially had been the case in April 1978 in neighboring Afghanistan, where the counterpart communist party Peoples Democratic Party of Afghanistan had seized power in a bloody coup), then the lack of attention paid to the ayatollahs would have been fully justified. Indeed, there were some 30 articles in the course of 1978 which mentioned the Tudeh Party, most of them from sources to which the intelligence community at the time was paying much greater attention, like the Soviet papers *Pravda* and *Trud*, or the French communist paper, *L'Humanite*.

Another reason the critique above is unfair is that it is based on a technology that was completely unavailable at the time – rapid search of digitized text. As has already been pointed out, the *Daily Reports* at the time existed *only* as physical, typed text, with at best periodic indexing of the titles of articles and their sources. The only mechanism for "searching" for previous mentions of a name or for comparing articles from the various area booklets was human memory and attention.[55] Also important was the problem of physical storage and retrieval – Jervis writes that when he asked in 1979 to see what analyses had been written in 1964, when Khomeini had been expelled from Iran after leading protests against a small American military presence, he was told that it would "take weeks to retrieve them from dead storage."[56]

What probably is most unfair, however, is that neither the collectors nor the analysts really failed at the jobs to which they were set. Although Jervis never quite makes the statement explicitly, his critique returns again and again to the point that collectors and analysts alike were responding to what they understood to be significant, and also – most importantly – to be what the policymakers expected and wanted. To be sure, as he points out, collectors and analysts shared significant assumptions – no one credited opposition charges that the Shah was an American puppet because, from the US point of view, he wasn't. Even more significantly, as noted, none of the Americans could understand how something as old-fashioned as religion could be the basis of political activity, to say nothing of the massive upheavals which soon were to topple the Shah. James Schlesinger, DCI for six months under President Nixon, has remarked that Stansfield Turner, DCI at the time of Iranian revolution, regarded Khomeini as "just another politician," running as it were on a "platform" of Islam, whose government would be forced to "go on pretty much as they had before, that they would have to sell us oil and so forth."[57]

Though such preconceptions were debilitating, it seems likely that even had people been more wary of their assumptions and mind-sets they still would not have noticed the growing danger that the clergy and their supporters presented to the Shah. To the degree that collection and analysis were driven by questions at all (rather than by collection require-ments), those questions seem to have been primarily tactical, rather than strategic. Thus everyone involved – collectors, analysts, and policymakers – all were intently searching for signs and clues about the future moves of the existing structures, rather than asking broader questions about what *might* or what *could* happen in Iran. There was nothing secret about the stresses and cleavages that ran through Iran – there was an active opposition press, albeit published entirely in the US and in Europe; there were a number of foreign academics who had written extensively on various aspects of Iranian society, including the clergy; and there were knowledgeable, on-the-spot newspaper correspondents who wrote about the riots, the students, and the clergy, often with direct interviews. The *Washington Post*'s William Branigan wrote about the riots in Qom in January 1978,[58] noting that they had been caused by an article in one of the state papers which was considered to have insulted the exiled Khomeini (not translated by FBIS). Branigan also interviewed Khomeini's rival, Shariatmadari, who, while not precisely supporting Khomeini, warned that "the people are still against the government. There will be more demonstrations." Jonathan Gage, of the *New York Times*, Liz Thurgood, of the *Manchester Guardian,* and Jonathan Randal, of the *Washington Post*, all wrote series of articles in their respective papers during May 1978, exploring the yawning gulf between the clergy and Shah. In other words, answers to questions about what might happen in Iran lay all around – the real problem was that no one saw a reason to ask the questions.

The IC and the end of the USSR: "superb in 'factology'; not very good in 'politology'"

The question of whether or not the CIA, the intelligence community, or the policymakers (or any combination of these) "missed" the collapse of the USSR is too large an issue to be answered in this chapter, or indeed even in a book. There is a large, and growing, body of literature which debates the question, sometimes alone, but also with increasing frequency as part of the even larger issue of "intelligence failures" and the general efficacy of intelligence in general. While there is a wide range of views – which to a great extent can be predicted based on whether or not the authors approve of the CIA in general – it probably is a safe generalization to say that most would tend to agree with Zbigniew Brzezinski's comment, that the CIA (and, by implication, the IC more generally) was "superb in 'factology' [but] not very good in 'politology,'"[59] meaning the understanding, anticipation, and prediction of political behavior.

While open source intelligence was only a part of the total effort against the USSR, it has the advantage of being more easily available for investigation, and thus can help to illustrate the ways in which – just as with Iran – the collectors, analysts, and policymakers did a superb job of answering the questions that they posed themselves, but also failed to see how these questions were blinding them to other, and ultimately more important questions. As has repeatedly been shown in this book, collectors and analysts did a splendid job of extracting fundamental information about the capabilities of the USSR from all-source and open source alike. Indeed, for many topics, such as Soviet economics, most of the information was obtained from sources which the Soviets published themselves. James Noren, author of the article "CIA's Analysis of the Soviet Economy," describes how "over the years, CIA's estimates of GNP growth [in the USSR] were refined to take advantage of new information released by the Soviet Union,"[60] while "successive publication of portions of Soviet input-output tables" allowed Duke University professor Vladimir Treml – like Murray Feshbach, another pioneer in the exploitation of data published by the Soviets themselves – to provide continuously improving views of the Soviet economy. Douglass Garthoff, who contributed the article "Analyzing Soviet Politics and Foreign Policy" to the same volume, does not directly credit open source information, but he does write in his conclusion that "it was not that the CIA often had especially confidential 'insider' information to give value or cachet," thus suggesting that much of the analysis in this realm was interpretation and hypothesis-making based on non-secret, non-stolen information (though he does add "there were instances" when that kind of information was used).[61]

As one of the commentators on Noren's paper pointed out, however, even the apparently straightforward reporting of GNP or other economic data required so much interpretation and hypothesizing that, just as with the esoteric communication methodology, the analysts' findings were "difficult for policymakers to understand"[62] – which is another way of saying that policymakers found them unconvincing. Garthoff is even more direct, pointing out that, just as had been the case with the Sino-Soviet split, analysts had to contend with the fact that policymakers had their own views and convictions. He argues that community practices were such that it was usually better: to be pessimistic than optimistic; to look for and identify threats rather than opportunities; and to focus on military issues first and foremost.[63]

None of this much mattered until the Gorbachev era, when it suddenly began to matter much faster than the IC could adjust to it. Whereas traditional Soviet censorship was fully in place for at least a year after Gorbachev became General Secretary – the immediate aftermath of the 26 April 1986 Chernobyl disaster is generally recognized as the start of *glasnost* – within about 18 months the information landscape in the USSR had been dramatically transformed. Perhaps the best indicator of the degree of attention that FBIS was paying to the Soviet and broadcast world by this point was the so-called "Danchev Episode" – on Monday, 23 May 1983, announcer Vladimir Danchev was heard on the 1100 GMT, 1200 GMT, and 1300 GMT readings of the Moscow World Service English language news to call the Soviet forces then in Afghanistan "occupants" and "invaders." This startling reversal of the usual formulae was instantly noted and flagged, both by FBIS and, presumably, also by the Soviets, because by 1400 GMT the reader was Vladimir Obratson, and the "invaders" were coming from Pakistan, not the USSR.[64]

As *glasnost* – a Russian word meaning essentially "publicizing" or "saying aloud" – evolved, it quickly changed from the apparent first intentions, which was to give Soviet citizens a means to correct official sloth and inefficiency, to become an all-out effort to fill in the "blank spots" of history. Just a year after the cautious introduction of *glasnost* the quantity, and even more, the content, of Soviet publications had been radically transformed, as an article written in 1987 notes:

> A Soviet population which for years had been told it has full employment, few social problems, good harvests, and the approval of history, is now suddenly confronted with widespread accounts of drug abuse, AIDS, bribery, kidnappings, infanticide, riots, atomic disasters, [and] shipwrecks.[65]

And that was just the beginning. In February 1988 the Party introduced "self-financing," requiring that publishers and broadcasters pay more of their own costs, which, not surprisingly, was immediately followed by a burst of detective fiction, translations of foreign mass market authors like Stephen King, and a corresponding drop in what party ideologues called "necessary" books. The demand for newspapers and journals, especially those which were particularly aggressive about filling in "blank spots," so dramatically outstripped supply that near-riots broke out at newspaper kiosks, and the authorities spoke of having to ration purchases.[66] Of course, not all publications were equally popular – while *Komsomolskaya Pravda*, a paper aimed at younger Party agitators, evolved into a muckraking quasi-tabloid with a circulation of many millions, the main Party newspaper, *Pravda*, saw its circulation drop from 6.87 million in 1990 to 2.8 million just a year later, leading the editor to predict that, absent a substantial infusion of Party cash, the paper would go bankrupt by mid-1991.[67]

Matters grew even worse as the once reliably quiescent republic presses began to sharply differentiate from one another, and from the center. By 1989 the Warsaw Pact countries had all become independent of Moscow entirely, making their publications and broadcasts entities of a different type altogether. Even big central papers like *Pravda* and *Izvestiya*, which had always spoken essentially with one voice, were now frequently at odds with one another, airing significant policy battles. In face of such turmoil, and with obviously avid interest on the part of its customers, FBIS/JPRS and its partner struggled heroically, trying to stay ahead of the burgeoning flood. Nevertheless, the question of what was being selected for translation and what was not grew ever sharper.

To its credit, in April 1991 FBIS undertook a serious examination of whether its time-honored analytic technique – by now known as media analysis – still was valid. The author of the study, a senior, long-time analyst, while cataloguing all the dramatic changes that had occurred, also noted that FBIS had long used less strict versions of the methodology for "extracting intelligence from the media of several Middle East and other Third World countries that have varying degrees of autonomy from state control," and, in addition, "Yugoslav media for many years have been less rigidly controlled than those of the rest of East Europe" but still "analysts have been able to use these media for serious analysis."[68] After a thorough study of the various changes in Soviet press laws, the paper and ink shortages, the back-and-forth political battles, and all the rest, the FBIS self-study came to the conclusion that:

> Although the policies initiated under the banner of *glasnost* have greatly changed the restrictions on Soviet media, they have not and will not eliminate all controls. Soviet media will continue to reflect the interests and intentions of major Soviet political forces. Political parties, in particular the CPSU [Communist Party of the Soviet Union] ... have demonstrated that they intend to use the media as essential instruments to advocate policy, influence opinion, and guide the actions of their adherents.

Thus, the report concluded, "with some adjustments to fit the new situation, the traditional techniques of media analysis can still be used to draw inferences" via media analysis of the Soviet press.

What analysis of the Soviet press could not do, however, was to see the demise of the Soviet Union itself. Four months after the FBIS report was disseminated, a group of disgruntled communists attempted a coup, which collapsed three days afterwards. Before the end of August the CPSU's property and archives had been transferred to the control of the Russian Federation, the red flag with its hammer and sickle had been replaced by the pre-revolutionary Russian tricolor, and Gorbachev had resigned. In early November the party was outlawed, and, on Christmas Day 1991, the Soviet Union was officially dissolved.

The response in Washington is perhaps best captured in the book *Western Intelligence and the Collapse of the Soviet Union*,[69] which opens with quotes from: then-Secretary of State James Baker; his then Assistant Secretary, Lawrence Eagleburger; former Secretary of State George Schulz; Robert Blackwell, CIA analyst and senior Soviet specialist on the National Intelligence Council; *New York Times* correspondent Serge Schmemann; CIA nationalities expert Paul Goble; and prominent Sovietologists Dmitri Simes and Richard Pipes.

All of these experts and officials are reported to have said the same thing: "I was surprised."

Notes

1 V. N. Vasiliyev, *et al.*, *Sekrety Sekretnykh Sluzhb SShA* [Secrets of the Secret Services of the USA] (Moscow: Izd. Politcheskoy Literatury, 1973), p. 189.

2 "The Doctors' Plot," CAESAR-1, 15 July 1953, p. 7, at: http://www.foia.cia. gov/CPE/CAESAR/caesar-01.pdf, accessed 14 August 2010.

3 Vasilyev, pp. 190–91. Google has not heard of the "Buck Rogers Bureau" (in English) but Yandex, Russia's premier search engine, shows 24 mentions, most of them copies of the 1973 text. The Vasilyev book, of course, was published before James Grady's *Six Days of the Condor* (Norton, 1974), which was set in a secret CIA unit devoted to reading mystery and spy novels for possible nuggets of usable intelligence.

4 One of the best, and most complete, profiles of Feshbach and his work is Cullen Murphy, "Watching the Russians," *Atlantic Monthly*, February 1983.

5 Senator Daniel Patrick Moynihan used Feshbach's work as the basis for his January 1980 speech predicting that "the defining event of the decade [to come] might well be the breakup of the Soviet Empire" – a claim even more astonishing for having been delivered just two weeks after the Soviets invaded Afghanistan. See John Diamond, *The CIA and the Culture of Failure* (Stanford, CA: Stanford University Press, 2008), p. 32.

6 BBCM was created in 1939, for much the same purpose as had been FBMS – to monitor and analyze German shortwave broadcasts. See Michael S. Goodman, "British Intelligence and the British Broadcasting Corporation," in Robert Dover and Michael Goodman (eds), *Spinning Intelligence: Why Intelligence Needs the Media, Why the Media Needs Intelligence* (New York: Columbia University Press, 2009), p. 119.

7 Roop, pp. 164–72.

8 Kalev Leetaru, "The Scope of FBIS and BBC Open Source Media Coverage, 1979–2008," *Studies in Intelligence*, vol. 54, no. 1, 2009, p. 19.

9 The *New York Times* began writing about the growth of Soviet TV as early as 1954. See Harry Schwartz, "Report on Television in Russia," 23 May 1954.

10 Admiral William Studeman, "Teaching the Giant to Dance: Contradictions and Opportunities in Open Source within the Intelligence Community," speech delivered December 1992. See http://www.fas.org/irp/fbis/studem.html, accessed 14 August 2010.

11 Vasiliyev, p. 190.

12 Studeman, "Teaching the Giant to Dance." This same example – with the same figures – is cited in Patrick Radden Keefe, *Chatter* (New York: Random House, 2005), p. 199, where it is used to suggest the capacities of ECHELON, an automated signals intercept system which has never been acknowledged to exist.

13 See John Hutchins, "The Georgetown-IBM experiment demonstrated in January 1954," at: http://www.hutchinsweb.me.uk/AMTA-2004.pdf, accessed 14 August 2010. See also Neil Macdonald, "Language Translation by

Machine: A Report of the First Successful Trial," *Computers and Automation* 3(2), February 1954.

14 Norman C. Miller Jr, "Computer Firms Push New Systems to Dig Data out of Libraries," *Wall Street Journal*, 3 November 1961.

15 Paul Borel, "Automation for Information Control," *Studies in Intelligence*, vol. 11, no. 1, 1966.

16 Alexander George, "The Scientific Status of Propaganda Analysis," RAND Study P-616, 15 December 1954, p. 15.

17 Richards J. Heuer, "Adapting Academic Methods and Models to Governmental Needs," in Richards J. Heuer (ed.), *Quantitative Approaches to Political Intelligence: The CIA Experience* (Boulder, CO: Westview Press, 1978), p. 1.

18 Richards J. Heuer, "Content Analysis: Measuring Support for Brezhnev," in Heuer (ed.), p. 105.

19 CACI, Inc., "The Application of New Methodologies to Analyze the Soviet Perceptions of US Policies," vols I & II, 31 October 1975, and "Further Development of Soviet Perceptions: Content Analysis," 17 November 1975.

20 Abbey Newsletter, vol. 15, no. 8. December 1991. At: http://cool. conservation-us.org/byorg/abbey/an/an15/an15-8/an15-801.html, accessed 1 October 2010.

21 *Newsweek*, 24 January 1966.

22 George Getze, "Soviet Lead Observed in Science Data," *Los Angeles Times*, 17 August 1962.

23 "Technology: Figures in a Flash," *Time*, 21 August 1964.

24 Committee on Scientific and Technical Communication, National Academy of Sciences, National Academy of Engineering, *Scientific and Technical Communication: A Pressing National Problem and Recommendations for its Solution* (Washington DC: National Academy of Sciences, 1969), p. 27.

25 Walter Sullivan, "Physicists, Deluged by Data, Turn to Computers," *New York Times*, 25 December 1969.

26 Heuer, p. 121.

27 CACI, Inc., vol. I, p. 82.

28 "A Review of the Intelligence Community" prepared by the Office of Management and Budget under the direction of OMB Deputy Director James Schlesinger, 10 March 1975, pp. 1, 10, 10a. At: http://www.fas.org/irp/cia/product/review1971.pdf, accessed 15 August 2010.

29 The source of these words is the CIA internal report of 1974, at: http://www.gwu.edu/~nsarchiv/NSAEBB/NSAEBB144/document%208.pdf. As given in the text, these appear to be quotes from the Cunningham original, but the author of the 1974 report does not use quotation marks, so it may be that this is summary, not quotation.

30 Church Committee Report, p. 274.

31 Cunningham, as quoted in the CIA 1974 report.

32   Church Committee Report, p. 275.

33   Cunningham, G-1.

34   Cunningham, D-2.

35   This issue was addressed with some vigor in an exchange in 1964. John Alexander noted the paradox that "the higher the level of the intelligence product, the less complete is its visible documentation" (*Studies in Intelligence*, vol. 8, no. 3, 1964, p. 2) and urged that analytic products should be buttressed with explanatory footnotes. That set off no fewer than three rejoinders in the next issue (*Studies in Intelligence*, vol. 8, no. 4, 1964). State Department analyst Allen Evans said that "customers won't read fat papers" and "don't want to be bothered with documentation." In any event, the premier product, NIEs, are supposed to be about the future, and "who will footnote the future?" Two supporting letters said that even if customers wanted to access the material in footnotes, in most cases they couldn't, because of classification issues, and, in any event, the whole point of the system is to trust the insights and intuitions of the analysts.

36   Ford, pp. 65, 67.

37   Jack Davis, "Sherman Kent's Final Thoughts on Analyst-Policymaker Relations," The Sherman Kent Center for Intelligence Analysis Occasional Papers: vol. 2, no. 3, 2003, p. 3.

38   Denis Hilton, "Causality vs. Explanation: Objective Relations vs. Subjective Interests," *Interdisciplines*, Institute of Cognitive Sciences, University of Geneva, at: http://www.interdisciplines.org/medias/confs/archives/archive_6.pdf, accessed 17 September 2011.

39   Church Committee Report, p. 274.

40   Schlesinger, p. 10a.

41   In fact, if the intelligence community had a prize for "Worst Week," the week in which Khrushchev was ousted would be a strong contender. 14 October 1964 was the date of the ouster, followed the next day, 15 October, by the unexpected victory of the Labour Party in British parliamentary elections, thus returning Labour to power for the first time since 1951. The day after that, 16 October, China conducted its first nuclear test. Unable to decide which story took precedence, *Time* magazine's cover for 23 October 1964 offered a quadrant, with the fourth corner taken by the one scandal for which the IC did not have any responsibility, the resignation of President Lyndon Johnson's personal secretary and close friend, Walter Jenkins, who for the second time had been caught misbehaving in a men's bathroom.

42   Writing in the inaugural issue of *Studies in Intelligence* (vol. 1, no. 1), in fall 1955, Kent claimed "Intelligence today is not merely a profession, but like most professions it has taken on the aspects of a discipline: it has developed a recognized methodology; it has developed a vocabulary; it has developed a body of theory and doctrine; it has elaborate and refined techniques. It now has a large professional following. What it lacks is a literature." See: https://www.cia.gov/library/center-for-the-study-of-intelligence/kent-csi/vol1no1/html/v01i1a01p_0001.htm

43 R. A. Random, "Intelligence as a Science," *Studies in Intelligence,* vol. 2, no. 2, 1958, p. 75. Random is identified as a "professional logician," but the name is a pseudonym (probably intended as a joking one) for someone who worked in operations (see Michael Warner, "Wanted: A Definition of 'Intelligence,'" *Studies in Intelligence,* vol. 46, no. 3, 2002, p. 19). Random defined "intelligence" as being distinct from other "policy sciences" only in that all its work is secret and covert.

44 Charles R. Shrader, *History of Operations Research in the United States Army,* vol. 2 (Washington DC: Government Printing Office, 2008), pp. 40–41.

45 Sherman Kent, *Writing History* (New York: F.S. Crofts & Co, 1941), p. 4.

46 As quoted by John McLaughlin, CNN.com, 10 December 2007, at: http:// articles.cnn.com/2007-12-10/politics/mclaughlin.commentary_1_nuclear-weapons-national-intelligence-estimate-iran?_s=PM:POLITICS, accessed 30 September 2010.

47 Sherman Kent, "A Crucial Estimate Relived," *Studies in Intelligence,* vol. 8, no. 2, 1964, p. 118.

48 Robert Jervis, *Why Intelligence Fails* (Ithaca, NY and London: Cornell University Press, 2010).

49 Annabelle Srebreny-Mohammadi and Ali Mohammadi, *Small Media, Big Revolution: Communication, Culture, and the Iranian Revolution* (Minneapolis: University of Minnesota Press, 1994), p. xx.

50 As indexed by the Newsbank Corporation, which has digitized all of the *Daily Reports* from 1974 through 1996. See: http://www.newsbank.com/

51 Jervis, p. 21.

52 *Daily Reports* were region-specific, and bound separately, with different identifying cover colors. Usually end-users subscribed only to the area of their interests and responsibilities.

53 This was a Teheran Domestic Service relay of an Agence Presse-France (APF) report that Kuwait had denied "Khomeyni" a visa to enter the country, forcing him to return to Iraq, where he is described as living in exile. The report is odd, because Khomeini at the time lived in Paris.

54 Jervis, p. 39.

55 Digitalization can create problems as well as solve them – a search for Khomeini's name in 1978 brings up an interview with Iranian Prime Minister Shapour Bakhtiar from the French socialist daily *Le Matin,* in which Bakhtiar threatens those who speak of civil war with imprisonment or death. It takes close re-reading of the piece to notice that the date is a typographical error, and in fact was published in 1979, not 1978. In the original format this would be an obvious typo, because the article is contained in a booklet dated 5 February 1979. In electronic form, it is harder to notice the error, and therefore easier to put Khomeini – and, for that matter, Bakhtiar – in the wrong place and wrong function.

56 Jervis, p. 25.

57 Address by James R. Schlesinger at conference devoted to "CIA's Analysis of

the Soviet Union, 1947–1991," in Gerald K. Haines and Robert E. Leggett (eds), *Watching the Bear: Essays on CIA's Analysis of the Soviet Union* (Washington DC: Center for the Study of Intelligence, 2001), p. 265.

58 The articles appeared on 11 and 20 January 1978.

59 *Watching the Bear*, p. 275.

60 *Watching the Bear*, pp. 19–20.

61 *Watching the Bear*, p. 101.

62 *Watching the Bear*, p. 53.

63 *Watching the Bear*, p. 100.

64 A follow-up *New York Times* article on 15 December 1983 reported that Danchev had been sent for psychiatric treatment and was now back at work, though no one was sure what he was doing. The article also adds the intriguing details that Danchev was from Tashkent, and that he would have gotten sterner treatment "but his position had been helped by the fact that his father was a [Communist] party official in Tashkent."

65 Anthony Olcott, "*Glasnost* and Soviet Culture," in Maurice Freidberg and Heyward Isham (eds), *Soviet Society under Gorbachev: Current Trends and the Prospects for Reform* (Armonk, NY: ME Sharpe, 1987), p. 115.

66 Brian McNair, *Glasnost, Perestroika, and the Soviet Media* (New York: Routledge, 1981).

67 *Komsomolskaya Pravda*, 24 November 1990.

68 FB AR 91-10005, Analysis Report, "Media Analysis in the Era of *Glasnost*," 5 April 1991.

69 David Arbel and Ran Edelist, *Western Intelligence and the Collapse of the Soviet Union* (London and Portland, OR: Frank Cass, 2003), p. ix.

PART TWO

The "information iceberg" tips over

CHAPTER FOUR

Collecting puzzle pieces while mysteries abound

The end of the Soviet Union did not, as the popular (and widely misunderstood) book of the early 1990s seemed to suggest, herald *The End of History*. Institutionally, however, the disappearance of the adversary which for four decades had been the main *raison d'etre* of the intelligence community brought serious challenges. Even if the collapse of the USSR was truly a victory of the combined forces of US intelligence and US policy, as many claimed it to be, there nevertheless remained the very reasonable question of whether the intelligence community continued to be necessary, now that the Soviets were gone.

Unsurprisingly, the CIA and other components of the IC argued strongly that the need remained undiminished, and perhaps had even grown, while other parts of Washington began casting about for the "peace dividend," the money once spent on intelligence and defense that now, they said, could be directed elsewhere. Senator Patrick Moynihan twice submitted bills calling for the abolition of the CIA (in 1991[1] and 1995[2]), and Senator Boren in 1992 submitted a National Security Act which would have subordinated the CIA and other agencies to a newly created Director of National Intelligence. None of these bills passed, but the issue of major reform was raised again in 1996, in the Report "IC21: The Intelligence Community in the 21st Century" by the Aspin-Brown Commission (also known as the Commission on the Roles and Capabilities of the US Intelligence Community).[3] The proposed legislation, the studies, and a considerable volume of media coverage in the 1990s all swirled around the question of what the IC should do, whether it was capable of doing whatever that was, and how the problems (if indeed there were problems) should be remedied. The turbulence wrought by those questions, and the even greater distractions of the Clinton presidency scandals, the change in Congressional power in the 1996 election, political upheavals in Africa and among the shards of Yugoslavia, and a number of other issues obscured another process that was beginning to gather force during the same decade, one which in retrospect may have proven to be of even greater impact than were all the unsuccessful attempts at intelligence reform. Although the full nature of this change remains murky – in part because it is so profound, and in part because it has only just begun, so that the effects continue to work themselves out, often in completely unexpected arenas and ways – some of the general outline of that transformation is now clear.

As has already been noted, the notion of an "information explosion" had entered the lexicon as early as the mid-1960s, while scholars like Marshall McLuhan and Herbert Simon had begun speculating even earlier about the possible consequences of the ever-burgeoning information mass that people increasingly could access. Somewhere in the 1990s, however, this quantitative transformation slipped over a line, to become a fully qualitative change. Dramatic transformations in information availability occurred everywhere – in the Middle East, for example, long a bastion of tightly controlled state media empires, the experience of the first Gulf War, and the role that CNN had played in bringing that war to the world's living rooms (ironically enough, CNN was able to go global because it was carried via a Soviet satellite[4] – the Soviets having pioneered satellite TV in order to tie their vast country together into a single information system[5]), prompted officials and investors in the Middle East to begin experimenting with satellite transmission as well. MBC (Middle East Broadcasting Center), the region's first TV satellite broadcasting facility, was opened in 1991, followed in 1994 by Arab Radio Television (ART) and Orbit. Although the intention of this effort was clearly to try to insure that information transmission remained under government control – the first satellite, Arabsat, was put into orbit by a consortium of Arab League member states – the pressure of competition and the burgeoning transmission capacities ignited what one scholar of the region has called "a media explosion in the Arab world."[6] The term seems apt, considering that when the 1990s began, most viewers across the region had their choice of one to four state-run terrestrial TV stations – so-called "leader TV" with content that has been called "mind-numbingly dull"[7] – yet by 2003 had access to about 86 free-to-air Arab language stations (a number which by 2008 had reached 377, plus another 140 pay channels, augmented in many countries by an increased number of terrestrial stations, including in some places, private, for-profit stations[8]).

The transformation in China was, if anything, even more dramatic. Deputy Director of National Intelligence for Analysis Thomas Fingar has remarked that one of his first tasks as a young China analyst, in 1975, had been to try to determine how many publications there were in China. "We didn't necessarily have them," he said, "but we had some reason to believe [that there] were 73 publications."[9] By 2004, according to official Chinese statistics, there were more than 11,000 licensed newspapers and magazines.[10] The transformation in Chinese radio and TV may have been even more dramatic. What had been a mere handful of stations during the worst days of the Cultural Revolution had grown by the 1990s to number more than 1,000 stations – a number which a standard reference work[11] characterizes as "out of control and chaotic," causing the government to re-regulate the industry, so that by 2000 that number had been reduced to 670, augmented by more than 368,000 satellite download and relay stations, serving an audience of 270 million TV sets, the greatest number in any one country in the world.

Similar expansions took place everywhere, although the numbers were not always as dramatic. Across the former Eastern bloc media battles raged as fledgling political parties, emerging oligarchs, and foreign would-be investors opened new newspapers and magazines, took over old state TV stations or started new ones, and began to experiment with popular format radio. Even long-established media environments underwent wrenching transformation in the 1990s – in the UK, for example, the Broadcasting Act of 1990 dramatically reduced regulation of TV and radio, resulting in the growth of outlets such that there were hundreds of terrestrial, cable, and satellite channels by the end of the decade; in France TV deregulation came somewhat earlier (in the 1980s), but also somewhat less completely, so that by 2000 the number of stations were not hundreds, but still scores; and even in the US, where in 1979 the average TV got fewer than seven stations, the average by 2008 had grown to be more than 100.[12] Africa too enjoyed a media boom at the end of the century, although newspapers and, particularly, radio were the new providers of information, rather than TV.[13]

Transition from sender to receiver

Although the details of this proliferation – or, more properly, these proliferations – are specific to their various times and countries, all of them have in common at least one thing – that the balance of power in the communication relationship was shifting from the producer to the audience. As has already been noted in Chapter 2, the foundation for what became open source analysis in the last half of the twentieth century was the theoretical work done by the Rockefeller Group on Mass Communications Research, and Harold Lasswell in particular. The formula that Lasswell had popularized as defining a "communication act" had encouraged analysts to focus on the initiator of communication – the sender – as well as on the secondary issues of the choices that the sender had made in crafting the message, the medium (or media) selected for transmission of the message, and the audience that was targeted to receive it. The *purpose* of that communication act, however – which was to get the recipient to *think* something or *do* something – was generally forgotten in the analytic methodologies which developed from the communications theories insights. There are probably a number of reasons why that was so, but at least one was that the technology of communication at the time was such that it was easy to assume that a message sent was the same thing as a message received and acted upon.

"Media effects" is the general name for the study of how audiences receive and act upon messages. Most of the early work in the field was done by refugees from Nazi Germany, who tended to see the mass mobilizations that characterized the 1930s and 1940s as the product of mass media, which were presumed to be so powerful that they could, in effect, inject political views directly into people's brains – thus the names given to this sub-branch of the field, the *hypodermic needle* or *magic bullet* theory of media effects.[14] Sociologists Paul Lazersfeld and Elihu Katz later modified the theory, based on their findings in a series of election studies that voters were as likely, or more likely, to be influenced in their choices by friends and families as they were by the media. Among those "influencers," however, there proved to be people who paid more attention to media than did those to whom they gave their opinions, thus giving rise to the "two-step theory" of media effects.[15]

The continued failure to find strong data support for so-called "transmissional models," which viewed the audience as passive recipients of messages sent by others, led to a counter tendency, as some communications theorists began to argue that it is audiences who determine what they are willing to receive, and what they will do with it. Clustered together as the "uses and gratification" theory of media, studies done by scholars of this persuasion argued that audiences select media content for certain specific purposes. At least in its early days, the uses-and-gratifications approach generated considerable skepticism, because the number of potential media sources, though larger than it had been in the 1940s, was still small enough that it was not possible to untangle whether audiences were selecting what they genuinely wanted, or simply settling for what was *least unwanted*. Further complicating matters was the emergence of the "agenda setting" school of media effects studies, which argued that, in the famous phrase, "the press may not be successful much of the time in telling people what to think, but it is stunningly successful in telling its readers what to think *about*."[16]

Even as the various media effects scholars quarrel back and forth, some placing greatest emphasis on the message sender, others on the structure of the message itself, and still others on the audience's preference for one kind of message over another, all share the assumption that media remain an important clue to determine human behavior. Lying behind that assumption, although not always conscious or well articulated, is a further assumption, that those who send messages are the elite, while those who receive them are the masses. Through the end of the twentieth century that assumption remained generally correct, although it was already beginning to become clear that the reasons behind that assumption had more to do with accidents of available technology than with any other factor.

Although the 1990s were marked primarily by the spread of extremely cost-intensive media technologies, such as satellite transmission of TV and wide-distribution newspapers printed simultaneously in many places, the consequent increase in media choices was already building in the conditions for the next phase of what is proving to be a profound revolution in how information is produced, distributed, and consumed (this is examined at greater length in the next chapter). Even in the 1990s, though, the rapid increase in outlets from among which consumers could make choices was having the noticeable effect of eroding the authority that control of media had once conferred on elites.

Until the twenty-first century, production and dissemination of information via media required large capital investment. Even in states where media are comparatively unfettered, the requirements of capital investment – taxes, licensing, financial reporting – and the attendant vulnerability to financial penalties – anti-trust laws, libel laws – gave governments a strong hand. This was even more true in the case of the electronic media, which require government regulation of the frequency spectrum, and so can also incur such interventions as "equal time" legislation, as in the US, or content-origination and language requirements, as in France and Canada. Add in censorship laws, "decency" laws, and the general tendency of media outlets to cluster around what author Daniel Hallin had identified in 1968 as a "sphere of consensus,"[17] and it is no surprise that even where media were not strictly instruments of government, they were indisputably instruments of "the establishment," representing the views, concerns, and prescriptions of a country's elite.

When content choice is limited, there is a natural quality about what is available, as if life could offer nothing else. As choices grow, however, the arbitrary nature of what is available becomes increasingly evident, even if the fact is not fully recognized or acknowledged. When the only choice is to watch the evening news or turn off the TV, human nature is such that most people will keep the set on, although the amount of attention they pay may plummet. If they have the choice, however, of switching to, for example, MTV – as became the case across wide swaths of Eastern Europe in the 1990s – particularly if they also have a remote control in hand, thus not requiring them to get up from their chairs – then the question of "why watch the news at all?" suddenly becomes more immediate. Even if the choice remains as it was in the early days of pan-Arab TV broadcasting, between the state news of one's own country and the state news of a neighbor, the artificiality of "leader TV" becomes immediately clear simply through duplication. As Middle East media scholar Abdallah Schleifer noted, "Perhaps the visit of a minister to inaugurate a chicken farm is not terribly interesting, but since there is nothing else to watch, and at least it's our minister and our chicken farm, we watch it. But who wants to watch some other country's minister visiting some other country's chicken farm?"[18]

The details of how this process worked out varied across countries and across regions, but all shared the same basic result, which was a dilution of top-down authority. That can be measured in various ways – for example, a ten-fold increase in the number of channels available to a given household has been found[19] to correspond only to a four-fold increase in the number of channels actually watched, meaning that while the overall TV audience may grow, the share of that audience enjoyed by any one channel is less than it was when there were fewer channels. Another measure of the same effect is evident in writer Ken Auletta's calculation[20] that, whereas in 1965 advertisers could reach 80 percent of the US homes with TV by buying time on just three networks, by 2004 that degree of penetration could be achieved only by buying time on 125 channels. Importantly, this is not just a US phenomenon – writers in the Middle East agree that the media market suffers from "major fragmentation," with the consequence that "too many stations are chasing too small a market." Rather than the "10 or 15" stations that might be commercially viable across the region, there are "60 or 70,"[21] with the consequence that "the majority of channels are fighting for survival" and "eating from each other's plates."[22]

As the figures above suggest, attention is not uniformly distributed across all channels – no matter how many choices are available, once a certain quantity threshold is crossed patterns of usage generally begin to emerge such that the so-called "80–20 rule" (or "Pareto rule") is roughly in evidence, meaning that about 20 percent of whatever is being chosen among is selected by about 80 percent of those choosing.[23] Thus for example it is estimated that just 10 of the 450 stations easily available across the Middle East attract 70 percent of the viewers (and 50 of them account for a full 95 percent, meaning that the other 400 essentially compete for 5 percent of the viewers).[24] The consequences of this kind of audience fragmentation may also be seen in the US, where even the 111 million people who watched Super Bowl XLV on 6 February 2011, the largest TV audience ever gathered (to that date) in America,[25] were still fewer than half of the number which had the physical ability to access the game.[26]

What may be harder to grasp, however, is that these blocks of greater and lesser audiences result from the aggregated behavior of individuals, not the movements of what once were considered to be mass audiences. Thus it is wholly possible that one viewer may join others in enjoying, for example, MBC 1 (the most watched station in the Middle East), but then not watch any of the other "top ten," choosing instead to watch Al-Manar (the Hezbollah-controlled station broadcasting from unknown locations in Lebanon) and also, perhaps, watch music videos of steamy Lebanese chanteuse Haifa Wehbe[27] on one of the Rotana company channels.

As producing and transmitting grow ever cheaper ...

Even in the 1990s, when, as noted, the cost of media production and transmission remained high, the fragmentation effect suggested above was in increasing evidence. One of the first examples of how erosive of traditional authority the simple ability to choose could prove to be was the emergence in Egypt of "televangelist" Amr Khaled.[28] A technocrat with no formal religious training or degree, Khaled began talking about Islam informally to groups in mosques and private homes around Cairo sometime in the mid-1990s. Although his theology is described as wholly consonant with mainline Sunni religious practice, Khaled's style of preaching is more open, more accepting, and more conversational than is the practice for more traditional Islamic clerics – he is described as part Dr. Phil and part Billy Graham, or by another description, Rick Warren[29] – thus drawing him ever larger audiences, particularly among young Cairenes who were trying to balance a westernized lifestyle with the desire still to be Muslim. When the first regional religious channel, *Iqraa*, began to air in 1998, Khaled was among the channel's offerings (where by one account he was for a time responsible for generating 80 percent of the station's ad revenue[30]), and soon afterwards he was also picked up by ART. He was also selling cassette tapes, video tapes, and CDs, creating such a strong presence across the region that by 2002 Khaled drew the ire of established authorities – secular and clerical – and was forced to leave Egypt (he is now based in England).

As described by commentators from the region, what authorities found threatening about Khaled was not his message, but rather that his authority – sufficient by 2007 to have *Time* magazine include him among their choices for "the 100 men and women whose power, talent or moral example is transforming the world" – derived from his popularity, rather than having been bestowed by the traditional hierarchies. Khaled is seen as part of a wider phenomenon in which, rather than having to rely on the wisdom and judgment of the clerical authorities in the place one lives, satellite TV began to make it possible for people to look for clerics, and views, they found more to their liking. On a mundane level, this has resulted in what one journalist dubbed "*fatwa* shopping"[31] and another called "a travesty" of "strange *fatwas*"[32] as people took advantage of the combination of competing *sheikhs* (the title of the cleric who can offer *fatwa* judgments) and the desire of the religious channels to draw viewers essentially to keep looking for the answers they *wished* to receive, rather than having to live with the ones that their local cleric had given.

The same phenomenon was amplified by the emergence of the world-wide web, which is generally dated from the early 1990s.[33] Although the early web was still a "push" medium, meaning that originators created and disseminated messages that receivers could either accept or ignore, but not change, the consequent growth in available information (which had already swelled enormously because of the earlier technologies of CD-ROMs and even video and audio tapes) led to what several Middle Eastern scholars have characterized as a religious revolution. Although Islam had always been split into various schools and traditions, technology was such that most believers inherited the teachings of the clerical establishment where they lived. As scholars have argued, the appearance of new media channels allowed would-be teachers to search for audiences directly, and would-be adherents to pick and choose among them, creating what scholar Peter Mandaville dubbed "syncretism."[34] Mandaville has written that

> new media such as the Internet also make it relatively easy for almost anyone to produce and disseminate information ... the combination of [the rise of mass audiences and reduced production barriers] makes for considerably increased conversation and deliberation across a multitude of communicative spheres [so that] scales of participation are markedly augmented [while] the relatively low cost of setting up a presence on the Internet and the ability to host it beyond the reach of state authorities make it possible for individuals and groups to have a political voice far less susceptible to official censorship.[35]

Although there is considerable merit to the argument of Mandaville and others that the new media were big drivers in the growth of more extreme and more radicalized forms of Islam, it may well prove in the future that what was even more important was the simple fact that people got ever more accustomed just to *choosing*, rather than having elites provide them with opinions, views, and issues. In China, for example, one of the first manifestations of the pleasures of choice was the *Super Girl* contest run on a regional Chinese station in 2005, as a joint promotional effort by the station, a company that was trying to induce Chinese consumers to eat yogurt (this in a country where most people don't consume milk products), and the local cellphone provider. Ignored the first year by central authorities, the *American Idol*-style show let young women compete against each other as singers, with the winners of each round determined by the numbers of SMS-text messages that supporters sent as votes.[36] The eventual winner, Li

Yuchun, who got more than 3.5 million votes in the contest's finale, wore her hair, dyed Kool-Aid red, in a spiky punk cut as she belted out her winning song, her version of an Irish band's hit song, "Zombie" – none of which were elements that might warm the hearts of senior Party officials (who indeed the next year rigged the contest so that a more wholesome act won).

There is merit to the argument that what unsettled authorities was the speed with which the Chinese people adapted to the idea of voting, including the formation of "proto-parties" that lobbied to build support for one singer or another. Similar arguments have been made for the Middle East, where local variations on the *American Idol* and *Big Brother* TV concepts stimulated the same kinds of intense popular following and sulfurous fulminations from offended authorities. *Star Academy*, which incorporated the contest elements of *American Idol* and the "live-together" elements of *Big Brother*, was first offered in December 2003 in the Saudi-owned, Lebanon-based LBC. As described by scholar Marwan Kraidy, the show was an instant "hyper-media event," capturing more than 80 percent of the youth audience in Lebanon, and also generating strong interest in Saudi Arabia. In Kraidy's words, each broadcast set off

> five days of voting and campaigning during which viewers build coalitions with friends, schoolmates, neighbors or family members and send text messages to be aired on music television channels, all in support of the nominee they want to stay in the program. These 'democracy-like' activities ... peak during the Friday "prime" when the weekly round of voting ended and the results were released [so that] discussion boards, fan sites and blogs in Arabic, English and French animated the internet [and] text messages sent by viewers extolling favorite contestants were played on moving screen tickers by music television channels and talk-shows and newscasts on Al-Jazeera.[37]

The show ran counter to so many traditional practices that Saudi viewers in particular flooded local authorities with so many requests for fatwas – rulings as to whether or not their religion permitted them to watch – that eventually the "Permanent Committee for Scientific Research and the Issuing of Fatwas" concluded, after close study, that not only could good Muslims not watch the show at all, they also had the obligation to stop others from watching.[38]

Super Star, more similar to *American Idol*, and broadcast by Future TV in 2003, caused riots in downtown Beirut when the Lebanese contestant was voted out in favor of a Syrian and a Jordanian, because, the rioters charged, the Syrians had rigged the contest. The following week, before the finale between the Syrian and the Jordanian, long-simmering conflicts between the two neighbor states came to the top as the entire national apparatuses, including in Jordan's case, the army, were mobilized in support of their respective national candidates. Egged on by heavy advertising from the cellphone service providers (which stood to reap windfalls from the increased SMS traffic), more than 30 million viewers watched the final show, and 4.8 million voted (52 percent of them for the Jordanian), thus making plain a "division of passions and votes according to national affiliations [which] undermines claims that Pan-Arab satellite television is uniting Arabs ... in one community."[39]

From listening to talking back to talking to one another ... to just plain talking

Although the Chinese and Middle East media environments differ greatly from one another (just as do their respective political, religious, cultural, and other environments), and the responses to the phenomena of increased choice also differed, the *Super Girl*, *Star Academy*, and *Super Star* episodes did all share at least one characteristic: the activation of a large popular base that was not condoned or created by higher authorities. This was – in the strictest sense of the word – "democratic," meaning that suddenly the "demos" – the rabble, in Greek – had been able to choose something *they* were interested in, and cared about. As a Chinese sociologist remarked about *Super Girl*, the run-away success of that first year was "a victory of the grass-roots over the elite culture."[40]

That "democratic" quality began to sneak up on authorities around the world with the start of the new century, as technology increasingly moved from web-based versions of old "push" media toward a new breed of websites, so-called "pull" media which allowed users to interact with content, or even to create their own content easily – what usually is called the move from Web 1.0 to Web 2.0. Paternity and primogeniture are disputed, but it is generally acknowledged that the online personal diary – at first called a "web log" and then "we blog" and finally "blog" – emerged in 1997,[41] thus allowing ever-increasing numbers of people to put their own thoughts online, offering them up to the world. Blogs in turn became "micro-blogs" in 2005, spawning phenomena such as Twitter, which by 2010 was claiming 105 million subscribers and more than 180 million unique visitors every month.[42]

The parentage and birth of the wiki is undisputed – Microsoft programmer Ward Cunningham worked out software in 1995 that allowed any user to add, subtract, or edit content on a webpage, a process and a product that he called a "wiki," using a Hawaiian word for "fast."[43]

Photo-sharing sites began in the late 1990s as commercial services tied to companies that would print digital photos, but quickly mutated to become services like Flickr, which let the first users upload photos to free sharing sites in 2004 and, by 2010, boasted more than 5 billion photos.[44]

User uptake was even more astonishing for the online video sharing service YouTube, which uploaded its first video in early 2005, and by 2010 was serving viewers more than two billion videos *per day*, which, according to the company, generates an audience more than two times larger than the prime-time audience of all three US TV networks combined.[45]

Social networking platforms are perhaps most difficult of all to track, because it is a dizzying progression from Friendster (2002) to MySpace (2003) to Facebook (2004), with rival claimants and regional variants such as LiveJournal (a US platform started in 1999 which immediately came to dominate the Russian space, so that it is now owned by a Russian company), Bebo (US-begun in 2005 but dominant for a time in the UK, Ireland, and New Zealand), Orkut (a Google product launched in 2004 but successful mostly in Brazil, where it is now hosted), Hi5 (US-launched, but dominant in Central America, Mongolia, and a handful of other places), Renren (a 2005 Chinese knock-off of Facebook that now has millions of users), Cyworld (South Korea's most popular site, begun in 2004), and scores of others. The Wikipedia list of what it says are only the "notable, well-known [social networking] sites" has 195 entries, from Academia.edu to Zoopa – and Wikipedia itself, of course, is an encyclopedia with more than 3 million articles in 51 languages, all created by volunteer contributors from around the globe since Wikipedia's inception, in 2001.[46]

As huge as some of the numbers above may be, and the speed with which they grew, in some senses even they are dwarfed by the user uptake for hand-held mobile devices, which in 2010 were announced to number more than 5 billion,[47] grown from about 12 million in 1990.[48] Although the types of service and their capabilities vary, most of these phones have the ability to take photos and video; to send these to web-based services; to create text; to send that to web-based services; and to access, and interact with, most of the important social-networking sites. An increasing number are also GPS-enabled, so that people can let one another know where they are (or, in many cases, be tracked by authorities who wish to know where they are). Indeed, some service providers are experimenting with services that automatically let your friends know where you are, just as some of the social network sites are experimenting with letting you know what your friends have purchased (and they you).

The intelligence community and the new information environment

The terrorist attacks of 11 September 2001 were a fundamental blow to the intelligence community (as well of course to the nation as a whole, and the thousands of families affected by the suicide bombers). Whether it is fair to claim, as former Director of CIA Stansfield Turner did, that it was a "failure of our system of collecting and evaluating information" that "ranks even higher than Pearl Harbor,"[49] is not for this book to decide. What does seem clear, however, is that the attacks demonstrated how completely the task of intelligence had changed since the last days of the USSR. Although Al Qaeda had a territorial base and some apparent government support in Afghanistan, it was not a government, or indeed even a traditional terrorist organization of the sort with which intelligence and law-enforcement agencies had dealt previously, like the IRA, the Basque separatist ETA, or indeed even the earlier Middle East terrorist organizations like Al Fatah. Those non-governmental groups had the kinds of hierarchical structures and ideological purposes that the IC could comprehend and deal with; indeed, the inclination in the early days of the IC to view "communism" as a transnational movement (or potential movement) made traditional insurgencies something relatively familiar, to the point that some analysts were inclined to see terrorists as instruments of state policy, and thus as phenomena to be dealt with on a state-to-state basis.

Al Qaeda was different, in a number of fundamentally important ways. The organization was dispersed and non-hierarchical, more resembling a franchise system than a command-and-control structure. For all that its adherents talked of returning to the "golden age" of the Caliphate, the group's goals seemed not to be territorial, but rather to be spiritual. Although the group and its loosely-affiliated spectrum of adherents, followers, hangers-on, and sympathizers – what one group of IC analysts dubbed "the ziggurat of zealotry"[50] – devoted a huge amount of discussion to social issues like education, economics, justice, family relations, and others, the drivers, justifications, and consequences of adopting or ignoring those injunctions lay in the next world, not as with Marxism, Nazism, or other more familiar ideologies, in this one.

Because the common judgment was that, as the Executive Summary of the 9/11 Commission Report put it, "The 9/11 attacks were a shock, but they should not have come as a surprise,"[51] a significant portion of the post-9/11 recommendations focused upon a perceived need to greatly increase the role played by open source collection and analysis in the intelligence process. The 9/11 Commission itself recommended the creation of an Open Source Agency that would be (according to the organization chart produced for the report) independent of and equal in stature to the CIA.[52] That report did not explain its recommendation, nor specify what this "OSA" might do, but the same theme was picked up, with much greater detail, by the Commission on the Intelligence Capabilities of the United States Regarding Weapons of Mass Destruction (WMD Commission). That report called for the creation of an "Open Source Directorate in the CIA," with responsibility for "collecting and storing open source information" and also for inventing or acquiring "tools to assist users in data searches."[53] Although a step down in status from the body envisioned by the 9/11 Commission, this "OSD" would still have had a significantly higher profile than had FBIS, which was merely a sub-unit within the Directorate of Science and Technology, rather than a Directorate of its own.

In the event, there was nothing in either the 9/11 Commission Report or the WMD Commission Report which made it inevitable that FBIS would become the foundation for what, in November 2005, became the Open Source Center. As Doug Naquin, Director of OSC (and FBIS before that) expressed it in a luncheon address he gave to retired intelligence officers,[54] "the 1990s was not a good decade for FBIS." In the mid-1990s there had been a strong movement to close the organization entirely, which was averted only through the intervention of the Federation of American Scientists (FAS), which alerted the scholarly community, who in their turn lobbied Congress to save what FAS described (in a letter to National Security Adviser Anthony Lake) as being "among the most important research tools of the U.S. intelligence community, and it is certainly the most important resource provided by the intelligence community to the American public."[55]

Though saved from death, FBIS was not flourishing in its final years. By Naquin's account the organization shrank by half between 1993 and 2002, a number which included many long-time employees in bureaus overseas, as those too were down-sized or closed entirely. Perhaps even more important, increasing numbers of competitors, both from within government and, even more so, from the private sector, began to move into the business of open source intelligence. That process may have been specifically encouraged by the Aspin-Brown Commission, which (in the report's words) "conducted an impromptu test to see how readily information could be obtained exclusively from open sources on a subject of current national security interest and how that information compared to what could be obtained from the Intelligence Community."[56] Further detail is supplied by entrepreneur Ronald Steele, founder of the OSS company, and a bitter critic of FBIS and OSC; he has described how he was asked by committee members in August 1995 to pit "me and my Rolodex against the entire US intelligence community" on a question having to do with Burundi.[57] Steele describes how he was able over the course of a weekend to purchase maps, names of journalists, regional specialists, and satellite photographs from a group of six companies, to produce what the Aspin-Brown Committee described as information that was "substantial and on some points more detailed than that provided by the Intelligence Community," although the Report also noted that "the information that came from open sources took longer to produce, required validation, and failed to cover many key aspects of the situation important to policymakers."

Although not mentioned by Naquin, the 1990s also saw the vigorous growth of a different kind of open source intelligence, as businesses made ever greater use of the growing body of data that could be easily accessed, developing the field now known as "business intelligence" or "competitor intelligence." Practitioners of this kind of intelligence, who had legal access *only* to open source information, argued (in the words of one of its most prominent exponents) that "information is a relatively inexpensive and easily obtainable commodity" because "electronic databases, CD-ROMs and other information vehicles allow anyone the freedom to ask almost any question imaginable about the competition," with the result that "the companies that convert information into actionable intelligence will end up winning the game."[58]

In contrast, FBIS, and to a great extent the larger policymaking and intelligence communities, continued to equate open source intelligence primarily with newspapers and other news media. The WMD Commission, for example, writes repeatedly of the "massive amount of 'open source' information now available on the Internet and in other publicly available sources,"[59] but the only specific examples the report offers of what part of that information it would have the OSD use is the "digital newspapers and periodicals available over the Internet," which the new OSD would "gather and store."[60]

The Commission's chapter on improving analysis was more specific about how it envisioned open sources being used. The main value of open sources, the report implied, lay in complementing and corroborating material from "the clandestine collectors," as well as in helping analysts working on "lower priority accounts" who have trouble getting "the clandestine collectors" to help them. Of course, the report notes, ability to use a lot of that open source material requires knowledge of foreign languages, so that a third function of this OSD would be to purchase or invent better machine translation tools, as well as tools that would make it easier for analysts to achieve "prioritization and exploitation of large volumes of textual data without the need for prior human translation or transcription."[61] The report envisioned a cadre of no more than 50 "evangel-analysts" who would be "trained specifically in open source research" and then "assigned to offices willing to experiment with greater use of open source material, where they would be expected to answer questions for and provide useful unclassified information to analysts. They would also produce their own pieces highlighting open source reporting but drawing on classified information as well." The report clearly envisioned that this small group of "evangel-analysts" was a temporary measure, who would migrate their skills and insights back into the traditional analytic workforce, "as a result both of their education outreach efforts and of the influx of younger, more technologically savvy analysts." Both because it was "a center of excellence for linguistics" and because its analysts "must surf a data avalanche every day,"[62] the NSA was proposed as the joint owner, with CIA, of this hypothetical OSD.

Collection, dot-connection, and the primacy of secrets

It is clear from the WMD Commission Report that intelligence is conceptualized much as it always had been, an activity that is defined by and is dependent upon secrets. Open source information is valuable only to the extent that it complements clandestine collection, or, in low priority instances, can be a reasonable low-cost substitute for it, thus allowing expensive clandestine collection resources to be shifted to higher-priority targets. The challenge of open source, then, is to build bigger machines that will "store history," in a "robust" program that can "gather data to monitor the world's cultures and how they change with time."[63] In other words, despite all the apparent support for open source information, the way in which even proponents see it being used is still within the canonical "collect-process-analyze" framework which was laid down in 1947.

As has been argued above, that model did not work particularly well in the comparatively more meager information environment of 1970s Iran, and the swelling flood of information from among which collectors might choose to satisfy collection requirements only made the problem worse. Author John Diamond has highlighted the preference for secret over open information, as well as a tendency to shape collection based on certain *a priori* assumptions, as a big part of the explanation of why India's resumption of nuclear testing in 1998 came as such a surprise – in spite of clear statements by Bharatiya Janata Party (BJP) spokespeople in the newspapers and other media during the election campaign that, if they came to power, as they in fact did, they would resume nuclear tests.[64]

The surprise that the BJP actually did what they said they would is categorized as yet another "failure to connect the dots," or to notice the significant pattern among available data before an event occurs. The traditional answer to this problem, both in the intelligence community and among lawmakers and policymakers, is to build bigger and bigger systems to collect more and more data[65] – an approach already criticized by the Schlesinger Commission Report in 1971. A look at the available open source information that was collected, however, makes plain that "more" would have done nothing. FBIS published 125 pieces mentioning the BJP between 1 January 1998 and the actual test, on 11 May 1998. These included reports that "The BJP (Bharatiya Janata Party)-led government will re-evaluate India's nuclear policy and exercise the option to induct nuclear weapons" (*Deccan Herald*, 19 March 1998); that "Neither the Clinton administration nor Congress has raised any apprehension over the Bharatiya Janata Party's election manifesto, advocating India going nuclear" (*Deccan Herald*, 17 February 1998); and that "BJP President L K Advani has said his party is 'undeterred' by the United States's criticism of the commitment to induct nuclear weapons if BJP came to power and asserted there will be no compromise in exercising nuclear option" (*Deccan Herald*, 8 February 1998). There was even a report that the BJP might deliberately be trying to circumvent US monitoring as it worked to reactivate its nuclear capability (Hong Kong AFP, 28 April 1998).

What is not addressed in the "unconnected dots" accusations, however, is what there is about this information that would prompt an analyst to select the five or six pieces which mention the nuclear issue – or ten, if one were also to include pieces on BJP-backed missile tests – from among the 125 which mention the BJP in that period, or the 772 which mention India.

The problems inherent in "category collection" show particularly clearly in an article published in *Studies in Intelligence*[66] by scholar Kalev Leetaru which dissected what FBIS had collected and disseminated between 1994 and 2004, when materials were made available to the public on a quarterly basis via CD-ROMs, thus allowing Leetaru a convenient way to extract a high-level, large-scale view of the entire corpus of FBIS collection (or at least of that portion of it that was made available to the public through the World News Connection).

According to Leetaru's article, FBIS compiled more than 4 million reports in that decade, with the volume of collection rising steadily from about 17,000 reports a month in 1993 to about 50,000 per month in 2004. As indicated by the topic tags that FBIS began to add to documents at the start of 1999, that material was devoted overwhelmingly to the monitoring of traditional state activities, as reflected in the traditional press (albeit in the internet versions of that press). Thus in the five-year period 1999–2004, almost half of the total material was tagged "domestic political" (44.94 percent), with just a slightly smaller portion deemed to concern "international political" (43.45 percent). Since a document might have more than one topic tag, another 34.59 percent concerned "leader," "military" was the topic of 17.16 percent, and economics – 15.36 percent "domestic" and 13.34 percent "international" – made up the six most frequently applied tags. Perhaps surprisingly, given that more than half of the period measured came after 9/11, the topic tag "terrorism" was applied only to 10.36 percent of the collected material.

To put that figure into perspective, however, that ten-plus percent still represents more than 277,000 documents. If a normal analyst's ability to digest material remained as it had been in 1994, when a study quoted by the WMD Commission spoke of analysts having to "scan 200 to 300 documents" every day,[67] then it would have required between about 900 and 1400 "analyst days" to read only the material marked "terrorism."

Of course, reading that material was not the responsibility of any one analyst – which suggests a problem of a different sort. The number of analysts in the intelligence community and the ways in which they are deployed against issues is not disclosed, but recent figures for the IC as a whole range from 100,000[68] to 200,000 people,[69] suggesting that there was no shortage of potential readers. Alfred Rolington, who was long-time CEO of the Jane's Information Group, highlighted the problems inherent in spreading information across too many people and offices, in an editorial he published in one of his company's journals to mark the first anniversary of 9/11. The company had devoted an entire issue of one of their journals to Al Qaeda, with the cover date August 2001. The issue contained material that had been written between May and June 2001, some of which had been posted on the company's website in June and July, and the rest of which was gathered in July to be published in a hard-bound journal with an August date. That special issue was merely the latest, and most complete, of what proved to have been several hundred articles that the Jane's publications and websites had produced since 1995.[70] As Rolington wrote, the articles in that special "talked in detail about Bin Ladin's organization and, buried in the flow, we reported that he was known to be training individuals as commercial pilots." The importance of that detail was "easy to see with 20/20 hindsight, but like everyone we were swamped by massive information flows."[71]

What Rolington was highlighting, in other words, is that the existing system of information collection for intelligence purposes only filters the "massive information flows" to a certain degree, without providing a clear means for distinguishing what the Cunningham Report in 1966 had called "secondary material" from "significant material."[72] Leetaru's *Studies in Intelligence* article shows that partial filtering quite plainly – nearly a quarter of the reports filed by FBIS in the decade studied by the article came from just 25 sources (nearly all of them wire services like XINHUA and ITAR-TASS). Indeed, 20 percent came from just 10 sources, suggesting that the FBIS source profile would exhibit precisely that same kind of "80–20" behavior as do the TV viewing choices across the Middle East (described above). As the article notes, these are "outlets with national stature and international importance." They are, in other words, precisely the "authoritative sources" that the esoteric communication analysts had relied upon, and which the defenders of the FBIS "media analysis" methodology had continued to defend.

However, just as official Iranian media would not provide evidence that the Shah was losing his grip, or the official Soviet media that the CPSU was doomed, so would those "authoritative voices" not capture – for instance – the emergence of Usama bin Ladin. To its credit, FBIS began processing statements by bin Ladin in 1994, and had issued at least 20 newspaper articles about him before bin Ladin issued his famous "jihad fatwa" against Americans in February 1998.[73] Those various reports, however, came from a broad spectrum of outlets, published in locations as diverse as London and Rawalpindi, virtually guaranteeing that they would be "swamped by massive information flows." In addition, as the *Studies in Intelligence* article shows, the bulk of attention both at FBIS and at its partner organization,

BBCM, continued to be focused on Russia and, to a somewhat lesser extent, China, which between them accounted for nearly 21 percent of the total 1994–2004 output.

The organization of information by countries suggests another reason why it would have been easy for information about bin Ladin or Al Qaeda to be "swamped," for neither topic was confined to a single country. Examination of the pre-9/11 reporting on bin Ladin, for example, shows that a wide variety of country and region tags were used, suggesting that, if analysts were also arrayed in a country-account taxonomy, not all analysts would have seen the same materials, thus diluting the impact that the reports might have had if aggregated. This suggests still a further problem, which is that the available dissemination platforms measure output, not uptake – there is no way to ascertain how many of the reports that FBIS and BBCM put out were actually read, and if so, by whom.[74] The combination of bin Laden's death, in May 2011, and the battle in Libya which has kept that country in the news through spring 2011 has highlighted another element which would have made it hard to aggregate available information, which is the complexity of rendering Arabic names in English. While the "Osama bin Laden/Usama bin Ladin" difference is not large, it would still affect search engine performance. Just the last name of Libya's embattled leader can be rendered in about 100 different ways in English, and there are some names which can have as many as 130,000 variant English renderings.[75]

The same taxonomic problem pervades the entire intelligence effort, and not just that of open source intelligence. As explained by the office of the Director of National Intelligence, a key means by which the "senior policy community" informs the intelligence community about "issues of critical interest" is through the National Intelligence Priorities Framework (NIPF).[76] As described, the NIPF is a meta-tagging system that is "updated semi-annually" in order to "guide and inform decisions concerning the allocation of collection and analytic resources as well as the prioritization of collection requirements." Although the contents are of course not revealed, former AD/DNI Thomas Fingar has described the NIPF as a matrix of "about 280 national actors" that are arrayed against "32 intelligence topics" which furthermore are grouped into "three categories" of urgency, resulting in, by his calculation, "about 9,100 cells," or collection categories, of which "almost 2300 issues had been assigned priorities higher than zero."[77]

Intelligence, open source and otherwise – always a puzzle, never a mystery

The dominant metaphor for the intelligence process has long been the jigsaw puzzle – that is, something of defined shape from which pieces are missing, and must be collected. For most of its history "OSINT" – open source intelligence – has been assigned the role of being, as Joseph Nye put it, "the outer pieces of the puzzle without which one can neither begin nor complete the puzzle."[78] Gregory Treverton, who has held senior positions on the National Security Council (NSC) and on the Senate Select Committee on Intelligence, has written extensively on how the puzzle metaphor is a legacy artifact of the Cold War, and a serious constraint for the challenges of modern intelligence. Echoing Brzezinski's criticism, that the CIA was "superb on 'factology,' not very good in 'politology,'"[79] Treverton notes that most traditional espionage targets are puzzles, so that the end product is "*the* answer: North Korea has X nuclear weapons; Soviet missiles have Y warheads" – in other words, "factology." By contrast, Treverton notes, "no evidence can definitively solve mysteries because, typically, they are about people not things" – the intentions and other human dimensions the analysis of which Brzezinski dubbed "politology." The first kind of problem depends upon information for solution; the second kind can never be solved definitively, no matter how much information is gathered.[80]

Author Malcolm Gladwell made the point even clearer, in his study of the Enron financial collapse. Gladwell argues that, although Enron executive Jeff Skilling was sent to jail for withholding information about the company's real financial picture, in reality there "are several millions of pages of documents that are all a matter of public record," which make it abundantly clear that the company was in fact not making money. The problem was that there was *too much* information, not too little, and the people in charge of understanding it – "the entry-level accountants at Arthur Andersen actually performing the audits" – were unable to understand what they were reading. This highlights an important distinction made both by Treverton and by Gladwell, that "hidden information and secrets are 'transmitter-dependent,' while information overload is 'receiver dependent.'"[81] In somewhat simpler terms, in the world of puzzles, the absence of information is the fault of the enemy – we do not know something that we consider to be of importance because the enemy has done his best to keep that information from us. In contrast, the solution of mysteries – indeed, even the perception that mysteries may exist – require that those who are responsible for creating understanding must do more than simply collect "more information." Gladwell based much of his argument on the work of law professor Jonathan Macey, who had argued in a law review article about the Enron collapse, and the Sarbanes-Oxley disclosure regulations which that scandal provoked, that "disclosure is a necessary but insufficient condition to accomplish the objective" of making sure that financial institutions are functioning properly. For the monitoring bodies to function properly, however, "there must also be in place an adequate infrastructure to receive, analyze, and interpret the information that is disclosed."[82] Gladwell made the same point even more starkly, arguing that, in order to prevent future Enrons, "it is vital that there be a set of financial intermediaries who are at least as competent and sophisticated at receiving, processing, and interpreting financial information ... as the companies are at delivering it."

Intriguingly, the joint Senate-House investigation into intelligence activities before and after 9/11 made essentially the same point about the analytic community, arguing that "many [counter-terrorism] analysts were inexperienced, unqualified, [and] under-trained ... there was a dearth of creative, aggressive analysis targeting Bin Laden and a persistent inability to comprehend the collective significance of individual pieces of intelligence."[83] While it is not the purpose of this book to criticize the analytic workforce or to address broader issues of analytic shortcomings, it is worth drawing out the implications of what Treverton, Gladwell, Macey, and others have argued about the need to transition from "sender-dependent" puzzles to "receiver-dependent" mysteries. Those tasked to search for puzzle bits do not need to understand the function or role of the information they are asked to find. Provided the missing or desired material can be described adequately, then what is required to find the needed piece is industry, ingenuity, and, perhaps, courage. After all, those seeking generally know where the desired piece is, for the enemy has locked it away, and has further signified its importance by making it super-secret – thus the only challenge (not a small one) is to steal what the enemy wants to keep hidden.

In the world of puzzles even open source intelligence operates under those rules. Those doing analysis of esoteric communication knew where the secrets were hidden – behind the arcane language and byzantine rules of Communist propaganda. The importance of what was being hidden could be judged by the rank of who was credited with having conveyed the veiled message, and the authoritativeness of the medium in which that message was carried. Moreover, since the "keepers of the secrets" at the top of the information chain were presumed also to command the attention of all those who were beneath them, it was safe to assume that – to the degree that anyone cared about the issue – "the masses" could be presumed to think as the elites told them to. Thus, just as almost any spy, provided he or she were spry enough, could be tasked with stealing a crucial widget (or plans to that widget), so could almost any open source analyst be told to watch the standard media roll by, with the purpose of noting changes. The meanings of those changes were less important than they were noticed, because the slow accumulation of those changes over time would, it was assumed, reveal the meaning through the process itself, as the puzzle filled itself in.

At least for the world of open source intelligence, the steady, almost exponential, growth of publicly available information made the assumptions and processes of a "puzzle-solving" approach appear ever more arbitrary. As elites everywhere were discovering, it was no longer enough simply to push out a message, and assume that the masses would do as they were told. Even if the masses remained basically obedient, the emergence of other newspapers to read, and other TV channels to watch, to say nothing of the spread of mobile devices that increasingly let them talk to one another made it ever more unsure whether the masses were even listening when the elites tried to talk to them. As the translators of FDD and JPRS were finding even in the late 1950s, the swelling flood of available information was making puzzle-solving an increasingly quixotic task.

This does not mean, however, that a transition to mystery-solving is imminent, easy, or, indeed, even possible. The challenges of such a transition are implied in the further charge of the Joint Senate-House Committee report, that many analysts were "without access to critical information." In context, those words refer primarily to the failure of various components of the intelligence and law enforcement communities to pool information which they had gathered in their various separate systems. The notion "critical information," however, suggests that conceptually the analytic process is still envisioned primarily as puzzle-solving, or as the means to answer the "Who? When? Where? How Many?" questions of tactical or current intelligence. Even in 1966, when the Cunningham Report was written, there was nothing inherent in information which would have allowed collectors and analysts to sort what they collected to "significant" and "secondary." By 2001, and even more so 2010, the challenge of information is not to store it, collect it, access it, or even necessarily to share it. The real challenge is to understand where in all the information that you have available to you is the part that will answer the question which you need to answer.

Notes

1 The first bill was submitted in May 1991, even before the USSR had collapsed. Bud Shuster, "DIALOGUE – American Intelligence: Do We Still Need the C.I.A.?; Independence Means Integrity," *New York Times*, 19 May 1991.

2 See Abolition of the Central Intelligence Agency Act of 1995, submitted 4 January 1995, available at: http://www.fas.org/irp/s126.htm, accessed 29 October 2010.

3 "IC21: The Intelligence Community in the 21st Century," Report of the Commission on the Roles and Capabilities of the US Intelligence Community, Washington DC: Government Printing Office, 1 March 1996, available at: http://www.access.gpo.gov/congress/house/intel/ic21/ic21_toc.html, accessed 28 October 2010. Hereafter "Aspin-Brown".

4 See "CNN Milestones" at: news.turner.com/press_kits_file. cfm?presskit_id=66&pfile_id=111.

5 V. SIforov, "Space Television Broadcast from Vladivostok to Moscow," *Current Digest of the Soviet Press*, 19 May 1965.

6 S. Abdallah Schleifer, "Media Explosion in the Arab World: The Pan-Arab Satellite Broadcasters," *Transnational Broadcasting Studies (TBS)*, vol. 1, Fall 1998, at: http://www.tbsjournal.com/Archives/Fall98/Articles1/Pan-Arab_bcasters/pan-arab_bcasters.html, accessed 29 October 2010.

7 Gordon Robinson, "The Rest of Arab Television," Report by the USC Center on Public Diplomacy, June 2005, p. 3.

8 Naomi Sakr, "Social Talk on Multi-channel Arab TV," in Graeme Turner and Jinna Tay (eds), *Television Studies After TV* (Oxford and New York: Routledge, 2009), p. 170.

9 Conference speech, 21 August 2006, at: http://www.dni.gov/speeches/20060821_2_speech.pdf, accessed 29 October 2010.

10 Open Source Center, PRC Media Guide, 21 March 2007, at: http://www.fas.org/irp/dni/osc/prc-media.pdf, accessed 29 October 2010.

11 Horace Newcomb (ed.), *Encyclopedia of Television* (New York: Taylor and Francis, 2004), vol. 1, p. 510.

12 Eli M. Noam, *Media Ownership and Concentration in America* (New York: Oxford University Press, 2009), p. 102.

13 Kwame Karikari, "African Media Breaks 'Culture of Silence," *Africa Renewal,* August 2010, at: http://www.un.org/ecosocdev/geninfo/afrec/vol24no2-3/, accessed 29 October 2010.

14 There is a vast number of articles and books on this subject. A good succinct explanation is available on the online catalogue of communication theories maintained by the University of Twente, the Netherlands, at: http://www.utwente.nl/cw/theorieenoverzicht/Theory%20clusters/Mass%20Media/Hypodermic_Needle_Theory.doc/, accessed 29 October 2010.

15 Elihu Katz, "The Two-Step Flow of Communication: An Up-to-Date Report on an Hypothesis," *Public Opinion Quarterly*, vol. 21, no. 1, 1957.

16 Bernard C. Cohen, *The Press and Foreign Policy* (Princeton, NJ: Princeton University Press, 1963), p. 13.

17 Daniel Hallin, *The Uncensored War: The Media and The Vietnam War* (Oxford and New York: Oxford University Press, 1986). Hallin saw the media as agreeing that certain topics were not subject to debate – the US troops in Vietnam, for example, could not be criticized until quite late in the war – and also agreeing that certain other topics were legitimately open to debate (the "sphere of legitimate controversy"). Views which did not fall into either were in what he called "the sphere of deviancy" and – in a world where access to media was costly and therefore difficult – simply did not make it into the public arena.

18 Schleifer, "Media Explosion in the Arab World."

19 Charles B. Goldfarb, *Cable and Satellite Television Network Tiering and à la Carte Options for Consumers: Issues for Congress,* Congressional Research Service, 9 June 2004, p. 4.

20 Ken Auletta, "The New Pitch: Do Ads Still Work?" *The New Yorker*, 25 March 2005.

21 Robinson, pp. 10, 11.

22 Gazbeya El-Hamamsy, "Carving Up the Dish," *Business Today Egypt*, September 2005, at: http://www.businesstodayegypt.com/article. aspx?ArticleID=5714, accessed 2 November 2010.

23 A classic discussion of this phenomenon may be found at Clay Shirky, "Power Laws, Weblogs, and Inequality," 8 February 2003, at: http://shirky.com/ writings/powerlaw_weblog.html, accessed 2 November 2010.

24 Ben Flanagan, "Multi-screen Complex," *Media Week Middle East*, 17 May 2009, p. 15.

25 See http://www.examiner.com/pop-culture-in-oklahoma-city/ super-bowl-nielsen-ratings-name-super-bowl-xlv-most-watched-show-history

26 The Neilsen rating, meaning the percentage of *potential* viewers who *actually* watched, was reported to have been 47.9. See: http://www.associatedcontent. com/article/7728146/2011_super_bowl_ratings_record_setting.html

27 As of 2 November 2010 her official fan club site was: http://www.haifafans. net/fanclub/

28 Except where noted, the following is based upon Lindsay Wise, "'Words from the Heart': New Forms of Islamic Preaching in Egypt," M.Phil. dissertation, St. Antony's College, Oxford University, 2003, at: http://users.ox.ac.uk/~metheses/ Wise.pdf, accessed 2 November 2010.

29 Asra Nomani, "Amr Khaled," *Time*, 3 May 2007.

30 Yasmin Moll, "Islamic Televangelism: Religion, Media and Visuality in Contemporary Egypt," *Arab Media & Society*, Issue 10, Spring 2010, at: http://arabmediasociety.com/?article=732, accessed 2 November 2010.

31 Neil MacFarquhar, "Fatwa Overload," *Foreign Policy*, 17 April 2009.

32 Nelly Youssef, "Spiritual Guidance, Political Indoctrination, and Financial Profit" at: http://en.qantara.de/Spiritual-Guidance-Political-Indoctrination-and-Financial-Profit/8001c165/index.html, accessed 31 May 2011.

33 As with most important technologies, the parents and birthdate of the web are all disputed. The first computer-to-computer transfers were made in 1969, via ARPANET, a US-government structure, and hyper-text, a main enabler of the present-day web, was made public in 1989 (by Tim Berners-Lee). Another enabler was the development of good browser tools like Mosaic and then Netscape. In terms of the number of users, and therefore the massive number of nodes, which is probably the quality that best defines the web, critical mass was reached somewhere in 1994 – and thus make a convenient point from which to begin to talk about widespread effects.

34 Peter Mandaville, "Reimagining Islam in Diaspora: The Politics of Mediated Community," *Gazette*, vol. 63(2–3), 2001, p. 184.

35 Peter Mandaville, *Global Political Islam* (New York: Routledge, 2007), p. 324.

36 Gady Epstein, "Golden Cow," *Forbes Asia Magazine*, 27 September 2010.

37 Marwan Kraidy, "Saudi Arabia, Lebanon and the Changing Arab Information Order," *International Journal of Communication*, vol. 1, 2007, p. 143.

38 Kraidy, *IJC*, pp. 146–47.

39 Marwan Kraidy, "Reality Television and Politics in the Arab World," *Transnational Broadcasting Studies*, vol. 1, no. 2, 2005, p. 13.

40 "China Rockin' to 'Super Girl'," *China Daily*, 30 August 2005, at: http://www.chinadaily.com.cn/english/doc/2005-08/30/content_473432.htm, accessed 4 November 2010.

41 Declan McCullagh and Anne Broache, "Blogs Turn 10 – Who's the Father?" CNET News, 20 March 2007, at: http://news.cnet.com/2100-1025_3-6168681.html, accessed 4 November 2010.

42 "Twitter Snags Over 100 Million Users, Eyes Money-Making," Reuters, 14 April 2010.

43 Todd Bishop, "Microsoft Notebook: Wiki Pioneer Planted the Seed and Watched it Grow," *Seattle Post-Intelligencer*, 26 January 2004.

44 The 5 billionth photo was announced on the Flickr blog on 19 September 2010. See: http://blog.flickr.net/en/2010/09/19/5000000000/, accessed 4 November 2010.

45 Jason Kincaid, "Five Years in, YouTube is Now Streaming Two Billion Views per Day," TechCrunch, 16 May 2010, at: http://techcrunch.com/2010/05/16/five-years-in-youtube-is-now-streaming-two-billion-videos-per-day/, accessed 4 November 2010.

46 All figures as accessed on 4 November 2010.

47 BBC News, "Over 5 billion mobile phone connections," 9 July 2010, at: http://www.bbc.co.uk/news/10569081, accessed 4 November 2010.

48 http://www.worldmapper.org/display.php?selected=333, accessed 4 November 2010.

49 Stansfield Turner, *Burn Before Reading* (New York: Hyperion, 2005), p. 1.

50 Jonathon Shainin, "The Ziggurat of Zealotry," *New York Times Magazine*, 10 December 2006.

51 Executive Summary, Final Report of the National Commission on Terrorist Attacks upon the United States, p. 2, at: http://www.9-11commission.gov/report/911Report_Exec.pdf, accessed 4 November 2010.

52 9/11 Report, p. 23.

53 WMD Commission Report, at: http://www.fas.org/irp/offdocs/wmd_report.pdf, accessed 5 November 2010, p. 351.

54 "Remarks by Doug Naquin, CIRA Luncheon, 3 October 2007," *CIRA Newsletter*, vol. 34, no. 4, 2007.

55 Letter to Anthony Lake, 3 January 1997, at: http://www.fas.org/irp/fbis/jjslake.html, accessed 5 November 2010.

56 Aspin-Brown, p. 88.

57 "Memorandum from Robert David Steele Vivas," OSS.Net, 1 May 2004, at:

www.oss.net/dynamaster/file.../The%20OSINT%20Story%202.1%20RTF.rtf, accessed 5 November 2010. The six companies Steele names are Lexis-Nexis, Oxford Analytica, Janes, Institute of Scientific Information, EastView (a US distributor of Soviet-produced materials, including maps), and SPOT, a French company selling commercial satellite photography.

58 Leonard Fuld, *The New Competitor Intelligence: The Complete Resource for Finding, Analyzing, and Using Information About Your Competitors* (New York: John Wiley & Sons, 1995), pp. 25, 24.

59 WMD, pp. 352, 353.

60 WMD, p. 379.

61 WMD, p. 396.

62 WMD, pp. 397–98. This oddly mixed metaphor is symptomatic of how much problem people have finding appropriate metaphors for the huge volume of open source information.

63 WMD, p. 379.

64 Diamond, pp. 260–71.

65 WMD, pp. 396–98 (Recommendation 3) envisions several potentially enormous machines for collection, translation, storage, and data processing.

66 Leetaru, p. 23.

67 WMD, p. 401.

68 "Remarks and Q&A by the Director of National Intelligence Mr. Mike McConnell," Harvard University, 2 December 2008, at: http://www.dni.gov/speeches/20081202_speech.pdf, accessed 6 November 2010.

69 Walter Pincus, "DNI Cites $75 Billion Intelligence Tab," *Washington Post*, 17 September 2009.

70 See slide 10 in a talk given by Rolington in May 2008, at: www.osif.us/images/Presentation_US_Intelligence.ppt, accessed 6 November 2010.

71 Alfred Rolington, "9/11 in Search of Context and Meaning," *Jane's International Security News*, 11 September 2002. Apparently no longer available on the Jane's website, but archived at: www.oss.net/dynamaster/file.../CEO%20Janes%20on%20OSINT.doc, accessed 6 November 2010. A Powerpoint slide showing the number of articles on Al Qaeda published in Janes, and when, is available on the slide deck referenced in endnote 70.

72 Cunningham, Report, p. D-2.

73 FBIS Report, Compilation of Usama bin Laden Statements 1994 – January 2004," January 2004, at: http://publicintelligence.net/compilation-of-usama-bin-ladin-statements-1994-january-2004/, accessed 7 November 2010.

74 In fact, although there is no way to prove it, it is quite likely that the massive FBIS data, if examined, would show the same kind of "80–20" characteristics as do all other large data sets, with a small number of items accessed by large numbers of users, and the great bulk accessed by only a few.

75 "Usama bin Ladin" is the transliteration used by the Open Source Center when it does its own translating. BBC and other sources use "Osama bin

Laden." For the source of the other numbers see: http://www.theatlanticwire. com/global/2011/04/freezing-qaddafis-assets-harder-cant-spell-name/36802/, accessed 11 May 2011.

76 National Intelligence Priorities Framework, at: http://www.dni.gov/content/AT/ NIPF.pdf, accessed 7 November 2010.

77 Thomas Fingar, "Reducing Uncertainty: Intelligence and National Security – Using Intelligence to Anticipate Opportunities and Shape the Future," talk on 21 October 2009, at: http://iis-db.stanford.edu/evnts/5859/lecture_text.pdf, accessed 7 November 2010.

78 As quoted in Best and Cumming, "CRS Report for Congress," p. 5.

79 *Watching the Bear,* p. 275.

80 Gregory Treverton, *Intelligence for an Age of Terror* (Cambridge: Cambridge University Press, 2009), pp. 18–19, 146.

81 Lou Agosta, "Interview with Malcolm Gladwell," 5 November 2009, at: http:// www.b-eye-network.mobi/view/11625, accessed 8 November 2010.

82 Jonathan Macey, "A Pox on Both Your Houses: Enron, Sarbanes-Oxley and the Debate Concerning the Relative Efficacy of Mandatory vs Enabling Rules," *Washington University Law Quarterly,* vol. 81:329, 2003, p. 330.

83 Congressional Reports: Joint Inquiry into Intelligence Community Activities Before and After the Terrorist Attacks of September 11, 2001, Part 1, p. 59, at: http://www.gpoaccess.gov/serialset/creports/pdf/part1.pdf, accessed 8 November 2010.

CHAPTER FIVE

Six qualities of information...

The greatly increased interest in open source information evidenced by the various studies and reports cited in the previous chapter was in part official recognition that the information "iceberg" which had been in place when the IC was first established had, in effect, flipped over – the quantity of information that could be freely obtained had so far outstripped what might be obtained through clandestine methods that the concentration solely on secrets was understood (at least by those outside the IC) to be in effect a self-imposed blindness. That perception was further fed by the demonstrations of various "data-miners" – for example, that of Las-Vegas-security-expert-turned-IBM-chief-scientist Jeff Jonas, who argued in a widely circulated presentation that publicly available records could have tied 19 of the suicide terrorists together in advance of their spectacular attack[1] – thus adding increased urgency to the push for more collection, better integration of data, and more "dot-connecting."

One of the biggest impediments to that effort, however, was general confusion about what precisely constituted open source information. One of the reasons for that confusion was the tendency to treat such information as OSINT, or "open source intelligence," in parallel to the other "-ints": SIGINT, or intelligence derived from captured signals; MASINT, or intelligence based on "measurement and signature," or the remote sensing of things like temperature, electronic "signature," and other physical properties of "items of interest and concern"; and HUMINT, or intelligence based on covert collection of secrets provided by humans. In that schema, OSINT tended inevitably to be viewed very narrowly, primarily as media-based information (most often derived from newspapers) that had been mostly – and, as critics of the IC argued after the collapse of the USSR and, even more so, the disaster of 9/11 – ineffectually deployed against issues of "leadership intention." Thus OSINT was held in general disregard, derided as being of little use even as the charge was also made that the IC was relying on it too heavily, because it was incapable of getting worthwhile intelligence from its other, far more expensive sources. Thus *Washington Times* editor Wesley Pruden scoffed that the CIA relied so heavily on information from newspapers that its director should be called the "Pastemaster General,"[2] while, somewhat earlier, CIA Inspector General Frederick Hitz was quoted as dismissing all open source intelligence "inside and outside of government" as "merely a collection of newspaper stories."[3]

Competing with that view, which turned OSINT into a particular *type* of information, was the argument that OSINT was rather a *source* of information, which could have a variety of forms. Even in the earliest days of OSS's R&A, useful information about geography and infrastructure – what later might have been considered MASINT, and perhaps IMINT – was derived from libraries, industry bulletins, and other open sources, thus showing that what is important is the information itself, rather than the way in which it was procured.[4] As has already been noted, even in the 1960s intelligence analysts were complaining that the outpouring of information from easily accessible Soviet journals was greater than they could cope with, despite the best efforts of JPRS and the other government translation services.

What became apparent by the beginning of the twenty-first century, however, was that OSINT increasingly was part of a spectrum of information sources, rather than a distinct entity. Information taken from a compromised fiber optic system, for example, remained clearly SIGINT, and as such top secret, but what of information derived from a commercially available cell phone scanner? As cell phones increasingly went digital, and thus were easier to encrypt, it may have become more difficult to overhear the actual contents (the embarrassing potential of which had been more than adequately illustrated by the "Squidgy-gate" and "Camilla-gate" scandals which hit the British royal family in the mid-1990s[5]) but it remained possible legally to buy a person's record of calls, as a blogger did with the cell phone of General Wesley Clark.[6] Some of the cell phone providers – Apple being a particular example – also have geolocation equipment built into their devices, thus allowing the companies, and those who know how to access that data, to track a cell phone user's precise locations.[7] Even cheaper, perhaps, are "offline satellite internet downloaders"[8] that allow hobbyists and others to capture free-to-air (FTA) transmissions from satellites, including movies, TV … and the videos from military unmanned drones.[9] Similarly the kind of overhead IMINT that had once required the global brinkmanship of a U2 program to acquire, or the fantastically expensive top-secret satellite systems that had replaced the U2, had become increasingly available – for payment – from any of the several commercial companies active in this market,[10] or for free, from Google Earth. As for HUMINT, in an era when the President of Iran, the Prime Minister of China, and the President of Russia all have blogs, Facebook pages, and appear to use Twitter,[11] the case can certainly be made that, again, this type of information lies along a source spectrum, from totally open to completely closed.

Perhaps to reinforce the idea that the new push for improved exploitation of "OSINT" referred not to content but to sources, several official and semi-official definitions of what is meant by "open source" were set down after 9/11. Intelligence Community Directive 301 (ICD 301), signed by DNI Negroponte on 11 July 2006, which established the "National Open Source Enterprise," defined "open source information" as being "publicly available information that anyone can obtain by request, purchase, or observation," with "open source intelligence" being further defined as "Produced from publicly available information that is collected, exploited, and disseminated in a timely manner to an appropriate audience for the purpose of addressing a specific intelligence requirement"[12] (it is worth noting that the document which ICD 301 replaced, which had become effective in 1994, had essentially the same definition, but also added what seems a further category: "Open source information also includes any information that may be used in an unclassified context without compromising national security or intelligence sources and methods"[13]).

More laconic, the Department of Defense Dictionary of Military and Associated Terms defines "open source intelligence" only as "Information of potential intelligence value that is available to the general public."[14] A somewhat clearer "semi-official" definition was provided in a Congressional Research Service report[15] issued in December 2007. As will be seen, this "definition" was really two definitions:

Open source information, according to some observers, generally falls into four categories: widely available data and information; targeted commercial data; individual experts; and "gray" literature, which consists of written information produced by the private sector, government, and academe that has limited availability, either because few copies are produced, existence of the material is largely unknown, or access to information is constrained. Within these four categories, open source information can include:

• media such as newspaper, magazines, radio, television, and computer-based information;

• public data such as government reports, and official data such as budgets and demographics, hearings, legislative debates, press conferences, and speeches;

- information derived from professional and academic sources such as conferences, symposia, professional associations, academic papers, dissertations and theses, and experts;

- commercial data such as commercial imagery; and,

- gray literature such as trip reports, working papers, discussion papers, unofficial government documents, proceedings, preprints, research reports, studies, and market surveys.

Although there are some clear problems with this list – not least of which is the off-handedness with which the largest single source of information ("and computer-based") is specified – this list at least has the clear virtue of making plain that there is a great deal more to "publicly available information" than the IC had been willing to grant. What perhaps was not so clear, however, were the consequences which came with accepting the definitions laid out in the CRS report, and trying to incorporate those into the production of intelligence. The CRS report lists several impediments to the greater use of open source information in the IC, in addition to a pronounced preference for secrets over all other kinds of information, but most of those are structural or cultural: analysts lack training in open source methods; analysts work in environments without access to the internet or other open sources; analysts lack good tools for dealing with internet information; and security concerns prohibit easy open source access. Only one of the impediments highlighted has to do with problems inherent in the information itself – its mind-boggling volume.

Volume: how much information is there?

There have been at least four efforts to calculate how much information humans are now producing. The first two were undertaken by the University of California Berkeley School of Information Sciences, in 2000 and 2003. The third was done by a private company in 2007–2008, using a somewhat different methodology and focusing more on data storage than data production, and the fourth was begun (but apparently not yet finished) by the University of California San Diego's Global Information Industry Center, in 2009.[16] Despite very carefully explained methodologies and well-declared assumptions, the findings of all of these studies could basically be captured in the simple statement with which the authors of the 2007–2008 began their report: the information universe "is big. Bigger than anything we can touch, feel, or see, and thus impossible to understand in context." And, they might have added, it seems to be getting bigger, increasing by somewhere between 30 and 60 percent – *per year.*

More granular answers quickly become meaningless, partly because of the various studies' differing assumptions about what constitutes "information" – this is particularly clear in the University of California, San Diego (UCSD) study, which defines "information" by three different metrics – but mostly because the answers are so large as to be incomprehensible. The 2003 study, for example, concluded that "print, film, magnetic, and optical storage media" had produced "about 5 exabytes" of information in 2002. Even those capable of understanding just how a big an "exabyte" is are unlikely to be able to visualize what that quantity of information might look like in a useable form – which probably is why the study's author made the further comparative calculation, that 5 exabytes is approximately the same amount of information as would be "contained in 37,000 new libraries the size of the Library of Congress book collections." The 2007–2008 report claims that 281 exabytes had been "either created, captured, or replicated in digital form" in 2007 – so does this then mean that the equivalent of more than 2 million Libraries of Congress had been created (or that the same report's prediction that in 2011 the production would rise to 1,800 exabytes, or 13.3 million Libraries of Congress)?[17] Even comprehension aids such as the one given in the UCSD report – that the amount of information annually available to Americans would, if printed, cover the entire country, including Alaska, with a stack of books seven feet high – are ultimately as impossible to grasp as are "exabytes" themselves.

Somewhat easier to contemplate are the consequences of this volume – one of which certainly is that any figure used as an example here is guaranteed to be out of date by the time this book appears. One often-used such figure – the time it would take to watch all the video loaded onto YouTube every minute – has grown from 24 hours in March 2010 to 36 hours in November 2010.[18] This is the equivalent of 176,000 full-length feature movies *every month*, and, what is more astounding, that figure was projected to increase to 48 hours just months after, meaning the volume will have doubled in just a year. It is worth recalling too that YouTube, while the largest of the DIY video hosts, is far from being the only one – Wikipedia lists[19] 37 video hosting companies, including two Chinese ones, Youku and Tudou, which claim 150 million and 55 million daily downloads, respectively; a French one, DailyMotion, which claims 60 million daily, and several others with a million or more daily views. In addition, increasing numbers of online news services also offer video.

Similar problems plague more focused applications. Unmanned drone airplanes, for example, which are used for reconnaissance and weapons deployment by the US, France, Israel, and others, produce ever-larger amounts of footage, all of which must somehow be monitored if the information is to have military value. According to newspaper reports,[20] in 2011 these drones were capturing so much footage that analysts had to process 1,500 hours worth of video (plus another 1,500 still images) *every day.* Even more daunting, the so-called "Gorgon Stare" programs projected for the near future are said to require 2,000 analysts *per drone* in order to process the data (as compared to the present ratio of 9 analysts per drone). A February 2011 Defense Science Board Task Force report on shortcomings in counterinsurgency efforts specifically identified this volume as a problem, noting

> The Department of Defense (DoD) has not balanced technical collection capabilities with the PED [processing, exploitation, and dissemination] required to more broadly make sense of the data and employ it effectively … The DoD is also seeing a dramatic growth in the variety, velocity, and volume of data collected by defense ISR [intelligence, survey, and reconnaissance] platforms. However, the rapid increase of collected data will not be operationally useful without the ability to store, process, exploit, and disseminate this data. The programmed expansion of broad area, full motion video and other advanced sensors will further exacerbate this problem … Current collection generates data that greatly exceeds the ability to organize, store, and process it.[21]

Industry reports suggest that, while the military is aware of the problem, it does not yet have the means to deal with it.[22] Civilian authorities report similar problems with the growing army of closed-circuit TV (CCTV) surveillance cameras, which are generally acknowledged to be useful for investigations but not for prevention – meaning that, as in the case of the London Tube bombers, the CCTVs can be used to track a crime after it has happened, but thus far has not been proven to help much in seeing crimes (or potential crimes) in advance. As a British police official lamented at a conference in Singapore, using CCTV footage in this way can mean that "even minor cases can require the review of hundreds of hours of video footage which is a huge drain on police resources. In the long run, this is not a sustainable approach."[23] Some scale of the human hours required for an investigation came to light in 2010, when officials in Dubai released photos which they had culled from more than 1,700 hours of surveillance tape to accuse what they charged was the Israeli assassination team responsible for the death of Hamas leader Mahmoud al Mabhouh.[24]

Some of the consequences of this widening gulf between information produced and the ability to process that information were noted in Chapter Four – including erosion of traditional authority hierarchies, the atomization of audiences, and what some researchers have called increased "homophily," or the tendency to use the greatly increased access to information to find people like one's self, who share the same ideas, attitudes, and convictions.[25] There are other strategies emerging for coping with information overload which are, if anything, even more potentially disruptive than is a tendency to "info-cocooning." The UCSD report cited above, for example, found that the average American's ability to process (or consume) information seemed to be growing at more than 5 percent a year. Although clearly inadequate for mastering the corresponding growth in information available (which the same study put at 30–60 percent per year), this growth was ascribed to an increasing tendency to "multi-task" – meaning do several things at once – with a corresponding drop in the degree to which any of the tasks received deep or prolonged engagement. Although there does not seem to be conclusive evidence on either side of the argument[26] – despite the enormous amount of attention paid to the question in the popular press – anecdotal evidence suggests that people are ever more inclined to skim the material they read, and to search for media content in ever smaller sizes (magazine articles rather than books; blogs rather than articles; "tweet" micro-blogs rather than blogs). Other studies indicate that the ability to pay attention, to process information, may have certain physical properties such that it can be depleted, making it impossible, for example, for people asked to pay attention to one task to notice something else – as is vividly illustrated by the famous experiment of asking viewers to count how often a basketball is passed among some students, as a result of which well over half of the viewers fail to notice when an actor in a gorilla suit walks through the middle of the milling ball-passers.[27]

Even before they can pay attention to them, people must *find* things they want within this ever-burgeoning information swell – meaning that information navigation aids have an ever-larger and more powerful role. The primary tool for this is, of course, the internet search engine, which is emerging as an increasingly strategic, and poorly understood, shaper of information. Although Google is the dominant such engine, it is far from being the only one. According to the company's own figures,[28] the company's market share ranges from a high of 98 percent, in Lithuania, to a low of 3 percent, in South Korea. Although the Korea market share is much lower than the next lowest figure (18 percent, for Taiwan), Google's market share figures for Asia, where there are strong competing search engines (Baidu for China, Naver for South Korea), and also for Russia (dominated by Yandex) tend to be much smaller than is true for languages and places which use Latin alphabets.

Even where Google dominates, however, the results of searches done with other engines can differ significantly from the result of a Google search. According to a study done in 2006,[29] only 3 percent of the websites found by identical search terms turned up on three major US engines (Google, Yahoo, and Ask Jeeves). In contrast, about 25 percent of the websites found were unique to one of these sites (meaning that a site would be found by one search engine but not the other two), while approximately another 10 percent were found by some combination of two of the search engines, but not a third. For those who lament that the rise of search engines has meant the decline of "stack-browsing" and the serendipity of finding a useful book next to the book for which one has been searching on a shelf, it is worth pointing out that libraries also have a similar lack of "search result overlap." A study of the "shelf neighbors" (within 25 tomes either side) of important or frequently-searched-for texts in two major university libraries, one of which uses Dewey Decimal cataloging, and the other of which follows the Library of Congress, found that, on average, the "neighbor sets" in the two libraries contained from 5 to zero common titles 82 percent of the time, while the most common result – in 25 percent of the cases – was that there was *no* overlap. In the authors' words: "how knowledge in general is organized in these two cataloguing systems seems to be almost completely different."[30]

Indeed, there is ample evidence that one of the main purposes of search engines may be to tailor how "knowledge in general is organized" to the individual user. Author Eli Pariser, who has written about the way Google and other search engines use "learning" algorithms to become increasingly adept at figuring out what kinds of web pages an individual user is likely to access, has found that even two very similar users, when seated side-by-side, can get quite different results. In his example, two "educated white left-leaning women who live in the Northeast" performed simple Google searches on "British Petroleum" during the 2010 oil spill; one was offered mostly news stories, while the other was given primarily investment-related information.[31]

Even for a single searcher, search results can differ dramatically within a single search engine, depending upon how an inquiry is phrased. This has become increasingly an issue as Google and several other search engines have begun to offer query prompts – essentially algorithmic "guesses" based on the first few letters that one types into the query box and the huge volume of similar queries that others have built around what the search engine perceives as the searcher's intent. As Pariser has documented, even the intent of those who live in the vicinity from which the searcher is looking can affect the prompts, since people in one area may choose a certain kind of response or prompt more often than do people in another area. The prompt feature has proven controversial, in part because some users complain that this has a normative pressure, pushing queries toward a default setting (and thus certain websites) that might not otherwise result, and partly because these prompts can suggest totally new lines of inquiry, as some bloggers complained was the case when the appointment of Timothy Geithner as Treasury Secretary apparently caused large numbers of Google searchers to wonder whether he is Jewish, thus offering anyone who started typing in the new secretary's name the prompt "Geithner Jewish."[32]

Table 1, based on searches performed on 29 November 2010 within the US (all important factors for results), shows how significant something as simple as including or omitting quotation marks can be (the top line shows the queries, with the number of results given in the columns below).

Table 1: Search results compared, by query and by search engine

	"Is Obama a Muslim?"	Is Obama a Muslim?	Obama Muslim	Obama's Religion	What is Obama's Religion?
Google.com	53,200	20,100,000	20,800,000	4,910,000	12,500,000
Bing	283,000	11,800	105,000	196,000	25,700
Yahoo	347,000	12,000	111,000	208,000	28,700
Yandex.ru	5219	2,000,000	2,000,000	3,000,000	51
Google.bg	51,500	66,400,000	66,300,000	69,400,000	69,200,000
Baidu	645	7,720	263,000	231,000	330,000

Perhaps even more important than the number of responses, however, is the order in which they appear. As wildly as the search results shown in Table 1 differ, they all share one quality – they are all far larger than the average search engine user is likely to bother to look through. Even Yandex's 51 results would require more than five pages to list (although default settings can be changed, most search engines return results in groups of 10) – which is about four more pages than the vast majority of users are likely to access. Nearly 90 percent of search engine users either use what they have found on the first page or rephrase their question; another 6 percent or so may look at a second page of results; perhaps 2 percent will look as deep as page 3; 1 percent will go to page 4; and 0.5 percent may go as far as page 5.[33] The fact that websites basically live or die by "page rank"[34] has spawned a wide array of subsidiary activities, including:

- "google-bombing," or the manipulation of links among sites so that, for example, a search for "French military victories" will offer as its first site a blog with the words "your search did not match any documents" or one for "Arabian Gulf" will return as the top site the question "Did you mean Persian Gulf?" and the admonition "make sure you read some history books"[35];

- Search engine optimization (SEO) industries, dedicated to teaching individuals, companies, and organizations how to shape their various messages in ways that make search engine spiders more likely to find them, and thus to bring the proprietor's website nearer to the top; and

- Whole series of litigations, as advertisers claim that Google is punishing them or rewarding their competitors,[36] or indeed competitors claim that the search giant is systematically downgrading them, thus prompting anti-trust action.[37]

As grave as the possible consequences of search engine manipulation may seem, or even just the realization that the information one is offered may have a deeply random character, depending upon how the query is phrased, in which search engine it is typed, and how deeply one cares to go in the results, these pale in comparison to the realization that search engines themselves are capable of finding only a tiny percentage of what actually is available on the internet. Because web crawling programs ("spiders") can only follow links, they are incapable of finding information that is in fact easily accessible. This so-called "deep web" (or "dark web" or "invisible web" – all three terms are commonly used) is estimated (more properly "guess-timated") to contain anywhere from 100 to 1000 times[38] as many pages as does the "surface web" that is indexed by the spiders. The total amount of potential information is literally incalculable. Google announced in 2008 that it had reached the milestone of 1 trillion indexed pages,[39] which is reckoned to be at best about 40 percent of the total "surface web." Examples which the readers of this book might find interesting include:

- the complete texts, fully searchable, of FBIS's *Daily Report* from 1974 to 1996 (through the NewsBank company);

- more than 5 million declassified documents related to CIA and national intelligence (at George Washington University's National Security Archive); and

- the complete contents of the US Patent Office archive (which author Patrick Keefe used to confirm his surmises in his book *Chatter* about some of the surveillance equipment at NSA).

None of this can be discovered by simple search, but all of it is easily available to those who know how to look in the "deep web."

Velocity – information is faster too

Until the invention of the electric telegraph, information could only move as fast as a horse, or perhaps one of the Rothschild's carrier pigeons,[40] thus making information essentially a local affair. Once the telegraph was adopted, however, as author James Gleick points out, "information that just two years earlier had taken days to arrive at its destination could now be there – anywhere – in seconds." Telegraphic cables spanned the Atlantic by 1858, allowing heads of state – Queen Victoria and President Buchanan – to "exchange pleasantries" directly.[41] The ability to gather information from several places at once also quickly transformed weather from being a local phenomenon to something which people were beginning to understand as a system, and so start to create the science of weather forecasting. The notion of forecasting is a reminder that the value of information lies in context as well as in what it contains. One of Sherman Kent's last remarks about strategic intelligence was that a successful warning depended not only on accuracy, but also on timing. If the warning is received the same day as the event being warned, then it is "too late." If, however, it is sent a year in advance of the event, it is "too early," because policymakers will be concentrating on other issues.[42] Much of the dynamic of secrecy depends upon timing – governments and other organizations want to control the pace with which certain kinds of information travel, and so impose classifications, news embargoes, or other restrictions on information; conversely, they expend enormous resources to try to ferret out other kinds of information in advance of the time when those controlling the information wish to have it made known. Timing is particularly important, for example, in psychological warfare – the Nazis were adept at releasing information about their military capabilities just prior to attacking, which served to paralyze their opponents in advance of the actual attack. Because they usually did not boast of capacities before they actually had them, however, their talk of a "secret weapon" near the end of the war was taken as a credible threat by the Allies, thus prompting them to bomb V-1 rocket facilities earlier than they might otherwise have done.[43]

The ease and ubiquity of information production and dissemination platforms are making the control of information ever more difficult. One good indicator of this process is the constant shrinking of the units into which news is chunked – the monthly digests (*Scribners Monthly*, *Atlantic Monthly*) became weeklies (*Business Week*, *Newsweek*), then became daily (*USA Today*). The "news" – which in itself is an odd social construct, discussed more below – came as 5-minute headline snippets on radio shows, or as 30-minute nightly segments like the iconic *CBS Evening News*, or, equally iconic, *Vremya* (in the USSR), the Six O'Clock News (BBC), or the Eight O'Clock News (France's TF1). In 1980 CNN invented the 24-hour, all-news format, thus transforming news from a series of discrete units into something more like a flow – a process which continues to accelerate (for a sense of what news felt like before it became a flow, see the cover of *Time* magazine which bears one of America's most remembered dates – 22 November 1963; the cover story for the day that President Kennedy was killed was about "Washington Hostesses," and featured the wife of the then French ambassador, Nicole Alphand).

One of the consequences of the proliferation of fast, cheap information dissemination devices (most notably mobile phones, but now beginning to include new hybrids like the iPad 2 tablet) is that the traditional lines between producers of information and consumers of information are blurring. Particularly for certain kinds of events – fires, accidents, natural disasters, but also celebrity sightings, political "gaffes," acts of police brutality, and others – the ability of by-standers to photograph (or video) the events as they occur, and then to send the results out to the world has resulted in what essentially is "real-time news." Ironically, Google and other cache & index search engines are finding themselves judged "too slow" in this environment, with people increasingly turning to services like Twitter for updates on events of interest as these unfold. On 1 September 2010, for example, an armed gunman entered a building in Silver Spring, Md. – and his picture was snapped by someone with a cell phone even before he entered the building. Twitter messages flashed information as soon as anything occurred, meaning that by the time the media arrived, the story was already 30 minutes old.[44] Even more dramatically, the death of Michael Jackson (on 25 June 2009) was "tweeted" even before the singer had been declared dead – a full two hours before any more mainstream medium released the story. By the time the story had fully broken, however, there were so many messages being sent and searches being done that both Twitter and Google temporarily crashed.[45] Still more dramatic, although not immediately understood for what it was, were the series of tweets sent from Abbotabad, Pakistan, by IT consultant Sohaib Athar just before midnight on Sunday, 1 May, commenting on unusual helicopter activity near his house, thus making him, as he soon realized, "the guy who liveblogged the Osama raid."[46] The "end of bin Laden" story was a milestone for the Twitter service in other ways too – the company reported that the hour following President Obama's announcement of the raid's success saw 12.4 million tweets (which, curiously enough, is not the record for tweets-per-second, which was set in Japan on New Year's eve, when 6,000 tweets *per second* were recorded, "a perfect metaphor," the now-bypassed media upstart CNN noted grumpily, "for everything that's right and wrong" about microblogging).[47]

Wikipedia has emerged as a prominent (and generally reliable) news aggregator, often getting the "stub," or first element, of a breaking story up within 30 minutes of an occurrence. Someone who examined the way that Wikipedia (or, more properly, contributors to the platform) handled the 2008 Mumbai terrorist attacks noted that "by the end of the first day of the Wikipedia article's life, it had been edited more than 360 times, by 70 different editors referring to 28 separate sources from news outlets around the web." The story, moreover, continues to evolve – by March 2010 the story had grown to be "nearly 43,000 words with over 150 different sources cited and 1,245 unique editors."[48]

Information is fast now too in a slightly different sense – the speed with which it can be reproduced. As Clay Shirky highlighted in his book *Here Comes Everybody*, in 1992 the Catholic Church hierarchy in the Boston area was able to contain a scandal about priests accused of sexually abusing parishioners largely because the existing information transmission tools were one-to-one (telephone or letter) or one-to-many (people faxing photocopies of newspaper clippings to lists of people). The result was serious, but only on a local level. A decade later, when a similar scandal erupted, the information became universal almost instantaneously, because of the ease with which people could share information instantaneously among their various networks – *no matter how big the networks were.*[49] Kevin Kelly, one of the founders of *Wired* magazine, and a much-quoted student of the internet, has characterized the internet as "a copy machine ... [which produces] a river of copies ... [which are] not just cheap, they are free."[50] That combination of speed and low cost has proven devastating to organizations which are more familiar with the days when information was slow and costly to reproduce. One need only contrast the Pentagon Papers – about 3,000 pages which it took Daniel Ellsberg and Anthony Russo about a month to photocopy, and the *New York Times* four months to decide to publish – with the several major Wikileaks "data dumps," which (to date) include: more than 92,000 documents related to the war in Afghanistan; 400,000 documents related to the Iraq war; and 250,000 State Department cables (which is rumored to be only about one-tenth of the total number of cables Wikileaks possesses[51]). Although the details of how those documents were taken have not been made public, even at relatively slow data transfer rates that volume would require at most a few hours to reproduce, not weeks or months, and could moreover be shared almost instantly with as many recipients as the sender desired. Even when attempts are made to block the Wikileaks server with so-called "distributed denial of service attacks" (DDOS attacks) – which means to bombard the host server with so many electronic requests that it can't handle them, and so crashes – replication from other sources makes it effectively impossible to contain. As Kevin Kelly observed in the same blog post quoted above, "even a dog knows you can't erase something once it's flowed on the internet."

There is another kind of velocity in the internet as well – the differential velocity to be seen between content which catches attention on a large scale, or "goes viral," and that which does not. Contrast for example the YouTube clip which shows a "flash mob" which convened in a shopping mall food court on 13 November 2010 to sing the Hallelujah chorus from Handel's "Messiah,"[52] with another YouTube clip put up at approximately the same time, an interview with a California doctor about the virtues of a vegan diet.[53] The first drew about 6.5 million viewers in two weeks, and generated nearly 10,000 comments on the YouTube page, while the second drew 116 viewers and 1 comment in the same period (despite being subtitled in 16 languages). This difference in the velocity of dissemination is important, because the nature of the network is such that something which is able to garner a lot of attention immediately is far more likely to "go viral" – meaning that viewers will alert one another to the piece of content, thus rapidly enlarging the network of those who watch or read something – while something that fails to grab attention immediately is likely to sink into obscurity. Although studies suggest that YouTube videos may have a window of as much as ten days in which to gather an audience before being consigned to oblivion,[54] that is actually a fairly generous amount of time, especially when the comparative cost of production is factored in. By contrast, movies, which traditionally used to be allowed three or four weeks in which to attract audiences before being dubbed "flops" are now finding that the fates of their multimillion-dollar efforts are effectively decided in the single night of the film's opening, because the first viewers immediately share their opinions with others via Twitter, Facebook, and other social media, thus "almost instantaneously neutralizing the ability of a studio's multimillion-dollar marketing blitz to get moviegoers to keep going to see a crummy movie" (as one industry account complained).[55]

This tendency of some kinds of information to "go viral" has had more tragic consequences as well. After initial hesitations about possible security implications of social media use, and also natural concerns about the strain content-heavy platforms such as YouTube and Facebook might place on IT infrastructures in areas of forward deployment, the military has generally embraced social media as a way to help military families stay in closer contact despite being deployed in various places around the world. The speed of such decentralized communication, however, has also meant that military families are now learning of casualties almost a day faster than the military is able to inform them officially.[56]

The vector of information has changed too

As the last example above suggests, the traditional flow of information – which generally was from the top down – has now changed dramatically as well. The shape of that change, and many of its important consequences, were explored at length in Chapter Four, and so will not be repeated here. There is at least one consequence, however, which deserves further exploration – this is the continued erosion of expertise as authority. Although this erosion is also in part a function of two other facets of the new information environment (veracity and verifiability, both explored below), the ability of almost anyone to send information, and of people to choose from whom they wish to receive it, has played havoc with the ways in governments and other authorities have traditionally controlled "reality" within their boundaries (this was demonstrated in the White House's attempt to control the newsflow about the bin Laden death in order to reserve the announcement for President Obama – the news, however, had broken almost an hour earlier, tweeted by former Secretary of Defense Rumsfeld's Chief of Staff, Keith Urban[57]).

That statement may seem exaggerated today, but in the mid-seventeenth century, when the Peace of Westphalia was signed, the agreement that sovereigns had the right to declare, and to defend by force if required, what would be the religion of the territory they controlled – a principle called *cuius regio, eius religio* (whose region, his religion) – was precisely that, a state-controlled definition of the nature of reality in that space. The development of the modern state also gave it formidable tools for enforcing that information-defined "reality," which allowed states to privilege some kinds of information and impede, suppress, or forbid other kinds. States developed economic levers (taxation, subsidization, privileging distribution), legal levers (censorship, libel laws, anti-trust laws), and administrative controls (licensing, spectrum allocation) for the better control of information.

In retrospect, however, the mightiest tool in the hands of the state was technology, or, more precisely, technological imbalance. As this book has repeatedly argued, the biggest single change in information creation, transmission, and storage is that it has become cheap. Before that revolution, the concentration of financial resources necessary to fund large information outlets, and the concentration of physical assets in which that resulted, provided governments with significant levers of control. It was precisely for that reason that one of the first targets of any coup attempt was the main radio or TV station in the capital city. In some places, it was the already powerful who added media to their portfolios, while in others they created power for themselves by acquiring the means of media production – but in both cases, the fact that information was far cheaper to receive than it was to create and send meant that elites within particular spaces could continue to impose their definition of "reality."

The fact that information can now come from below as well as above (or indeed can come from anywhere) means not just that that control is gone, but, even more importantly, that the nature of "reality" is up for grabs. Non-conforming opinions probably always existed in every society, but until the new cheap technologies arrived the only way they could be marshaled and promulgated was through instruments like the Soviet-era samizdat – barely legible carbon copies of manuscripts laboriously hand-typed and physically passed from hand to hand. Today those who believe (or profess to believe) that, for example, President Obama is Muslim[58] or that the 9/11 attacks were the work of US or Israeli intelligence[59] can not only press their case with text and video, but they can continue to recruit fellow-thinkers, so that their numbers can continue to grow – in spite of all the "facts" that are issued in refutation. Indeed, the cheap ubiquity of information has made it possible for people to begin to revisit controversies that – it would have seemed – had already been settled by the time the Peace of Westphalia was signed; see for example the websites[60] maintained by the Association for Biblical Astronomy, which argue that the sun revolves about the earth. Similar websites exist for Muslims too.[61]

Veracity and verifiability are problems too

That geocentric Muslim blog offers a classic example of the problem that "fact" has always presented to officials, in the 30 November 2010 entry which states "60 million Americans know that the sun revolves around the Earth." The source of that "fact," to which the geocentric blog provides a hyperlink, thus allowing anyone who wishes to do so immediately to check it, is a Gallup Poll from 1999 which announced that 79 percent of Americans, when asked, "correctly respond that the earth revolves around the sun."[62] Mathematically the blog is not quite correct, in that the "60 million" figure represents about 21 percent of the US population at the time, rather than the 18 percent of poll respondents who actually declared themselves believers in geocentricity (Gallup does not explain what the other 3 percent thought), but, within the generally acceptable bounds of a rhetorical argument, the geocentric blog is not wrong, or at least no more "wrong" than is the poll claiming that 221 million Americans got the answer "correct." The difference in the emphasis, however, and the inference which may be drawn from either, is quite clear.

What this illustrates is that information is never context-free – a single data point is essentially meaningless. It is only when that data point is aggregated with others, when it is put into the context of an argument, that it acquires meaning, but, just as the 79-percent-vs-21-percent figures above suggest, that meaning derives entirely from the context. Paul Linebarger, in his classic text *Psychological Warfare*, put the matter succinctly: "the facts [in the example he provides] are *true* in each case ... but the interpretation placed on them – who communicates these facts to whom? why? when? – makes them into propaganda ... the questions of truth and of interpretation are unrelated categories ... You can dislike an interpretation ... but you cannot sit down and *prove* it is untrue."[63]

What governments or other authorities *could* do in the past, however, was control the contexts in which information was imparted. For a variety of cultural and historical reasons, Westerners in general, and Americans in particular, came to be what are called "low context" information users, because, at least until recently, they have generally trusted their newspapers, TV shows, and other sources of information, and so tend to respond more to the content of information than to the manner in which it is conveyed – what Linebarger called the "To Whom? Why? When?" of information – so that it still remains a general conviction in the West that "the facts will speak for themselves." One of the things that has become increasingly clear as information has become cheaper and more ubiquitous is that information is more context-dependent than we had assumed. In the past, when information flowed through well-defined channels, it seemed easy to know how to weight information derived from, for example, the *New York Times*, as compared to information from the *National Enquirer*. In part that assurance was eroded by the behavior of the outlets themselves – the *Times* suffered a series of scandals such as the revelation that reporter Jason Blair had been making up his stories, or that the memoranda purporting to describe President Bush's behavior while in the Air National Guard had been forgeries (leading the *Times* to offer the startling headline "Memos are Fake But Accurate"[64]) while the *Enquirer* drew journalistic accolades, and even some speculation the newspaper might be a candidate for a Pulitzer Prize, for the persistence with which it had followed the story of politician John Edwards' infidelities and untruths.

The larger problem, however, is that the growing number of information outlets in and of itself makes it ever harder to know how to contextualize, and therefore to value information. Although there are ample clues that, for example, the "Federal Vampire and Zombie Agency"[65] is a spoof site – including a pop-up disclaimer to the effect that "This site is fictional and is for entertainment purposes only [and] not affiliated with the U.S. Government in any way" – in many important ways the site looks as "official" as do most US government sites. A YouTube video[66] urging Twitter-users to support the international campaign to help save the endangered "Galvao bird" was viewed more than 1.5 million in the first week it was up, and the requested support slogan "cala boca Galvao" was among the most-tweeted phrases for more than two weeks. The entire campaign, however, was a spoof, engineered by Brazilian soccer fans who had disliked the World Cup commentary of a TV announcer, one Galvao Bueno, and so manipulated the "twitosphere" to get the unwitting world to tell the announcer in Portugese to "shut your mouth."

The information offered in the websites above at least has the advantage that it is demonstrably untrue; there is no such thing as a "Galvao bird" nor do zombies exist, despite their current ubiquity. It is much more complex to navigate among the many purveyors of what each claims is "the truth." In the past few years there has been a proliferation of national news broadcasters which use cable TV and the internet to present the point-of-view of their respective national sponsors on ongoing events. Thus on any given day an interested English-speaking viewer could watch the international news through the prism of Russia (www.rt.com), France (www.france24.com), China (www.cctv.com), Iran (www.presstv.ir), Japan (www.nhk.or.jp), and Qatar (http://english.aljazeera.net/video/). What makes this competition for viewer attention so complicated is that none of the information provided is *false*, but neither do any of the sources agree entirely with one another. Each of the various services places the items it chooses to highlight – which often enough are the same items that the other services feature – into the larger context of each sponsoring nation's "narrative" (the artificiality, or conventionality, of each approach becomes particularly evident when viewed with

a satirical news site such as The Onion's "Today Now!" online TV: http://
www.theonion.com/video).

It is to address this kind of ambiguity that educators, librarians, and
others are beginning to develop curricula for teaching skills variously
called "media literacy" or "information literacy," with the goal of setting
standards for how information is evaluated and used. The Association
of College and Research Librarians, for example, defines "information
literacy" as the development of a life-long ability to:[67]

- Determine the extent of information needed;

- Access the needed information effectively and efficiently;

- Evaluate information and its sources critically;

- Incorporate selected information into one's knowledge base;

- Use information effectively to accomplish a specific purpose; and to

- Understand the economic, legal, and social issues surrounding the
  use of information, and access and use information ethically and
  legally.

As sound as these principles may seem, they obscure some of the important
issues raised by the problems of veracity and verifiability. The huge quantity
of information available on any given topic makes the question of "the
extent of information needed" difficult to answer. Even as early as 1956
information pioneer Herbert Simon, who later got the Nobel Prize, argued
that living beings navigate their environments not by seeking optimal
returns (as the then-current economic and political models of "rational
theory" suggested) but rather tried simply to "satisfice" their needs,
meaning to gather sufficient resources to satisfy a given need at the minimal
functional level possible.[68] More recently this notion of information-
adequate-to-need has been explored by author Farhad Manjoo, in his book
True Enough. In his view, the proliferation of information, and the disappearance of the kinds of validating markers that top-down information
delivery systems used to provide, has meant that "no longer are we merely
holding opinions different from one another; we are also holding different
facts."[69] One vivid demonstration of the ways in which velocity, volume,
and a diminishing need to verify can quickly create "facts" was the speed
with which a quotation misattributed to Martin Luther King zipped around
the internet in the wake of bin Laden's death, gathering millions of retweets
and thousands of Google hits in fewer than 24 hours.[70]

There is another issue concerning verifiability and veracity of information – that of its permanency and the ease with which it might be
recovered. The printed information of the past had a fixed, archivable form,

which gave the information it contained some longevity. That was the world in which, for example, Sherman Kent said that the main task of the intelligence analyst was to stand behind policymakers "with the book opened at the right page, to call their attention to the stubborn fact they may neglect."[71] In the electronic environment the situation is more complicated, and in many ways is contradictory. On the one hand, digital information has proven famously persistent, so that, for example, such things as Sarah Palin's appearance in the Swimwear Competition portion of the 1984 Miss Alaska contest,[72] an OSS Field Manual on "Simple Sabotage," from 1944,[73] or a graduate school article on how Russia's economy ought to be run written by (at the time not yet) Russian Prime Minister Vladimir Putin[74] all remain easily accessible on the web. On the other hand, information is equally famously ephemeral. Search engine links break, websites are taken down or content deleted from them, effectively erasing the information which may once have been there. Even more fundamentally, data coding and reading devices evolve rapidly, making formats and devices quickly outmoded. In their book *Blown to Bits: Your Life, Liberty, and Happiness After the Digital Explosion*, authors Hal Abelson, Ken Ledeen, and Harry Lewis give the example of the BBC's attempt to commemorate the 900th anniversary of the Domesday Book (completed in 1086) by creating a video disc version of England as it appeared in 1986. By 2001, neither the discs nor the equipment required to read them were manufactured anymore, making the discs impossible to use.[75]

Finally, the problems noted above are true of all information in the digital environment, but are even more true for the huge mass of visual information that is being created. Part of the problem is that no effective search tools for visual content have yet been devised, leaving them dependent upon textual tags that may or may not correspond to the terms that a would-be user would employ in searching. Equally important, however, is the enormous amount of storage required by visual material. There are some efforts to preserve at least the internet portion of the new information environment (the best known of which is archive.org), but that effort is massively out-matched by the quantity of information with which the archive is trying to cope.

And a final problem – information has become vulgar

The ongoing debate about whether the internet, social media, and the other cheap means of communication have had a "democratizing" effect and, if so, whether that is a good thing, has tended to ignore (or forget) that *demos*, the root word for "democracy," has two meanings in Greek: "the people," but also "the mob." That ambiguity remains more evident in Latin, where *vulgus* continues to be evident primarily in the adjective "vulgar" – meaning low, common, and prurient.

It takes no more than a five-minute acquaintance with the internet to be convinced that the new cheap media are deeply vulgar, in precisely that sense. In addition to pornography, which constitutes an enormous portion of internet content, the new media are rich in embarrassing pictures, stupid jokes, salacious tee-shirts, and a never-ending string of internet fads and crazes – of which the apparently unlimited supply of LOLcats is sufficient evidence. What this reflects, of course, is the fact that most people's interests tend precisely to be "common" (tautological, but often overlooked). In the old, expensive media days, content was bundled, so that a person who wished to read the comics, do the crossword, or see how his or her team had fared, had to buy the entire newspaper – thus also acquiring the "serious" news on the front page, the lofty ruminations of the editorial, and other less "vulgar" content. The limitations of technology obscured the fact that it was impossible to tell how many of the purchasers actually were paying attention to the high-minded instructive materials that the newspapers' owners, or the government, were trying to impose upon their readers.

Scholars who study the development of printing have argued that one of the most important consequences of Gutenberg's invention was that it made it possible increasingly to give knowledge a taxonomy, and therefore a hierarchy. For example, Tom Pettitt, a European scholar, noted while speaking at Harvard's Nieman Lab that, after Gutenberg, "people like to categorize – and that includes the things they read. So the idea clearly was that in books, you have the truth. Because it was solid, it looked straight, it looked like someone very clever or someone very intelligent had made this thing, this artifact. Words, printed words – in nice, straight columns, in beautifully bound volumes – you could rely on them."[76] To be sure, author Andrew Pettegree has argued[77] that even from the earliest days of Gutenberg, people were more interested in "vulgar" content than they were in the high-minded and uplifting, one proof of which is that only the big, expensive, and ponderous printed projects have survived (most of which, interestingly enough, bankrupted their printers, as his Bible project did Gutenberg). What made the newly-invented printing business profitable were (in the words of a review of Pettegree's book[78]) "posters, handouts, pamphlets, pictures, almanacs, prophecies, topical poems, hoaxes and one-page documents," all ephemera that fed a Renaissance-era "market for news, sensation and excitement," almost nothing of which survives precisely because it was used, and mostly used up.

The internet and its "democratized" – or "vulgarized" – capacities provide similar ephemera, taking aim at the order which Gutenberg's more "serious" offspring appeared to create. It is no longer possible to determine the value of information solely from its author or its publishing house, the quality of its paper, or the footnotes to which it may refer. Expensive media tend to have august names – *Le Monde, New York Times, The Independent, The Economist* – while cheap media take a deliberate delight in silly, almost childish names – *Yahoo, Google, Twitter.* One of the most informative, and longest-functioning, Egyptian bloggers calls himself "Egyptian Sand Monkey," while a prominent Venezuelan one has dubbed his blog "The Devil's Excrement"[79] – neither of which is likely to reassure those not familiar with the internet about the quality of the information. Countries and cultures which hold the printed word in particularly high reverence have reacted especially harshly against the "vulgarity" of the new cheap media. France, for example, has battled Google, first trying to create its own search engine, Quaero ("I seek" in Latin – and thus serious, not silly), then forbidding Google to digitize French books, insisting that it will undertake that project itself, in order not to be "stripped of our heritage" (President Sarkozy's words). In Iran, where regard for the written word is even higher – written Persian is meant to be poetic, allusive, and elliptical – the quick popularity of what there is called "weblogestan" sent critics, journalists, and clerics into paroxysms of rage. The reaction of one literary critic was characterized as typical: "Blogging, after laying waste to the Persian script and language, has been able to drag every serious and intellectual topic into the scum of the disease of vulgarity, grow like a cancerous tumor, and trash the writer, the reader and everyone else."[80] In China a different kind of language-based "vulgarity" has emerged, as people trying either to protest or evade the country's heavy internet censorship adopt so-called "Martian language,"[81] a mix of computer symbols, slang terms, and characters which play on the tonic qualities of Chinese words (which uses the same word for different meaning, with the precise meaning derived from the pitch with which it is pronounced). Most of these are playful, but in at least one case – that of the "Grass Mud Horse," which has been widely adopted as a symbol of protest against censorship – the result was vulgar in all senses, for the innocent-looking symbols of this invented animal, when pronounced differently, results in the classic "mother" oath.[82]

There are a number of strands in this issue. One certainly is that the internet and cheap media allow people to indulge in the things that really interest them, rather than make do with what a cultural or political elite thinks they should be watching, reading, or listening to. Another is that the ease with which the internet can make absolutely perfect copies of an original has cut the knees from beneath whole ranks of assumptions about what constitutes property and how it should be defended. In the expensive media days, it was costly to make an original and almost impossible to make even a reasonable copy, let alone multiple copies, thus providing some tangible physical justification for why, for example, music or movie companies should be paid so much for their products. As digitization spread, and people came to understand how inexpensive perfect copies were to make, the protection of intellectual property rights began to look ever more arbitrary, even greedy – thus spawning an entire culture of piracy. A companion strand to content control is ideological and political control, which the internet has attacked with enthusiasm. Whether or not the ultimate effect is to make the world more "democratic" in a political-system sense,[83] there can be little disagreement that, at least in the sense of the rabble's ability to shake up the ruling elite, the cheap media-internet is deeply "democratic." Free tools permitted, for example:

- Tunisian political activists to combine online plane-spotting hobbyists and Google maps to demonstrate that President Ben-Ali's wife was using the state airplane to take shopping trips to Paris;[84]

- Parties unknown in Myanmar to make public, via YouTube and other video hosting services, the lavish scale of the wedding staged by a senior member of the Ministry of Commerce;[85]

- Political rivals in Kazakhstan to post an entire series of audio tapes of intimate conversations between President Nazarbaev and his unacknowledged third wife;[86] and

- Russian rapper Noize MC to make a biting satiric video and song, condemning Lukoil vice president Anatoly Barkov to Hell for his part in a fatal collision, caused when his Mercedes collided with another car while driving on the wrong side of the road.[87]

Perhaps the best illustration of this "peasants-storming-the-castle" quality of the vulgar internet is Wikileaks, already mentioned above. As internet expert Geert Lovink noted,[88] even before the spectacular data-dump that came to be called "Cablegate," the Wikileaks phenomenon shows the most extreme extension to date of the power that cheap information creation, storage, and transmission is unleashing. For one thing, Lovink points out, the sheer volume of leaked information that digitization now makes possible has created qualitative differences, not least of which is that one individual – Julian Assange – and a very small group of helpers (Lovink speculates that the entire core of Wikileaks cannot number more than a dozen people) has managed to grab the attention, and probably change the future behavior, of the world's most powerful nations, in much the same way that the Al Qaeda hijackers managed to do when they flew their planes into the World Trade Towers and the Pentagon. Lovink does not use that comparison, instead calling Wikileaks the "Talibanization" of the "flat world theory," but the disproportion between the numbers of participants, the scale of their resources, and their vastly out-sized effect make the Al Qaeda comparison seem even more appropriate. Either comparison, of course, suggests vividly that information has followed the same path of ever-wider availability, and ever-more "democratic" (or vulgar) effect, as has violence – once a state monopoly, mostly because weapons of scale required great resources to build, violence has become vastly asymmetrical. Lovink points out that Wikileaks proves that the same is now true of information – Assange has made himself and his organization a central actor on the world stage, with none of the resources that such prominence once required. Lovink also notes that Wikileaks is a product of the hard-core computer "geek and hacker" community, which has particular characteristics which make it deeply hostile to what might be called the "Westphalian world," of hierarchies, authorities, and physical possession. The attitude of the Wikileakers seems similar to that of what the music and video industries have called "digital pirates." The strenuous efforts of industry bodies like the RIAA (Recording Industry Association of America) to defend intellectual property rights in the digital environment – which include securing the creation of legislation which not only makes it possible for an individual to be fined as much as $1 million for an iPod's worth of music files, but also makes it theoretically possible for Apple to be fined as much as $1 *trillion* if every iPod owner were to download files for which RIAA claimed copyright[89] – has generated considerable resentment, and also ingenuity, among the "geeks and hackers."

Even before the "Cablegate" dump prompted the US to try to use legal and *ad hoc* means to silence Wikileaks, the "geek and hacker" community had been angered by the US Department of Homeland Security's decision in late 2010 to begin seizing domain names which it deemed to be facilitating illegal activities.[90] Among the initial 82 seized were sites offering child pornography and drug counterfeiting, but also sites facilitating file-sharing and other violations of intellectual property rights. As Lovink predicted might be the case, parts of the computer-savvy *"demos"* (or *"vulgus"*) responded by mounting an attack on the top-down, hierarchical structure of the internet domain name system (DNS), making palpable a danger about which people have been warning ever since the powers of the internet and the Web began to become apparent, the creation of an anarchic, ungovernable "darknet" where people – or those people with the skills and interests to do so – would be able to create, share, and pass information unhindered. As Lovink noted ominously, Wikileaks may prove to be "the 'pilot' phase in an evolution towards a far more generalized culture of anarchic exposure, beyond the traditional politics of openness and transparency."

Even without that dystopic possibility, however, the Wikileaks episode has demonstrated that digitization, the internet, and the web are all powerful agents of "vulgarization," exposing the paradoxes and weaknesses of the hierarchical, top-down world. Microsoft, for example, has had to decide whether or not to side with Russian police, who were using possible copyright violation as the grounds on which to seize computers belonging to environmental activists and other groups distasteful to the Kremlin (in the end they did not).[91] Similarly, the US faces an increasingly complex landscape as it continues to push China to open up its internet while at the same time moving to shut down Wikileaks, or forbidding its own workers – or even potential future workers[92] – to view materials it considers "secret," even though they are freely available around the world. Even Google itself – in some ways the party responsible for having begun so much of this "vulgarity" – has begun to face criticism that its search optimization algorithms are disadvantaging texts which use wit, humor, or puns, increasingly forcing a kind of bland standardization into what until now had been a creative free-for-all.[93]

Closing Gutenberg's parenthesis?

It has become a commonplace of discussions of the new information environment to invoke the myriad disruptions loosed upon the world by Johannes Gutenberg's invention of the moveable type printing press. To a greater or lesser degree the invention of cheap printing has been cited as whole or part cause of the scientific revolution, the age of global discovery, the Reformation (and the Counter-Reformation), the Enlightenment, the American Revolution, the French Revolution... In short, the argument runs, the printing press created the modern world as we know it. The "digital optimists" tend to argue that the web, and the various attributes of information sketched above, will have a similar –but similarly unpredictable – effect on that world, overturning it as surely as the post-Gutenberg world upended the pre-Gutenberg world before it.

It is worth noting, however, that there is another school of thought, which views the Gutenberg era as an exception – what adherents of this school call "the Gutenberg apostrophe."[94] Before Gutenberg, information was local, non-hierarchical, and ephemeral. There was no shared audience, no "imagined community." People believed whatever they wished to believe, or whatever those who had immediate physical control over them forced them to believe. Gutenberg changed all that, allowing information to be standardized and organized and structured. What the web may be re-introducing, these scholars argue, is a world in which information is returning to the informal, free-flowing, non-specific, and non-hierarchical state it has had for most of human history. Once again people are increasingly able to believe what they wish to believe, and to think what they want to think. The notion of authority, or at least information authority, is eroding. Alfred Rolington, formerly the CEO of Jane's Inc., has noted that "few respect information's authority" because "the clients believe they have as much to contribute as the specialists."[95]

Given that almost three centuries passed between Gutenberg's invention and the appearance of a recognizably modern world, it seems premature to draw conclusions about the effect of a process which is at best fewer than five decades old (if counted from the birth of DARPANET). The ongoing collapse of the newspaper industry, the apparent collapse of the music industry, the uncertain future of the movie industry, and the growing paradoxes, contradictions, and outright inabilities shown by governments as they try to control the flow of fast, cheap, out-of-control information makes a very strong case that – at the very least – the open source analyst of tomorrow must approach the job differently than it was done before.

Notes

1 http://jeffjonas.typepad.com/SRD-911-connections.pdf, accessed 28 November 2010.

2 Wesley Pruden, "The Spies Go AWOL when Kabul Falls," *Washington Times*, 27 November 2001.

3 As quoted in a press released accessed at: http://www.highbeam.com/doc/1P2-18852570.html, accessed 28 November 2010. In fairness, there is reason to be skeptical of this quote, because the person to whom it is sourced, Robert Steele, is a vigorous advocate of his own open source company. Hitz's statement does not seem to be available elsewhere, and it contradicts what Hitz himself seems to argue in his own book, *Why Spy?* (New York: Thomas Dunne, 2008) when he writes of how "Google and Wikipedia are revolutionizing the way information is gathered, organized, and communicated around the word" (pp. 155–56).

4 A backhanded confirmation of that importance was that, as psychological warfare expert Paul Linebarger, caustically observed, "most of [R&A's reports] were carefully classified SECRET even when they were copied out of books in the Library of Congress." *Psychological Warfare* (Washington DC: Infantry Journal Press, 1948), p. 91.

5 "Government Blocked Probe into 'Squidgy-gate' and 'Camilla-gate' Affairs," *Daily Mail*, at: http://www.dailymail.co.uk/news/article-513900/Government-blocked-probe-Squidgy-gate-Camilla-gate-affairs.html, accessed 28 November 2010.

6 http://www.americablog.com/2006/01/americablog-just-bought-general-wesley.html, accessed 28 November 2010.

7 This became a big scandal in April 2011, but the fact that Apple was doing this had been in their terms-of-service consent form since mid-2010. See: http://www.washingtonpost.com/blogs/post-tech/post/tracking-on-the-iphone-catches-the-hills-attention/2011/04/21/AFE7akJE_blog.html and: http://www.theregister.co.uk/2010/06/22/apple_location_terms_and_conditions/

8   See for example: http://www.skygrabber.com/en/index.php, accessed
    29 November 2010.

9   http://dangerousintersection.org/2009/12/17/
    drones-dollars-and-the-open-source-insurgency/

10 Wikipedia lists at least four such companies.

11 Presumably the politicians do not maintain the content for these sites
    themselves, but some sites – an example being President Medvedev's
    video blog ("vlog" at: http://archive.kremlin.ru/eng/sdocs/vappears.shtml)
    maintained on the official Kremlin website – clearly have their principal's close
    participation.

12 http://www.fas.org/irp/dni/icd/icd-301.pdf

13 Director of Central Intelligence Directive 2/12, at: http://www.fas.org/irp/
    offdocs/dcid212.htm, accessed 29 November 2010.

14 http://www.dtic.mil/doctrine/dod_dictionary/?zoom_
    query=open+source&zoom_sort=0&zoom_per_page=10&zoom_and=1,
    accessed 29 November 2010.

15 CRS Report for Congress.

16 The 2000 study is at: http://www2.sims.berkeley.edu/research/projects/
    how-much-info/

    The 2003 study is at: http://www2.sims.berkeley.edu/research/projects/
    how-much-info-2003/

    The 2008 study is at: http://www.emc.com/collateral/analyst-reports/diverse-
    exploding-digital-universe.pdf

    The 2009 study is at: http://hmi.ucsd.edu/pdf/HMI_2009_ConsumerReport_
    Dec9_2009.pdf

17 Another use of the "Library of Congress" as a unit for measuring
    information volume was that NSA alone collects one "Library of Congress"
    worth of information *every six hours*. See: http://www.readwriteweb.com/
    archives/every_day_the_nsa_gathers_4x_the_amount_of_info_in.php?utm_
    source=feedburner&utm_medium=feed&utm_campaign=Feed%3A+readwrite
    web+%28ReadWriteWeb%29.

18 Cited on YouTube's official blog, at: http://youtube-global.blogspot.
    com/2010/11/great-scott-over-35-hours-of-video.html, accessed 29 November
    2010.

19 As of 29 November 2010.

20 Elisabeth Bumiller and Thom Shanker, "War Evolves with Drones, Some Tiny
    as Bugs," *New York Times*, 19 June 2011.

21 Defense Science Board Task Force on Defense Intelligence, *Counterinsurgency
    (COIN) Intelligence, Surveillance, and Reconnaissance (ISR) Operations*,
    February 2011, p. 49.

22 See article from Mitre Corporation, "War, Drones, and Videotape: A New Tool
    for Analyzing Video," on corporate website, at: http://www.mitre.org/news/
    digest/defense_intelligence/05_10/video.html, accessed 29 November 2010.

23 Asian Security Review, at: http://www.asiansecurity.org/articles/2009/may/21/ cctv-safe-city/, accessed 29 November 2010.

24 "Dubai Security Cameras 'Everywhere'," at: http://www.suite101.com/content/ dubai-security-cameras-everywhere-a252288, accessed 5 June 2011.

25 For example, see Hady W. Lauw, *et al.*, "Homophily in the Digital World: A LiveJournal Case Study," Internet Computing, March/April 2010 (vol. 14, no. 2).

26 Contrast for example Nicholas Carr, *The Shallows: What the Internet is Doing to Our Brains* (New York: Norton, 2010) and Steven Johnson, *Everything Bad is Good for You* (New York: Riverhead, 2005).

27 Christopher Chabris and Daniel Simons, *The Invisible Gorilla* (New York: Crown, 2010). A video of the experiment may be viewed at: http://www. youtube.com/watch?v=vJG698U2Mvo

28 The figures are for February 2010, in a graphic at: http://www. visualeconomics.com/2010-02-03-planet-google-from-philosophies-to-market-shares/, accessed 29 November 2010.

29 A. Spink, *et al.*, "Overlap among Major Web Search Engines," *Third International Conference on Information Technology: New Generations*, 2006, at: http://ieeexplore.ieee.org/xpl/freeabs_all.jsp?arnumber=1611621, accessed 29 November 2010.

30 Thomas H. Hammond, *et al.*, "Intelligence Organizations and the Organization of Intelligence: What Library Catalogs Can Tell Us About 9/11," presentation at the Conference on Innovation, Institutions and Public Policy in a Global Context, sponsored by the Structure and Organization of Government Research Committee of the International Political Science Association and the Elliott School of International Affairs of George Washington University in Washington DC on 22, 23, and 24 May 2003, at: www.sog-rc27.org/Paper/DC/hammond.doc, accessed 2 June 2011.

31 Eli Pariser, *The Filter Bubble: What the Internet is Hiding From You* (New York: Penguin Press, 2011), p. 2.

32 http://weblog.blogads.com/2009/03/26/google-search-prompt-geithner-jewish/ and: http://www.election-trends.com/2009/creepy-google-search-trends-is-geithner-jewish/, accessed 30 November 2010.

33 http://www.eightfoldlogic.com/blog/2008/05/search-engine-referral-rates-by-page-in-serps/, accessed 29 November 2010.

34 An interesting, if irrelevant, bit of trivia – Google's "page rank" algorithm is not named for what seems to be intuitively obvious, where a web page "ranks" in the engine's result, but rather is named for its first programmer, Google co-founder Larry Page.

35 Both searches were executed 30 November 2010.

36 Hal Abelson, *et al.*, *Blown to Bits: Your Life, Liberty, and Happiness After the Digital Explosion* (Upper Saddle River, NJ: Addison-Wesley, 2008). PDF version downloaded from: http://www.bitsbook.com/wp-content/ uploads/2008/12/B2B_3.pdf, pp. 150–53.

37 See: http://www.engadget.com/2010/11/30/google-to-face-formal-eu-investigation-over-unfair-downranking-o/, accessed 30 November 2010.

38 See Chris Sherman, Gary Price, *The Invisible Web* (Medford NJ: Information Today Inc., 2001).

39 See: http://googleblog.blogspot.com/2008/07/we-knew-web-was-big.html, accessed 30 November 2010.

40 James Gleick, *The Information: A History, A Theory, A Flood* (New York: Pantheon, 2011), Kindle version, location 2481 (chapter 5). Gleick also explores jungle drumming and the mountain-top bonfire relay signals, both of which could move information over fairly long distances quicker than an animal could move.

41 Gleick, Kindle location 2608 (chapter 5).

42 Davis, "Kent's Final Thoughts."

43 Linebarger, pp. 129–30.

44 Paul Farhi, "Twitter Breaks Story on Discovery Channel Gunman James Lee," *Washington Post*, 2 September 2010.

45 See: http://www.dailymail.co.uk/sciencetech/article-1195651/How-Michael-Jacksons-death-shut-Twitter-overwhelmed-Google–killed-Jeff-Goldblum.html

46 See: http://www.poynter.org/latest-news/making-sense-of-news/130724/how-4-people-their-social-network-turned-an-unwitting-witness-to-bin-ladens-death-into-a-citizen-journalist/, accessed 11 May 2011.

47 See: http://www.cnn.com/2011/TECH/social.media/05/05/twitter.reveals.limitations.taylor/index.html, accessed 13 May 2011.

48 "Why Wikipedia Should Be Trusted as a Breaking News Source," at: http://www.readwriteweb.com/archives/why_wikipedia_should_be_trusted_or_how_to_consume.php, accessed 1 December 2010.

49 Clay Shirky, *Here Comes Everybody* (New York: Penguin Press, 2008). See especially chapter 6, "Collective Action and Institutional Challenges."

50 Kevin Kelly, The Technium blog, at: http://www.kk.org/thetechnium/archives/2008/01/better_than_fre.php, accessed 2 December 2010.

51 http://www.techeye.net/internet/wikileaks-promises-leak-seven-times-bigger-than-iraq, accessed 2 December 2010).

52 http://www.youtube.com/watch?v=SXh7JR9oKVE, accessed 2 December 2010. A "flash mob" is a group of individuals who suddenly convene in a shared space for an activity and then quickly disperse.

53 http://www.youtube.com/watch?v=QZFMWvmAstA, accessed 2 December 2010. The video has subsequently been made private.

54 Gabor Szabo and Bernardo Huberman, "Predicting the Popularity of Online Content," Social Science Research Network, at: http://papers.ssrn.com/sol3/papers.cfm?abstract_id=1295610, accessed 4 December 2010.

55 Simon Dumenco, "Could Twitter Destroy Hollywood's Marketing Magic?" at: http://www.businessinsider.com/could-twitter-destroy-hollywoods-marketing-magic-2009-8, accessed 4 December 2010.

56 Greg Jaffe, "Facebook Brings the Afghan War to Fort Campbell," *Washington Post*, 5 November 2010.

57 See: http://mashable.com/2011/05/02/osama-death-twitter/#13399Dan-Pfeiffer. According to another account, Urban then tried to walk back from his announcement, but it was too late. See: http://www.geektown.ca/2011/05/bin-ladens-death-how-news-first-broke-on-twitter.html.

58 A Pew Research Center poll conducted in August 2010 found that the number of Americans who believed the President is Muslim had grown from 12 percent, in March 2008, to 18 percent, when this poll was conducted. See: http://pewresearch.org/pubs/1701/poll-obama-muslim-christian-church-out-of-politics-political-leaders-religious

59 A Scripps Howard poll done in 2006 found that about one-third of Americans believed that the US government had staged the 9/11 attacks in order to create a pretext for war. See: http://www.scrippsnews.com/911poll. A poll conducted in 2008 by the World Public Opinion Organization found that, for example, 43 percent of respondents in Egypt blamed the attacks on Israel, while 36 percent of Turkish respondents, 30 percent of Mexican respondents, and 23 percent of German respondents said the US had staged the attacks. See: http://www.worldpublicopinion.org/pipa/articles/international_security_bt/535.php

60 See: http://www.geocentricity.com/

61 For example, see: http://mando2u2003.blogspot.com/

62 See: http://www.gallup.com/poll/3742/new-poll-gauges-americans-general-knowledge-levels.aspx, accessed 5 December 2010.

63 Linebarger, p. 117, original emphasis.

64 See: http://www.nytimes.com/2004/09/15/politics/campaign/15guard.html?_r=2&scp=1&sq=%22Memos%20on%20Bush%20are%20Fake%20But%20Accurate%22&st=cse, accessed 5 December 2010.

65 See: http://www.fvza.org/, accessed 5 December 2010.

66 See: http://www.youtube.com/watch?v=bdTadK9p14A, accessed 5 December 2010.

67 ACRL, "Information Literacy Competency Standards for Higher Education," adopted January 2000, at: http://www.ala.org/ala/mgrps/divs/acrl/standards/informationliteracycompetency.cfm#ildef, accessed 5 December 2010.

68 Herbert Simon, "Rational Choice and the Structure of the Environment," *Psychological Review*, vol. 63, no. 2, 1956.

69 Farhad Manjoo, *True Enough* (New York: Wiley, 2008), p. 2.

70 See: http://www.theatlantic.com/national/archive/2011/05/anatomy-of-a-fake-quotation/238257/.

71 Kent, *Strategic Intelligence*, p. 182.

72 See: http://www.youtube.com/watch?v=rSdFIDygFwM, accessed 5 December 2010.

73 See: http://www.scribd.com/doc/3316541/CIA-Simple-Sabotage-Manual, accessed 5 December 2010.

74 See: http://www.uralgold.ru/expert/28.htm, accessed 5 December 2010.

75 Abelson, p. 105.

76 See: http://www.niemanlab.org/2010/04/the-gutenberg-parenthesis-thomas-pettitt-on-parallels-between-the-pre-print-era-and-our-own-internet-age/, accessed 6 December 2010.

77 Andrew Pettegree, *The Book in the Renaissance* (New Haven: Yale University Press, 2010).

78 Robert Pinsky, "Start the Presses," *New York Times Book Review*, 13 August 2010.

79 Apparently this was the disparaging name given to oil when it was first discovered in Venezuela.

80 Alireza Doostdar, "The Vulgar Spirit of Blogging: On Language, Culture, and Power in Persian Weblogestan," *American Anthropologist*, vol. 106, no. 4, December 2004, p. 652.

81 See: http://news.xinhuanet.com/english/2008-05/22/content_8225456.htm, accessed 6 December 2010.

82 Probably the fullest discussion of this is on Wikipedia, at: http://en.wikipedia.org/wiki/Grass_Mud_Horse.

83 This recently has been the subject of heated disagreement, with Evgeny Morozov leading the argument that the internet facilitates tyranny as much as it may encourage the opposite. See *The Net Delusion: The Dark Side of Internet Freedom* (New York: Public Affairs Books, 2011).

84 See: http://globalvoicesonline.org/2007/08/30/arabeyes-who-is-using-the-tunisian-presidential-airplane/, accessed 6 December 2010. In January 2011 Ben-Ali was forced from office and fled the country. This early act of "digital resistance" is worth commemorating even if Ben-Ali himself is now gone.

85 See: http://www.guardian.co.uk/world/2006/nov/02/burma.jonathanwatts.

86 See for example: http://www.youtube.com/watch?v=ggE8-xxN8KY, accessed 6 December 2010.

87 See: http://www.youtube.com/watch?v=UPXtawGmZgQ, accessed 7 December 2010, and: http://www.rferl.org/content/Scandal_Erupts_Over_Fatal_Car_Crash_Involving_Russian_Oil_Executive/1973679.html, accessed 7 December 2010.

88 Geert Lovink, "Twelve Theses on Wikileaks," at: http://networkcultures.org/wpmu/geert/2010/12/07/twelve-theses-on-wikileaks-with-patrice-riemens/, accessed 31 May 2011.

89 Abelson, p. 208.

90 See: http://arstechnica.com/tech-policy/news/2010/11/fed-up-with-icann-pirate-bay-cofounder-floats-p2p-dns-system.ars, accessed 7 December 2010.

91 Clifford Levy, "Undercut by Microsoft, in the End Russia Drops Piracy Case," *New York Times*, 5 December 2010.

92 See: http://www.fastcompany.com/1707699/state-department-reading-wikileaks-could-endanger-security-clearances.

93 David Wheeler, "'Google Doesn't Laugh': Saving Witty Headlines in the Age of SEO," *The Atlantic*, 12 May 2011, at: http://www.theatlantic.com/technology/archive/2011/05/google-doesnt-laugh-saving-witty-headlines-in-the-age-of-seo/238656/

94 See for example Tom Pettitt, "Containment and Articulation: Media, Cultural Production, and the Perception of the Material World," at: http://web.mit.edu/comm-forum/mit6/papers/Pettitt.pdf, accessed 7 December 2010.

95 Rolington, Powerpoint presentation.

CHAPTER SIX

So what? Addressing the signal-to-noise problem

A moment comes in any presentation about the issues raised in the previous chapter when someone in the audience will object that, sure, there may be lots of information available now, but "most of it is junk" (or ruder words to the same effect). That is a golden teaching moment, for it allows the presenter to point out that *all* information is "junk" – until someone has a use for it.

As has been shown repeatedly in this book, there is a persistent assumption in the intelligence community, and also in the policy-making community it is meant to serve, that there are innate qualities in information which make it "useful" or "secondary" (to quote again the Cunningham Report). Although experience shows (as was explored in depth in the Jervis report on Iran, for example) that information is valuable only to the degree that it provides insight, or answers a question of some sort, the belief lingers that "better intelligence" is primarily a function of getting "the right information."

The most recent iteration of this continued belief in the existence of objectively "valuable information" is Intelligence Community Directive 203 (ICD 203), signed on 21 June 2007.[1] Intended to address what were understood to be analytic shortcomings which had been manifest both in the failure to foresee the 9/11 attacks and in the intelligence leading up to the 2003 invasion of Iraq, ICD 203 imposes a series of fixed requirements on IC analysts and their "finished intelligence" products, with the goal of assuring recipients that the analysts have met "the highest standards of integrity and rigorous analytic thinking." There are five broad requirements. Four of these are that intelligence analysis should be: objective, independent of political considerations, timely, and meet eight specified standards of analytic "tradecraft" (each analytic unit is further mandated to conduct regular audits of how well their analysts have observed seven of those eight standards – the eighth, "accuracy of assessment," has proven too slippery to assess in a meaningful way). Although there are epistemological questions which might be raised about several of the standards – what, for example, is the difference between being "objective" and being "free of political consid-erations," or, in the case of the tradecraft standards, what is the standard of logic by which it is judged whether or not an argument is "logical"? For present purposes, though, the largest problem is presented by the fifth standard: "analysis should be informed by all relevant information that is available to the analytic element."

Presumably this requirement was inserted in ICD 203 to address the problems of information "stove-piping" which the WMD and 9/11 Commissions had uncovered, because various parts of the intelligence community possessed information that it had not shared with other parts or, alternatively, that some parts of the community gave much greater weight to the information sources or types with which they were most familiar, and so ignored other kinds of information which might have had an impact on their analysis. As is made clear in other directives (ICD 208, on Writing for Maximum Utility;[2] ICD 204, on Roles and Responsibilities for the National Intelligence Priorities Framework;[3] and ICD 900, on Mission Management[4]), the model that shapes how intelligence is to be gathered and used remains unchanged from the earliest days of the CIA, when information was understood to be in short supply. Thus the main charge is to collect as much information as possible on what ICD 204 calls "intelligence topics approved by the President," after which, as the intel-ligence cycle dictates, that information will be "processed" and "analyzed." Perhaps in part because the belief persists that intelligence involves only secrets, the requirement that intelligence be "informed by all relevant information" has continued to be interpreted as meaning primarily secret information – with the result that most of the potential riches suggested in the previous chapter remain discounted or ignored.

Competitive intelligence vs "intelligence"

Secrecy is so central to most understandings of "intelligence" that it is useful to compare the methods of IC analysts with those who work in the field of competitive (or competitor) intelligence, a business specialization which emerged in the late 1970s. Now formalized as a profession with its own organization (Strategic and Competitive Intelligence Professionals, or SCIP), journals (*Journal of Competitive Intelligence, Competitive Intelligence Review*), and various credentialing programs, competitive intelligence intends to be an organized means of helping corporate decision-makers to make better decisions about the tactics and strategies which they will deploy against their competitors. Leonard Fuld, one of the leaders of the competitive intelligence industry, acknowledges that, while "intelligence" can be hard to define precisely, it is "analyzed information" that "helps a manager to respond with the right market decision or long-term decision."[5] In another place he writes that "intelligence is using information efficiently, making decisions on a less-than-perfect picture ... seeing your competition *clearly*, understanding its strategy, and acting *early* on that knowledge."[6] Unlike IC intelligence, however, competitive intelligence is emphatically "not spying, stealing, or bugging"[7] – indeed, the SCIP has developed a professional code of ethics which specifically forbids the use of "misrepresentation, improper influence, covert collection, [and] unsolicited information" in the conduct of competitive intelligence[8] – which means that everything the competitive analyst does derives, of necessity, from open sources.

According at least to one history[9] of what its author calls the "classic CI model," the competitive intelligence industry began with an information process model that was explicitly derived from the government's intelligence cycle ("CI" here should not be confused with "counter intelligence," the usual IC use of the term, but rather should be understood as "competitor intelligence"). Thus for the first decade or so of formalized activity, the competitive intelligence industry focused on collection of technical data about competitors, with the goal of creating "information aids" to company executive officers who may require them. As the author points out, "there is no mention of how it is that the intelligence director determines what information is needed or exactly what are the needs of [the] company." In the 1990s the process was modified by the inclusion of what was called a Key Intelligence Topics dimension, or KIT, a process intended to push CI analysts and senior management more closely together, replacing the once self-generated data acquisition approach with a formal interview process, in which senior management worked with CI professionals to try to help both sides get a better understanding of the information a given company really required. While modeled on the US government's National Intelligence Topics process, the KIT process was more specifically intended to be what another article[10] called "an interactive dialogue between CI professionals and key decision-makers" of a given organization.

Thus, although the CI process retains a superficial resemblance to the government intelligence process, it has the important difference of this in-built "interactive dialogue" between those who initiate intelligence requests and those who fulfill them. As a history of CI points out, "the [competitive] intelligence cycle may seem to be reactive ... [because]

intelligence is only produced through the requests of managers [but] the process is actually dynamic and interactive [because] throughout the intelligence cycle, feedback and updates from CI professionals allow for midcourse adjustments and new issues to surface."[11] What that process of dialogue and midcourse correction is doing, of course, is described even more succinctly by CI "guru" Leonard Fuld, who noted that the very first step of successful analysis is to "Define the question: make sure you know what you and your client want to know."[12]

Fuld's use of the word "client" highlights a subtle but significant difference between competitive intelligence and the intelligence activities of the IC. Traditionally the recipients of intelligence products have been called "consumers" or "customers," rather than "clients." A major reason for this, as has already been suggested in Chapter Three, is that Sherman Kent and the other founders of the IC analytic practices distrusted the abilities and motives of the recipients of the IC's products. A "client" is one who controls a process, by defining the goal that is to be reached and also by making decisions about how resources are to be allocated, how great a risk is to be incurred, and other potential costs and benefits of various means of reaching that goal. The adviser offers expertise – knowledge and opinions – but it remains the client who makes the choices and who is in charge. A "customer" or "consumer," by contrast, has the choice only of using or not using a product. Although the highly saturated markets of the early twenty-first century have generally changed the relationship between producer and consumer so that it is the former which must woo the latter, at the time that the CIA was established most producers enjoyed the ability to define what it was that the consumers would buy. When Kent wrote that an intelligence organization should have the characteristics of "a large university faculty," "our greatest metropolitan newspapers," and an "organization engaged in the manufacture of a product"[13] he was picturing a world in which university curricula were established by an educational elite with uniform views, newspapers had set identities and editorial positions, and the attitude of manufacturers to consumers was best defined just a few years later by GM president Charles Wilson in his 1952 confirmation hearing to become Eisenhower's Secretary of Defense, when he said "what was good for our country was good for General Motors and vice versa"[14] (in spirit not all that far from Henry Ford's equally famous remark about the car buyer getting "any color he wants, as long as it's black").

In that kind of hierarchical world, questions are primarily those of fact – which indeed is how Kent visualized the function of the analyst, whose job it is "to see that the doers are generally well-informed." He then adds that "at [the doers'] request" they may "analyze alternative courses without indicating choice." Even Kent, however, argued that good analysis required "the kind of guidance that any professional man must have from his client." Lack of that kind of guidance, he warned, is "the chief contributor to the worst sickness which can afflict intelligence … the sickness of irresponsibility … [which is shown by analysts becoming] satisfied with dishing up information without trying to find out what lies behind the order for them."[15]

Asking Better Questions

As has already been noted, when the IC was established the greatest single concern was the nearly total absence of basic information about the Soviet Union. In spite of the fact that, within a decade, the amount of available information about Soviet activities was already greater than the capacity of the IC to absorb it, the preferred method for dealing with the USSR was to continue to collect information. The reasons this was so are stated explicitly in, for example, a 1976 National Intelligence Estimate (NIE) about the comparative strengths and weaknesses of NATO and Warsaw Pact troops. That document states: "We do not have access to the Soviets' war plans but we can infer the general nature of their military contingency plans from the information available from Warsaw Pact exercises, from Pact writings on military strategy, and from the current disposition of Pact forces."[16] It is not difficult to understand why analysts and policymakers alike tended to assume, in a world where those kinds of assumptions reigned, that what was "good information" and what "secondary information" was more or less self-evident.

As has already been noted, this approach is a puzzle-solving one. There is nothing innately wrong with this approach – indeed, many of the hardest intelligence problems we confront are precisely of this sort. Some examples of such "puzzles" might include:

- How many nuclear devices does North Korea possess and where are they kept?

- Where is Osama bin Laden?[17]

- What are the range and speed capabilities of the latest generation Chinese surface-to-air missiles?

- Which of the cabinet ministers in Country X takes bribes, and from whom?

It should be noted that while some of these questions appear to be ones for which only clandestine information might provide the answer, this is not necessarily a condition of puzzles – the second question, for example, received its answer entirely through clandestine means[18] – even the hardest of the others have dimensions for which open sources could provide important clues. It is worth recalling in this regard what competitive intelligence specialist Leonard Fuld calls "the cardinal rule of intelligence" – "Wherever money is exchanged, so is information."[19] Thus the equipment and expertise required to manufacture, store, and test nuclear devices or surface-to-air missiles (SAMs) all might conceivably leave commercial trails.

More important to understand, however, is that all of the questions above are ones for which more information will always prove useful. While there may be disputes about the reliability of a particular source, and evidence may be inconclusive, the answer to questions of the *Who?* *What?* *When?* *Where?* type is ultimately going to be a simple statement of fact. Since the collapse of the USSR, and the movement of radical Islamic terrorism to the world's center stage, a considerable body of literature has emerged from the IC and elsewhere which stresses the importance of two other sorts of questions: ones responding to the questions *How?* and *Why?*, and, perhaps even more so, ones addressing concerns about the future, of the "*What might happen?*" and "*what could happen?*" variety. The first of these are normally dubbed "mysteries," while the second are "unordered problems" or, even more colorfully, "wicked problems."

One important difference between a *Who?* *What?* *When?* question and a *Why?* or a *How?* question is that the latter does not have a correct or factual answer – it can only have a *plausible* answer. As was discussed in Chapter Three, answering a "why?" question requires, in effect, constructing two stories – one which constructs causal connections which the analyst finds convincing, and a second which the person or persons to whom the analyst relays his or her hypotheses of causality finds convincing. The wording for this point is convoluted, but deliberately so, for it stresses a point which is too often forgotten, that causality is never *provable*, in the sense that a mathematical equation may be said to be provable, but rather is based on belief. The role of additional information when dealing with this kind of question can be quite tricky. Perceiving a pattern of causality requires a certain amount of data, but once a pattern is seen (or hypothesized), additional information can be used in one of two ways. The soundness of the explanation is best tested, of course, when information is sought which might contradict, weaken, or otherwise fall outside the governing hypothesis, thus suggesting that the hypothesis is insufficiently inclusive. Note that this is different from "provability" – virtually no mysteries are "provable" or "disprovable," but rather rise or fall on the degree to which analysts and those for whom they are analyzing accept the assumptions on which a particular causality is hypothesized to rest. Human nature being what it is, however, most people tend to sort information in order to support the hypotheses to which they have already committed themselves, which means that all more information does is tend to make a reigning hypothesis even more entrenched. The preceding chapters have shown many examples of this process – the dispute over the Sino-Soviet split; the inability to see the threat to the Shah which was posed by the clerics; the assumption that India would not begin nuclear testing again; and, of course, the entire process by which WMD were not found to be in Iraq. ICD 203 has attempted to address this problem in a formal way, both by requiring that analysis be based on "all available information" and also by imposing the specific tradecraft requirement that, when putting forward a hypothesis, analysts are supposed to state whether some alternative hypothesis might explain the chain of causality which they are advancing, and then further to state why that alternative has been rejected, or is less preferred. While praiseworthy as an attempt, in practice these "alternative analyses," when performed at all, tend to remain within a rather narrow band of causal explanations which have been generated and "sanctified" by Western social science. Thus, to take one example, the behavior of North Korean leadership will be explained in terms of games theory or rational choice or power politics, but the IC is less likely to accept the recent hypothesis of academic Brian Myers, who argues that there is extensive popular support for the leadership regime because the North Koreans are convinced that they are the last racially pure people on the planet, under constant threat of pollution by outsiders.[20] Just as the Iran analysts of 1978–1979 could not accept that religion was a criterion which might motivate profoundly disruptive political behavior, so can it be difficult now for analysts to understand the workings of convictions about "blood purity."

It is worth pointing out that constructing hypotheses to answer questions of "why?" and "how?" is the only activity of the IC which, strictly speaking, can be called "analysis," at least in the etymological sense of the Greek source word, *analyein*, meaning to "break down" or "reduce." "Analysis" thus can only be applied for phenomena which have already come about or which exist now. In the Soviet period, hypotheses about why certain things existed or had happened, and explanations of how things had been done or achieved were valued because it was assumed that the same conditions or explanations would be valid the next time the Soviets did something, and thus "analysis" had an implicitly predictive value.

One of the consequences of the existing "collect-process-analyze" model is that it obscures what policymakers are genuinely interested in, which is not the present, but rather the future. Although the CIA was established in large part to prevent the repetition of surprises such as the Japanese attack on Pearl Harbor, the IC has found warning to be extraordinarily difficult to do well. Willmoore Kendall, a colleague of Sherman Kent in R&A who stayed on for the early days of the CIA but then returned to academia, argued in his review of Sherman Kent's *Strategic Intelligence for American World Policy* that the problem was hard-wired into the way that Kent conceptualized the universe. In Kendall's words: "The course of events is conceived [by Kent] not as something you try to influence but as a tape all printed up inside a machine; and the job of intelligence is to tell the planners how it reads."[21] Indeed, Kent said essentially the same thing in his own book *Writing History*, which defends the value of history as being "an extension of memory that permits us to draw upon experience and ... allows us to establish a common pool of wisdom." The past in Kent's description is the guide to the future, and he urges that his students study it in accordance with the recommendation of German historian Ernst Bernheim, who laid out what looks very much like today's intelligence cycle: the writing of history has "four steps: 1. *Heuristik*, the gathering of historical evidence; 2. *Kritik*, the evaluating of this evidence; 3. *Auffassung*, the moment of comprehending the true meaning of the evaluated evidence; 4. *Darstellung*, the presentation of the new idea in terms of the evaluated evidence."[22] Thus understanding the "true meaning" of the past will always serve, Kent suggests, as a guide to what the future will bring.

Kendall contrasted what he called Kent's "absolute prediction" ("General DeGaulle will come to power this day six months") with "contingent prediction" ("The following factors, which can be influenced in such and such a fashion by action from the outside, will determine whether, and if so, when, General DeGaulle will come to power"). "The latter is what the government needs," Kendall wrote, "especially in peacetime." The term more commonly in use now is "unordered problems" or "wicked problems," but the structure is the same – a number of analytic hypotheses about past causalities are used to characterize a new or emerging situation (usually a process of analogizing, or commensuration) with the goal of identifying where in the further development of that situation might lie danger, opportunity, or both, while also recognizing that interacting with the problem in any way will also change the problem, thus affecting the further interaction of contingent factors.[23]

Indeed, as one of the original papers on the subject made clear,[24] "wicked problems" lie entirely within the realm of policy – they do not have "correct" or "incorrect" answers, but have only "better" and "worse" ones, which, moreover, can be better for some and worse for others *at the same time*. Although there is nothing inherent in the nature of wicked problems which makes them resistant to analytic input or to the possibilities of the changing information environment, in the specific environment of the IC it is almost impossible for analysts to contribute meaningfully to the "wicked problem" process (another of the characteristics of such problems being that they have no clear beginning or end points, and so cannot be solved, resolved, or answered). The primary reason for this is Walter Lippmann's firewall between "the staff which executes" and "the staff which investigates,"[25] laid down by Sherman Kent at the foundation of the IC, and now made hallowed by time, tradition, and – most important – workflows, budgetary processes, and other bureaucratic "exoskeletons."

Kent's firewall has important implications for the way that information is used, particularly in the emerging world of cheaper, faster, and more out-of-control information. As already has been noted, Malcolm Gladwell defined puzzles[26] – the *Who? What? Where? When?* questions – as transmitter-dependent, meaning that it is the creator of the puzzle who is responsible for supplying, or failing to supply, required information, while the only responsibility of those wanting the information is to try as hard and as imaginatively as they can to look for it. It is clear from documents such as ICD 203 that this remains the way most information is envisaged in the IC – describing the reliability of sources, as that ICD requires, is another way of making clear that the value of information lies in the source that provides it. Thus also the insistence in the esoteric communication methodology upon the "authoritativeness" of media, and the assurance (or concern) that most of what is to be found on the internet is "junk."

Gladwell contrasts those to "receiver-dependent" mysteries, which rely upon the receiver to understand and assemble available information in a way that makes sense, or has meaning, for the purpose at hand. Information here is less source-dependent, because its value lies in the way it informs the hypotheses which the analyst is trying to form, or defend. In mystery-resolution it is not important to decide how factual or authoritative the information is, but rather how it impacts the hypothesis. Thus an analyst constructing a hypothesis in answer to a question like "why are so many people in the Middle East anti-US?" would not be concerned about whether or not it is true that the US (or Israel) was responsible for the 9/11 attacks on the World Trade Towers, but rather would use that information as part of the hypothesis-building process.

In practice, however, it is precisely here that the proliferation of information is most likely to unsettle both analysts and policymakers. Thus in 1954, the question of whether or not the first letter of Nikita Khrushchev's title was capitalized in *Pravda* seemed of enormous value, because the choice was between that as a source of information and nothing. Today, when Google suggests that there may be more than 53 million websites with the "dot ru" country extension, plus about 5 million Russian blogs,[27] plus who knows how many Russian YouTubes, RuTubes, and other sources – to say nothing of streamed versions of Russian broadcast TV and projects like the news service Russia Today – it is all but impossible to decide which information to access, and even harder to understand how to value any of it. This is undoubtedly a large part of why IC analysts continue to prefer to base their analyses on information provided through the "collect-process-analyze" procedure – the value of that information is pre-determined by the process of acquisition,[28] and thus analysts are spared making that difficult decision for themselves. Thus the phrase "based on all available sources of information" often enough comes to mean "based on all the information supplied to me," even though that assumption ignores the long history of problems which the IC has suffered because what has been collected and what needs to be answered fail to match up.

It is in dealing with unordered or wicked problems, however, that the Kent-era assumptions about information become genuinely closed circles. In terms of the original article about wicked problems, what Kent and the early IC had been dealing with were "tame problems," or perhaps more precisely, questions which were *assumed* to be "tame." As the authors Rittel and Webber explained, a tame problem is one which has clear outlines, responds to or is a product of a known or discoverable law or rule, and may be solved by asking questions about it for which there are descriptive answers – *Who? When? How many?* Even the *Why?* question is essentially descriptive, although the answers supplied will be hypotheses, rather than facts.

In contrast, the questions asked about wicked problems are always prescriptive, because, as Rittel and Webber write, "one of the most intractable problems is that of defining problems (of knowing what distinguishes an observed condition from a desired condition) and of locating problems (finding where in the complex causal networks the trouble really lies)." One consequence is that "the information needed to *understand* [a wicked] problem depends upon one's idea for *solving* it."[29] To take again the example of violent radical Islam, if the problem is defined as a military one, then the information sought and gathered will revolve around security, enemy capacities, insurgency tactics, and other such issues. If the problem is viewed rather as a social one, then the information required to address it will be anthropological, sociological, and perhaps historical. The problem may even be defined in theological terms, in which case the information gathered will be that which shows that elements of Biblical prophecy are being fulfilled by the course of current events.[30]

Information vs "news"

Where the policymaker–analyst relationship goes persistently awry is in the tension between the desire of the former to ask prescriptive and predictive questions ("What will happen? What might happen? What should happen?") and the reluctance of analysts to take on anything other than descriptive and, at best, explanatory questions. As has already been discussed in previous chapters, most of what have been characterized as "intelligence failures" could more usefully be described as the consequences of having asked the wrong questions. Rather than asking questions like "what could happen to the Shah?" or "why are the clerics so angry at the regime?" or even "what are our interests in Iran and how can we best protect them?" the collectors and analysts instead provided policymakers with a steady flow of information about the up-or-down movement of a previously defined set of what were understood to be indicators of the likely future course of events.

In this regard the IC behaves very much like news organizations, providing a steady flow of information about a bounded set of topics, with the greatest single value being the freshness of the information. As one of the foremost critics of "the news" as a social phenomenon, Neil Postman, pointed out, the ability to pass around decontextualized "facts" about distant parts of the globe is a technological artifact that has woven itself into the modern world without having an obvious or clear further purpose.[31] Some factors which do seem important, however, include the notion that "news" serves as a form of social capital, binding a group together with shared concerns, and also providing a means by which the group can determine rank relative to one another – the first to receive "the news" in his or her circle gains status by then sharing it with the other members of the circle. In this regard, the two most important characteristics of "news" are freshness and exclusivity. Less immediately obvious, but clearly operative, is "salience." In ICD 203, and in most discussions of the IC's information function, the word more commonly used is "relevance," but what in fact is meant is "salience." "Relevance" can only be measured in relation to something else, whereas "salience" is the name for the general process by which information is ranked, valued, and sorted. Thus ICD 203 requires that analysis demonstrate "relevance to US security" but does not specify how that is to be determined. It takes only a quick glance at, for example, the *National Security Doctrine 2010*[32] to see that "US security" is a classic "wicked problem" for which the definition of the problem also pre-defines the information that will be used in the study of the problem. In terms of "the news" this means a set group of countries and topics – reflected in the IC by the 9,100 "slots" of the National Intelligence Priorities Framework – about which reporters or collectors provide a steady stream of updated information. One of the persistent mysteries about "the news" is what precisely the recipients are supposed to *do* with the information they receive. Some scholars have gone so far as to argue that the purpose of this news flow is essentially emotional – that is, the topics are ones of high salience for a particular group, while the individual items which relate to those various topics form basically one of two stories: *this reinforces stability* and *this threatens stability.* Traditionally news does not carry direct prescriptions for action or for remedy (though these can be implied in a number of indirect, even subliminal ways), but rather attempts to elicit an emotional response. The appearance of a TV channel dedicated to a 24-hour presentation of news about the weather gave this a name – the Weather Channel phenomenon[33] – but it was something that already worried Walter Lippmann in 1920:

The world about which man is supposed to have opinions has become so complicated as to defy his powers of understanding. What he knows of events that matter enormously to him, the purposes of governments, the aspirations of peoples, the struggle of classes, he knows at second, third, or fourth hand. He cannot go and see for himself … News comes from a distance; it comes helter-skelter, in inconceivable confusion; it deals with matters that are not easily understood; it arrives and is assimilated by busy and tired people who must take what is given them.[34]

One other phenomenon of news which Lippmann does not mention is that it comes in a uniform, steady flow – although newspaper people will talk of a "slow news day," in practice they will fill as many pages as they have advertising support to print, just as the TV evening news always fills 30 minutes (with commercials). Although the content and nature of the President's Daily Brief (PDB) are among the most closely guarded of all the IC's secrets, people who should know have described it as being much like a daily newspaper. Certainly the eleven PDBs which have been fully or partially declassified[35] are basically indistinguishable from newspapers.

This problem is further compounded by the explosion of places where policymakers, and others, may now find "news." In the early days of the IC, analytic products had authority because there were few competing sources of information, particularly about the topics on which the IC was reporting. Now there is an essentially unlimited supply of sources from which policymakers (and everybody else) can draw the information they wish. Paul Miller, an analyst detailed to support the Afghan team at the National Security Council, wrote that IC analytic products had to compete for attention and believability with a policymaker's "[remembered] under-graduate professor of political science, [his or her] personal experience, [and] the headlines of the *New York Times*."[36] More anecdotally, a senior IC official remarked in late 2009 that in his experience most policymakers get their information from: first, TV news; then the *New York Times* and other newspapers of record; then their own trusted associates and friends; then the Internet, either directly through their own searches or through those of their staff; and only fifth from the IC.[37] As was already noted in the previous chapter, Alfred Rolington, former CEO of Jane's, said much the same thing when he remarked that "few respect information's authority" because "the clients believe they have as much to contribute as the specialists."[38]

Law professor Jonathan Macey has made a strong case that at a certain level of complexity, information actually compounds problems, rather than helps to solve them. As Macey points out, "the bedrock principal on which all of U.S. securities law is based" is that publicly traded companies are required to disclose massive amounts of information about themselves and their activities. The only debate, Macey writes, is about how much they must declare, and in what form. The collapse of several high-profile companies including, most notably, Enron prompted the extremely stringent reporting requirements of Sarbanes-Oxley; however, as Macey writes, "Enron rose and fell in the context of [what was already] one of the world's strictest regimes of mandatory disclosure and reporting," suggesting that "more information" or "more disclosure" would be unlikely to improve the situation. In words which sound very similar to the many "post-failure" studies which the IC has undergone in the past decade, Macey writes that "In the Enron collapse, the U.S. mandatory reporting system worked fairly well ... Enron did make disclosures that should have led reasonable market participants to uncover grave problems within the company. Thus, the corporate governance problem that Enron unmasked was not a problem with the controversial U.S. system of mandatory disclosure. Rather, the problem was that the market did an astonishingly poor job of both interpreting Enron's disclosures and 'decoding' the information contained in the trades conducted by Enron insiders."[39]

Macey's explanation of why he thinks the market – by which he means the aggregate self-interest of all the parties who are involved in buying and selling on the stock market – performed so poorly is also similar to critiques which have repeatedly been leveled at the IC. The question most participants seem to have been asking themselves was essentially whether or not Enron was reporting as it ought to be doing – which it was. Almost no entities had an incentive to ask what the information that was being reported *meant*. It was only a Cornell University Business School class that had the incentive to ask, in essence, how is Enron functioning, and what does the information it has submitted *mean*? It was on that basis that the class urged investors to sell, a full three years before the company actually collapsed.

There is a similarity here to another famous incident in the use of information – as told in Malcolm Gladwell's *Blink*,[40] British intelligence officers were assigned to intercept and transcribe German Morse code signals. The texts themselves were encoded, so that the information was, in effect, sent, but was not understood. A part of the war effort was devoted to trying to decipher the codes, and many ways that proved successful. As the transcribers grew more familiar with the messages they were intercepting, some of them began to recognize patterns in how various Morse code operators were keying in their messages – a pattern that is called a "fist." This allowed the operators to begin to triangulate location, so that they could tell the locations from where an identified Morse code operator was sending. This then allowed them to make informed hypotheses about the kinds of units to which the various operators were attached, which in turn gave them some insight into how hard-pressed that given unit might be. This also allowed them to make good hypotheses about what was going on when the locations changed, allowing them to inform their superiors about enemy troop movements before any other information was available.

From gathering to hunting – but you have to know what you are hunting for

Among the many phrases that emerged in the aftermath of 9/11 was that of NSA's Maureen Baginski, who urged that her SIGINT colleagues (and by implication all of the various collectors) had to become "hunters rather than gatherers."[41] That is a more succinct formulation of the same point that Macey was making, and indeed what the Morse code transcribers were demonstrating, that information really only has a chance to function when it is being used in an attempt to answer a question. The impulse behind the "collect-process-analyze" model is the same as behind the financial reporting requirements, that there is something innate within the information that – given enough time and enough collection – the answer will somehow emerge. The best refutation of that assumption is Google itself (or any other large search engine). What Google provides is an enormous *index* of where its web-crawlers have found information – very much like the back of a scholarly book will have a list of topic words and phrases with an indication of the page on which they will be found. Although the difference in scale is mind-boggling, the function is the same. Nothing in Google's enormous store of indexed material means anything, however, *until a question is typed in the query box.* It is the question that sorts the material, indicating what information is irrelevant and suggesting other information that may be relevant.

As anyone who has spent time web-searching quickly learns, there is both an art and a science of how to maneuver through the web efficiently, but both are based on the way that questions are conceptualized and framed. In a similar vein, one of the skills which librarians are taught as they are trained is how to help library patrons learn to ask more meaningful, productive questions; this "reference interview" is designed to help move the patron from asking what are essentially collection questions ("Do you have anything on polar bears?") to more potential fruitful kinds of questions ("What are some potential effects of climate change?").

The problem that the intelligence analyst faces, however, is that he or she has little chance to move beyond the collection regime requirements. Contrast with the analyst of competitive intelligence, who is able to ask such potentially enlightening questions as:

- Who is our main competitor?
- What are their strengths and weaknesses?
- What are our strengths and weaknesses?
- What are our resources for competition and how might we best deploy these?

- What would be the best indicators of competitor activity that would be disadvantageous to us, and where might we find those?

Trying to imagine a situation in which an intelligence officer might be able to ask similar questions about his or her "company" – the US – makes it clear why it was that Willmoore Kendall, unlike Sherman Kent, saw a fundamental difference between the purposes of intelligence in wartime and those in peace. In war information requirements are overwhelmingly tactical, because the strategic goal is clear: defeat the enemy. In peacetime, as the questions above suggest, the situation rapidly becomes an entire complex of "wicked problems." It is for that reason that another of Kent's contemporaries, George Pettee, proposed in his own book, *The Future of American Secret Intelligence*, that what was required for US intelligence in peacetime is "a doctrine of method," by which he meant "what data to seek as essential to the solution of a problem." In words rather similar to what the Cunningham Report criticized the IC for *not* doing, Pettee argued that collectors could not proceed on their own, without this guiding doctrine, because "individual initiative can only lead to disorder unless the individual understands the purposes and structure of the program in which he plays a part."[42]

Not stated, but implicit, is that the "purposes and structure" would have to be articulated at the level of policy, not as collection requirements, but rather almost as an inventory, of the kind suggested by the questions above. The degree to which such a process is unimaginable within the current structures of the IC and the government is a good indicator of how difficult it usually proves for the IC to ask better questions. That inability, however, also brings up in regard to the IC the same question that Macey asked of the US financial regulatory system: is it worth the cost?

His answer is unambiguous:

> The story of the rise and fall of Enron suggests that the billions spent on legally mandated corporate governance systems and regulatory infrastructure in the U.S. may be largely a dead weight social loss. Investors pay dearly for such systems and infrastructure but do not receive the safeguards and other protections they are told they might receive.

Notes

1 http://www.fas.org/irp/dni/icd/icd-203.pdf

2 http://www.dni.gov/electronic_reading_room/ICD_208.pdf

3 http://www.fas.org/irp/dni/icd/icd-204.pdf

4 http://www.fas.org/irp/dni/icd/icd-900.pdf

5 Leonard Fuld, *The New Competitor Intelligence* (New York: Wiley, 1995), p. 23.

6 Leonard Fuld, *The Secret Language of Competitive Intelligence* (New York: Crown, 2006), p. 20.

7 Fuld, *New Competitor*, p. 23.

8 John Prescott, "The Evolution of Competitive Intelligence," *Journal of the Association of Proposal Management Professionals*, Spring 1999, p. 49.

9 John McGonagle, "An Examination of the 'Classic' CI Model," *Journal of Competitive Intelligence and Management*, vol. 4, no. 2, 2007.

10 Meera Mody, "Key Intelligence Topics (KITs) in Competitive Intelligence and Global Business," in David Blenkhorn and Craig Fleisher (eds), *Competitive Intelligence and Global Business* (New York: Praeger, 2005), p. 18.

11 Prescott, p. 44.

12 Fuld, *New Competitor Intelligence*, p. 48.

13 Kent, *Strategic Intelligence*, pp. 74–75.

14 According to Wilson's obituary in *Time*, the newspapers "edited" his remark, to be the more famous "What's good for General Motors is good for the country." See "Armed Forces: Engine Charlie," *Time*, 6 October 1961.

15 Kent, *Strategic Intelligence*, pp. 182, 183.

16 WARSAW PACT FORCES OPPOSITE NATO (NIE 11-14-79), p. 11, at: http://www.foia.cia.gov/docs/DOC_0000255681/DOC_0000255681.pdf, accessed 14 December 2010.

17 This puzzle was solved while this book was being written. It will be noted, however, that solving the puzzle left a great many mysteries still unresolved.

18 See Nicholas Schmidle, "Getting Bin Laden," *New Yorker*, 8 August 2011.

19 Fuld, *New Competitor*, p. 27.

20 See Brian Myers, *The Cleanest Race: How North Koreans See Themselves and Why it Matters* (New York: Melville House, 2010).

21 Willmoore Kendall, "The Function of Intelligence: Review," *World Politics*, vol. 1, no. 4 (July, 1949), p. 549.

22 Kent, *Writing History*, pp. 1, 6.

23 The origin of the term "wicked problem" and the implications the concept has for intelligence is explored at length in David Moore, *Sensemaking: A Structure for an Intelligence Revolution* (Washington: NDIC Press, 2011).

24 Horst Rittel and Melvin Webber, "Dilemmas in a General Theory of Planning," *Policy Sciences*, no. 4, 1973, pp. 155–69.

25 Lippmann, *Public Opinion*, p. 384.

26 Malcolm Gladwell, "Open Secrets," *The New Yorker*, 8 January 2007.

27 The figure is from late 2009. See: http://blogs.law.harvard.edu/idblog/2009/11/20/yandex-on-the-russian-blogosphere/, accessed 15 December 2010.

28 It has been argued that one of the easiest ways to decide the value of information is by the price one has paid to receive it – one reason why clandestine, top-secret information is so much more valued than is open source information.

29 Rittel and Webber, p. 161, original emphasis.

30 There is an astonishing number of websites which track the approaching End of Times. Some examples include www.prophecyupdate.com "Today's headlines – already written in the Bible thousands of years ago!"); www.secretsofsurvival.com ("America has more false gods and false religions than any other nation in Earth's history … is God's wrath imminent?"); www.inthedays.com ("Current news events in the light of Biblical prophecy");and, for an Islamic perspective, www.maqasid.wordpress.com ("Khurasan: Signs of the End of Times").

31 Neil Postman, *Amusing Ourselves to Death: Public Discourse in the Age of Show Business* (New York: Viking, 1985, reissued 2004), p. 12.

32 Available at: http://www.whitehouse.gov/sites/default/files/rss_viewer/national_security_strategy.pdf, accessed 17 December 2010.

33 Steven A. Holmes, "It's Terrible News! And it's Not True!" *New York Times*, 27 July 1997.

34 Lippmann, *Liberty and the News*, pp. 37–38.

35 http://www.gwu.edu/~nsarchiv/NSAEBB/NSAEBB116/index.htm

36 Paul D. Miller, "Lessons for Intelligence Support to Policymaking During Crises," *Studies in Intelligence* 54, no. 2, 2010, p. 8.

37 Josh Kerbel and Anthony Olcott, "Synthesizing with Clients, Not Analyzing for Customers," *Studies in Intelligence*, vol. 54, no. 4, 2010, p. 26.

38 Alfred Rolington, slide deck.

39 Jonathan R. Macey, "A Pox on Both Your Houses: Enron, Sarbanes-Oxley, and the Debate Concerning the Relative Efficacy of Mandatory Versus Enabling Rules," *Washington University Law Quarterly*, vol. 81:329, pp. 330, 349. 330

40 Malcolm Gladwell, *Blink* (New York: Little, Brown, 2005), pp. 27–29.

41 Keefe, *Chatter*, p. 123.

42 Pettee, *American Secret Intelligence*, p. 97.

PART THREE

So what now?

CHAPTER SEVEN

Improving information "food searches"

Somewhere in the late 1980s or early 1990s the discipline of IR (information retrieval) that had been born in the "information explosion" of the 1960s began to fission under the pressure of increased computerization. A part of the field remained focused on what essentially were cataloging and coding problems, trying to devise systems that would improve the ability of a system to find the information that it contained within itself. Another part of the field, however, turned increasingly to the behavior not of the computer or other sorting device, but rather of the human who was trying to use the machine to access information. One of the biggest drivers of this switch of attention, it seems, was the growing ubiquity of online information, which, as has already been discussed, lacks many of the taxonomic features that were so well established for non-online information, which was stored neatly and hierarchically in library catalogs, book indexes and footnotes, encyclopedias, and other well-bounded and well-defined "information arenas." The online environment by contrast was chaotic and unbounded from the beginning, for which reason, perhaps, those writing about it began to use metaphors derived from the natural world, rather than from the world of traditional taxonomies.

One of the earliest of these was a paper called "Orienteering in an Information Landscape: How Information Seekers Get from Here to There."[1] Using the geographic metaphor of people trying to navigate an "information landscape" from a starting point to some desired (or at least acceptable) end point, the authors studied how a group of professionals drawn from various professions ("financial analyst, venture capitalist, product marketing engineer, demographer, management consultant, logistics specialist, research assistant, statistician, merger and acquisition specialist, college finance officer, and sales/planning staff") acquired the information that they considered necessary to do their jobs. One of the things that emerged from this study was that there are three quite distinct types of "search modes":

- *Monitoring*, or following an established topic or set of variables over time;

- *Planned information gathering* using an established process or one suggested by a typical approach to the task;

- *Exploring* a topic in an undirected fashion.

As the researchers note, each of these activities uses information sources in very different ways. In the first case, monitoring, the source is unchanging, and the purpose of accessing it is to check the content for changes since the last time it was accessed. Clearly this is the foundation of the esoteric communications methodology (or propaganda analysis). Somewhat less clearly, it is also very close to the daily activity of most IC analysts, who – just as the intelligence cycle suggests they should – return daily to their in-boxes, to search through the information delivered to them by the collectors and the processors. Vast as that information may be in volume, it nevertheless represents a pre-defined source, just as the much less voluminous Soviet daily newspapers did.

The second activity – following an established search method to learn about a topic – is what usually constitutes "research." This was more true, perhaps, in a pre-digital environment, but it continues to characterize a lot of search activity today, despite the fact that established search methods are of diminishing value as the quantity of available information continues to mushroom. In a pre-digital environment, when most information was held in rigid taxonomies, searches that were conducted in a way that duplicated those taxonomies had a reasonably good chance not only of being confident that the sources they were consulting would be the ones that anyone else conducting the same search would encounter (thus speaking to the researcher's traditional fear of having "missed something") but also of having confidence in how the information sources would be judged by those who used them (so speaking to concerns about "reliability" and "authoritativeness"). This search mode is also common in the IC, where, just as in the earliest days of the OSS R&A, analysts are asked to write what amount to inventories of established physical, political, and (if of people) psychological characteristics of countries, organizations, and persons of interest. One result of this approach is what no doubt is the best-known of the CIA's publications, *The CIA Fact Book*.

For all the virtues of this methodical approach to information acquisition, its potential shortcomings also have become increasingly evident as the sources of potential information have multiplied, especially those which do not fit into established taxonomies or which might arguably fit into several.[2] As many writers have noted, taxonomies impose assumptions upon those who use them; the Dewey Decimal System, for example, assigns all books on "Religion" to the 200 category, of which the sub-categories of 220s through the 280s are assigned to various topics of Christianity, while the 290s are reserved for "Other and Comparative Religions," with "Islam, Babism, and Bahai Faith" all grouped at 297. It is also worth recalling here the study noted in Chapter Five, which found that results of grouping books according to the Library of Congress system, rather than the Dewey system, would result in almost entirely different ordering.[3] Similarly, a study of the *Cumulative Book Index* (CBI – a publishing industry product which catalogs annual book production in the US by subject) conducted by two librarians who followed the general topic "women" through the CBI's annual editions found that, in essence, the entire social history of the twentieth century might be written in the changing categories, sub-categories, and "see also" headers (this last, for example, showed that "single women" was a "see also" for 1961–1975, while "spinster" was a "see also" for 1912–1917, 1928–1952, and 1959–1962).[4]

Clearly this second type of search mode is threatened by the information explosion, because the methodical approach makes it difficult to incorporate new information sources as these become available. This may perhaps be illustrated by the difference between Leonard Fuld's *The New Competitor Intelligence*, published in 1995, and his *The Secret Language of Competitive Intelligence*, published in 2006. Eighty percent of the first book is mostly lists of various resources which a competitive analyst might consult, depending upon the question that is to be answered. Tellingly, virtually none of those addresses or resources is available online, meaning that the analyst would have to have access to a good library. By 2001, it was possible for authors Chris Sherman and Gary Price to publish a book, *The Invisible Web: Uncovering Information Sources Search Engines Can't See*,[5] which provided URLs to several hundred pages worth of similar kinds of resources, but now online. By 2006, the amount of information that is easily available online had grown so vast that Fuld didn't bother to list URLs, and devoted his book instead to discussing various strategies for asking questions which then might point a good analyst toward a resource set.

The third kind of search mode, however, is even more clearly dependent for its outcomes upon how well the researcher understands what resources may be available, and how they might be accessed. The metaphor of "information landscape" and the conflation of information searching with nourishment seeking led to the emergence of several food-based metaphors, which were put forward to help researchers understand the problems of searching. Marcia Bates, a librarian at UCLA, wrote an influential article[6] in which she compared the actions of someone searching for information to that of someone picking berries. Unlike the classic IR model, which depended on the query to return a single "information output set," the berry-picking model was advanced as iterative, cumulative, and self-modifying. Thus (to continue the berry analogy), one might start out with the goal of accumulating enough huckleberries to fill a pie, and so would wander from bush to bush. Huckleberries, however, might be hard to find, or one might be distracted by an abundance of raspberries, and so the task itself might change, in the end achieving a goal that is not the one for which the searcher set out, but which would be as good, and might even be better.

The apparent aptness of the metaphor led other researchers to access a body of work done by field biologists who studied the actual foraging practices of animals. Because food for most creatures is clumpy, with large empty or non-productive spaces in between areas where their food may be found – areas which themselves are of varying degrees of richness – animals were found to engage in a constant struggle to strike the best balance among the factors of: how much nourishment is being gained in one place; how rapidly the resources of that place are being depleted (meaning that it takes more energy expenditure to get the same amount of nourishment); the nourishment gains that might be realized by moving to a new foraging area; and the potential costs of traveling to the new area, including those incurred if the new area must first be discovered. As Peter Pirolli, author of the book *Information Foraging Theory*, put it, "the optimal forager is the one who has the strategies, mechanisms, diets, and so forth, that maximize the calories per unit of effort expended." By analogy then, "the optimal information forager is one who maximizes the value of knowledge gained per unit cost of transaction."[7]

Steps toward optimal foraging[8]

Although the *information=food* metaphor can be taken too far, it does offer some suggestive elements. Part of efficient foraging, for example, is knowing the relative ease with which information may be gained in one domain as compared to another. In more concrete terms, when IC analysts (most of whom have backgrounds in social science) are asked to research a particular industry or company, they commonly conduct the kind of intensive searches via conventional search engines (such as Google) that they would have done for a social-science topic, not realizing the wealth of information available through services such as Dun & Bradstreet, SEC filings, and other required company financial disclosures. Analysts asked to get physical specifications of certain kinds of equipment, processes, or applications may not be aware that a large part of what they are seeking could be available through a patent registry, most of which are now available online. Patrick Keefe, for example, argues that a series of openly available US patents "confirms more or less precisely what we know of the dictionary system" which lies at the heart of the ECHELON system, which is purported to be (but has never been acknowledged as) the complex of systems by which NSA processes its trillions of signal intercepts. Keefe also found NSA patents for ways to detect text messages hidden in color images (steganography), automated file identification protocols, speech identification software, and ways to discern encoded file transmissions– all of which Keefe argues describe core NSA activities.[9]

If *information=food*, then how might an analyst become a better forager? One of the ways in which the analogy does *not* help is that it takes for granted the purpose of searching. Simply to eat and survive is too close to the criticisms which have been leveled against the IC since at least the mid-1960s – that it engages in activities largely to suit its own ends and purposes (discussed at length in Chapter Three). It cannot be stressed enough that *no information foraging process can be efficient if it does not begin with a defined question*. The question may mutate and evolve as the analyst picks his or her berries, but the "nutritional imperative" (if the metaphor is to be maintained) must always be in the form of a question. Indeed, as the authors of the orienteering article write, they found four general reasons why the people in their study continued to research. One reason was simply mechanical: the research plan mandated the next step. The other three reasons, however, arose from the interaction of information and the original question. People continued to research because: they found a change which required explanation; they were missing needed data; and "something interesting arose which prompted exploration."[10]

Assuming then that the analyst has a question, how ought he or she to proceed? Certainly part of increased efficiency assumes knowledge of the search tools available, and how they might best be used. Learning how to construct more productive search terms is time well spent. Google, for example, has a whole series of pages which explain how to limit or bound searches in useful ways, and there are also books such as Tara Calishain and Rael Dornfest's *Google Hacks: 100 Industrial Strength Tips and Tricks*[11] which provide ways to, for example, have Google return only pictures of faces in response to an image search (type &imgtype=face at the end of the results search string), search within a specified date range (insert the search limiter **daterange:** start date-end date[12]), or search for phrases using "wildcards" (for example: "**three * mice**" – * is the wildcard, and Google will return any phrase that starts with "three," ends with "mice" and has one word in between. Two asterisks will give two words, and so on). Other repositories will share some of these features, but will also have search protocols unique to that system. LexisNexis, ProQuest, and the Russian database Integrum, for example, all have very powerful search engines which will serve an analyst well, provided he or she takes the time to learn how to use them.

The fact that these last three (and many others) are available only on a for-pay basis (usually provided through libraries) highlights another important part of the efficient search process. The "orienteering" article, published in 1992, still regarded research as primarily a library-based activity, conducted in concert with, or indeed, solely by, trained librarians. One of the great ironies of the information and digitization explosion is that, even as librarians are increasingly transforming themselves into "information scientists" (with "information science" replacing "library science" in many universities), the ubiquity of individual computers, and the ease of using search engines, has convinced many organizations (and individuals) that librarians (and even libraries) are no longer necessary. This is a huge mistake – librarians are probably the single most important resource any research analyst might employ while trying to "maximize the value of knowledge gained per unit cost of transaction."

There are at least three ways in which librarians can prove of enormous assistance to a research analyst. The first is that librarians are formally trained in the art of how best to ask questions. Normally aspiring librarians must take an entire course devoted to what is usually called "the research interview." This is a structured way to assist a library patron in framing and reframing the original question with which a patron approached the reference desk. The second service that librarians can provide is simply to know about the ever-expanding wealth of online resources, and how these might help a researcher with a specific question. Examples of this have already been noted above – showing someone how to expand company profile searches by using financial disclosure information, or perhaps helping to find university master's or doctoral theses on a topic of interest (theses can be particularly rich sources, because one of the requirements is exhaustiveness of the research).

It may be worth adding here an additional librarian "sub-service" for those who are concerned about the footprint they may be leaving as they search for information. This of course is a concern for many IC analysts, but it can (or should) also be a concern for those engaged in competitive intelligence, investigative journalism, and any other activity which might be compromised by the ability of the system administrators at the target website or data repository to infer interests from a search pattern. Libraries, even if they are part of intelligence organizations and are identified as such, are generally considered to have legitimate purposes when conducting searches, and so are less likely to raise concerns than might the presence of an individual researcher or analyst.

A third service that a librarian might perform is to help the analyst construct a search strategy. Although perhaps related to the "research question," this service engages more closely with the researcher, with the goal of stimulating imaginative approaches to information seeking – to return again to the berry analogy, this seeks to improve the likelihood that an analyst will find rich "berry patches" quickly. One of the fundamental questions that a librarian might ask is "who else might want (or need) this information?" Leonard Fuld gives the example of someone trying to research a competitor's R&D plans. Rather than proceed directly, Fuld urges that the researcher assume various roles, and then try to imagine how the people in those roles might get the information they require. An equipment supplier, for example, would want to know how much equipment and of what type the company was buying; this role might encourage the researcher to look for bid solicitations, buy-sell boards, or requests for quotes (RFQs). If the researcher were to don the hat of someone trying to organize a scientific conference, the focus then would be on scientists or engineers affiliated with the company, who may attend conferences, or even give papers; the analyst might then search for conference write-ups, agendas, and proceedings. Thinking like a recruiter or head-hunter, an analyst might research job listings, help-wanted advertisements, and online ads, thus getting a sense of the areas of the given company's growth, and also how rapidly they might be growing.[13]

A particularly vivid example of how this method might prove useful for intelligence was offered in 2009 by two geographers at UCLA, who as an experiment applied the principles of biogeography – "the study of how plants and animals distribute themselves over space and over time"[14] – to the question of where Osama bin Laden might be living. Using openly available information about bin Laden's physical needs (his height, for example, requiring buildings with tall ceilings) and equally public satellite imagery, the two authors and their class applied the principles of "distance-decay theory, island biogeography theory, life history characteristics, and remote sensing data ... over three spatial scales" to build concentric "probability rings" within which, they hypothesized, bin Laden might be found. As reported by the media,[15] Abbotabad, the town where bin Laden was found to be living, was an area that the geographers' method had assigned at "88.9 percent" chance of being an appropriate location for the terrorist leader's needs.

Security consultant Tom Ryan offered a related but different demonstration of the "who else is interested?" principle in 2009, when he created a fictitious persona, "Robin Sage,"[16] whom he used to build a social network that targeted particularly young men who work in the IT, intelligence, and security fields. Using the various data fields offered by social media, and helped no doubt by the choice of a deliberately attractive young woman's picture to be the face of "Robin Sage" (the photo in fact was taken from a pornography site), Ryan was able to demonstrate how a potential attacker might conceivably penetrate a given organization, or at the very least construct a network of how the various people who "friended" the fictitious

"Robin Sage" were connected to one another, and perhaps even more important, what they were interested in and working on. Although a highly effective demonstration of the potential power of "social engineering" in the social media, as well as another reminder of the cumulative portrait of each of us that may be formed from the "digital exhaust" we all now trail behind us, it should be pointed out that Ryan's experiment probably violated several tenets of the Code of Ethics developed by the Society of Competitive Intelligence (SCIP).[17] Identity representation (and misrepresentation) online is also an area to which law enforcement and legislatures are paying periodic (and often rather confused) attention.[18]

There are other ways of finding who else may be interested in a given question. Google has a function which is specific to groups, allowing a researcher to sift through literally millions of interest-focused discussion forums. The Google interface (groups.google.com) allows a researcher to sort not only by topic, but also by the number of members in a group, the number of postings per month (a measure of activity), and the language. Some of the groups are open for viewing by anyone who accesses them, while others are by invitation only. The open pages can provide such information as (to take just one example) the activities, interests, and concerns of students at the Virtual University of Pakistan (at: http://groups.google.com/group/virtual-university-of-pakistan-2009?lnk=srg, 32,141 members, 3,451 messages per month). Even the latter, however, can be informative, if only because they allow a researcher to find, for example, a discussion group for Ugandans (in-country and in the diaspora) who want to "analyse the political, social, health and economical issues in Uganda" (at: http://groups.google.com/group/ugandans-at-heart?lnk=srg, 7377 members, 5035 messages per month).[19]

Internet search guru Russ Haynal has devised another way that researchers might make their own job easier. Called "upsteam surfing,"[20] the technique allows a researcher to find, first, who links to a site of interest (using the Google command link:http://www.siteofinterest.com – NB: "siteofinterest" means whatever site one is interested in) and then, if he or she finds a site of similar interest among those returns, to see which sites link to both (using the Google command link:http://www.siteofinterest.com link:http://www.secondsiteofinterest.com). Quite often the result is the discovery that someone else has already assembled the URLs of interest for a given question. One of Haynal's examples is to "surf upstream" from the URLs of two world ports, which leads not only to three large portals for shippers (http://www.lumutport.com/weblinks/majorworld.asp, http://www.armadahull.com/shippinglinks.php, and http://www.sinorikex.com/show.php?contentid=22) but also to a vast wiki, maintained by someone named Hans Dekker, which aggregates any information about world shipping that a researcher might want (at: http://crazycustoms.pbworks.com/w/page/16268636/FrontPage).

There are other ways as well to discover who else is interested in a particular subject, with the opportunity to leverage the work that others are doing or have done. Social bookmarking sites (well-known examples, at least as of December 2010, include deli.cio.us and StumbleUpon) allow users to bookmark sites or web pages which they find valuable, useful, or interesting. Unlike traditional taxonomic systems, the social bookmarking services rely upon so-called *folksonomies*, or user-defined metadata tags. The various tags, and the numbers of people who have bookmarked a particular site, are visible to anyone who uses the sites, which allows an interested researcher both to leverage the finds that others have made, and also perhaps to identify unknown experts in a particular domain. There is a similar suite of tagging sites for favored news stories (Digg, Reddit), as well as a system for locating bloggers who are frequently referenced by others (Technorati). Yet another way that the social media can be harnessed for information finding purposes is through the microblogging services (of which Twitter is the best known). One of the most important means that people have for accumulating social capital in the "microblogosphere" is to point others toward articles of shared interest – analysts who locate a group of "tweeters" who share their interests can, by following the tweeters' stream of postings, basically allow these others to do a big part of the information search for them. Although more hit-or-miss, Facebook can also perform this service, provided someone has established an account for a particular arena of interest (see for example the Facebook page for an IBM research team in Haifa, Israel, which offers a number of papers and links; at: http://www.facebook.com/pages/IBM-Research-Haifa/111268028905735).

Social information foraging

As might be deduced from the epistemological model on which the IC was originally based, analytic tasks are generally assigned in a hierarchical, specialized way. Following what is essentially a Frederick Taylor-like model, one analyst will be assigned the task of following one topic or topic cluster. John McLaughlin, former Deputy Director of the CIA, describes how in 1992, new to the job, he was introducing himself to the analysts, and so discovered that among the approximately 800 who were assigned to study Russia was a "canned goods analyst" and a "timber analyst"[21] – both suggestive of the high degree of specialization that the IC favors.

One of the findings of information foraging theorists is the demonstration that the single-forager model is markedly less efficient than is group foraging. The model that Peter Pirolli advances is of a group of researchers with discrete tasks who share a larger common domain – in his book, this is a business intelligence agency whose researchers each had responsibility to cull 600 trade magazines monthly to find material to put in newsletters for clients on a variety of set topics. What Pirolli discovered was that analysts routinely found and forwarded material pertinent to accounts other than their own, a kind of "cooperation which enhanced the individual's search capacity and reduced the risk of missing something relevant to a specialty area that had emerged in a non-specialty publication."[22] The general driver of this behavior, Pirolli asserts, was the recognition that such sharing enhances the social capital of the one who shares, which in turn can create a virtuous circle of "social capital competition," as each member becomes increasingly conscious of the benefits of sharing (which include that he or she will also gain better information in the process). Alfred Rolington, long-time head of Jane's Information Group, noted another benefit of this group approach to information when he described how he discovered that the only people in his company who had an overview of total production were the bookkeepers, who were responsible for paying Jane's freelance authors for their various articles. It was only they who were in a position to see when otherwise non-communicating groups or individuals were working on identical or related topics. This is consistent with another of Pirolli's findings, which is that, while any group foraging is likely to be more efficient than single-researcher foraging, some group foraging is more efficient than others. A particular danger, Pirolli discovered, is a group which is too tightly bound, so that everyone in it looks at essentially the same sources. Using network analysis, Pirolli found that groups tend to clump together, so that a graph of relationships will form many clusters, spaced by what Pirolli called "structural holes." The network members who are most likely to draw the greatest benefit from group information foraging, Pirolli found, are those who serve as bridges to two or more groups. Such people serve as "information brokers," benefiting not only from the information they are able to access from their multiple groups, but also from their enhanced social capital acquired by bridging the "structural holes." As explained by a quote Pirolli offers in his book:

> Given greater homogeneity within than between groups, people whose networks bridge the structural holes between groups have earlier access to a broader range diversity of information and have experience in translating information across groups. This is the social capital of brokerage.[23]

It is for this reason that IBM, for example, has invested large resources in trying to make it easier for people to become conscious of their network groups, and to reach out beyond them. IBM has developed, studied, and deployed such internal tools as *Fringe*, a so-called "people-tagging" service,[24] *Answers*, an internal Q&A board which not only connects people who have and who need information, but also ranks them according to how often and how accurately they participate,[25] and *SaNDVis*, a tool which "uses writings, meetings attended, personal profile information and previous work experience to map these connections with lines showing who is closest to whom," thus creating a "web of relationships around a search term to reveal who within IBM has expertise on a topic"[26] – all with the goal of making it easier for IBM's globally distributed workforce to be aware of one another and of the capabilities of the organization as a whole. In contrast, a 2010 study suggested that the single-searcher model may cost US government agencies as much as a month of lost time every year (at a cost estimate of $15 billion), searching for information that the various systems with which they are working already possess.[27] Several causes for this inefficiency are cited – bad cataloging, poor standardization, inadequate training – but not considered is whether performance might improve if "information foraging" were made more social.

ICD 205 – mandated outreach

Although the study above was of the government as a whole, rather than just the IC, the findings are consistent with a tension that has grown steadily since 9/11. There is wide agreement in the many studies, commissions, and reports that have been done about the IC's performance that the single-analyst model must change, and that analysts must share information. A number of well-publicized initiatives have begun to facilitate that sharing, including *Intellipedia*, a Wikipedia-type wiki which operates at three levels of classification,[28] and *A-Space*, a Facebook-like social networking site that is designed to foster information sharing and online collaboration.[29] Similar efforts are underway in other organizations. The Department of Defense has created the *Horizontal Fusion* suite of tools, including NORA (Non-Obvious Relationship Awareness), Project Garnet (a secure collaborative workspace for NSA analysts), and Tearline Reporting (a platform which permits excision of classified portions so that material can be shared as widely as possible).[30] The State Department also has a wiki-based information sharing platform, called *Diplopedia*,[31] and the FBI has *Bureaupedia* (although the announced purpose of this space is not so much to share information as it is to try to capture the knowledge and expertise of veteran agents before they retire).[32]

One of the problems with the internal wiki approach, as Pirolli's research indicated, is that social information foraging favors demographic diversity. Closely affiliated groups tend to lack or have trouble developing the information brokers that enrich an overall system. One of the criticisms most frequently aimed at the IC is that it is precisely the kind of closed environment which tends to recycle the same information, viewpoints, and practices. As early as 1976 the Church Committee report had observed:

"The CIA is thought by many observers to be technologically one of the most innovative research centers in the country, and it allocates considerable funds to continue the search for new technology ... [but] the intelligence community still expends relatively little effort on R&D in the analytic field." The primary reason for this, according to the report, is "the secrecy that surrounds the work of the intelligence community as a whole," which creates an "insulation [which] is recognized to have had a detrimental effect on the quality of analysis."[33]

Perhaps the most concerted effort to address that insularity has been Intelligence Community Directive 205 (ICD 205),[34] released in 2008. Stating that the overt purpose of the directive is to *require* analysts to "leverage outside expertise as part of their work," the ICD notes that in order "to explore ideas and alternate perspectives, gain new insights, generate new knowledge, or obtain new information" analysts must "network in the U.S. and internationally to develop trusted relationships ... [which] could include, as appropriate, experts in academia; think tanks; industry; nongovernmental organizations; the scientific world ... state, local, and tribal governments; other non-Intelligence Community U.S. government agencies; and elsewhere."

As admirable as the goal appears, implementation has proven difficult, for reasons about which the ICD itself warns. The entire fifth section of the ICD is concerned with potential security problems[35] which might arise from attempting to reach beyond the IC, including that analysts "shall never discuss classified or sensitive information with outside experts who are not appropriately cleared. This prohibition includes intelligence sources and methods; military and operational information; gaps in IC collection capabilities; or insights, assessments or judgments derived from sensitive intelligence collection. Discretion will be exercised regarding foreign policy and other political sensitivities and, when the degree of latitude allowed is uncertain, analysts should consult their immediate supervisors."

A study conducted by the Center for Strategic and International Studies (which, to be fair, was attempting to sell the virtues of an open source collection system of its own devise) charged that these security concerns, as well as a community-wide failure to commit funds in support of outreach, have resulted in a situation in which "only a few analysts" are able to enjoy "systematic, formalized, and sustained access to tailored groups of US and foreign non-governmental experts." Most IC analysts, that report charges, are deprived of "critical subject matter expertise residing outside the IC that could fill intelligence gaps and improve analysis." The CSIS report concludes that "for many parts of the IC, analytic outreach remains too burdensome to be practical," so that "the resulting lack of outreach leaves analysts with a smaller, less diverse peer group," which "limits analyst creativity and constrains the generation and consideration of alternative ideas."[36]

Essentially the same criticism was leveled by Kenneth Lieberthal, a China expert at the Brookings Institution, who argued in a 2009 paper that IC analysis of China is fundamentally flawed because "few analysts in the IC who work on China have spent much time there interacting with Chinese," so that there is little of what he calls "finger feel" for nuances of Chinese behavior or utterance. Lieberthal, like the authors of the CSIS report, cites security concerns as being the major reason that the IC prefers to hire people with as little in-country experience as possible: "The types of people who get outside of the highly structured [study] programs that attract many foreign students and immerse themselves in Chinese society off the beaten track typically are those who develop the keenest understanding of the country, its aspirations, and the ways people think and operate there. Those are precisely the people whose experiences in China are most likely to disqualify them from working as analysts in the IC on China," with the result that "to the IC analyst China – even as it has opened up to an unprecedented extent – is overwhelmingly a place that exists on paper but not one that provides personal experiences that generate real insights." Even worse, Lieberthal argues, "Security concerns have also sharply reduced the ability of most IC analysts to benefit from interaction with the non-IC academic, think tank, NGO, and business communities. CIA analysts must now, for example, as a matter of policy receive specific clearance to attend any event at a downtown Washington, D.C. think tank."[37]

Richard Russell, a 17-year veteran of the CIA's analytic corps who later became an academic, has argued that the problem lies even deeper than just security concerns, and instead reflects a general discomfort with and contempt for information that comes from outside of the IC itself. Devoting an entire chapter of his book, *Sharpening Strategic Intelligence*, to what he calls "analysts who are not experts, " Russell charges that current IC work practices "place a premium on analysts who are generalists and can write well and quickly meet tight deadlines," while disadvantaging the careers of "analysts who would prefer to specialize and work on 'slower' … issues for longer periods of time." Many analysts, and most managers, Russell charges, do not have advanced degrees and often do not have degrees of any sort in the areas of their responsibility. Analysts are discouraged from reading scholarly or professional material about their areas of responsibility, and, Russell charges, security concerns make it virtually impossible for people who have travelled extensively in areas of interest then to enter the IC, because it is safer to have analysts who "have little to no travel experience." This compounds the problems which arise because "management gives no time, resources, or attention to having analysts read or study the publicly available scholarship on the countries or topics they are responsible for before assuming their analytic responsibilities on an account."[38]

Whatever the justice of their charges, critics of the IC's efforts at outreach should in fairness also note that the reluctance to engage often goes both ways. In part because of IC abuses of academic relationships in the past, and in part because of genuine concerns about how to keep academic interests and "taskings" clearly separate, academics too are often reluctant to engage with the IC. The American Anthropological Association has been particularly militant in trying to keep its members from contact with the IC. There is also considerable controversy about the so-called Pat Roberts Intelligence Scholars Program, which funds the study of about 100 graduate students – the identities of whom are not revealed to their professors. [39] In part to address this problem, an effort was made to create a web-based platform that would facilitate virtual analytic outreach without incurring the many problems of trying to do so physically. Called BRIDGE, the effort was focused on an unclassified, password-protected website that had most of the social networking features that users now expect. [40] Although BRIDGE was enthusiastically received by some members of the IC and also by some outside it, [41] the program was dropped after about a year of existence, for reasons that were never made public. The cancellation coincided with the dropping of another platform which some analysts had begun to use to make outreach easier – the *ugov.gov* email service, which did not flag IC users as flagrantly as do the agency-specific email addresses – which in concert seemed to signal to analysts that "outreach is over." [42] Even the adoption of Intellipedia and A-Space is widely perceived to have stalled, with little hope for greater uptake beyond the group of "early adopters and enthusiasts" [43] who had immediately embraced it.

Collection and outreach confused

Gregory Treverton has made a persuasive argument that the impediments to outreach are inherent in the institutions of the IC, rather than in faint-heartedness, ill-will, or other sins of which critics complain. In a study of the outreach efforts of several US and foreign intelligence agencies, Treverton notes that "reaching outside fellow intelligence services is something of an unnatural act," in large part because "too often the [information] flow is only in one direction, with intelligence officers listening but not talking," thus making "government-sponsored seminars or workshops seem mere collection opportunities, with outsiders giving and officials receiving." [44] As Treverton notes, "the mind-set of collection is hard for organizations to shake." [45] The only US intelligence unit which is entirely analytic (as opposed to combining collection and analysis) is the State Department's Bureau of Intelligence and Research, which therefore "finds outreach a less unnatural act." The "collection mindset," Treverton argues, tends to have a "short-term, slightly predatory perspective," [46] which makes information sharing almost impossible.

In another study of the IC's analytic culture and capabilities Treverton made the even stronger point, that a variety of circumstances have more or less driven the IC out of the analysis business entirely, so that the "vast majority of what all those analysts do is current and tactical, more question answering than producing deep understanding of critical issues." The question that the IC faces, he argues, is "whether the analytic community is in the information business or the secrets business."[47] By his description (and that of others), the IC has tended to circle around the provision of secrets as the one unique thing it has to offer the President, while "analysis" – a term which usually is used to imply longer-term contextual or explanatory work – is of less interest to the policymakers. Treverton also repeats a theme raised by Russell, that the IC simply does not have (and does not have the means or desire to develop) the skills and knowledge which lead to deep analytic expertise. In Treverton's words: "World-class work of this sort does not occur inside the Intelligence Community."[48] That being the case, it is not surprising that IC managers and analysts alike continue to cluster around fast-turnaround questions that may be given the kind of short, concise answer that fits easily into a format like the President's Daily Brief (PDB). In that kind of work environment, "collection" remains a core function, while – as Treverton notes – "outreach" seems superfluous, "something additional, not a fundamental part of the job."[49]

The 2008 Open Source Innovation Challenge

A good illustration of the problems confronting better use of open source information in the IC was the Director of National Intelligence (DNI)'s Open Source Innovation Challenge, offered as part of the 2008 Open Source Conference, held in Washington DC. Advertised as a "unique occasion for representatives from academia; think tanks; industry; the media; federal, state, local, and tribal government; and other diverse sectors to use open source information to address real intelligence challenges," the contest was supposed to "provide illuminating information" and also "provide creative ideas or employ new ways of researching and analyzing current issues" using only open sources.[50]

Just as had been the case in the 1995 Burundi experiment (described in Chapter Four), the 2008 Challenge asked what essentially were collection questions, not insight questions, and also replicated the quick-turnaround, short-answer format by requiring that answers be no more than three pages long, and that they be produced within the span of a week. Contestants, who had to be registered participants in the conference, could choose to address one of the two questions posed:

1 Using the best open sources to inform your answer, is Al Qaeda a cohesive organization with strong and centralized control, intent and direction?

2 According to open sources, who will be the global leader in alternative fuels and why?

It is clear that both of the questions could have been improved upon. The first raises a persistent IC concern (indeed, almost paranoia) with the use of the term "best open sources" (as measured how?), and then begs what can only be a "yes or no" answer, excluding the possibility of an answer that, for example, Al Qaeda might be found to be a cohesive organization *without* centralized control. The second question is even more problematic, since, as written, it is entirely a bibliographic question, not asking who might become the global leader, but rather who does a group of sources say will become the leader – plainly the intellectual construct behind the phrasing is from a collection environment, not an analytic one. Even granting that the question is clumsily worded, and intends in fact to ask not about sources but instead about the subject of alternative fuels, the phrase still reveals a great deal about how questions are asked in the IC. Just as Willmoore Kendall had remarked in his review of Sherman Kent's book in 1949, this type of question begs "absolute prediction," rather than "contingent prediction," thus suggesting that there can only be one immutable answer to the question, rather than a range of possible outcomes, dependent upon inputs, circumstances, and other events.[51] The question is unbounded in time, and lacks important qualifying information – "global leader" in what terms? Research funded? Output? Sales? Percentage of alternative fuel used versus overall usage?

What most reveals the "collection mindset" behind the questions, however, is that neither question has a policy dimension – contributors are asked simply to offer what in reality is an opinion, but which will be presented as if it were an immutable fact. What might be done with the information, or what purpose the questions might serve, simply fall outside the scope of the innovation challenge.

Although the winners were announced at the 2008 gathering, there does not appear to be an available write-up of the contest, nor of any lessons which may have been learned. Indeed, there does not seem even to be a list of entries or winners. The only information that can be discovered by an open search is supplied by a couple of independent bloggers, and also a monthly newsletter put out by a Japanese think tank, published in Switzerland. The latter[52] describes the Open Source Conference and the nature of the challenge, promising a fuller write up of the results of the challenge "in the next issue," but does not appear to have done so. The only publicly available notice of the winners appears to be that offered by a blogger at Mercyhurst College, in an entry[53] which celebrated that college team's victory, and also noted that "the other winning entry" came from iJet Intelligent Risk Systems,[54] although without making clear whether both winners answered the same question, or whether each question had one winner.

In any event, the Mercyhurst entry was in response to the Al Qaeda question, and deployed many of the imaginative, "new media" collaborative possibilities that the IC claims it is seeking to incorporate[55] (in this regard recalling the UCLA biogeography search for bin Laden, described above, as well as the Cornell business school class which studied Enron, mentioned in Chapter Six). The college took a "crowdsource" approach to the question, setting up a wiki-style information aggregation site and widely publicizing its existence through a network of bloggers who work on intelligence questions in the open arena. The call drew responses from several organizations in the US, and also from students of security in Switzerland and England. In addition to traditional information resources, the team also used deep web search engines, and then used online software to run their hypotheses through an ACH (Alternative Competing Hypotheses) framework and also to visualize their data. Their presentation was further enriched by use of an embedded video – resulting in a rich, informative, and tightly argued final product.[56]

As noted, although the Mercyhurst entry has obvious virtues, there is no available explanation of why this was chosen over the other entrants (of which there was a total of 24, according to another blogger[57]), nor is there any explanation of how (or whether) this entry satisfied the original terms of the contest, by providing "creative ideas." The closest thing available to an official (or corporate) response is that given by the anonymous blogger who writes the blog "Kent's Imperative" (at: http://kentsimperative. blogspot.com/, begun in 2006 and apparently inactive since October 2008). Although that blog does not explain who the author is, evidence and voice suggests he (or she) is an experienced CIA analyst who desires to preserve the methodological legacy of Sherman Kent. If that is indeed the case, the blogger's response to the Mercyhurst effort is revealing:

> The most critical issue that we see in crowdsourced OSINT strategies is the problem of denial and deception. **One of the enduring tenants [sic] of OSINT tradecraft is that the sources consulted ought not ever know the use to which the information will be put** [emphasis added]. The divorcing of content from use context goes a long way towards reducing the problems created by sources which may attempt to influence rather than inform (at least in terms of deliberate active messaging tailored for IC audiences)… Crowdsourcing seems particularly vulnerable to denial and deception given that it relies on explicit calls for participation… the publication of the specific indicators sought by the project coordinators essentially provides a roadmap for potentially successful deception themes and associated messaging, as well as the essential elements of information to be protected by adversary operations security and other denial measures. While source validation measures may provide some defense against such deception, it is unlikely to defeat a well-crafted

campaign executed through appropriate cover organizations and other agents of influence.

This blogger's response is an eloquent statement of the distrust with which most IC analysts tend to regard information, particularly if it is freely supplied (as it might be in the kind of intellectual exchange envisioned by ICD 205). The blogger's confidence that material which is collected without the source being aware of the purpose to which the information will be put is unchanged from the convictions of the IC's collectors in Iran in 1978, that information about the clerics was unimportant – or, worse, might be an attempt to deploy a "well-crafted campaign" for "successful deception themes."

We don't need help to be deceived – we can do that ourselves

The IC's continuing fear of "D&D," or "denial and deception," seems particularly odd given the fact that most of the entries on the IC "intelligence failure" list[58] could be viewed as the product of the IC's decision to trust its own information, and its interpretation of that information, above other inputs or interpretations. Although the various authors of the many books that constitute the ever-growing library on intelligence and analytic reform vary in their explanations for those failures – or lapses, to use Treverton's more generous term – none of them seem to question whether the fundamental assumptions of the process may not be at fault. As a fear of D&D suggests, the IC has a fundamental belief in the existence of "true facts." Indeed, as yet another book on intelligence reform puts it, "a typical goal of intelligence is to establish facts and then to develop precise, reliable, and valid inferences … for use in strategic decision making or operational planning."[59] The problem, however – as even that book acknowledges – is that most "facts" are situational and contextual. Even something as intuitively "objective" and "immutable" as the temperature of an object is changed by the act of measuring it.[60] Just as Leonard Fuld argued that there is no one "factual" approach for understanding what a competitor is planning, so is there no one "factual" interpretation for an intelligence issue. As David Moore points out in his *Sensemaking: A Structure for an Intelligence Revolution*, a "steer is a steak to a rancher, a sacred object to a Hindu, and a collection of genes and proteins to a molecular biologist."[61]

As has been argued repeatedly in this book, the IC was established with the assumption that information was difficult to find, but – once it was – it would be unambiguous and absolute. By viewing the analyst, as Kent did, to be the one whose job it is to call the attention of policymakers "to the stubborn fact they may neglect,"[62] the IC has in effect (to return to the foraging metaphor) become like the panda, an animal over-specialized in one particular kind of food.

As Chapter Three has already demonstrated, the assumption of scarcity was already proving itself false within a decade of the founding of the CIA (if indeed it had ever been true), and by now, as Chapter Five has shown, is clearly absurd. Nevertheless, somewhat like the Vikings in Greenland whom author Jared Diamond describes in his book *Collapse* as starving to death despite an abundance of fish,[63] the IC continues more or less steadfast in its belief that the only valuable "information nutrition" lies in the secrets which it has acquired itself. The distrust of the kind of wide-flung "information foraging" that the Mercyhurst College team demonstrated in its Innovation Challenge submission substantiates Russell's charge that the IC has come to view the *process* of intelligence to be an end in itself, rather than judge it by the utility of what that process may result in.[64]

Notes

1 Vicki O'Day and Robin Jeffries, "Orienteering in an Information Landscape: How Information Seekers Get From Here to There," Hewlett-Packard Lab Reports, HPL-92-127 (R.1), September 1992.

2 It is impossible to write about taxonomies without citing the Jorge Borges short story "The Analytical Language of John Wilkins," which invents: "a certain Chinese encyclopedia entitled 'Celestial Empire of Benevolent Knowledge'" in which "the animals are divided into: (a) belonging to the emperor, (b) embalmed, (c) tame, (d) sucking pigs, (e) sirens, (f) fabulous, (g) stray dogs, (h) included in the present classification, (i) frenzied, (j) innumerable, (k) drawn with a very fine camelhair brush, (l) et cetera, (m) having just broken the water pitcher, (n) that from a long way off look like flies." The story is available at: http://www.alamut.com/subj/artiface/language/johnWilkins.html. The Adobe Bookshop in San Francisco has experimented with another taxonomic approach for its used books, grouping them by the color of their covers. For results see: http://www.npr.org/templates/story/story. php?storyId=4182224, accessed 2 June 2011.

3 Hammond, *et al.*, "Intelligence Organizations and the Organization of Intelligence."

4 Carole L. Palmer and Cheryl Knott Malone, "Elaborate Isolation: Metastructures of Knowledge about Women," *The Information Society*, vol. 17, 2001, p. 187.

5 Chris Sherman and Gary Price, *The Invisible Web: Uncovering Information Sources Search Engines Can't See* (Medford, NJ: Cyber-Age Books, 2001).

6 Marcia Bates, "The Design of Browsing and Berrypicking Techniques for the

Online Search Interface," *Online Information Review*, vol. 13, no. 5, 1989, pp. 407–424.

7   Peter Pirolli, *Information Foraging Theory: Adaptive Interaction with Information* (New York: Oxford University Press, 2007), p. 15.

8   One of the difficulties of this chapter is that the available resources change so fast that any examples offered here are likely to be outdated or displaced by the time the book appears. Thus examples should be considered more as strategic suggestions than as prescriptions to be followed.

9   Keefe, *Chatter*, pp. 121–23.

10 O'Day and Jeffries, p. 6.

11 Tara Calishain and Rael Dornfest's *Google Hacks: 100 Industrial Strength Tips and Tricks* (Santa Rosa, CA: O'Reilly Media, 2003).

12 The dates however must be expressed in Julian form, which computers can use because that calendar counts the number of days since God created the Universe – which, on 1 April 2011, is 2455652.5. Gregorian-to-Julian converters are available online, e.g. http://www.csgnetwork.com/juliangregcalconv.html or: http://www.fourmilab.ch/documents/calendar/

13 Fuld, *New Competitor Intelligence*, p. 50.

14 Thomas W. Gillespie and John A. Agnew, "Finding Osama bin Laden: An Application of Biogeographic Theories and Satellite Imagery," *MIT International Review*, 17 February 2009, at: http://web.mit.edu/mitir/2009/online/finding-bin-laden.pdf, accessed 12 May 2011.

15 See: http://news.sciencemag.org/scienceinsider/2011/05/geographers-had-calculated.html?ref=hp, accessed 12 May 2011.

16 Tom Ryan, "Getting in Bed with Robin Sage," Black Hat Briefings and Training, at: http://media.blackhat.com/bh-us-10/whitepapers/Ryan/BlackHat-USA-2010-Ryan-Getting-In-Bed-With-Robin-Sage-v1.0.pdf, accessed 4 June 2011.

17 See: http://www.scip.org/publications/ProductDetail.cfm?Itemnumber=1209 and also: http://www.scip.org/content.cfm?itemnumber=2654&navItemNumber=2660.

18 California, for example, has made it a misdemeanor to "credibly impersonate" someone online (see: http://arstechnica.com/tech-policy/news/2010/09/california-outlaws-using-a-fake-identity-online-in-some-cases.ars). Use of false identity is violation of Facebook's terms of service, and, if discovered, will result in the user's page being blocked. After the Arab Spring of 2011, this has become controversial, as it has made it more difficult, even dangerous, for activists to use the Facebook platform. See for example: http://www.helium.com/items/2094886-facebook-fake-identity-policy-under-microscope and: http://news.cnet.com/8301-13577_3-20034879-36.html.

19 These URLs changed between the writing of the text and the editing, and the Pakistan university site now appears to be closed. This is a reminder that the internet changes constantly – and also a reminder that, if you find something of value to you on the internet, *print it!* It may well not be there the next time you look for it.

20 http://navigators.com/search_upstream.html, accessed 30 December 2010.

21 John McLaughlin, "Remarks," in *Watching the Bear*, p. 244. The "800 analysts" figure is a rough guess, based upon Rae Huffstutler's comment in the same volume that in the 1980s there were "over 1600 analysts in CIA's Directorate of Intelligence alone, half of them working on Soviet issues" (p. 15).

22 Pirolli, p. 150.

23 Pirolli, p. 155.

24 Stephen Farrell and Tessa Lau, "Fringe Contacts: People-Tagging for the Enterprise," IBM Research Report, RJ10384 (AO606-027), 20 June 2006.

25 http://infostory.wordpress.com/2010/10/07/the-future-of-the-social-network-according-to-ibm/, accessed 31 December 2010.

26 Noam Cohen, "Computers Help Social Animals to See Beyond Their Tribes," *New York Times*, 19 December 2010.

27 http://ohmygov.com/blogs/general_news/archive/2010/10/20/New-study-finds-government-workers-terribly-inefficient-at-searching.aspx, accessed 31 December 2010.

28 Massimo Calabresi, "Wikipedia for Spies: The CIA Discovers Web 2.0," *Time*, 8 April 2009.

29 Ben Bain, "A-Space Set to Launch This Month," *Federal Computer Week*, 3 September 2008.

30 These and others are described at: http://horizontalfusion.dtic.mil/initiatives/page2.html, accessed 2 January 2010.

31 See: http://gcn.com/articles/2010/12/07/state-department-diplopedia.aspx, accessed 2 January 2010.

32 Ben Bain, "FBI Creates Knowledge Wiki," *Federal Computer Week*, 26 September 2008.

33 Church Committee, p. 273.

34 Text available at: http://www.dni.gov/electronic_reading_room/ICD_205.pdf, accessed 2 January 2010.

35 For a much fuller exploration of why the interests of security and of analytic outreach are fundamentally at odds, see Anthony Olcott, "The Challenges of Clashing IC Interests," *International Journal of Intelligence and Counterintelligence*, vol. 23, no. 4, 2010.

36 Arnaud de Borchgrave, Thomas Sanderson and David Gordon, *The Power of Outreach: Leveraging Expertise on Threats in Southeast Asia*, CSIS Report, April 2009, pp. 3–4.

37 Kenneth Lieberthal, *The US Intelligence Community and Foreign Policy: Getting Analysis Right*, Brookings Institution, September 2009, pp. 27, 33–34.

38 Richard Russell, *Sharpening Strategic Intelligence* (New York: Cambridge University Press, 2007), pp. 119–48.

39 David E. Kaplan, "Hey, Let's Play Ball," *US News and World Report*, 29 October 2006.

40 A slideshow explanation of BRIDGE, from a presentation given in July 2009, is available at: http://1105govinfoevents.com/OGI/OGIPresentations/OGI09_3-4_Doney_BRIDGE.pdf, accessed 3 January 2010. A description, and an interview with IC BRIDGE "sponsor" Don Doney, is available at: http://radar.oreilly.com/2009/04/building-bridges-with-the-us-i.html, accessed 3 January 2010.

41 In addition to the blog above, see also: http://bobgourley.sys-con.com/node/1095702/mobile, accessed 3 January 2010.

42 Marc Ambinder, "Shutdown of Intelligence Community E-mail Network Sparks E-Rebellion," *The Atlantic*, 6 October 2009.

43 Joab Jackson, "Intellipedia Suffers Mid-Life Crisis," *Government Computer News*, 18 February 2009.

44 Gregory Treverton, *Approaches to 'Outreach' for Intelligence*, Center for Asymmetric Threat Studies Report, December 2008, p. 6.

45 Treverton, pp. 6–7.

46 Treverton, p. 15.

47 Gregory Treverton and Bryan Gabbard, *Assessing the Tradecraft of Intelligence Analysis*, Rand Technical Report, 2008, p. 46.

48 Treverton and Gabbard, *Tradecraft*, p. 16.

49 Treverton and Gabbard, *Tradecraft*, p. 6.

50 See: http://www.dniopensource.org/Challenge/Guidelines.aspx, accessed 4 January 2011.

51 Moore, *Sensemaking*, p. 549.

52 Masaaki Kikuchi, "Open Source Conference Organized by the US Government," *IISIA Monthly Report*, October 2008.

53 See: http://sourcesandmethods.blogspot.com/2008/09/we-all-of-us-won-dni-open-source.html, accessed 4 January 2011.

54 Confirmed with a one-line entry on the company's website. See: http://www.ijet.com/news/awards/index.asp, accessed 4 January 2011. This page has been removed.

55 See for example the DNI's publication *Vision 2015: A Globally Networked and Integrated Intelligence Enterprise*, available at: http://dni.gov/Vision_2015.pdf, accessed 4 January 2011.

56 The Mercyhurst entry may be seen at: http://sourcesandmethods.blogspot.com/2008/09/and-winner-is-dni-open-source.html, accessed 4 January 2011.

57 See: http://kentsimperative.blogspot.com/search?q=Open+Source+Innovation+Challenge, accessed 4 January 2011.

58 For a representative list of "failures," see Treverton and Gabbard, *Tradecraft*, p. 10.

59 Robert M. Clark, *Intelligence Analysis: A Target-Centric Approach* (Washington DC: Congressional Quarterly, 2007), p. 9.

60 Clark, p. 236.

61 Moore, *Sensemaking*, p. xvii.

62 Kent, *Strategic Intelligence*, p. 182.

63 Jared Diamond, *Collapse: How Societies Choose to Fail or Succeed* (New York: Viking Books, 2005).

64 Russell, p. 142.

CHAPTER EIGHT

Narratives of persuasion and the battle for attention

As was explained in Chapter Four, the esoteric communication methodology (also known as propaganda analysis and, somewhat later, and more misleadingly, called media analysis) springs from the "transmission model" school of communication theories. It is not surprising, given how many of the early theorists were refugees from a Europe which in the space of two decades had been seized by no fewer than three totalitarian social orders (Bolshevism, Nazism, and Fascism), that the members of the Rockefeller Foundation's Communication Group would take for granted that a message sent would have a strong and lasting effect on the recipient. Harold Lasswell, one of the leaders of that group, throughout his career saw media information to be a "stimulus-response" phenomenon, in which a message sent would have a predictable and repeatable effect – one reason why, as he wrote, "Democracy has proclaimed the dictatorship of palaver, and the technique of dictating to the dictator is named propaganda."[1]

It was also Lasswell who is credited with having declared that "the job of research in mass communications is to determine who, and with what intentions, said what, to whom, and with what effects."[2] Later that dictum was modified to become what is now called the "Lasswell formula," which defines an act of communication as having five parts:[3]

Who → Says What → In Which Channel →
To Whom → With What Effect

Although research (based on American voting behavior) was demonstrating as early as the mid-1950s that the "hypodermic needle" theory is not in fact correct – most people appeared more likely to be influenced by the behavior and views of those around them than they were directly by the media[4] – Lasswell's theory remained the foundation on which open source intelligence analysis was built. Because policymakers were interested in the thoughts and intentions of hostile foreign leaders, open source collectors monitored the available media to see how the shape of leader messaging changed (or didn't change) over time, which they used as the best-available surrogate for interpreting those otherwise unavailable thoughts and intentions.

Even as transmission models take for granted that a message sent will have a predictable effect, however, they overlook another dimension of communication, which is that there is nothing in this model which requires the audience to whom a message is addressed actually to pay that message any attention. The obvious importance of the role played by the audience led other groups of researchers and communications scholars to study the behavior not of message senders, but rather of the would-be recipients: the audience. Their work is grouped together as the "uses and gratifications" (U&G) theory of communication, which studies (in the words of one scholar) "the gratifications that attract and hold audiences to the kinds of media and the types of content that satisfy their social and psychological need."[5] What U&G approaches argue, in other words, is that audiences have at least as great an impact on message senders as the message senders do upon them. People access – or fail to access – media because they see the content provided by the media as meeting certain specific needs. Those needs are defined slightly differently by various theorists, but the conclusion is the same – that a message sender whose message fails to entertain, educate, or engage a particular audience is unlikely to have the target audience even notice the message, let alone be affected by it.

Although the experience both of the fall of the Shah in Iran and of the collapse of the USSR suggested the salience that a U&G approach might have had for open source intelligence analysis (since in both instances significant numbers of people were choosing media and media content other than that created and sent by the central authorities), the IC has been reluctant to incorporate the dimension of audience into open source collection processes. There are a number of reasons for this reluctance, but in fairness, until the very recent past, many of them were simply technical – as has already been explained, until the twenty-first century, the cost of creating and disseminating information was so large, relative to the cost of receiving it, that only messages sent by powerful actors and elites were in media that could be readily accessed. Indeed, this was one of the objections most often raised to U&G theory in general, that, while it may be true that end-users might prefer one type of medium to another, the overall choice spectrum was so narrow that the whole of it could be effectively controlled by the elite. Even when people went to great lengths to try to express other points of view – as was the case, for example, with the Ayatollah Khomeini's cassette tapes or the many hand-typed carbon copies of Soviet-era *samizdat* literature – those hard-to-access alternate media were generally responding to or arguing with the dominant message. Thus, for most of the twentieth century, even if the reality was that many parts of an audience might prefer other content, technological infrastructures were such that it was the powerful elites who controlled, or at least appeared to control, the flow of information in society.

Lasswell rebooted

As Chapter Five has already shown, however, the era of "mass media" has passed. Although the overall volume of information available has grown logarithmically, the share of "mass audience" that any one channel or medium enjoys has shrunk dramatically. This does not mean that media no longer have influence, but rather that the sizes of the audiences which they do influence are smaller and – more importantly – can be quite disparate one from another.

Hierarchical structures in general – among which must be numbered governments and the intelligence communities which serve them – have had difficulty imagining how to navigate this new environment. The reason is easy to understand – the information environment of old was, as has been explained, a top-down authority structure, in which information buttressed authority, and authority gave information its power. As part of that authority structure, it is only to be expected that open source intelligence analysts would look to the corresponding authorities in other countries, and the channels which they use to address their peoples. That tendency is also reinforced by the legacy message-senders themselves, who have difficulty understanding that they have lost their previous prominence – even if their circulation figures and financial positions argue strongly that that is the case.[6] Probably the biggest challenge, however, is simply deciding where best to pay attention in the ever-more cacophonous bazaar of would-be message senders now competing for the attention of the world, and of one another.

Curiously enough, the Lasswell formula can actually prove to be a useful tool for making those decisions. Although enormously complex, this new media environment in fact provides far greater opportunities to exploit "verbal intelligence" (David Kahn's term) than has ever been true before. Although there are probably other tools which can help to unlock this environment, Lasswell proves to be strikingly useful, in spite of having been derived from a quite different information environment than exists today. As has been stressed before – but, based on continued current IC practice, seems cannot be stated too often – efficient use of the Lasswell formula, or indeed any intelligence methodology, requires starting with an explicit question. In traditional open source intelligence analysis, the usual question, explicitly or, more often, implicitly, was "what are the leaders saying?" The media environment, of course, continues to make it possible to answer that question, since leaders and other official organs continue to issue press releases, hold news conferences, be written about in major newspapers, and appear on TV (especially if they own the stations). What has changed in the new environment, however, is that it is now also possible to ask what other parts of a given society might be saying as well. To some extent this means simply that the web allows us to view lower-level authority structures which earlier would have required physical presence "on the spot" for that type of information to be accessible. Now, though, the web can offer, for example:

- the platforms and appeals of the top 25 political parties in India;[7]

- the daily doings of the akim (or governor equivalent) of the Kazakhstan province of Zhambyl;[8]

- or the schedule that the city works department of Narvik, Norway, will be following in replacement of water mains in certain neighborhoods in Europe's northernmost city (which warns politely that "subscribers will be able to be without water for short periods," according to Google's translation).[9]

Potentially far more interesting, however, is the ability to see other message senders, many of whom in the pre-digital era would have had to content themselves with passing out leaflets or perhaps pasting posters on walls in the middle of the night. Now it is possible for would-be activists and organizers to use any number of platforms, of which the following list is the merest suggestive sketch:

- The Russian pro-government youth group Nashi, which has strong nationalistic, even xenophobic tendencies, and often seems to have an agenda independent from that of the Kremlin, has a well-developed portal site at: www.nashi.su (the SU domain extension was assigned to the USSR, but is still used by nearly 92,000 websites[10]).

- The Anglo-American "campaigning community" Avaaz (which, as the group's homepage states, means "voice" in many languages) serves to bring "people-powered politics to decision-making worldwide," particularly about environmental, human rights, and disaster relief issues. The group claims more than 7 million members in 193 countries, and may be found through its multi-lingual website: www.avaaz.org.

- The Warwickshire (England) chapter of the Freemasons, which claims 4,500 members, in 190 lodges, provides information, schedules, and history at: http://www.warwickshirepgl.org.uk/.

- The Union Romani, an organization for Roma people in Spain, offers news, advice, legal services, and other information at: http://unionromani.org/.

- Ottawa-Cuba Connection, which claims to be a citizen group promoting closer ties with Cuba, may be found at: http://ottawacuba.org/.

And so on . . .

Self-organizing communities

Analysts trying to use this new information environment should constantly remind themselves that, no matter how granular the web now makes it possible for message sender appeals to be, the fact remains that, just as was true of the largest of the mass media decades ago, for a message to have the chance to produce an effect, it must at the very least be paid attention by someone. The structure of the web makes it possible to get some measure of how many people visit a given website, how many pages they read there, and how quickly they leave the page again.[11] Still, just as newspaper circulation figures tell only how many people purchased a newspaper, and not how many read what parts of it, or what they thought or did after that reading, so do website traffic figures give only the basic information, that someone has seen the site.

Although it might be argued that a personal page, such as a blog, a Facebook page, or a Twitter feed, is no more than the smallest possible unit of the message-sender communications paradigm, experience over the past half decade has begun to suggest that the ability to create online personal representation can prove to be a powerful new promoter of communities.[12] Beginning with the "anti-FARC" rallies of February 2008, which brought millions of people to the streets of Colombia (with many more in sympathy demonstrations in other countries),[13] there has been a steady stream of what have come to be called "Facebook revolutions" or "Twitter revolutions" – Moldova in April 2009, Iran in June 2009, Kyrgyzstan in April 2010,[14] Tunisia in January 2011, and Egypt in January–February 2011 (with rumblings in Jordan, Iraq, Bahrain, Yemen, Libya, Algeria, Syria, and Iran[15]). An acrimonious battle has broken out among various pundits over the issue of whether or not the social media have in some sense "caused" these events.[16] Although the nay-sayers bring some good points to their argument (Malcolm Gladwell, for example, is quite correct when he points out that the French Revolution occurred without help from Facebook), the issue is, from an analytic point of view, largely irrelevant. For an analyst at least, the question is not whether or not these platforms in some way provoke or stimulate discontent (which they probably do not, though they probably can help amplify it), but rather that they can help make discontent *visible*.

The really important thing about social media platforms for analysts is that these provide what is probably our best available indicator of what people are in fact most interested in. As has already been suggested, most media analysis is still based on the assumptions of transmission models – as indeed are such giant concerns as the advertising industry, the mainstream media, government functions such as public diplomacy and strategic communications, covert influence operations, and others. All of those tend to measure what has come to be called "push" – how many units of X have been sent down the assembly line. The social media, by contrast, rely upon aggregation – anyone can put a page up or send out a tweet, but that message has no impact unless and until it begins to attract the attention of others. A vivid example of that phenomenon as this book was being written was the "We Are Khaled Said" Facebook page which had been anonymously established and curated to commemorate an Egyptian blogger whom police beat to death.[17] However, this was not the first such page, or the first such event – similar pages had been created in 2008, for the April 6th movement,[18] and Egyptian bloggers had been aggregating, for example, amateur videos of police brutality since 2005.[19]

What the various social media platforms allowed analysts to see, in other words, were the issues and interests around which a growing number of people were linking up. Although one of the goals of trying to identify new Facebook pages or tweeters as they start to "snowball" may be prediction (a notoriously risky activity), it is probably more useful to understand the social media as a new version of what is no doubt the oldest source of "verbal intelligence" that exists – the rumor. Ironically, rumor was well studied and widely used by the intelligence community during World War II, in part because of the power that rumor appeared to have on morale (both among the enemy and domestically – there were many "anti-rumor" bureaus set up in the US during the war), but also because rumor was pretty much the only medium of communication with enemy populations that existed.

Although the study of rumor has become a somewhat isolated sub-speciality in communications theory since the war, a few of the principles that students of rumor have laid out seem valid for understanding the social media platforms. Robert Knapp, a psychologist who headed an anti-rumor bureau for the Massachusetts Committee of Public Safety during World War II, was the author both of an article on rumors[20] and also of a secret memo[21] (now declassified) about how the military might best use rumor as a weapon. In both Knapp makes several points about rumor which also apply to social media:

- successful rumors are "self-propelling," meaning that people themselves do the work of accessing them and passing them along (though not stated, the corollary is also important, that rumors in which no one is interested do not "self-propel," and therefore die) – the counterpart activity in social media is "going viral";

- a good rumor "exploits the emotions and sentiments of the group," and "serves to articulate a sentiment common to the group";

- Rumor has "the unique distinction of both expressing and at the same time forming public opinion." As Knapp noted, "Somehow the more a rumor is told, the greater is its plausibility."

A later student of rumor, Tamotsu Shibutani, elaborated on Knapp's observation, characterizing rumor as "improvised news,"[22] by which he meant that rumors are explanations generated *and edited* by people as they are passed along. As he pointed out, rumor transmission involves both additions and omissions as people shape and reshape the body of a rumor to better fit their own needs and interests. A particularly vivid example of this occurred during the January 2011 change of power in Tunisia, which to an undetermined degree coalesced around the figure of Mohammed Bouazizi, a fruit vendor who set fire to himself after a contretemps with a minor official, and later died. Most of the early accounts described Bouazizi as a university graduate who had been unable to find work worthy of his degree and so had turned to fruit vending, only now to find himself harassed and shaken down by corrupt officials.[23] After Bouazizi died, however, some journalists travelled to the man's home town to do more in-depth profiles, including interviews with Bouazizi's family and friends; their accounts state that Bouazizi in fact had never even completed high school, let alone received a university degree.[24]

Narratives of persuasion

To many analysts in the IC, and perhaps to policymakers as well, that sort of discrepancy – or factual inaccuracy – is one of the reasons why media information is distrusted in general, and information obtained from social media is deeply distrusted, or ignored, in particular. However, to ignore or downplay media information simply because it may contain incorrect information is to profoundly misunderstand the nature of "verbal intelligence." Even a committed "transmission model" theorist like Lasswell understood that part of a communication act was the shaping of the message that was being sent. Even in a strictly textual environment the creation of a potentially effective message required a number of choices, ranging from:

- the language in which it was written (to illustrate – many Middle Eastern and South Asian countries have parallel newspapers, with at least one major one in English; very clearly part of the audience at whom messages printed there are aimed is the US and the West, as well perhaps as the educated elites, but certainly not the peasantry, who may not even be literate in any language);

- through the level of vocabulary (the *New York Times*, for example, is generally considered to be written with an 8th grade vocabulary in mind, while *USA Today* is said to be pitched at a 5th grade level[25]);

- down to choice of particular words and phrases (for example, are the Chechens fighting against Russia "insurgents," "terrorists," "guerrillas," "rebels," "freedom fighters," or "separatists"? A Google search shows all the terms have been used, with more or less the same frequency);

- and even down to such seeming minutiae as the choice of fonts (while apparently trivial, most organizations have official fonts – the State Department drew wide attention in 2004 when it switched the official font from Courier 12 to Times New Roman 14[26]).

As will be explored in the next chapter, the choices grow even more complex when text is combined with visual material, or visual materials alone are the basis of the communication.

The time-honored term for this process of choice is "rhetoric," which originally meant simply the art of capturing and holding the attention of an audience, for purposes of persuading them. However, the small difference which many people perceive between being persuaded and being fooled has caused the notion of "rhetoric" to become tainted with connotations of falsehood, "spin," or disingenuousness. This book has already highlighted the deep conviction both of the founders of the IC and of many of its senior leaders that there is something called "truth" which somehow lies behind rhetoric or other information – best formalized, perhaps, by the Biblical verse inscribed on the walls of CIA's headquarters: "And Ye Shall Know the Truth, and The Truth Shall Make You Free."[27]

However, as psychological operations agents like Knapp, or even Nazi Propaganda Minister Goebbels well knew, truth is multi-faceted. Paul

Linebarger, a "psy-ops" (psychological operations) officer in World War II, wrote in his book *Psychological Warfare* that "the facts [of a news item] are true in each case ... but the interpretation placed them ... makes them into propaganda. Interpretation can be no more true or untrue than a Ford car can be vanilla or strawberry in flavor ... all good propaganda is true. It uses truth selectively."[28]

   This is a fact of human information processing that the IC and US policy-makers (as well as a good-sized chunk of the US advertising industry) have forgotten. As a recent paper on the advertising industry – tellingly titled "Fifty Years of Using the Wrong Model of Advertising"[29] – demonstrates, virtually all advertising is based on positivist assumptions. Advertisers (and, by extension, most public communicators) assume that "consumer opinion" is based on error or ignorance, while the job of opinion-makers, including advertisers, is to correct and educate by providing "factual information." As the authors of that paper point out, those assumptions themselves were deeply nested in "rational actor" theories of social behavior, which posited that humans process information in order to make choices which will lead logically to their greatest personal advantage. Thus communication is viewed as an entirely one-way transaction, with information being trans-ferred from those in possession of "the facts" to those who are in error. Although several examples of the inefficacy of "telling truth" were noted in Chapter Five (the growing numbers of Americans who appear to believe that President Obama is foreign-born, a Muslim, or both; the persistently high degree of conviction across the globe, and especially in the Middle East, that the terrorist attacks of 9/11 were the work of the US, Israel, or both), perhaps an even more vivid example of how poorly "argument by fact" actually works occurred when US Ambassador to South Korea Alexander Vershbow characterized concerns about the safety of US beef as "disinformation," and expressed the hope that "Koreans will begin to understand more about the science and about the facts of American beef."[30] The result was several days of large anti-US demonstrations and widespread condemnation by public figures, who universally characterized the ambas-sador's remarks as "an insult to all Korean citizens."[31]

   Rather than concentrate upon whether information being communicated is true or false, which leads to the establishment of quixotic efforts like the State Department's Rapid Response Unit,[32] analysts would be better served by trying to understand the rhetorical shape which the communication is being given. Just as communicators – or at least potentially successful ones – know better than to use a language that the target audience does not speak, so should they understand (whether consciously or more subliminally) how to phrase their communication attempts in narrative structures that the target audience is familiar with, and can use easily to process information. There is a large, and growing, body of literature which demonstrates that humans may not even be able to perceive information that does not fit into the narrative frameworks that they already possess, let alone be persuaded by it.[33] Furthermore, numerous studies suggest that one consequence of the explosive growth in the easy availability of information is that people increasingly use information tools to seek out information resources that reinforce what they already believe, among communities of the like-minded.

Scholar Christian Smith has written a particularly illuminating study of the power of persuasive narratives, in his book *Moral Believing Animals: Human Personhood and Culture*. Arguing that "we not only continue to be animals who make stories but also animals who are *made* by our stories," Smith defines narratives as:

> a form of communication that arranges human actions and events into organized wholes in a way that bestows meaning on the actions and events by specifying their interactive or cause-and-effect relations to the whole ... narratives seek to convey the significance and meaning of events by situating their interaction with or influence on other events and actions in a single, interrelated account.[34]

To illustrate his point, Smith sketches a few major narratives:

- The "American experiment" narrative, which celebrates the journey of a people from the Old World of darkness, religious persecution, and oppression, to the New World of freedom, where, by hard work and bravery, they carved a better world.

- The "Militant Islamic Resurgence" narrative, which laments that Islam, which had once enjoyed a flourishing civilization while Europe was floundering in medieval darkness, had been crushed by invading infidels, who for the past five centuries have continued to humiliate, divide, and conspire against Muslims, who can only reclaim their birthright by submitting themselves to Allah and fighting to drive the infidels from their lands.

- The "Capitalist Prosperity" narrative, which celebrates the eighteenth-century invention of untrammeled commerce, limited government, technological innovation, and enlightened, rational self-interest. Though threatened by government regulation, utopian egalitarians and anti-entrepreneurial freeloaders, capitalism can, if left alone, provide freedom and prosperity to the world.

- The "Progressive Socialism" narrative, which saw the early communalism of humankind eroded by the greed of rapacious exploiters who seized the means of productions and grew fat on the labor of others, until the contradictions of raw capitalism opened the eyes of a progressive minority who understood their own duty to lead the rest of humankind to overthrow capitalism and build a society based on fraternity, justice, and equality.

- The "Expressive Romantic" narrative, which views people of the distant past as free, uninhibited, and untrammeled, but now smothered beneath the restrictions of encroaching "civilization," which has replaced authenticity and spontaneity with convention and repression, which can only now be thrown off by the flouting of conventional mores and a return to the earlier authenticity of experience.

- The "Scientific Enlightenment" narrative, which celebrates how the understanding of objective truth and the development of a scientific method gradually led humans out of their centuries-old ignorance to come to truer understandings of the world, ourselves, and the universe, so that we can increase health, reduce suffering, and overcome, perhaps, mortality itself.

Although narratives can seem crude and stereotypical when expressed directly, particularly in the quick sketch forms given above, it is not hard to see how any particular "fact" could look quite different when inserted into one narrative rather than another. To cite just one example from among the myriads possible, US attempts to argue in favor of "rule of law" when lecturing Russia about the development of civil society have failed to realize that, in the Russian narrative, "law" is generally regarded as a human construct, which is therefore inherently biased toward the interests of those powerful elites who drew up the "laws" in the first place. Contrasted with this is "justice," which is something that only God (or perhaps blind nature) can supply.[35] To most Russians, it was "rule of law" that allowed a small group of powerful oligarchs to seize control of the country's assets, and then to snatch those assets back and forth between themselves, without regard for the interests or needs of the citizens – and thus it should be little surprise that US exhortations about the importance of "rule of law" would be ignored.

Thus, to return to the five-part structure of the Lasswell formula, anyone wishing to send a communication that has at least the chance of being noticed and paid attention would be wise to structure the rhetorical argument in such a way that the assumptions, linkages, and appeals of the message are congruent with a narrative that the target population accepts. Similarly, open source analysts trying to understand whether or not a particular message, or group of messages, has the potential at least to have impact needs to understand the narrative structures, cultural references, and other rhetorical elements of the messaging. As has already been noted, it is here that social media platforms can perform their greatest service for analysts, because – just like rumor, save more visibly – communication attempts on social media live or die according to whether they suit the needs, requirements, and interests of a particular audience. Indeed, as with the case of Mohammed Bouazizi, the elements of the story – the narrative – will be shaped by the audience, thus providing important insight about the concerns and fears of the audience which has embraced a particular message or group of messages. Reporting of events in Tunisia and later in Egypt in early 2011 illustrated particularly clearly how narratives can be in conflict – western news narratives tended to flip back and forth between a stability narrative (Ben Ali and, even more so, Hosni Mubarak as a reliable ally, even if regrettably corrupt, in an unstable region) and one of "rising Islam" (since the Muslim Brethren or a wider, more inchoate, "Islamic fundamentalism" were seen as the only non-governmental political forces in the region), in contrast to regional bloggers, Facebook and YouTube posters, and Twitter-tweeters who had been rehearsing narratives of lost dignity, a future denied, and the "failed generation" of their fathers.

Viewed through the lens of Knapp's rumor studies, what the social media were aggregating was what Knapp termed "intelligence" about that particular audience's "fears, hopes, and hostilities," as well as their "customary and traditional ways of expressing their anxieties, hopes, and aggressions, especially in conditions of national crisis." Some sense of how such "intelligence" might have been used, had it been mined in the social media, is suggested by an ingenious MA thesis[36] (later published in shortened and revised form as a journal article[37]) written by Captain Stephanie Kelley, a student at the Naval Postgraduate School, in 2004. After grounding her proposal in a thorough reading of the available literature about rumors, Kelley proposed that information officers should aggregate, categorize, and – most important – *listen* to the rumors that were circulating in Iraq in the aftermath of the US invasion. Using the approximately 1,000 rumors that were collected and published in *The Baghdad Mosquito* between October 2003 and August 2004, Kelley argued that these rumors could be grouped into eight "overarching concerns" – ranging from concerns about the politics and governance of Iraq (the subject of about 27 percent of the rumors), through "quality of life" issues (18 percent), the nascent insurgency (17 percent), questions about the US military and what they were doing (7 percent), and, of least apparent concern, the Abu Ghraib detainees (subject of just 2 percent of the rumors collected).

The shock and revulsion that the pictures of the abused detainees provoked in America, in contrast to the seeming indifference to that issue in Iraq, suggest how rumor (or the new equivalent, social media) might be leveraged to improve information campaigns or to analyze public opinion in places of interest. Not only were the detainees apparently of little concern, but Kelley's rumor taxonomy also suggests that concerns about "communication" were only slightly higher, at about 3 percent of the collected rumors. Her findings suggest that what was the greatest concern of the US communicators – explaining that the Abu Ghraib pictures were not representative of American values or American behavior – was not of much concern to the presumed target audience, who would much rather have gotten more detailed and more reliable information about the emerging political environment, and how their country was to be governed.

Micro-sliced audiences and their platforms

There is of course at least one difference between a rumor and a posting on a social media platform – all that it takes to be able to spread a rumor, in theory at least, is the presence of another human, while a social medium, just like any medium of communication, has certain infrastructure requirements. The point may be obvious, but it is nevertheless surprising how often message senders ignore the question of how their message will be disseminated. A case in point is the Shared Values Initiative (SVI), a high-profile, multi-million-dollar effort mounted to reach out to Muslims across the globe in the aftermath of the 9/11 terrorist attacks. Crafted by advertising mogul Charlotte Beers, who was brought to the State Department specifically for the purpose of improving America's global "approval rating," particularly among Muslims, the SVI resulted in the production of five short films that were intended to be aired during Ramadan in 2002. There were a variety of reasons why the initiative proved to be so grand a flop that it was shut down just six weeks after it began with (the telling detail of its inefficacy) less than half the allotted budget spent, but certainly part of the problem was that the producers of the films had not taken into account their reliance for delivery on the state-owned TV companies of the target countries – most of which refused outright to air the films. Although the SVI films came out a few years before it would have been possible to envision platforms like YouTube, even at the time there were other platforms that the films' producers might have considered using – jihadists and other anti-American message-senders, for example, were already using Adobe Flash to make sound-and-picture slide decks that travelled easily, and very widely, on the internet.

Traditional open source intelligence, as has already been shown, did pay relatively careful attention to the first three elements of the Lasswell formula, developing sophisticated ways to derive meaning from the message sender, the shape (or rhetoric) of the message, and the medium chosen for its dissemination. The element of audience was largely ignored, however, partly because the greater analytic interest lay in what the message senders were saying, but also because, in that era of mass media, it was generally assumed that it was precisely "the masses" which media messages reached. The atomization of audiences, however, also has brought with it a much larger requirement to understand the interconnection between channel and audience. This can work in either direction – a message sender trying to reach a particular audience (for example, South Korean teenagers) has to understand the media accessing habits of the target, which in this case might include that, not only do they not read newspapers, but they also do not use the social media platforms that their counterparts in, say, France or Brazil might (as of this writing, the dominant social media platform in South Korea was Cyworld, and the search engine of choice was Naver – but, *caveat lector*, these are usage habits that can change very quickly). Similarly, Russians tend to prefer the blogging platform LiveJournal and the Facebook look-alike Vkontakte, meaning that a would-be message sender using Blogspot or Facebook would greatly diminish the chances of being noticed. From the point of view of trying to find and monitor messaging of interest, the same holds true – sometimes, for example, political discussion will move to unexpected platforms in order to evade authorities, but also because the platforms are ones that like-minded people might use. Thus for example Iranian political discussion for a time moved to a book discussion forum hosted in southern California, and Chinese dissidents were gathering (as avatars) in online gaming environments like World of Warcraft.

Because there are so many platforms that people can now use to communicate with one another, or can try to attract like-minded, the kind of broad-brush "media monitoring" that provided the basis for open source analysis in its classic form no longer seems possible. One of the most important first steps for any would-be open source analyst should be the question of who precisely is to be monitored. As has already been implied, the proliferation of possible platforms and media makes it possible for groups to seek out their own platforms, which they use in their own ways. Good marketers already understand this, and spend enormous time, effort, and resources on trying to find micro-audiences on as detailed and granular a scale as they possibly can. In the advertising world this audience segmentation is usually done on the basis of income, lifestyle, and, perhaps, place of residence. While those distinctions can also be important for open source intelligence analysts, the sorts of questions in which such analysts are likely to be interested also require that audiences be segmented by beliefs, allegiances, modes of perceptions, and other components of attitude and allegiance.

The science of how this might be done in the IC is very young, and has not yet conquered even such basic questions as how to reconcile security concerns with the need to gather sociological and anthropological information that normally can only be gathered in the field, by people who have mastered the languages and cultures of the people under study, usually by having lived with them. It may be precisely because of their closer proximity (and the more immediate failures that can result from not understanding cultural nuances) that the need for this kind of cultural expertise building was recognized by the military. Rather as information scientists used geographic metaphors for their study of data search and retrieval, so have the military chosen to understand acquisition of this sort of fine-grained understanding of the various groups in a region of interest as one more aspect of what the military call the Contemporary Operating Environment (COE) – as Major Daniel Schmitt argued in a Master of Operations' thesis written for the Marine Corps' School of Advanced Warfighting, doctrine as of 2004 defined 11 crucial dimensions which defined the COE, and his argument was that "culture" had to become the 12th.[38] Another experienced Marine has gone even further, arguing that all of the US forces should be required to "view the cultural terrain as a co-equal element of military terrain."[39] Indeed, a blistering report on the failures and inadequacies of counterinsurgency intelligence, survey, and reconnaissance (COIN ISR) issued by the Defense Science Board Task Force on Defense Intelligence in 2011 argued that poor "human terrain mapping" was a significant contributor to sub-optimal COIN ISR performance in Afghanistan.[40]

The process by which such in-depth understanding might be achieved has come to be called "cultural terrain mapping" or "cultural topography." Although the processes for doing such mapping are still being developed, in general most approaches are similar to that elaborated by Jeannie Johnson, a CIA-analyst-turned-academic, who was one of the editors of the volume *Strategic Culture and Weapons of Mass Destruction: Culturally Based Insights*.[41] While acknowledging the enormous elasticity of the term "culture," Johnson argues in a methodological postscript to that book that one goal of efficient analysis must be "to narrow the world of variables to those that are most likely to have an effect on security policy."[42] Although the focus of the volume in which she writes is about very high-level weapons policy decisions, the limiting factors that she advances seem a good starting point for almost any audience segmentation question that touches on security or intelligence issues.

The four dimensions she suggests "mapping" for any group of interest to the analyst are:

- **Identity**, meaning the "nation-state's [or other target group's] view of itself, comprising the traits of its national character, its intended regional and global roles, and its perception of its eventual destiny";

- **Values**, understood as the "sorts of goods – both material and immaterial – [that] this society values more highly than others";

- **Norms**, or the "accepted and expected modes of behavior" (which in practice often become most apparent when those norms are violated); and

- **Perceptive Lenses**, or the "beliefs (true or misinformed) and experiences or lack of experience that color the way the world is viewed."[43]

Humans all have multiple identities, based on family, place of birth, social role, occupation, religion, leisure-time interests, and myriad other factors. What is important for the analyst – and also for the would-be strategic communicator – is to identify the group or groups that are of specific interest for a specific purpose. How precisely those groups may be identified and understood is too complex and too detailed a question to answer here – in general, however, all of the many resources of the IC should be marshaled toward trying to capture and store as much information about the various features of the "human terrain." To give just one example, drawn from the events occurring in Egypt as this book was being written, the "human landscape features" most often used by US policymakers and IC representatives in their public statements were drawn from (as it were) an outdated map. Identifying the two major features as "Mubarak=stability" and "no Mubarak=Muslim Brotherhood" made it almost impossible to discern other features, such as (for example) that the leadership of the Muslim Brotherhood were as "digitally clueless" as were their counterparts in the ruling National Democratic Party (NDP); that Facebook communities had been forming among Egyptian youth – and mobilizing them – for at least three years before the January–February 2011 events[44]; that age cohorts could be as powerful as geographic or institutional affiliations; and others.[45]

It should also be noted that the capacity to do this kind of cultural mapping, and the understanding of why it is necessary, was well established during World War II. While it is not clear why the skills were forgotten (or at least neglected), it is striking to read Paul Linebarger describing ways to understand "the true terrain of psychological warfare – the private thoughts of the enemy people." Although Linebarger does not use Johnson's terms precisely, he asks that a would-be propagandist construct what he termed a "Propaganda Man," or a simulacrum of the target. Among the questions Linebarger would want answered are things such as:

- What does he like?
- What prejudices is he apt to have?
- What kinds of words disgust him?
- What did he think of your country before the war?
- What things does he dislike you and your people for?

Also important to understand, Linebarger asserts, is what other message-senders would like this Propaganda Man to do. Learning what the enemy leaders are trying to convince the Propaganda Man to do may reveal the enemy's needs and weakness. For example:

- Are the leaders trying to get this target person to get to work on time?

- To voluntarily forgo holidays to increase output?

- To be frightened that your side will kill him and his family if his side loses?

- To believe that bomb shelters are safe, so there is no need to evacuate?

The goal, in short, Linebarger wrote, is to make the Propaganda Man "your friend." If you know better what he wants, needs, and desires than does his own leadership, and if you furthermore are able to make your propaganda message seem to answer those needs better than does the propaganda of the leadership against which you are contesting, then "the terrain is favorable" to you and your goals.

"With what effect?"

There is one dimension in which the Lasswell formula must be modified for use in the new media environment. As transmission model theory suggests he should, Lasswell took for granted that a message sent would have a predictable effect. Indeed, the *purpose* of the first four parts of the Lasswell formula is all pointed toward the fifth element – that communication should have an effect. The largest single distinction between data and rhetoric (or physical intelligence and verbal intelligence) is that the second has as its purpose trying to get someone to *do* or to *think* or to *believe* something (which of course can include the opposites – don't do, don't think, and don't believe).

For more than 2,500 years, since Plato first laid out the elements and types of persuasive rhetoric in the work *Rhetoric*, message senders have assumed or, perhaps more often, *claimed* that a message *sent* is the same thing as a message *received*, and that a message *received* is the same thing as an *achieved effect*. Indeed, vast bureaucracies and huge industries have been built on precisely these beliefs – including, but not limited to, the advertising industry, the publicity and public relations industries, public diplomacy and strategic communications bureaucracies, and psychological operations and covert influence efforts. However, achieving a predictable effect or, indeed, even being able to demonstrate in a convincing way that your message has had an effect, is utterly beyond the control of the sender, despite the claims of generations of advertisers, strategic communicators, spin-*meisters*, propagandists, and others to the contrary. It is difficult to prove that statement, for a number of reasons, not least of which is that most message senders are heavily invested in believing in their own efficacy. The industries which serve them also need to have it well established that their advertising, their messaging, has achieved the ends they claim. A particularly vivid example of this (selected almost at random, because there are so many "advertising success stories") is the story of how the N.W. Ayer advertising firm teamed up with the Oppenheimer family and the DeBeers diamond cartel to, as an article on the process put it, convert "tiny crystals of carbon into universally recognized tokens of wealth, power, and romance."[46] It was because of advertising, the argument goes, that the sales of diamonds had in the four decades between 1939 and 1979 grown almost a hundred-fold (from $23 million to $2.1 billion), all because of an advertising budget that had begun at $200,000 per year and had gradually grown to be $10 million.

Characteristically of this type of success story, however, the article is unable to answer such questions as: whether a different type of sales approach (for example, mass-marketing diamonds rather than making them an artificially created, cartel-controlled "scarce good") might not have achieved even greater sales; whether it was primarily peer pressure rather than direct advertising that created the expectation that a man would give a woman a lump of carbon crystal as an "objective correlative" of emotion or desire (although advertisers of course claim both direct and two-step influencing as successes); and why it was that the Ayers/DeBeers team may have seemed able to create a retail diamond market in the US and, later, Japan, but – despite deploying the same efforts, skills, and tactics – the duo was (as the article notes but does not mention again) "unable to create a similar [diamond-gifting] tradition in Brazil, Germany, Austria, or Italy."

This alacrity in taking credit for successes and the equally quick dismissal of failures, even in efforts which would seem to be quite similar to the contexts which showed successes, is a characteristic of most studies of message efficacy. A massive compendium[47] of the results of state-by-state and national anti-smoking campaigns aimed at youth, for example, while attempting to paint a generally positive picture of the role that such campaigns might play in reducing tobacco use among youth, reported as successful apparent declines of tobacco use of 20 percent or less, and in one case even reported as a successful campaign result that, over the decade of the 1990s, use of tobacco products among youth in California, where there had been intensive anti-smoking campaigns, rose less than did youth consumption of tobacco nationally, without remarking that smoking *increased* among both populations. A "smaller increase" would seem at best a very pale result of that campaign's "media effect." More honest, perhaps, is that same report's evaluation of yet another anti-smoking campaign, which "found no statistically significant relation between smoking and campaign exposure among either youth or adults."

What may be even stranger about the "media effects" industry is that it has taught its customers to expect failure, or at least to accept it as part of the process. Within just a few years of the birth of the mass market advertising business, it had become axiomatic to accept that "half of my money spent on advertising is wasted, but I don't know which half" (a statement, probably apocryphal, usually attributed to department-store owner John Wanamaker or soap-maker William Levy). In fact, if by "wasted" the speaker meant "did not lead to a sale or other desired action," that 50 percent success rate is wildly overstated. Conventional wisdom in direct-mail marketing – a generally scorned lower-tier advertising activity which relies on mass mailings of postcards or coupons that interested recipients will then mail back or otherwise use an advertisement, thus demonstrating some kind of receiver involvement – is that a campaign may be judged successful if as few as 0.2 percent of the cards or coupons are returned. Even the Direct Mail Association, an industry trade organization, is reported to have acknowledged, based on a study of 1,122 targeted direct mail campaigns, that the industry average response for such efforts was 2.6 percent.[48]

Given the enormous revenues generated by internet-based advertising, which is widely imagined to allow for much more tightly targeted messaging, it is surprising to learn that response rates in that domain are not markedly different than they are for direct mail advertising. The standard measurement of online advertising efficacy is the "click-through rate," or CTR – meaning the percentage of those who after accessing a particular website also click on the advertising link the page offers. Here too – even according to the advice given by the Google AdWord advisory page[49] – a CTR of 2 percent would be considered a very good response. Unlike direct mail campaigns, online advertisers can also measure the so-called "conversion rate," meaning the percentage of those who click on the ad who actually *do* something. Discussions on advertising bulletin boards[50] suggest that "conversions" may be almost as small a proportion of "click-throughs" as "click-throughs" are of total visitors – meaning, for example, that (as one participant in the first discussion above calculated it), 10,000 "impressions" (or people who viewed a site) could result in as few as seven "conversions."

Duncan Watts, a biologist-turned-network-specialist, argued in 2008[51] that all of the work that has claimed to demonstrate cause-and-effect results in marketing is probably erroneous, for two reasons. The first, he said, is that the data sets used for such studies are too small. Disputing particularly the work of Malcolm Gladwell, who has popularized the two-step influence theories of the 1950s in his best-seller *The Tipping Point*, Watts ran a series of experiments designed to test whether or not – as Gladwell had argued was the case – there are some people who are more influential than others in initiating and sustaining fads or movements. Gladwell had posited three kinds of people whom advertisers would be wise to target – Mavens, who are deeply knowledgeable about particular topics, and eager to share their expertise with others; Connectors, who are more likely than other people to know large numbers of people, and especially from a mix of spheres; and Influentials, who play, Gladwell said, a disproportionate role in influencing the decisions of others. The goal of the new marketing strategy, then, is to identify the Influentials, and to target them with your messages.

What Watts' data seem to have demonstrated is that Influentials are no more likely to be able to begin fads than is anyone else. It is true, Watts says, that if a fad begun by an Influential does catch on, it is likely to spread more quickly than if it were begun by a non-Influential, but there is nothing in his data to suggest that any given person is more or less likely to start a successful fad than is anyone else. In fact, Watts' data suggests that the process by which fads are generated and spread may well be random, or – a more charitable explanation – that fads and trends are the result of so many factors, known and unknown, that they are ultimately mysteries which are impossible to create or control. Trends, Watts argues, are like forest fires – there are thousands every year, but only a few grow into monster conflagrations, and they do so because of the confluence of a whole variety of factors. In such cases, Watts says, "no one goes around talking about the exceptional properties of the spark that started the fire."

The other reason that Watts disputes Gladwell's argument is that – just as was the case with the diamond industry example above – the descriptive process is precisely *analytic*, identifying the driving parts which have caused something *that has already happened*. This kind of explanatory process is circular, but highly seductive – since the phenomenon being analyzed clearly already exists, the process of identifying the elements which "caused" the phenomenon allows analysts huge range for conjecture, without any ready means of determining whether, for example, the same phenomenon will result if the same process is repeated. Significantly, Watts' data suggests strongly that phenomena are contingent, not inevitable, since every iteration of his experiments produces different outcomes.

The process of intelligence analysis is similar. Just as the N.W. Ayers company was able to argue that it had "caused" the increase in DeBeers' sales, so have analysts tended to "explain" events such as (for example) the Rwandan genocide of 1994 as having been "caused" by the incendiary broadcasts of the government radio station Mille Collines. A representative statement of that view is the conclusion of a study of the genocide in the *Journal of Communication*:

> [T]his study suggests that the strong establishment of media dependency for political information, alongside media's agenda-setting and framing roles, and an absence of alternative voices, can set the stage for unusually powerful propaganda campaigns. Such campaigns, in turn, may spark extreme fear and mass panic with catastrophic outcomes, even genocide.[52]

Other students of the event, however, have argued that hate radio did not "cause" the genocide, although it clearly played a facilitating role. Indeed, one has argued that "the massacres would have taken place with or without the RTLM broadcasts."[53] A more nuanced argument was made by Kenyan journalist Mary Kirmani, who, after studying reams of transcripts from the Mille Collines broadcasts, came to the conclusion that government officials and radio journalists were responsible for about one percent of the station's incitements to violence, while the rest of the broadcast vitriol was aired by callers-in and other private individuals, who were able to use the station as a platform around which they could cluster, in the end creating what in effect was a shared community of hate. As she wrote: "Those who argue that RTLM was set up with the express aim of instigating mass murder ... miss the point. They fail to see the frightening process by which a station that was set up merely to air the political views of one group became the megaphone through which people were incited to mass murder."[54]

What Kirmani is arguing seems close to what Watts asserts in a very different arena, that media messaging can have an effect – indeed, sometimes a very powerful amplifying effect – but there is no clear formula for knowing in advance which messaging will have impact, or among whom. In fact, as efforts[55] by pro-Mubarak forces to turn Twitter back against the government's opponents suggest, media do not dictate to audiences, but rather groups now choose media to aggregate, reinforce one another, and form communities of shared interest. This nearly reverses the Lasswell formula – a group of people trying to achieve a certain effect cluster around a medium or media to find and build an audience that will share their interest and join in achieving the effect. As Kirmani demonstrated, that kind of self-editing and self-defining community was possible even in 1994, when technology was more constraining. By the twenty-first century, as we are seeing, information is becoming increasingly self-generating and self-refining, simply because a message that is not interesting or useful to a particular group of people does not survive in the "information bazaar." People studying Al Qaeda, for example, have discovered that this new enemy is not the traditional top-down, command-and-control entity that security forces are accustomed to battling, but rather is what has come to be called a "brand."[56] In the words of scholar Daniel Kimmage,[57] Al Qaeda is "a chaotic amalgam of international terror cells and localized insurgencies that espouse loosely articulated common goals yet lack the organizational cohesion of a movement and face an unprecedented global security clampdown. Both internal and external factors ... have impelled jihadists to channel their efforts through a variety of decentralized structures," including the cluster of media platforms that were the subject of Kimmage's study. Kimmage argues that the various Al Qaeda media platforms are caught in a constant tension, trying to establish the kind of "brand control" that characterizes other media such as CNN or ABC by using such devices as logos, "accredited" content producers, and other mannerisms of more mainstream media, while at the same time having to adjust to the ease with which anyone who desires to do so can inject content into the Al Qaeda production stream.

The fact that there is no good way of predicting what effect a given message may have does not mean, however, that the "media effects" dimension of the Lasswell formula should be ignored. What analysts can observe when examining messages sent to audiences of interest is the effect that the sender would *like* to achieve. In advertising, this is called "the ask" – what the message sender wants you, the message recipient, actually to *do* because of the message he or she has sent. Paying attention to "the ask" of a message or group of messages can be quite revealing, both about the message sender and the intended (and sometimes unintended) audience. One of the most striking things that can emerge from this sort of study is how often messages fail either to have an "ask," or, if they do have one, convey it in so muddled a way that even a recipient who pays the message attention does not know what he or she is supposed to do. The Shared Values Initiative, for example, gave no guidance to anyone who might have watched the five films what they were expected to think, feel, or do. Again, there is no guarantee that a recipient would necessarily do what the message sender asks, but it is particularly hard to heed a message when there is no indicator of what the sender expects you to do in response.

When there is a discernible "ask," an analyst should be able to place the intended effect along a continuum of possible response. In advertising terms this is usually called the "ladder of loyalty," with the various steps of this ladder moving from someone who is unaware of a product or service, to becoming a potential customer (aware and perhaps curious); then a first-time customer; then a repeat customer; then a client; then a brand advocate; and finally a brand evangelist. In political terms, the "ziggurat of zealotry" proposed by analysts in the CIA's Counter-Terrorism Center[58] suggests a similar vertical metaphor. Although that construct was meant to describe degrees of Islamic radicalization – with peaceful personal devoutness at the bottom, moving through attempts to increase the piety of one's local population; to more concerted efforts to overthrow existing governments; and, at the top, devotion to full-time violent jihad – one of the metaphor's purposes was to alert analysts both to attempts to move believers higher up the ziggurat, and also to make plain that this progress can be countered or halted at lower and less dangerous levels.

An important final reminder – analysts who are tracking the "ask" of a message-sender of interest must be extremely careful not to confuse desired effect with actual effect. One of the most persistent pitfalls of analysis is that the process of selecting causal factors for any phenomenon can quickly become arbitrary and "intuitive." Watts' argument, for example, stimulated enormous hostility in the advertising community, but provoked no data-supported refutations. Rather people simply argued that he was wrong, because their "gut feelings" or "experience" told them so – somewhat in the same way that Propaganda Minister Goebbels was said to have based his understanding of "public opinion" on the likes and dislikes of his mother.[59] The only reliable indicator of whether or not a given message is resonant with the interests and needs of a particular audience is the degree to which that audience picks up the message itself, embracing it, modifying it, and perhaps acting on it. In some rare cases it may actually be that a given behavior has been "caused" by a given message, but it is far more likely that an event, trend, or phenomenon is underway, and alert message senders are modifying their messaging in response, in the effort to keep the trend contained within their particular "brand."

Implications

The approach to using media-based information for intelligence purposes which is laid out above has serious implications for how such information is collected and used. While the traditional activities of open source intelligence – knowing the identities and connections of the message senders, understanding the various media channels available, and knowing rhetorical patterns well enough to see and understand changes – all remain important, a great deal more is now required, if the full potential of open source information is to be realized. Analysts have to be alert to the ever-expanding universe of communications channels, to understand how people use these, and – perhaps even more important – how the various channels *interact* with one another. A particularly important example of that last point is the symbiotic relationship between new media and traditional media, especially television. Aware of their comparatively much smaller audiences, users of the new media desiring larger audiences will try to craft their stories in a way that is likely to appeal to more traditional media which, for all that those audiences may be atomizing and shrinking, are still larger than the audiences of the average blogger or tweeter. Traditional media, however, increasingly are coming to believe that the stories their readers want to hear or their viewers to watch are to be found in new media, so to an ever larger degree they look for material – including now even video and pictures – in the new media.

Open source analysts also need to know as much about the various audience strata as they can. There is an ever-growing industry of audience measurement and analysis, the output of which the open source intelligence should constantly be acquiring and digesting. Even more daunting, it is probably the open source community which is the most likely agent for acquiring, codifying, and *understanding* all of the anthropological and sociological information that is required to map the world's cultural terrain. Having a sense of what kinds of messages *might* resonate with a particular audience of interest makes it somewhat simpler for an analyst to be sensitive to signs that a particular audience is beginning to coalesce around a given message, or a particular "ask."

Perhaps the greatest challenge that the new media environment presents to the intelligence community, however, is that, in order to maximize the benefits that may be drawn from it, most of the legacy intellectual and administrative structures that developed during the period of "mass media" will have to be dismantled, and their purposes re-imagined. It is outside the scope of this book to suggest how that might be done (though there is no shortage of books which do make various versions of that argument). What is clear, however, is that the period of the "mass media" has ended, and – in the rearview mirror of history – was something of an anomaly, because of the social consequences that resulted from the accident of technology, that it was far cheaper to receive information that it was to send it. Now that information is as cheap to send as it is to receive, in the realm of rhetoric – information conveyed with the purpose of persuasion – we have returned to what probably was always humankind's condition, save on a global scale. Plato in his *Rhetoric* said that communication consists of a speaker, a speech, and an audience. It can fail, or succeed, because of the nature of the speaker, the nature of the speech, or the nature of the audience. This pretty much describes the media environment of today, with the difference that the number of speakers is potentially as large as the planet's population, while the audience can range from that size down to one. The number of speeches, it would seem, might well be the product of those two numbers multiplied – which should give some sense of the scale both of challenge and of possibility for the intelligence analyst who wants, as the IC claims to do, to tell policymakers not just the "what" but also the "so what" of what is to be found in that ocean of information.

Notes

1 Harold D. Lasswell, "The Theory of Political Propaganda," *The American Political Science Review*, vol. 21, no. 3 (August 1927), pp. 630, 631.

2 This was the first formulation of the "Lasswell formula," made in the 1940 paper "Research in Mass Communication," issued by the Rockefeller Foundation's Communication Group. Quoted in Gary, *The Nervous Liberals*, p. 100. According to Jefferson Pooley, the formulation was actually a group creation, but because the first paper was classified "secret," attribution was assigned to Lasswell since he was the one who most often quoted it later. See Jefferson Pooley, "The New History of Mass Communication Research," in David Park and Jefferson Pooley (eds), *The History of Media*

and Communication Research: Contested Memories (New York: Peter Lang, 2008), p. 53.

3   Harold D. Lasswell, "The Structure and Function of Communication in Society," in L. Bryson (ed.), *The Communication of Ideas* (New York: Harper & Row, 1948), p. 37.

4   The book generally credited with disproving the hypodermic needle theory is Paul Lazersfeld and Elihu Katz, *Personal Influence: The Part Played by People in the Flow of Mass Communications* (Glencoe, IL: Free Press, 1955). However, it should be noted that by arguing that media influence influential people in communities, who in turn influence others, Lazersfeld and Katz remain within the transmission model, even if it is, as they see it, a "two-step" process.

5   Thomas E. Ruggiero, "Uses and Gratifications Theory in the 21st Century," *Mass Communication and Society*, vol. 3, 2000, p. 3.

6   For example, the three largest newspapers in France, including *Le Monde*, are essentially bankrupt, kept alive only by a handful of hopeful investors. Even the *New York Times* teetered on the brink of insolvency before getting a massive – and reportedly costly – loan from Mexican telecom billionaire Slim Helu. In a similar vein, NBC is in the process of being purchased by the cable-provider Comcast.

7   Mangesh Karandika, "Indian Political Parties Miss the Convergence Opportunity," available at: http://www.karandikars.com/convergence_in_indian_political_websites.pdf, accessed 4 February 2011.

8   http://www.zhambyl.kz.

9   https://www.narvik.kommune.no/artikkel.aspx?MId1=118&AId=3276, accessed 4 February 2011.

10 Information from registration site at: http://stat.nic.ru/en_su/2011/01/01/titul-20110101.shtml, accessed 5 February 2011. Figures on this site show that the number of SU site registrations continues to grow, albeit slowly.

11 There are a number of commercial services which claim to provide this type of service. The most comprehensive free service is www.alexa.com, although it only catalogues the top million most-visited sites. Alexa also offers some insight into the demographics of who visits a given site.

12 The most extended argument for this is made by Clay Shirky, *Here Comes Everybody*.

13 "Colombians in Huge Farc Protest," 4 February 2008, at: http://news.bbc.co.uk/2/hi/americas/7225824.stm, accessed 5 February 2011.

14 Although social media were not often credited with having organized this change of power, primarily because internet penetration in Kyrgyzstan is under 15 percent, the social media were used by all sides to push information out, including most prominently by Rosa Otunbaeva, who became president after Kurmanbek Bakiev was forced out. Otunbaeva tweeted actively throughout the revolution, in three languages.

15 This list changes every day as this text is written, so will undoubtedly be

out of date by the time this appears in print. The "Facebook Revolution" model may also be moving to Europe, in the "29 May Movement" (see for example the video at: http://www.youtube.com/watch?v=DskfLNJh_C4) or the "fed up" movement (see: http://www.thedailybeast.com/blogs-and-stories/2011-05-28/spain-protests-will-european-summer-follow-arab-spring/#). As further illustration of the internet's fluidity, these video clips, accessed at the end of May 2011, have now vanished.

16   The most strident nay-sayer has been Belarussian blogger Evgeny Morozov, whose book *The Net Delusion* (New York: Public Affairs Books, 2011) appeared just as crowds were forcing Tunisia's president to flee. Also prominent has been *New Yorker* columnist Malcolm Gladwell, who published two articles ("Small Change: Why the Revolution will Not be Tweeted," 4 October 2010, and "Does Egypt Need Twitter?" 2 February 2011) which argued that social media play an unimportant part in social movements. Bill Keller, editor of the *New York Times*, fired an influential anti-Twitter broadside, "The Twitter Trap," in *New York Times Magazine*, 18 May 2011.

17   http://www.facebook.com/ElShaheeed, accessed 8 February 2011. As of that date 562,704 people had "liked" the page, and individual postings were drawing 7–8 thousand comments and equal number of "likes." The page's originator proved to be Wael Ghonim, a Google employee whom Egyptian authorities kidnapped and held prison for nearly two weeks. See: http://thelede.blogs.nytimes.com/2011/02/08/subtitled-video-of-wael-ghonims-emotional-tv-interview/?hp, accessed 8 February 2011.

18   See: http://www.facebook.com/shabab6april, accessed 8 February 2011. As of that date there were 55,540 people who had "liked" the page, and comments were drawing hundreds of comments and "likes." According to an article in the *New York Times*, the creators of the April 6th page contacted the "We are Khaled Said" page to get help with their "marketing." See: http://www.nytimes.com/2011/02/10/world/middleeast/10youth.html?ref=world, accessed 10 February 2011.

19   Most prominent of these is Wael Abbas, whose blog *misrdigital.com* has been a focal point for anti-regime activism since at least 2005. See: http://abcnews.go.com/Blotter/egypt-police-brutality-documented-blogger-wael-abbas-now/story?id=12831672, accessed 8 February 2011. However, Abbas is far from the only one – Egypt has long had an active blogosphere; for background see: http://www.movements.org/blog/entry/pointing-the-spotlight-on-digital-activism-in-egypt/, accessed 8 February 2011.

20   Robert H. Knapp, "A Psychology of Rumor," *Public Opinion Quarterly*, vol. 1, no. 8, 1944.

21   Robert Knapp, OSS Secret Memo, "Criteria of a Successful Rumor" at: http://www.icdc.com/~paulwolf/oss/rumormanual2june1943.htm accessed 8 February 2011.

22   Tamotsu Shibutani, *Improvised News: A Sociological Study of Rumor* (Indianapolis, IN: Bobbs-Merrill Co., 1966).

23   See for example: http://www.guardian.co.uk/commentisfree/2010/dec/28/

tunisia-ben-ali, accessed 10 February 2011. Blog and Twitter sentiment is described at: http://globalvoicesonline.org/2010/12/23/tunisia-unemployed-mans-suicide-attempt-sparks-riots/, accessed 10 February 2011.

24 See for example: http://english.aljazeera.net/indepth/features/2011/01/2011116 84242518839.html, accessed 10 February 2011.

25 Based on: http://answers.yahoo.com/question/index?qid=20060804172645A AAg6cP, accessed 10 February 2011. The authority of these claims is open to question.

26 See: http://www.slate.com/id/2095809/, accessed 10 February 2011. There are three exceptions to this, including "treaty materials" and "documents prepared for the President's signature." This raises the intriguing question of whether or not a document that was properly signed but in the wrong font would be valid. The State Department memo has not been posted online, and the Australian newspaper which claimed the story no longer makes the article available. However, several references remain, including: http://forums. civfanatics.com/archive/index.php/t-77603.html, accessed 10 February 2011.

27 See: http://www.wired.com/science/discoveries/magazine/17-05/ff_kryptos

28 Linebarger, p. 117.

29 Robert Heath and Paul Feldwick, "Fifty Years of Using the Wrong Model of Advertising," *International Journal of Market Research*, vol. 50, no. 1, 2007.

30 http://english.hani.co.kr/arti/english_edition/e_international/287525.html

31 Choe Sang-Hun, "An Anger in South Korea Over More Than Beef," *New York Times*, 12 June 2008.

32 Set up during the administration of President George W. Bush under the guidance of Undersecretary of State Karen Hughes, the Rapid Response Unit (RRU) monitored global news for the purpose of issuing immediate rebuttals and refutations information that was considered "wrong." See the interview with RRU member Greg Barker on the PBS show "Frontline," aired 27 March 2007, http://www.pbs.org/frontlineworld/stories/newswar/war_reporter.html.

33 Prominent examples include George Lakoff, *The Political Mind* (New York: Viking, 2008); Drew Westen, *The Political Brain* (Cambridge, MA: Perseus Books, 2007); Kishore Mahbubani, *Can Asians Think?* (Singapore: Times Media Publishing, 1998); Richard Nisbett, *The Geography of Thought* (New York: Free Press, 2003); Charles M. Hampden-Turner and Fons Trompenaars, *Building Cross-Cultural Competence* (New Haven, CT: Yale University Press, 2000), and Farhad Manjoo, *True Enough* (Hoboken, NJ: Wiley, 2008.

34 Christian Smith, *Moral, Believing Animals: Human Personhood and Culture* (Oxford and New York: Oxford University Press, 2003), Kindle version, location 762–765 (chapter 4).

35 This argument is developed at length in Anthony Olcott, *Russian Pulp: The Way of Russian Crime* (New York: Rowman Littlefield, 2003).

36 Stephanie R. Kelley, "Rumors in Iraq: A Guide to Winning Hearts and Minds," Naval Postgraduate School Thesis, 2004, at: http://www.au.af.mil/au/awc/ awcgate/nps/kelley_sep04.pdf

37 Stephanie R. Kelley, "Rumors in Iraq: A Guide to Winning Hearts and Minds," *Strategic Insights*, vol. 4, no. 2, February 2005.

38 Major Daniel Schmitt, "Cultural Terrain – Mapping out the Future," thesis submitted 2007, at: http://dodreports.com/pdf/ada509524.pdf, accessed 15 February 2011.

39 Major Ben Connable, "All Our Eggs in a Broken Basket," *Military Review*, March–April 2009, p. 57.

40 Defense Science Board Task Force on Defense Intelligence, *Counterinsurgency (COIN) Intelligence, Surveillance, and Reconnaissance (ISR) Operations*, February 2011, at: http://www.acq.osd.mil/dsb/reports/2011-05-COIN.pdf, accessed 30 May 2011.

41 Jeannie L. Johnson, Kerry M. Kartchner and Jeffrey Arthur Larsen (eds), *Strategic Culture and Weapons of Mass Destruction: Culturally Based Insights into Comparative National Security Policymaking* (New York: Palgrave Macmillan, 2009).

42 Johnson *et al.*, p. 245.

43 Johnson *et al.*, pp. 245–52.

44 See for example the prescient blog post by Egyptian journalist Mona Eltahawy, "Generation Facebook," posted on 1 May 2008, which ends with the phrase "Egypt's Generation Facebook, unlike its octogenarian leader, has time on its side." At: http://www.monaeltahawy.com/blog/?p=48, accessed 17 February 2011.

45 Reporters David Kirkpatrick and David Sanger offered a particularly detailed explanation of the complex background that led up to the 26 January movement, in their article "A Tunisian-Egyptian Link that Shook Arab History," *New York Times*, 13 February 2011.

46 Edward Jay Epstein, "Have You Ever Tried to Sell a Diamond?" *The Atlantic*, February 1982.

47 M. C. Farrelly, *et al.*, "Youth Tobacco Prevention Mass Media Campaigns: Past, Present, and Future Directions," BMJ Journals Online, at: http://www.ncbi.nlm.nih.gov/pmc/articles/PMC1766092/pdf/v012p00i35.pdf, accessed 16 February 2011.

48 See: http://www.gaebler.com/Direct-Mail-Response-Rates.htm, accessed 16 February 2011.

49 See: http://www.google.com/support/forum/p/AdWords/thread?tid=7aeb3290fd8feccb&hl=en, accessed 16 February 2011.

50 See: http://www.webmasterworld.com/google_adwords/3424299.htm, accessed 16 February 2011, and: http://www.facebook.com/note.php?note_id=303041339135, accessed 16 February 2011.

51 In Clive Thompson, "Is the Tipping Point Toast?" *Fast Company*, 1 February 2008, at: http://www.fastcompany.com/magazine/122/is-the-tipping-point-toast.html, accessed 16 February 2011.

52 C. Kellow and H. Steeves, "The Role of Radio in the Rwandan Genocide," *Journal of Communication*, vol. 48, no. 3, 1998, p. 128.

53 Richard Carver, "Broadcasting and Political Transition," in Richard Fardon and Graham Furniss (eds), *African Broadcast Cultures: Radio in Transition* (Oxford: James Currey, 2000), p. 192.

54 Mary Kirmani, "RTLM: A Tool for Mass Murder," in Allan Thompson (ed.), *The Media and the Rwanda Genocide* (Ann Arbor, MI and London: Pluto Press, 2007), p. 123.

55 See for example: http://maddowblog.msnbc.msn.com/_news/2011/02/03/5983241-the-counterrevolution-will-be-tweeted, accessed 17 February 2011.

56 For an extended discussion of this, with a supporting bibliography, see Christina Archetti, "Fighting Brand al-Qaida," paper for presentation at the UK Political Science Association annual meeting, April 2009, at: http://www.psa.ac.uk/journals/pdf/5/2009/Archetti.pdf, accessed 4 February 2011.

57 Daniel Kimmage, *The Al-Qaeda Media Nexus*, at: http://docs.rferl.org/en-US/AQ_Media_Nexus.pdf.

58 Jonathon Shainin, "The Ziggurat of Zealotry," *New York Times Magazine*, 10 December 2006.

59 Leonard Doob, "Goebbels' Principles of Propaganda," *The Public Opinion Quarterly*, vol. 14, no. 3, Autumn 1950, p. 422.

CHAPTER NINE

A world awash
in images

In much the same way that the IC has tended to trust or value physical information more than it does verbal information (to use David Kahn's terms), so has it had an ambivalent, even contradictory approach to visual information. On the one hand, the perceived need to obtain "ground truth" information about adversaries, especially the USSR, was one of the strongest drivers of the growth and development of the CIA and other intelligence components, resulting in such programs as Operation Genetrix (which released unmanned balloons with cameras over Soviet and Chinese territory), the U2 project, the Project Oxcart development of the A-12 spy plane, and the entire range of satellite reconnaissance projects, beginning with the once-Top-Secret, now-famous Corona Project.[1] Indeed, it was the drive to acquire photographic evidence that eventually resulted in the creation in 2003 of the National Geospatial-Intelligence Agency (NGA), one of the 16 constituent entities under the umbrella of the Directorate of National Intelligence. NGA was aggregated over the decades from, first, the various aerial photography units active in the service branches in World War II, which later were gathered into the Photographic Intelligence Division of the CIA. That in turn became the National Reconnaissance Office (NRO), a top-secret entity that was not officially acknowledged even to exist for thirty years.[2] NRO in its turn became one of the founding parts of the National Imagery and Mapping Agency (NIMA) when that agency was set up in 1996.[3] Although NGA's mission includes the collection and interpretation of a broad range of information other than overhead photographs, it is nonetheless fair to describe NGA as the IC's prime collector of visual information, and as such a testament to the value that policymakers place on what NGA is able to collect.

At the same time, however, the collection of open source visual information has been a far more halting and *ad hoc* effort, with no open source equivalent of NGA remotely in evidence. To be fair, a certain part of the reluctance to deal with photographs and film has historically been due to the technological limitations inherent in monitoring visual media. As has already been discussed, the roots of FBIS lay originally in radio, and then moved with time to include newspapers. Although TV was firmly established as an object of collection by 1974 (the first date year for which FBIS Daily Reports have been digitized and thus made searchable), the volume of material reported by FBIS which came from TV was basically insignificant, constituting only about three percent of the publicly available total FBIS output for the period 1974–1996.[4] More importantly, however, all of that reporting treated TV as if it were "radio with pictures"[5] – what was collected were the texts of press conferences, leader speeches, and segments from national news broadcasts. Again, there were technological reasons for this – although it was physically possible for the whole of that period to capture images from TV (Sony introduced its Betamax video recorder in 1975), there was no obvious or low-cost way that visual material recorded from TV could have been easily or routinely distributed.

There is another issue with visual images that, while of less concern to the government (because the classification "For Official Use Only" is generally regarded as permitting reproduction of materials, even copyrighted ones, as required for the execution of duties) has a clear impact on – among other examples – this chapter. In addition to being generally more costly to print than is text, visual images are also extremely easy to copyright, since the image is, in effect, the entire whole, incapable of excerpting. The "Fair Use Doctrine" currently in effect in US law was last revised in 1961, and envisions "quoting" as an entirely textual activity. As the official website www.copyright.gov explains:

> examples of activities that courts have regarded as fair use [include]: 'quotation of excerpts in a review or criticism for purposes of illustration or comment; quotation of short passages in a scholarly or technical work, for illustration or clarification of the author's observations; use in a parody of some of the content of the work parodied; summary of an address or article, with brief quotations, in a news report; reproduction by a library of a portion of a work to replace part of a damaged copy; reproduction by a teacher or student of a small part of a work to illustrate a lesson; reproduction of a work in legislative or judicial proceedings or reports; incidental and fortuitous reproduction, in a newsreel or broadcast, of a work located in the scene of an event being reported.'[6]

There is no corresponding "fair use" for pictures, meaning that – as seems often to be the case – the challenges and rewards of using visual materials for intelligence purposes must unfortunately be done in text, in effect turning pictures back into words.

For all these reasons text has remained the default distribution for visual materials up to the present day, as may be seen in an Open Source Center report of the contents of a Taliban video, released in November 2009, and available on the Federation of American Scientists (FAS) website. The text of the report describes what the film shows, also describes what background music or voice overlay the film contains, and then transcribes what voices recorded in the film are saying – all of this in text. To be sure, technology now is such that the report also includes a link to the video itself, but in all other ways the treatment of the Taliban propaganda video is as it might have been 50 years earlier.[7]

Another issue which may have impacted the IC's general attitude toward open source visual information is that visual information is much more data-dense than is textual information, requiring much greater storage space and capacity, no matter what the form in which the visual material is stored. To take but one example, an electronic version of *War and Peace* is 1387.2 KB in size,[8] while a digital movie, a storage industry study warns, could require 1,600 *terabytes* of storage – or more than 1024 x 1024 x 1024 times greater than is required to store the novel.[9] The intelligence community had learned this lesson even before the CIA was created – in 1944 the OSS's Pictorial Records unit appealed to the US public for photos taken in Europe or Japan which might have intelligence value, after which they received "hundreds of thousands of photos ... showing equestrian monuments and sea gulls." Sherman Kent later judged that only about 1 percent of that flood had any value (and that only because it was produced by professional journalist-photographers); he may however have been off by a percentage point or two, because the flood of images was so great that the Pictorial Records unit simply stopped opening the mail bags when they arrived.[10]

Visual information is also generally much harder to process and "read" than is text – one indicator of which is that the CIA's Long-Range Plan of 1965, which was the first to take account of the suddenly enhanced capabilities for photographic reconnaissance offered by the fledgling satellite industry, projected that staffing requirements at the National Photo Interpretation Center (NPIC) would "account for over half of the CIA's expansion over the next five years" because of the need for "more trained photo interpreters ... essential to keep up with the flow of photography."[11] As has already been discussed, the problem of how to store *and retrieve* even just textual material was so great that, as a study done of DIA in 1968 charged, the existing storage and retrieval system was "too slow, poor in coding, and poor in reproducing documents," as a consequence of which it was "impossible to know what data was available [so] there was no ground to deny a requirement to collect more of the same," meaning that "distrusting central files, analysts set up their own in a duplicative and wasteful manner."[12]

While Google and other search engines may have created a solution for text IR (information retrieval), the search for a reliable, workable, high-volume version of what has been dubbed a VIRAT (Visual Image Retrieval and Analysis Tool) continues to be unresolved. Although search engines for video exist, all of those that are publicly available rely upon some form of meta-data – meaning either the textual tags that people apply manually to the videos (whether amateurs uploading video to YouTube or professional broadcast technicians annotating videos of sporting events), or the text that accompanies, for example, some TV broadcasts for closed-captioning purposes (or which can be created by voice recognition software). In either case such tagging relies upon humans who must be consigned to the tedious task of actually watching video. In the words of a DARPA bid solicitation for VIRATs, at present the only way that video can only be analyzed is through a process which is "very labor intensive, and limited to metadata queries, manual annotations, and 'fast-forward' examination of clips."[13] DARPA – the R&D body of the Pentagon – has become involved in the quest for good VIRATs because of the rapid increase not only in the number of unmanned photographic reconnaissance platforms (most of them UAVs such as the Predator and Reaper, the use of which has tripled between 2007 and 2010) but also because the number of cameras that each carries has grown from one to many – meaning that the total quantity of stored video that an analyst might wish to access, if it were possible, is growing exponentially.

A final technical impediment which might also be pointed out is that video is stubbornly linear, meaning that, unlike a text, it is extremely difficult to "skim" or "speed-read." There are also few good means available for "hand-delivery" of a video, both characteristics which make the briefers who deliver the President's Daily Brief (PDB) or give other types of briefings to high officials and policymakers reluctant to use video in their presentations. A clip running even a few seconds can seem endless in the office of a busy impatient official, particularly if the machine on which it is to be shown is balky or acts up.

"A crowd thinks in images"

For all the difficulties outlined above, however, there is another issue which has probably been the greatest brake on the IC's exploitation of the visual equivalent of Kahn's "verbal intelligence." This is a continued, deep-seated bias among analysts and policymakers alike which favors textual information over visual. A good part of this is simply legacy – people are taught how to "read" texts from their earliest days, and those who reach the ranks of IC analysts or major policymakers are likely to be those who have done particularly well at "text-reading" through the years. There is no equivalent process for learning what some call "visual literacy" or what others have called "visuality."

Although this term may smack of the "post-modern," visuality was first used as a term parallel to literacy in the 1830s by historian Thomas Carlyle, who was trying to create an approach to understanding history that moved beyond "facts" to also account for the imagination or "spirit" behind events.[14] Although Carlyle was attempting to create a historical prose style that would evoke the highly dramatic paintings of historical events that were popular at that time, his appeal to evoke emotion and some ineffable spirit larger than the recitation of facts would create was an effort to move beyond what he called the books authored by "Mr. Dryasdust" because of reliance on "the technical apparatus of historical research such as archives or even libraries."[15] Clearly such a view is in direct contradiction to that of Sherman Kent. As was pointed out in Chapter Six, in his 1941 book *Writing History* Kent had offered German historian Ernst Bernheim as the model for a would-be historian to emulate,[16] precisely because Bernheim believed that real history could come *only* from "*remains*," by which Bernheim meant physical objects which "testify to the factuality of the occurrence." Bernheim contrasted these to "*tradition*," by which he meant "the occurrence as it was interpreted by someone"[17] – precisely, it would seem, the kind of higher "visuality" for which Carlyle was arguing.

At least one scholar has argued that the antipathy of historians like Kent to "visuality" may run even deeper than a simple disagreement about what constitutes history. Stuart Ewen contends that French sociologist Gustave Le Bon had a profound effect on the course of western social science, particularly in the inter-war period, in the form of his book *The Crowd: A Study of the Popular Mind*, published in French in 1895 and, within a year, translated into 19 languages (according to Ewen, President T. Roosevelt kept a copy on his bedside table).[18] Based on his understanding of the Paris Commune of 1871, Le Bon argued that a crowd is a distinctively different creature than is any of the single humans which gather together to become a crowd. As Le Bon wrote:

> Moreover, by the mere fact that he forms part of an organised crowd, a man descends several rungs in the ladder of civilisation. Isolated, he may be a cultivated individual; in a crowd, he is a barbarian – that is, a creature acting by instinct. He possesses the spontaneity, the violence, the ferocity, and also the enthusiasm and heroism of primitive beings, whom he further tends to resemble by the facility with which he allows himself to be impressed by words and images – which would be entirely without action on each of the isolated individuals composing the crowd – and

to be induced to commit acts contrary to his most obvious interests and his best-known habits. An individual in a crowd is a grain of sand amid other grains of sand, which the wind stirs up at will.[19]

Although in this passage Le Bon credits both words and images with the power to stir up crowds, the "words" he means are those of a powerful speaker, not a text. Further on Le Bon merges the two, writing,

> A crowd thinks in images, and the image itself immediately calls up a series of other images, having no logical connection with the first… Our reason shows us the incoherence there is in these images, but a crowd is almost blind to this truth, and confuses with the real event what the deforming action of its imagination has superimposed thereon. A crowd scarcely distinguishes between the subjective and the objective. It accepts as real the images evoked in its mind, though they most often have only a very distant relation with the observed fact.[20]

The phrase "images evoked in his mind" recalls of course Walter Lippmann, who traced most of the problems of modern democracy to the "pictures in our heads,"[21] those stereotypes, largely erroneous, that people form about places, issues, and people that they do not know from first-hand experience. According to Ewen, the similarity of terms is not a coincidence – Le Bon was a strong influence on Graham Wallas, who was one of Lippmann's professors at Harvard, and a reason why, in Ewen's phrase, Lippmann became "the American interpreter of Gustave Le Bon."[22] As has already been noted, Kent shared Lippmann's disdain for those who take as reality the shadows on Plato's cave (the passage from *The Republic* which Lippmann used as the dedication page in *Public Opinion*). Although never fully agued out as such, the implication of much of Lippmann's writing, and with him Kent's, is the conviction that the visual is inherently erroneous, irrational, and not the stuff of which good analysis is made.

Welcome to the fishbowl

The problem which increasingly confronts both analysts and policymakers, however, is that visual information is playing an ever greater role in the shaping of public opinion – just as Lippmann feared. Unlike Lippmann's day, however, the technology of photo and video production is cheap, easy, and – as a consequence – ubiquitous. The confluence of mobile devices with digital photography (basically unanticipated a decade ago) has resulted in staggering amounts of visual imagery. The challenge of YouTube has already been mentioned in Chapter Five, but that is just part of the problem.

Facebook is generally acknowledged still to lag behind YouTube as a video provider, but nevertheless reported in June 2010 that the number of videos uploaded to the site was "more than 20 million per month" – up from "about 12 million a month" just three months earlier.[23] Unlike YouTube, though, Facebook also hosts photos. Here too Facebook is not the largest photo repository, but rather is one of five which, collectively, were reckoned in 2009 to hold nearly 50 billion photos.[24] What is more important than the volume of images available, however, is the role that visual imagery – particularly that which is produced by amateurs – is increasingly coming to play in world affairs. Examples are so numerous that any illustrative list will seem almost random, but might include:

- The cell-phone videos of Saddam Hussein's execution, which transformed what was to have been a solemn event into a Sunni-Shi'a confrontation, thus recasting the narrative which the Iraqi and US authorities were trying to shape;[25]

- Cell-phone stills and video played a large role in the creation and documentation of street protests and demonstrations in Iran during the 2009 parliamentary elections; in Tunisia in December 2010; in Egypt in January 2011; and in Syria in April 2011. Although the precise nature of the role is a subject of fairly intensive debate among pundits and policymakers, the fact that participants enthusiastically take and share videos and stills intuitively has to have some impact – one reason why when authorities shut off the internet Egyptian activists in Tahrir Square jury-rigged handmade directional antennas to download cell-phone videos and then leap-frog them out of the country, until their signals could reach computers outside of Egypt which still had access, and thus could beam the photos and videos to the world.[26] On the other hand, the ubiquity of shared photos and videos has reportedly also allowed Iran authorities to "crowd-source" identification of dissenters whom they wished to single out for punishment;[27]

- Tang Jie, a 28-year-old graduate student at Fudan University, in Shanghai, was able to use a combination of simple still photos taken from the internet, the movie-making equipment on his laptop, and a theme song he found on the internet to create his first video, "2008 China Stand Up!" – a passionate nationalist outburst by a young man who argues that China is being tricked, cheated, and undervalued by the rest of the world. In its first ten days on Sina.com, a major Chinese website, the video drew more than a million viewers – an average of more than two per second – and tens of thousands of positive comments. By the end of the month it was a kind of unofficial rallying video for the so-called "angry youth," an intensely nationalistic group of Chinese youth;[28]

- Even North Korea, traditionally considered to be at the bottom end of the media availability spectrum, is reported now to have significant access to foreign video, as at least one-fifth of the population is reported to have DVD players,[29] and state TV has played the British film *Bend It Like Beckham* and the US film *Titanic* (in addition to a steady flow of Tom and Jerry cartoons).[30] More significantly, defectors and anti-regime supporters outside of North Korea are reported to be training a cadre of "citizen journalists" to document and report on conditions inside the hermetic country, in part with small digital video cameras. With USB drives, video content is also viewable inside DPRK.[31]

This list has deliberately omitted the better known examples – the Abu Ghraib photos, for example, or the more recent iterations of the same phenomenon, the US soldiers in Afghanistan said to be posing with bodies,[32] or the videos of German soldiers, also in Afghanistan, playing with skulls and human bones.[33] It also omits well-known "gaffe videos," such as that which torpedoed the Senate campaign of George Allen,[34] and also omits famous fakes, such as the composite photo which claimed to show then-presidential candidate John Kerry as having spoken years before at an anti-war rally with Jane Fonda.[35]

This list also omits the cross-over visual platform of video games, which, according to a 2008 study by the Pew Foundation, are played for an average of an hour a day by 97 percent of US teens,[36] as well as by millions more people overseas. Almost certainly overlooked by intelligence collectors, these games, and especially the industry segment known as "serious games" or "games for change," are a huge, growing, and highly ideological phenomenon. Gaming scholar Ian Bogost has argued that gaming is becoming what he calls "procedural rhetoric," a way of making claims about "the rules" by which the world functions. In his words:

> Video games are not just stages that facilitate cultural, social, or political practices; they are also media where cultural values themselves can be represented – for critique, satire, education, or commentary. When understood in this way, we can learn to read games as deliberate expressions of particular perspectives. In other words, video games make claims about the world, which players can understand, evaluate, and deliberate.[37]

Anyone tempted to dismiss these as "merely games" might wish to look at, for example, *WeForest*[38] or *Tilt Flip*,[39] global-warming games that teach children it is good to plant trees. Or a person might play *Peacemaker*,[40] which negotiates a peace settlement between Israel and Palestine (and, the website claims, "challenges you to succeed as a leader where others have failed"). Another choice might be *PeoplePower*,[41] which in the course of play teaches practical ways to organize a non-violent struggle between "the Movement" and "the Regime" (a game played by the organizers of protests in Cairo's Tahrir Square, according to its creator, and soon to be translated into Arabic, Russian, and Spanish).

The point, in other words, is that visual imagery plays an enormous – and quickly growing – role in the formation of public opinion. As such, it should be a legitimate object of collection and analysis, just as is the case with text. In addition to the problems already listed above, however, must also be added the fact that there is no agreed-upon methodology for how best to analyze visual imagery.

Taking pictures into account

One of the difficulties of trying to impose an analytic methodology on visual material is that there has been an enormous quantity of literature written about images, but very little of it seems useful in an intelligence context. Given that even the mechanics of vision are not wholly understood (current thinking appears to be that, as one researcher puts it, "what we perceive accords not with the retinal stimulus, or the properties of the underlying objects, but with what the same or similar stimuli have typically signified in both the species over the eons and experiences of the individuals over their lifetimes"),[42] it is probably not surprising that there is far more surmise in the field of visual interpretation than there is hard evidence.

One of the reasons that this may be true is that, just as the quote above suggests, visual information "signifies" meanings – a word chosen because it attempts to capture the ways in which visual information bypasses the logical, calculating processes of the brain, and reaches more directly for emotion. Indeed, the process of transforming light energy into mental images ("seeing") appears to involve heuristics, or mental shortcuts that prompt the brain to pull up stored responses to stimuli, with the result that we can "see" things that aren't there, or, equally, fail to see things that are. As authors Christopher Chabris and Daniel Simons argue in their book *The Invisible Gorilla*,[43] our visual processing apparatus seems to be evolved for the purposes of perceiving patterns – even if those "patterns" are in fact non-existent (a phenomenon known as *pareidolia*). Indeed, as they point out, that "seeing" of a pattern can take place in seconds, or even milliseconds – a phenomenon which author Malcolm Gladwell explored at length in his book *Blink*.[44] As Gladwell noted, people make extraordinarily quick judgments about visual phenomena, in a process that appears completely to bypass conscious thought. Both books assume that this "blink" reaction must have conveyed adaptive advantage on our ancestors – reacting *as though* a pattern spells danger is probably a better long-range strategy than not responding, since the cost of "false positives" is so much lower than that of "false negatives." Implicit in both arguments, however, is that humans rely on heuristics – or, to use an older word, stereotypes – to judge visual information.

That has several consequences, of which the analyst needs to be mindful as he or she attempts to interpret images. Anthropologists have demonstrated, for example, that people from "holistic cultures" (a term which usually applies primarily to East and Southeast Asian cultures) and those from "analytic cultures" (Europeans and Americans) will notice very different elements in the same picture, and thus interpret them differently. In what has become known as the "Michigan fish test," American respondents shown animated pictures of three large fish swimming in an aquarium which also contains smaller fish, plants, and other objects, will "notice" only the three big fish, while respondents from Japan focus more on the picture as a whole, which the researchers interpreted to mean that the two groups would tend to respond very differently to the same visual stimulus.[45] That same study also seemed to indicate that "analytic culture" viewers were more easily able to separate a focal animal from a background, so that they could discern whether or not they were being re-shown an animal they had already seen, but with a different background, while the "holistic culture" viewers had more difficulty deciding whether the animal was the same if the background changed. By the same token, however, Americans took longer to decide, which the study's authors interpreted to mean that the process of analytic cognition was more time consuming than holistic or relational viewing. Given that the animals shown in this second test were wolves (or so the pictures in the text show), these findings suggest a potential for differential interpretation of whether or not something is threatening.

Heuristics also mean that the originator of visual imagery has very little control over how the message is interpreted. As ambiguous as text can sometime seem, that ambiguity is nothing in comparison to what happened, for example, to photographer Eddie Adams, who photographed South Vietnamese General Nguyen Ngoc Loan at the moment when he was shooting a Viet Cong prisoner in the head.[46] As Adams wrote in the obituary he penned for General Loan in 1998, he had taken the photo because he considered Loan to be an admirable soldier who was doing his duty – as Adams asked rhetorically in his obituary, "What would you do if you were the general at that time and place on that hot day, and you caught the so-called bad guy after he blew away one, two or three American soldiers?"[47] The picture, however, became what Adams called "a lie" because any viewer's sympathy inevitably will be with the man who is about to die, rather than with the man shooting. Whatever the context before the event (when asked why he had shot, General Loan said his victim, later identified as Viet Cong member Nguyen Van Lam, had killed many "South Vietnamese and even Americans"[48]) or afterward (when, as Adams put it, "I killed the general with my camera" because the photo "really messed up the rest of his life"[49]), the moment frozen in the picture has become one of the most famous ever taken, with its meaning totally beyond the control of its creator. The same might also be said of Cuban photographer Alberto Korda, whose photo of Che Guevara[50] has appeared on everything from Cuban banknotes to Bart Simpson tee-shirts.

A methodology for visual persuasion

That a picture can come to mean essentially the opposite of what its creator intended it to mean should be a caution for anyone attempting to impute a "meaning" to visual imagery. There have been periodic bursts of scholarly activity around this question, generally grouped together under the notion of "semiotics," or the study of signs. Intended to be a rigorous approach to interpreting visual imagery, the field has made some important contributions, in particular in its argument that images are representations of larger, more complex arguments (the "signifier" and the "signified" combining to become a "sign," which then can itself become a new "signifier," in an almost endless process[51]).

Unfortunately, semiotics has also managed to get itself so tangled in jargon and the general problem of trying to use words to interpret pictures (to say nothing of the further problem, that the interpretations can easily seem idiosyncratic) that the term has become almost a synonym for "irredeemably academic." That has complicated the efforts being made by the few government agencies which are taking concerted, if sometimes halting, steps toward developing a methodology for at least systematizing and categorizing visual persuasion items – ranging from still photographs through short videos to full-length movies – as a first step toward a more robust analytic method.

One of the most active in this effort is the DNI's Open Source Center, which – to judge by an article written by an Open Source Center analyst and two private-sector contractors[52] – seems to be returning to its FBIS roots, basing a nascent visual analysis methodology on a Lasswell-like foundation. According to the authors, the four most important parameters for visual analysis are identifying the "persuasive themes, master narratives, content and technical signatures, and indicators of audience resonance and effects"[53] in a given image or group of images. In essence, taking for granted that the reason a particular piece or set of visual material has been selected is because of interest in the sender (whether jihadist recruiters using the As-Sahab production and distribution network, the developing video production capabilities of the nationalist, pro-Kremlin youth group Nashi, or an independent outlier like Tang Jie), the rest of the elements adhere rather closely to the Lasswell formula.

As the authors argue, there is a surprisingly small "vocabulary" of themes to which visual message senders can appeal in their "rhetorical shaping" of the images they send. This is one of the consequences of the "blink" phenomenon noted above – among the reasons that visual messaging can bypass the logic processing parts of the brain is the library of heuristic stereotypes with which we all are born, augmented by those which we acquire as we grow up in particular environments. In this regard it is worth bearing in mind that today's media environment provides a steady stream of normative narratives, building and constantly reinforcing locally-specific notions of what is right and wrong, what good and bad.[54] Whether this flow leads to the inevitable "violence phenomena" that, for example, researcher George Gerbner has suggested (his "cultivation theory" research has attempted to establish that TV in particular teaches "the cultivation of fear and acquiescence to power"[55]), it is true that youth ages eight to eighteen in the US are said now to devote almost seven hours a day to consuming visual media,[56] while other studies suggest families (and not just youth) in the US and Europe watch anywhere from two and a half hours a day in Sweden to more than eight in the US.[57] As noted above, video games probably also increasingly serve this function.

The emerging OSC methodology suggests that a first step in visual analysis is to identify the rhetorical heuristics which the attempted communication is using. Aggregating information from several sources, the authors of the *Parameters* article provide several examples of what they call "persuasive themes" – which, although they do not make the point, seem to fall into almost binary oppositions, meaning that the themes into which a viewer might sort an image are even fewer than the authors suggest. Table 2 below shows some of the themes they name, but arrays these to further suggest how, for example, an image of a leader might be an attempt either to enhance or to degrade him or her.

As the authors argue, such persuasive themes "are appealing for neuro-psychological, cultural, and contextual reasons that make them an important weapon in the arsenal of any communicator. When systematically identified and catalogued, they can also prove invaluable in deconstructing a persuader's strategy, goals, and intended audiences."[58] Thus for example the Nazi images of strong, manly blonde warriors, contrasted to pictures of rat-like non-Aryans, can be understood as appealing immediately to heuristics of "strength and superiority," "intolerance and xenophobia," "righteous cause," and "dehumanization." Other categories might suggest

Table 2: Some persistent themes of visual persuasion

Positive Themes	Negative Themes
Strength and superiority	Weakness and inferiority
Humanization	Dehumanization
Resistance and struggle	Victimization
Righteous cause	Scapegoating
Leader glorification	Leader denigration
Traditional and nostalgia	Iconoclasm
Belonging and affiliation	Intolerance and xenophobia

themselves to a particular group of viewers as well, which illustrates two important phenomena about visual imagery – the first that, as has already been mentioned, imagery is more ambiguous than text, and so will evoke a wider range of reactions from a given audience, and the second that, even so, both experience and available research suggest that, despite some differences and disagreements, viewer responses tend to cluster around similar themes, meaning that it is very rare to find an image that evokes completely contradictory heuristics among viewers. Persuasive themes, as the authors argue, "are, at a high level, universal."[59]

This does not mean, of course, that viewers will necessarily be persuaded by a given set of images – those whom visual images attack and vilify, to state an obvious example, are unlikely to be swayed – but most viewers will recognize the same themes to which the appeal is being made. What makes them persuasive, or not, is how those appeals fit into the much more specific "master narratives" that were outlined in Chapter Eight. As is explained there, master narratives vary dramatically from culture to culture. As what one source calls the "formulas or 'scripts' that we often use when we tell stories," master narratives "embody our expectations about how things work."[60] It has already been pointed out in Chapter Eight that most current research indicates that people are unlikely even to perceive, let alone be persuaded by, messaging that does not fit within a master narrative which they do not accept. What the Eddie Adams story suggests, however, is that the visual elements of a photo or video can be so affective that the sender's intent can be lost entirely, and the material incorporated into a new master narrative. This sort of message "hijacking" is much less likely to occur with texts.[61]

What makes visual images both more powerful and more malleable than texts is, as the *Parameters* authors note, the multiplicity of non-verbal cues and clues that such messages employ, stimulating viewer responses in ways that often are quite unconscious. All humans are hard-wired to respond to facial expressions, for example, so that images of faces can evoke empathy, protectiveness, disgust, fear, or other emotions, simply by the way in which these are presented. The desired audience response can be further reinforced through technical means – a low camera angle can make a viewer feel as though he or she is beneath, and therefore lower than, the person being pictured (common with laudatory photos of leaders), while a high camera angle can have the opposite effect. A picture's composition can have important subliminal effects, making a leader seem exalted or isolated, or a crowd seem large or small, scattered or dense. Color too can have powerful subliminal effects – there are, for example, whole series of still photos taken in conflicts in the Middle East which focus on a child's toy, usually brightly colored, abandoned in a heap of rubble or other signs of devastation[62] (thus illustrating the adage that a good news photograph must capture an implied actor, an implied action, and an implied victim).

Color can also play subliminal affective roles, in very culturally specific ways. Green, of course, has a strong affective link for Muslims, as can black, particularly for Shi'a, who often wear the color as a sign of mourning for the death of Imam Husain in 680 CE, or, if in male headgear, as a sign of a claim to be a *sayid*, or descendent of the Prophet Mohammed. Iraqi TV broadcasts of Muqtada Sadr donning white robes as he urged his followers to resist the Coalition forces in Iraq in 2003 and 2004 are said to have been understood by fellow Shi'a as equivalent to the donning of a shroud, and as such an indicator that Sadr was prepared to fight to the death. In contrast, red is said to have no particularly significant resonance for Muslims, but does have for Chinese (as a color of good fortune) and also for Russians (as a synonym for beauty well before the Bolshevik Revolution – the reason why Red Square long predates the arrival of "the Reds"). Similar differences appear with white, which is the color of a wedding dress in the West, and of a mourner's suit in the East. Indeed, there is considerable controversy among scholars about whether "color" is even a constant thing, discernible by all peoples equally, whether historically or in the present moment.[63]

There are other technical qualities that can prove affective – the proliferation of amateur content has had the effect of making professionally produced content sometimes seem too slick and too "soul-less," while the very imperfections of amateur video or photos can seem "truer." This may be seen vividly in the contrast between the numbers who view, for example, an official, professionally produced recruiting video for the US Navy – 268,175 since 2007, in the case of one video (placed unofficially, and therefore allowing access to the viewing history),[64] or, in the case of an officially placed one (which does not allow access to the viewing history), which has been viewed 140,412 times since 2009[65] – with the almost 3.5 *million* who since 2006 have watched "Navy Carrier Squadron Pump It,"[66] a video shot by sailors themselves, then lip-synched to a song by the group Black Eyed Peas. In general, as an article in the service newspaper *Navy Times* acknowledged, "homemade videos are reaching more online viewers than the service's own pitches."[67]

So what?

The authors of the *Parameters* article end their discussion at the same point as does Chapter Eight above, and, indeed, as did Harold Lasswell, with the reminder that the first four parts of the formula (message sender → message → medium → audience) are only means toward the last element, which is the achieving of an effect. Discussion of how to measure the effect of a visual image is not substantively different than was the discussion of how to measure the impact of textual material from the previous chapter. Those wishing to send messages should, in the end, only be concerned with how well their messages are resonating with the audiences they wish to reach, and those who are trying to understand the effect of visual messages need concern themselves only with those messages which actually are resonating with a particular audience.

Although all the same points apply for visual communication attempts as were discussed for textual ones in the preceding chapter, there are nevertheless certain qualities of visual communication which present particular challenges to analysts and communicators alike. The "Eddie Adams" effect has already been noted – how people interpret images can become totally unhooked from what the senders intended. This also means that images cannot be controlled once they have gained public attention – the Iranian authorities battled hard but without success to discredit the powerful effect of the three videos which chanced to catch the death of Iranian Neda Agha-Soltan, whose image became an icon of the so-called "Green Revolution" in 2009.[68]

Another effect of visual material is the heightened reaction it can evoke for certain very basic human interests. Probably the most immediate, and most ubiquitous, is sex. As Paul Linebarger pointed out in his 1948 study *Psychological Warfare*, antagonists were making active use of the fact that, as he wrote "young human beings, especially young males, are apt to give considerable attention to sex," which – well before YouTube or Flickr – prompted the Japanese to bombard GIs with salacious pin-ups in the hopes this would "diminish morale," while the Germans offered a whole series, "The Girl You Left Behind," which showed what hijinks war profiteer "Sam Levy" was getting up to with "comely Joan Hopkins" while "tall and handsome Bob Harrison, Joan's fiancé, is on the front, thousands of miles away, fighting for guys like Sam Levy."[69]

Almost as ubiquitous, and as attention-grabbing, is humor. An excellent indicator of the differences in human interests were the results of the short-lived YouTube Video Awards, which were conducted just twice, in 2006 and then again in 2007. In both iterations a group of videos was selected by the YouTube staff, and users were given a week to indicate their favorites by watching.

Once they had "voted" for a favorite, no further voting in that category was allowed, thus providing a relatively "free and fair" result. The first year YouTube offered seven categories, and the second year, twelve. Figure 1 is based upon the total numbers of views received by the winner in each of the categories in that second year, as of the time that the winners were announced.[70] Even the least watched of these winners gathered approximately a million viewers – which only makes the obvious dominance of the "humor" category clearer – a phenomenon which has led some marketers to argue that the key to having a video "go viral" is to design so that it will appeal to what has come to be called the "Bored at Work Network."[71] Although this "BWN" responds well to humor, it also has a demonstrated penchant for the unusual, bizarre, and – a crucial element – the unpredictable. Just as filmmakers on a much larger scale have discovered, humans possess an uncanny ability to grow accustomed to novelty. Although early cinema audiences may have frightened their "social betters" by seeming literally to have been mesmerized by what they watched (Stuart Ewen cites

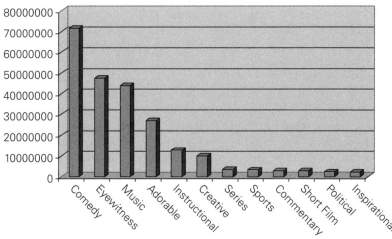

Figure 1: Number of views, winning clip by category, YouTube awards 2007

several commentators from the early twentieth century who noted the "dreamlike, hypnotic and/or suggestible state" into which viewers appear to fall as they watch cinema[72]), more recently cinema has proven to be an ever-escalating battle to gain the attention of jaded audiences (3D and computer animation, for example, appear to have become humdrum again, according to industry accounts[73]).

Just as was suggested in Chapter Five, this "BWN" phenomenon is part of the vulgarization that cheap media access has permitted. Vulgarization, it should be recalled, has two senses – one, that it is democratic, and two, that it caters to human instincts, interests, and responses of which elites unfailingly do not approve. That presents a real challenge both for IC analysts and for government communicators. While the continued high-level interest in anything having to do with North Korea might make it possible for analysts to write about the crude cartoon video that appeared, seemingly perhaps from within North Korea itself, or from recent refugees, making fun of heir-apparent Kim Jong-un and the trainload of birthday gifts intended for him which reportedly was blown up by unknown saboteurs,[74] it is far harder to imagine an easy way to discuss the importance of the "Grass Mud Horse" videos and blog entries which flooded the Chinese internet in late 2009 – both because the pun around which the videos revolved is a mother-oath and because the videos themselves are deliberately "childish."[75] It is no easier in an intelligence context to write about the work of Chinese artist "Pisan" (real name Wang Bo),[76] who manages somehow to maintain a respectable (and respected) career as an animator while also turning out dramatically critical cartoons such as the "2011 New Year's card" he created – in which high Party "tigers" (the sign of the outgoing lunar year) run over, gun down, set fire to, and poison with bad products their subservient "rabbit" subjects (the sign of the incoming year), until suddenly the rabbits grow teeth and counter-attack, reminding that they too have "two teeth standing up and can bite really hard when pushed."[77]

The problems that such interests create for those who work in government settings was made poignantly clear in a February 2011 Inspector General's report about the State Department's efforts to embrace the use of social media.[78] State has embraced the new media enthusiastically, creating the imaginative Democracy Video Challenge (DVC), and also encouraging all stations to make as much use of social media as possible, and as is consistent with the regulations. The DVC,[79] run annually since its beginning in 2008, asks people to submit their videos which in precisely three minutes or fewer will illustrate how they would complete the sentence "Democracy is …" Affiliated with but specifically not sponsored by State, the contest collects videos from six regions of the world and then asks interested parties to vote on them, just as the YouTube contest above. The contest has generated some extremely interesting videos, but it is difficult to gauge how effective the effort is. The entire channel has had 1.6 million views since 2008, and the

2010 winners, recently announced, have drawn between about 40,000 and 150,000 views each – a figure which is large compared to some of State's other videos,[80] but is nothing compared to, for example, the numbers of those who viewed "Dry Erase Girl Quits Her Job" – nearly six million *in the first 24 hours.*[81]

The Inspector General's report makes clear why this kind of imbalance is certain to persist. For one thing, the platform for the DVC, www.america. gov, is intended as the web portal to the outside world – and as such may not be accessed by Americans, since to do so would violate the Smith-Mundt Act of 1948, which forbids State from "propagandizing" American citizens. Equally athwart regulations is the notion that a video or other content might be funny (to say nothing of sexy) – as the IG report dryly states, Embassy staff "know they are supposed to focus on the MSRP [Mission Strategic and Resource Plan] but they fear that too great an emphasis on serious issues will make the site heavy, boring, and unable to attract an audience."[82] This report also notes the distance between the effort and expense required to function in the new media environment (text and visual), highlighting that posts must devote additional personnel to content creation, yet are able in the best of circumstances to generate around 150,000 "likes" on a Embassy post's Facebook page (to say nothing of the unresolvable problem that regulations require official websites to carry a "dot mil" or "dot gov" extension, which of course is impossible with a Facebook or Twitter feed).[83] The Pentagon has also faced these problems, banning social media in 2007,[84] but also establishing a DoD New Media unit (with a Wikipedia page – an unusual concession for the online encyclopedia) that cultivates bloggers, posts videos, and otherwise embraces the visual elements of this new arena. The ban was lifted in 2010,[85] but confusions and problems remain, as troops find themselves unable to disconnect from domestic problems back home, or even can find themselves busy texting or watching videos rather than being aware of the situation around them.[86]

To be fair, these problems relate to the entire new media sphere, and not just the visual ones. However, visuality is a large part of the appeal of new media – as evidenced recently by the Israeli soldier who posted pictures on her Facebook page of herself with Palestinian prisoners, and then refused to apologize.[87] Indeed, "visuality" appears to be on the verge of extending beyond photos and videos, as easy-to-use, DIY animation platforms have also begun to appear. XtraNormal, for example, requires only that a user have a script, which is then turned into a cartoon-style video using any of several possible formats, including ones which caricature leading US politicians.[88] The service has recently partnered with YouTube, which also has created easy-to-use portals for Stupeflix and GoAnimate,[89] virtually guaranteeing a rising flood of BWN-friendly content.

The chances that the analytic community will be able to cope with this new flood probably approach zero. For the time being, that may not be a problem. It is worth recalling, however, that YouTube itself was begun only eight months before FBIS was transformed into the DNI's Open Source Center, and now is viewed daily by more people than read all the world's newspapers combined.

Notes

1 See timeline provided on NGA's official website, at: https://www1.nga.mil/About/OurHistory/Documents/Chronology.pdf, accessed 15 March 2011.

2 "The NRO Mission," Report of the National Commission for the Review of the National Reconnaissance Office, 1 November 2000, at: http://www.fas.org/irp/nro/commission/nro.pdf, accessed 15 November 2011.

3 NGA timeline.

4 Based on source searches conducted on the Newsbank database, available by subscription at: http://www.newsbank.com/

5 It is worth pointing out that reducing radio broadcasts to "text-only" also forfeits considerable amounts of potential information. Harold Graves had written in 1941 that "the voice was the first means by which human beings communicated with each other. It is still the most subtle, the most used, and probably the most persuasive of all communications." *War on the Short Wave*, p. 61.

6 http://www.copyright.gov/fls/fl102.html, accessed 30 March 2011.

7 "Afghanistan – Taliban Propaganda Video Capitalizes on 'Capture' of US Base," Open Source Center Report, 30 November 2009, at: http://www.fas.org/irp/dni/osc/taliban-vid.pdf, accessed 26 March 2011. The link to the video itself is available at: http://www.fas.org/irp/dni/osc/taliban.html.

8 http://www.memoware.com/?screen=doc_detail&doc_id=9570&p=contributor_id^!162~!, accessed 18 March 2011.

9 See "2010 Digital Storage for Media and Entertainment Report," at: http://www.tomcoughlin.com/Techpapers/M&E%20Storage%20Report%20Brochure,%20033010.pdf, accessed 18 March 2011.

10 Winks, *Cloak and Gown*, pp. 106–107.

11 Cunningham Report, p. D7.

12 Cunningham Report, p. F2.

13 As quoted in an IT-industry blog, *The Register*, at: http://www.theregister.co.uk/2010/09/01/darpa_vid_search_dough/, accessed 18 March 2011.

14 Nicholas Mirzoeff, "On Visuality," *Journal of Visual Culture*, vol. 5, no. 1, April 2006, p. 55.

15 Mirzoeff, p. 56.

16 Kent, *Writing History*, p. 6. The book Kent cites, *Lehrbuch der historischen Methode und der Geschichtsphilosophie*, was first published in 1889 and was subsequently republished in five further editions, the last of which appeared in 1908 – the one to which Kent refers. Bernheim's book appears never to have been translated into English.

17 Patrick Kelly, "The Methodology of Ernst Bernheim and Legal History," at: http://www.scribd.com/doc/20021802/The-Methodology-of-Ernst-Bernheim-and-Legal-History-Patrick-Kelly, accessed 7 March 2011.

18 Ewen, "Reflections on Visual Persuasion," p. 811.

19 Gustave Le Bon, *The Crowd: A Study of the Popular Mind*, electronic version at Electronic Text Center, University of Virginia Library, http://etext.virginia.edu/etcbin/toccer-new2?id=BonCrow.sgm&images=images/modeng&data=/texts/english/modeng/parsed&tag=public&part=all, accessed 10 March 2011, p. 13.

20 Le Bon, pp. 23–24.

21 See Chapter 1 of Lippmann, *Public Opinion*, "The World Outside and the Pictures in Our Heads."

22 Ewen, "Reflections on Visual Persuasion," p. 813.

23 "Facebook: 2B Videos Viewed per Month," 8 June 2010, at: http://gigaom.com/video/facebook-2b-videos-viewed-per-month/, accessed 22 March 2011.

24 Those five, in order, are Image Shack, Facebook, PhotoBucket, Flickr, and Multiply. Google, which owns Picasa, refuses to divulge numbers, saying only that it holds "billions" of photos. See "Who Has the Most Photos of Them All? Hint: It is Not Facebook," at: http://techcrunch.com/2009/04/07/who-has-the-most-photos-of-them-all-hint-it-is-not-facebook/, accessed 22 March 2011.

25 See for example comments at: http://www.albionmonitor.com/0612a/copyright/saddamexecute4.html, accessed 22 March 2011; and at: http://hnn.us/articles/33747.html, accessed 22 March 2011.

26 "Signalling Dissent," *The Economist*, 17 March 2011.

27 "Iranian Officials 'Crowd-Source' Protester Identities," 27 June 2009, at: http://globalvoicesonline.org/2009/06/27/iranian-officials-crowd-source-protester-identities-online/, accessed 23 June 2011.

28 Evan Osnos, "Angry Youth," *The New Yorker*, 28 July 2008. The video may be seen at: http://www.youtube.com/watch?v=MSTYhYkASsA, accessed 23 March 2011.

29 Robert Boynton, "North Korea's Digital Underground," *The Atlantic*, April 2011.

30 See: http://www.nkeconwatch.com/2010/12/30/bend-it-shown-edited-on-dprk-tv/, accessed 23 March 2011.

31 Martyn Williams, "How Digital Technology Gets the News out of North Korea," at: http://www.itworld.com/personal-tech/125972/how-digital-technology-gets-news-out-north-korea, accessed 23 March 2011.

32 See: http://www.guardian.co.uk/world/2011/mar/21/us-army-kill-team-afghanistan-posed-pictures-murdered-civilians, accessed 23 March 2011.

33 See: http://www.spiegel.de/international/0,1518,445133,00.html, accessed 23 March 2011.

34 See: http://2010.newsweek.com/top-10/most-memorable-quotes/allen-let-s-give-a-welcome-to-macaca-here.html, accessed 6 April 2011.

35 See: http://articles.sfgate.com/2004-02-20/news/17414203_1_anti-war-rally-photo-agency-separate-photo, accessed 6 April 2011. The photo itself may be seen at: http://urbanlegends.about.com/library/bl_kerry_fonda.htm.

36 See: http://www.pewinternet.org/~/media//Files/Reports/2008/PIP_Teens_Games_and_Civics_Report_FINAL.pdf.pdf, accessed 30 May 2011.

37 Ian Bogost, "The Rhetoric of Video Games," in Katie Salen (ed.), *The Ecology of Games: Connecting Youth, Games, and Learning* (Cambridge, MA: MIT Press, 2008), p. 119.

38 http://theplaymob.com/weforest.html

39 http://www.tiltworld.com/

40 http://www.peacemakergame.com/

41 http://www.peoplepowergame.com/

42 Dale Purves, R. Beau Lotto and Surajit Nund, "Why We See What We Do," *American Scientist Online*, at: http://www.colorado.edu/MCDB/MCDB3650/PurvesWhyWeSee.pdf, accessed 24 March 2011.

43 Christopher Chabris and Daniel Simons, *The Invisible Gorilla* (New York: Crown, 2010).

44 Malcolm Gladwell, *Blink* (New York: Little Brown, 2005).

45 Takahiko Masuda and Richard Nisbett, "Attending Holistically versus Analytically: Comparing the Context Sensitivity of Japanese and Americans," *Journal of Personality and Social Psychology*, vol. 81, no. 5, 2001.

46 The photo may be seen at: http://en.wikipedia.org/wiki/File:Nguyen.jpg, accessed 25 March 2011.

47 See: http://www.time.com/time/magazine/article/0,9171,988783,00.html, accessed 25 March 2011.

48 Horst Faas, "The Saigon Execution," at: http://digitaljournalist.org/issue0410/faas.html, accessed 25 March 2011.

49 See: http://www.time.com/time/magazine/article/0,9171,988783,00.html, accessed 25 March 2011.

50 The photo may be seen at: http://en.wikipedia.org/wiki/File:CheHigh.jpg, accessed 25 March 2011.

51 Daniel Chandler's online book *Semiotics for Beginners* provides an excellent overview. See: http://www.aber.ac.uk/media/Documents/S4B/sem02.html, accessed 27 March 2001.

52 Martin Gurri, Craig Denny and Aaron Harms, "Our Visual Persuasion Gap," *Parameters*, Spring 2010.

53 Gurri *et al.*, p. 104.

54 For a good survey of the state of research into this question as it relates to

media and violence, see The Media Awareness Network website, at: http://www.media-awareness.ca/english/issues/violence/effects_media_violence.cfm, accessed 26 March 2011.

55 George Gerbner and Larry Gors, "Living with Television: The Violence Profile," *Journal of Communication*, April 1976, 173.

56 Kaiser Family Foundation report, at: http://www.kff.org/entmedia/entmedia012010nr.cfm, accessed 26 March 2011.

57 "Couch Potatoes," *The Economist*, 19 July 2007, at: http://www.economist.com/research/articlesBySubject/displaystory.cfm?subjectid=7933596&story_id=9527126, accessed 26 March 2011.

58 Gurri *et al.*, p. 104.

59 Gurri *et al.*, p. 105.

60 "What is a Master Narrative?" at: http://www.technology.ku.edu/~communities/PDFs/MasterNarrativeNEW.pdf, accessed 26 March 2011.

61 Anthropologist Laura Bohannan's amusing account of how the African tribe she was studying "rewrote" Shakespeare to fit its own cultural norms suggests such hijacking is not impossible. See "Shakespeare in the Bush," at: http://www.naturalhistorymag.com/editors_pick/1966_08-09_pick.html.

62 See "The Passion of the Toys," at: http://www.slublog.com/archives/2006/08/the_passion_of.html, accessed 25 March 2011.

63 For an extended discussion of these complexities see Guy Deutscher, *Through the Looking Glass: Why the World Looks Different in Other Languages* (London: Arrow Books, 2011).

64 See: http://www.youtube.com/watch?v=6fzK6EYWEo8, accessed 26 March 2011.

65 See: http://www.youtube.com/user/UnitedStatesNavy#p/u/29/6DriBYQvG_4, accessed 26 March 2011.

66 See: http://www.youtube.com/watch?v=DqaWdkdFb3Y, accessed 26 March 2011.

67 As reproduced in a blog entry at: http://www.kayesweetser.com/archives/25, accessed 26 March 2011.

68 See for example the documentary prepared by Press TV, Iran's official English-language internet TV, which argues that the death was faked, and she was later murdered – at: http://www.youtube.com/watch?v=Shp7HE2YA_c&skipcontrinter=1

69 Linebarger, *Psychological Warfare*, pp. 137–40.

70 "YouTube Awards," *New York Times*, 22 March 2008.

71 Mathew Ingram, "Lessons in How to Go Viral: Use the 'Bored at Work' Network," at: http://gigaom.com/2010/08/13/lessons-in-how-to-go-viral-use-the-bored-at-work-network/, accessed 26 March 201.

72 Ewen, "Reflections on Visual Persuasion," p. 816.

73 Brooks Barnes, "Many Culprits in Fall of a Family Film," *New York Times*, 14 March 2011.

74 The account of the sabotaged train may be read at: http://articles.nydailynews. com/2010-12-27/news/27085637_1_birthday-gifts-train-kim-jong-il, while the cartoon videos, which hackers placed on the pro-regime Uriminzokkiri site, may be seen at: http://www.youtube.com/watch?v=8sb7hiENZP4, accessed 26 March 2011.

75 Michael Wines, "A Dirty Pun Tweaks China's On-line Censors," *New York Times*, 11 March 2009.

76 See: http://www.whiterabbitcollection.org/artists/pisan-wang-bo/, accessed 26 March 2011.

77 A version with amateur-produced subtitles may be seen at: http://www.youtube. com/watch?v=XbAtMsz0dro&feature=related, accessed 26 March 2011.

78 Office of the Inspector General, "Review of the Use of Social Media by the Department of State," Report No. ISP-I-11-10, February 2011.

79 See: http://www.videochallenge.america.gov/ or the corresponding YouTube channel at: http://www.youtube.com/democracychallenge

80 For example, the YouTube of a talk by James Glassman, at the time Under Secretary of State for Public Diplomacy, entitled "Public Diplomacy 2.0," has been viewed 3,566 times since 1 December 2008. See: http://www.youtube. com/watch?v=X3NU4d81Ps4

81 The CBS page with the "nearly 6 million" figure has been taken down. A YouTube interview by Shira Lazar of CBS News, at: http://www.youtube. com/watch?v=CzG44v62xWc, accessed 24 September 2011, gives a figure of "400,000 uniques [unique viewers] an hour."

82 Office of the Inspector General, p. 5.

83 The America.gov website was quietly phased out of operation on 31 March 2011. Since there was no explanation given for this move, it is not possible to say whether or not the OIG report had anything to do with that.

84 http://www.zdnet.com/blog/ip-telephony/pentagon-bans-myspace-youtube-mtv-etc-on-dod-networks/1601, accessed 27 March 2011.

85 http://news.bbc.co.uk/2/hi/americas/8540236.stm, accessed 27 March 2011.

86 James Dao, "Staying in Touch with Home, for Better or Worse," *New York Times*, 16 February 2011.

87 Robert Mackey, "The Lede Blog," 16–17 August 2010, at: http://thelede.blogs. nytimes.com/2010/08/16/israeli-bloggers-copy-controversial-images-from-faceb ook/?scp=17&sq=Robert+Mackey&st=nyt and: http://thelede.blogs.nytimes. com/2010/08/17/israeli-ex-soldier-defends-her-facebook-snapshots/.

88 One example, which proved to be a big hit with IC analysts (though few would admit to having watched it), is entitled "Spies Like Them," viewable at: http://www.youtube.com/watch?v=VJsvI8TKPzo.

89 See: http://stuff.techwhack.com/11130-goanimate-stupeflix-xtranormal, accessed 27 March 2011.

PART FOUR

Conclusion

CHAPTER TEN

Don't be surprised by surprise

This book begins with a discussion of how open source information has traditionally been used in the intelligence community, and then passes to an examination of how dramatically the availability of information has changed, both over the 65 years since the IC was established, and, even more particularly, over the past few years. It has never been the book's intention or purpose, however, to take up the subject of intelligence or analytic reform. There are several reasons for this – not least of which is that there is already a groaning shelf full of books which chew at those issues in one form or another. Perhaps equally important, there is very little evidence of a corresponding concern, that those on behalf of whom IC analysts are laboring have any interest in changing the existing relationship between analysts and decision makers in any substantive way. Yes, policy-makers would be willing to be embarrassed less often, or to be taken by surprise less frequently, but there is no evidence of the willingness, or indeed even a perceived need on their part, to change the shape of the policy-maker–analyst relationship from that was which set out six decades ago by Sherman Kent, or indeed that which was advocated nine decades ago, by Walter Lippmann. Still, without modifying the initial reluctance to discuss or advocate reform, it does seem proper to close this volume with a look at the relationship between information and the decision-making process, particularly as practiced in government.

It is a given of human psychology that anyone who needs to make a decision, no matter how trivial, is going to want to get information that will make the decision feel less risky, or less arbitrary. Although the information desired will vary according to the decision that must be made, in general the information a would-be decision-maker senses he or she needs will be a combination of the descriptive – the *Who? Where? When? What?* – and the more predictive: *What is going to happen? What could go wrong? What are the chances my decision will prove to have been correct?* Although the mechanisms that we humans accept as causal are always changing, the process of seeking causal patterns within observed phenomena is probably as old as our species – and in many ways remains as fundamentally fatidic now as it did when our forebears relied upon auguries of weather signs, tortoise shell cracks, and animal entrails. Causality is a fantastically complex phenomenon, which we are forever abstracting, reifying, and "simplifying."

The enduring conviction that there is an order underlying the apparent chaos of daily life is another fact of human psychology, one which feeds easily into one of the fundamental "faith issues" of the IC – that "real intelligence" can only be done with secrets. As CIA historian Michael Warner concludes after a lengthy examination of the various definitions of "intelligence" previously offered by others: "Intelligence is secret state activity to understand or influence foreign entities."[1] Although this definition begs a lot of questions – such as, for example, where did the people from whom the spies are getting their information get *their* information? (a surprising amount of what passes for "secret" proves on closer examination to have come originally from the world of open information) – it does at least have the virtue of assigning a specific definition to the activities of the intelligence community. Following the logic of Warner's definition, then, it is the function of the intelligence community to collect, process, and disseminate *secret information*, and nothing more (as a contrast, scholars Charles Mangio and Bonnie Wilkinson examined more or less the same set of definitions of intelligence as did Warner, but decided that all they could conclude is that "intelligence analysis is analysis done by intelligence organizations").[2]

Where the IC repeatedly gets caught out is in the next part of that assumed function, that the information it disseminates (secret or not) will prevent surprise and reduce the uncertainty of decision-making. This suggests that what is desired is not a particular *kind* of information – whether secret or not – but rather an informational *function*. Although that function is generally presumed to be relatively straightforward – that is, a "proper" decision or "good" decision will be a product of the volume of information that is available as the decision is made – in fact, the process of decision-making, and the role that information plays in that process, is significantly more complex than people generally credit. Rather than being a straight linear curve – meaning rising information volume equals better decisions – the evidence suggests instead that the curve is more like an inverted U; that is, in a new or unfamiliar situation, particularly if the situation is stressful, the addition of a certain amount of knowledge will help bring a decision-maker closer to a decision, but at a certain point additional information becomes too abundant, too repetitive, too contradictory, and too cumbersome, thus actually making it *harder* to come to a decision. Thirty years ago clinical psychologists Siegfried and Susan Streufert, analyzing decision-making processes in complex and stressful environments, came to the conclusion that, after a certain point, the introduction of more information makes the decision process more difficult and even more stressful than when decisions are made in ignorance. Psychologists C. J. Bartlett and Calvin Green had found basically the same thing in the mid-1960s, when their examination of how clinicians make diagnostic predictions had concluded that "the efficiency of clinical prediction can be decreased by the inclusion of too many predictors." What appears to have confused Bartlett and Green is that all of the predictors that they loaded into their tests, which in sum had made prediction more difficult, "had [each individually] been shown by past research to be a valid set of predictors." That brought them to the paradoxical conclusion that, even though the addition of more information made clinical prediction harder, not easier, doctors should still continue to try to use all of them anyway, "until research evidence is available to indicate what the valid set of predictors should be."[3]

Of course, the notion of "too much information" is also well-known in the commercial sector. Stanford business professor James March, for example, has argued that:

> no rational decision maker will obtain all possible information ... [decision makers] can be expected to invest in information up to the point at which the marginal expected cost equals the marginal expected return. The cost of the information is the expected return that could be realized by investing elsewhere the resources expended to find and comprehend the current information. There are times when information has no decision value.[4]

Although it was argued in Chapter Seven that the process of information gathering for intelligence purposes has many similarities to (and much to learn from) the conduct of "competitor intelligence," there is at least one crucial difference between the two kinds of intelligence activities, as may be inferred from March's statement. The hypothetical "rational decision maker" in March's text is assumed to be functioning in a business environment, actively gathering information in order to make a commercial decision which will result in some sort of competitive advantage. In other words, the purpose of any commercial decision is basically *offensive* – attempting to seize and hold resources (markets, audiences, service niches, etc.) which are either unexploited or which may be snatched away from less adroit competitors.

This is in strong contrast to the normal situation in the policy-making and intelligence communities, where the posture is defensive. Although there may have been some surface elements of competition during the "zero-sum" Cold War years, even then the prevailing model was that of containment – the purpose of intelligence, as Harry Ransom wrote in his 1959 study of the CIA, is telling policymakers "the capabilities, vulnerabilities, and intentions of foreign nations"[5] which may be planning to attack us or our interests. Essentially the same words are still used today – the CIA's public homepage says the organization serves as "the nation's first line of defense" by "collecting information that reveals the plans, intentions and capabilities of our adversaries."[6] The same point was made more tersely in the 1950s by Henry Stimson (who served both as Secretary of War and, twice, as Secretary of State) when he called the CIA "a sentinel on duty at all times."[7]

Author David Kahn has argued that the information needs of offense and defense are fundamentally different, because of the profound differences between the two activities – attacking is finite in time, has clearly defined goals, and has markers of success or failure which are relatively easy to measure. In contrast, defending is a nebulous, unending process, in which the best one may say at the end of the day is that "we haven't been attacked ... yet." Kahn makes that point vivid by quoting Clausewitz: "Defense consists in the parrying of a blow. What is its characteristic feature? Awaiting the blow."[8] Intelligence may certainly be helpful to an attacker, but it is not crucial to success – given a clear goal, success or failure will depend as much upon things like persistence, fortitude, and even luck, as it will upon the quality of the intelligence. In contrast, for a defender, intelligence is vital to success – it is, as the CIA website states, the "first line of defense."

The business of collecting information on "the capabilities, vulnerabilities, and intentions of foreign nations," in the hope of parrying a blow, shapes the production of intelligence in an important way. As noted above, students of management like March envision the information-gathering process as an active one. The study conducted by the Streuferts, however, which was done in a war-gaming environment and thus is much closer to the "information needs environment" of the intelligence and policy-maker communities, found an important distinction between what they dubbed "active search" and "passive search" for information. The first is the type of search that March, or indeed any of the gurus of competitor intelligence, would advocate – what someone undertakes when he or she perceives that a piece of information necessary to decision-making is absent. The Streuferts, however, also interjected a constant inflow of *unrequested* information into their simulation, thus reproducing the daily flood of unsolicited, undesired, and often non-salient information into the "in-boxes" of collectors, analysts, and policymakers. Not surprisingly, there is no publicly available figure for how great the volume of that flood is (if indeed anyone even knows it), but such figures as are available suggest that the flow is relentless – former Assistant Director of National Intelligence for Analysis Thomas Fingar has spoken, for example, of "roughly 50,000 pieces of finished intelligence" appearing every year[9] (which works out to be one about every two minutes of the working day), while former National Security Advisor Zbigniew Brzezinski said that he calculated that the volume of information sent to the President by just the Secretary of Defense, the Secretary of State, and the Director of the CIA averaged about 300 pages *every day*.[10] Mark Lowenthal, at one time the CIA's Assistant Director for Analysis and Production, likened that daily ream of reports to bland, "corporate-voiced...cost-free subscriptions" that the recipients got whether they wanted them or not, and which cost them nothing to receive, thus making the products easy to ignore, particularly since there is nothing in that daily stream "that screams 'read me now.'"[11] At least one policymaker, Robert Blackwill, former US Ambassador to India and also an important figure in the early days of the US occupation of Iraq, has stated flatly that he paid no attention whatever to the IC's finished intelligence, and further claimed that he was not the only one of his rank who did so. Characterizing the typical IC product as "non-adhesive," Blackwill asked rhetorically, "Why bother to read what they write for a general audience of people who have no real responsibility on the issue?"[12] In a similar vein, CIA analyst Paul Miller, who served a rotation in the White House as part of the Afghan policy support team in the National Security Council (NSC), wrote that IC products can be "highly polished" but too often are "'duh' reports and analysis."[13]

The paradoxes of choice

As this book has tried to make clear, both active and passive searchers now have vastly more information available to them than ever was possible before. The benefits of that volume, however, are not distributed evenly. Just like the person who enters a search term into the query box on Google or other search engine, the active searcher has some criteria by which to sort that galaxy of possible information into more or less three piles – useless, maybe useful, and probably/certainly useful. The passive searcher, however, is more in the unhappy position of having to look at "everything," because, they fear, "something" might turn out to be crucial. Worse than looking for a needle in a haystack, which at least offers the comfort of knowing there is a needle in there somewhere, the passive searcher cannot even be confident that there is a haystack, let alone a needle.

The IC analysts and policymakers who must sift through those tells and middens of "passive search" are faced with what psychologist Barry Schwartz has called "the paradox of choice."[14] Although in theory an increase in the supply of things among which one may choose is usually regarded as desirable, in practice an increase in the number of things among which one must choose usually creates a whole series of problems – all of which can be seen reflected in the day-to-day work of the IC. Schwartz makes a distinction between "choosers" – those who consider each choice option carefully, weighing costs and benefits, pros and cons – and "pickers" – those who are either so indifferent to the outcome of their choice or, alternatively, so overwhelmed with the processes and possible consequences of making a selection that they tend simply to grab the first approximation of what they are seeking. In a world of hyper-abundance, neither approach works particularly well but (one of Schwartz's paradoxes), in some ways the picker may do better than the chooser. For one thing, choice requires effort, which means that those choosing can get tired or inattentive, and thus make mistakes. Not surprisingly, choosers also can take far longer to reach a decision than do pickers. The Streuferts for example found that in their war game exercises, "*more* information is acquired before a decision is made when the rate of information presentation increases."[15]

It is perhaps worth pausing here to note that "information overload" is not a new phenomenon. As early as 1621 Robert Burton, author of *The Anatomy of Melancholy*, and owner of one of the largest private libraries of the day (1,700 volumes!), lamented: "What a glut of books! Who can read them? As already, we shall have a vast Chaos and confusion of Books, we are oppressed with them, our eyes ache with reading, our fingers with turning."[16] Scholar Ann Blair has noted that this sense of being overwhelmed by all the written matter that clamors for attention actually predates Gutenberg and the advent of printing – in 1255 French nobleman Vincent of Beauvais wrote that "the multitude of books, the shortness of time and the slipperiness of memory do not allow all things which are written to be equally retained in the mind"[17]; he decided to solve this problem by creating *another* book, a four-volume compendium summarizing all the manuscripts he had read and found worthwhile.

Such statements capture two dimensions of information which seem to have remained as valid in the twenty-first century as they were in the thirteenth – the oddly intertwined senses of being overwhelmed by the volume of useless information and the haunting fear that a piece of valid, important, or vital information will be overlooked in the flood of the other. What the two highlight together is that all use of information requires making choices – which in turn requires that there be criteria by which selection may be made. Although Vincent of Beauvais may have thought otherwise, this can work reasonably well when the number of choices is small, and the differences between them relatively large, but the process will become dizzying when the number of choices grows and the differences between them grow ever narrower – as anyone who has tried to choose a paint color or buy a laptop or decide on a health or retirement plan or even just select a brand of toothpaste in a supermarket can probably attest. In other realms this sense of being overwhelmed by a plethora of basically identical things has been dubbed "analysis paralysis" or "the Curse of Knowledge."[18]

The choice process can have even more paradoxical consequences, for as the differences between choices grow ever more indistinguishable, there is a tendency for the entire choice array to seem inadequate and of little value – reflected in the marketplace by studies which show that when given too many things among which to choose, consumers tend to make no choice at all.[19] The mechanisms of "refusing to buy anything" in a passive search environment are different, but may be seen in the frequent fear of both analysts and policymakers, that no matter how much information may be inundating them, they still want more. This is similar to a companion paradox of overabundant choices, which is that, even after a choice has been made, "buyer's regret" is extremely common, leaving people wishing they had chosen something else. Again, in the IC-policymaker arena, the way this manifests itself most often is as a persistent worry that, no matter how much information one may have, still more is "needed," because (as the Church Committee report characterized the "jigsaw theory of intelligence" in 1975[20]) "one little scrap" could prove to be "the missing piece" that suddenly makes a picture whole.

The fact that processing information and arriving at a decision requires time and work has the further consequence, Schwartz argues, of making people tend to overvalue what they already possess, and to undervalue what they do not. In the intelligence-policymaking realm, this is manifested in what the Streuferts found, that the amount of information required to make a participant modify a decision once it has been taken is significantly greater than the amount required to come to the initial decision – thus suggesting how easily increased information can only serve to "lock in" a decision already made.[21] This is related to another, much-discussed phenomenon associated with choice – the problem of heuristics, or "decision shortcuts." Because it is impracticable to approach every potential decision as if it were both new and vitally important, people develop (or inherit) patterns which help them to navigate the choice process. If the subject of choice is, for example, toothpaste, then a convenient heuristic is simply always to buy the same brand, or even to select one's purchase from the same spot on the shelf in the market regardless of what is there, without agonizing over the differences between "multi-care with whitener" and "mint-flavored cavity fighter."

In the case of information necessary for decision-making, however, heuristics can prove more problematic. There is a huge literature[22] about the various errors, inefficiencies, and blunders that heuristics can cause in the decision-making process, which need not be rehearsed at great length. There are, however, a few such "mental shortcuts" worth pointing out here:

- The "representativeness" heuristic, which is closest to the common understanding of "stereotype"[23]; this constructs a mental model of what a "typical" member of a group should look like, thus allowing, for example, Sherman Kent to write "strategic intelligence ... deals with [people] as Frenchmen, Swedes, Russians, and Belgians, and it deals with them as military, political, or economic beings,"[24] as if everyone born in France or serving in the military were the same. This is the heuristic which prompted Stansfield Turner to assume that Ayatollah Khomeini was "just another politician" or allowed Dean Rusk to rebuff the CIA analyst who was trying to warn him that the Chinese had infiltrated their troops into North Korea with the assurance that "Young man, they wouldn't dare."[25]

- The "availability" heuristic, which makes people tend to extrapolate from their personal experience, judging the likelihood of something by the ease with which they can recall similar-seeming circumstances; this can cause people to over-estimate, for example, the frequency of co-occurrences ("Every time I wash my car it rains"), thus leading to incorrect or misleading imputations of causality. Evidence suggests that this heuristic will have particularly strong impact as people increasingly inhabit completely different "information eco-systems," so that things which are thought to co-occur in one system will never be considered in another – this was part of the reason why the "Talmudists" had so much trouble getting policymakers to accept their claims about a growing Sino-Soviet split, and almost certainly is one of the factors fueling the rancor in the debate over whether or not global climate change is occurring.

- The "anchoring and adjustment" heuristic, which has primarily to do with numbers but can also be reflected in other realms; this causes people to lock onto certain trajectories based upon their initial assumptions or understandings, and then derive their answers accordingly. Thus for example people who are given identical sets of facts about two parents in a hypothetical divorce and custody case are significantly more likely to favor one parent when asked to whom they would *award* custody than they are when asked to whom they would *deny* custody.[26] This heuristic also appears to cause people to over-estimate the likelihood of "conjunctive events" (the Tversky-Kahneman example is to draw seven red marbles in a row, with replacement, from a bag containing 90 red and 10 white marbles) and to under-estimate that of "disjunctive events" (pulling at least one white marble from the same bag). It is this heuristic which helped the analysts at FBIS to conclude that, despite all the changes being introduced into Soviet media, and Soviet life, by *glasnost* and *perestroika*, the USSR would continue to exist into the indefinite future.

The disintegration of the larger "heuristic"

The concept of master narrative, argued in Chapter Eight, could also be called a "master heuristic," a set of generally accepted rules that allow people to "know" what "life is like." As has repeatedly been argued in this book, the way that information has been used for most of the life of the IC was based on a set of heuristics which were not fully articulated – indeed, one of the characteristics of dominant heuristics is that they have become "naturalized" and so are not noticeable to those who inhabit them – but which may be seen, for example, in Sherman Kent's *Strategic Intelligence* and *Writing History*. Kent is not the only mid-century American who believed in what has been dubbed "scientific liberalism" – indeed, one of the reasons that Kent's arguments were so influential was that they were consistent with the heuristics that had governed American life for a century or more.[27] As already has been quoted, Kent considered an elite-led, scientific, "rational" government that would take as its task the "[doing] away with poverty, disease, and war; [the promotion of] happiness, health, and peace" to be "as typical of the American way as succotash and ham and eggs."[28]

Kent was not the only person who thought this; for most of the twentieth century there was a broad consensus across America's various elites about what constituted "the American way." Such a concept is a reflection of the definitions of modern statehood laid out in the Peace of Westphalia, in the seventeenth century, which had enunciated the principle "*cuis regio, eius religio*" ("whose region, his religion"), in effect saying that a state has the right to define reality within its boundaries (for what is religion, if not a description of the laws of the universe?). Although pursued with more stringency in some nations than in others, the sense that a primary purpose of information is to train and educate the populace has been a persistent feature of information environments everywhere. As James Fallows put it in a magazine article on the future of journalism, "giving people what they want as opposed to what they should want is a conflict as old as journalism ... for more than a century after the Civil War American readers and viewers were in various ways buffered from getting exactly what they wanted ... news, like education, aspired to be as interesting as possible, but to have an uplifting civic content." Fallows then lists various points of evidence, such as the "fairness doctrine," the requirement for "public service programming," the rules forbidding monopolization of news supply in a given area, and the perceived need to write about or broadcast such things as presidential news conferences, all of which combined to make the information industries "prestigious loss-leaders aimed at telling a broad Middle American audience what it needed to know."[29]

As has already been noted in Chapter Four, until very recently, there were some issues about which the country's various elites might disagree (what author Daniel Hallin had dubbed "the sphere of legitimate controversy"), but the effect of mass media, mass education, and a broadly shared cultural consensus was such that, as scholar Morton Halperin noted in his blistering attack on the bureaucratic behaviors which had helped lead the country into war in Vietnam, "a majority of American officials (as well as the American public)" had "a set of widely shared images," or convictions, which served as ready heuristics for deciding what was good and bad, what was (to echo the Cunningham Report) "secondary material" and what "significant material." In the case of Vietnam, Halperin argued, the dominant heuristic was that "the pre-eminent feature of international politics is the conflict between Communism and the Free World," making the "surest simple guide to US interests" be "opposition to Communism."[30]

There no longer is a "set of widely shared images," in no small part because the inexorable collapse of the cost of creating, disseminating, and storing information means that, in Fallows' words, "with each passing month people can get more of what they want and less of what someone else thinks they should have." As noted already, one effect of this is an accelerating atomization of publics, which – among other things – increasingly challenges the borders within which rulers attempt to contain their particular definitions of reality. The profoundly erosive effects of this proliferation of "realities" have been in full evidence across the Arab world as this book was being written. Clashing information is evident not only in challenges mounted to long-established leaders by persistent crowds in the various streets (of Tunis, Cairo, Damascus, Sana'a, and even Baku, proving "the Arab Spring" is not an ethnic phenomenon), but also in the various narratives (or heuristics) that all sides have tried to pin on one another – are the people in the streets democrats or rebels, Islamic militants or freedom-fighters, drug-crazed terrorists or the fresh face of a New Middle East?

Such clashing claims were always made, of course, but in the new media environment there is no elite, no controlling medium, to define which of them is "true." Daniel Patrick Moynihan is reputed to have said that "Everyone is entitled to his own opinion, but not to his own facts."[31] What the information environment of today is demonstrating is that people also now demand, *and find*, the facts they want. This is profoundly problematic for an intelligence system which still relies on Kent's epistemology (or understanding of knowledge). A system which believes that there are absolute Platonic truths has a set of criteria by which information choices may be made – the problem, however, is that other systems can intrude upon that system, creating difficulties and even wreaking havoc. This may be illustrated by the following test:

> *Which of these statements is true?*
> A) $2 + 2 = 4$
> B) $2 + 2 = 10$

The proper answer is actually another question: what is the base system in which the statement is being made? If the base system is 10 (as in our familiar 1–9, plus zero), then the answer is A. If, however, the system is base four, then the only possible "fact" is B (since the only digits will be 1–3, plus zero). This may perhaps seem like a gimmick, but in fact it is an important point – a similar clash of "master heuristics" might be seen in, for example, the inclusion of Mongolia as part of the Coalition of the Willing which overthrew the Saddam Hussein government in Iraq in 2003. From one heuristic, this illustrated how broad the international support for the action was, and also signaled Mongolia's switch from the Soviet-era "communist camp" to the Western one. From the point of view of many in the Middle East, however, this was a reminder of Baghdad's total devastation by the forces of Hulagu Khan, in 1258. An interesting illustration of how powerful that heuristic is to those who share it is the "backstory" for "the Ninety-Nine," a set of Islamic comic book heroes. As the series' website explains: "Hundreds of years ago, when Baghdad fell to the forces of Hulagu Khan, the Caliph and the librarians of Dar-al-Hikma captured the sum total of knowledge of world culture contained within their tomes and instilled this information into ninety-nine gemstones which had been crafted to absorb the very light of reason." Those stones were smuggled out of Baghdad and taken to Andalusia, where they formed the centerpiece of "a great hidden Fortress of Knowledge." That library too was destroyed, and the stones scattered "to the four corners of the world ... lost to time and tide."[32] The task of the super heroes, each of whom exemplifies one of the 99 virtues, is to fight to return those stones, and the knowledge they contain, to the world that the Mongol invaders destroyed – a heuristic of lost glory destroyed by rampaging barbarians which stands in strong contrast to that of a global liberating army.[33]

The Gutenberg parentheses?

The problem with any dominant heuristic, or narrative, is how to deal with those who do not accept it. In the Westphalian world of old, dissenters could be burnt at the stake, jailed, exiled, or otherwise punished – but the easiest way by far to impose a particular reality was to make it so that no other reality or heuristic was visible. Technology made this very easy – as has repeatedly been argued here, creation and dissemination of information was expensive, meaning that only those who were in the elite of a given society could participate in that creation and dissemination. This is turn had a credentialing function – the fact that people got their names and opinions into newspapers, their books published, or their faces and voices on the air implied that their views had gone through some kind of vetting process, which made it simple to accept what was offered as being true. Indeed, the structures of that technology made it fairly easy to assign comparative values to the "truths" being offered – hard-bound books were more serious and thus "truer" than paperbacks; both were "truer" than magazines and newspapers; while radio and TV were more slippery (since the presentation was oral), but also could have greater impact, because of the greater ubiquity of those media.

All of this is gone, washed away by the swelling tide of all-but-free information. There may be some very small areas in which Daniel Patrick Moynihan might be able to insist that there still exist inarguable facts, but for the most part the world has become one in which most narratives are visible, and indeed are immediately at hand. Some information theorists argue that what is being born now is a world very like that which existed before Gutenberg's printing press, but now on an ideological plane, rather than a spatial one. In the pre-Gutenberg days, the argument runs, information passed orally, and so depended on proximity. No one particularly owned any ideas or even works of art; rather they were shared, and in some ways an artifact of a community – "everybody knew" that things were as they were.

The introduction of text brought with it the hierarchies of authority, single-authorship, orders of knowledge, and all the other phenomena which, *in toto*, made the world of Sherman Kent's epistemology possible. As has already been argued, the only world in which information can be innately "significant" or "secondary" is one in which there is a clear absolute truth – which of course was the world that Kent, Schlesinger, and others believed to exist.

As this book has tried repeatedly to demonstrate, however, other truths and other heuristics become ever more visible as information becomes more accessible, with consequences that grow ever more complex and contradictory. Some students of information have begun to argue that we are entering a period of "secondary orality," when people again can cluster around the stories they find most congenial, rejecting those they dislike. Text no longer holds its power to, for example, confirm that President Obama was born a US citizen – the numbers of those who profess to believe he was not have approximately doubled since the question first arose, despite the many attempts to put the question to rest by textual explanations, and even photos of documents. The State Department has devoted an entire office to rebutting charges that, for example, 9/11 was staged by Israel, the US military, or a combination of both, or that US adoption overseas is actually a cover for a booming "body-parts" business – all with no discernible impact on the persistent vitality of those canards. Battles over whether or not there is global warming, the efficacy of childhood vaccination, ownership of Jerusalem, how many people killed President Kennedy (and who they were), whether immigration is a good thing or a bad one – all of these and more increasingly are waged with no shared assumptions, no common "facts," and thus no realistic way of one side swaying the other.

This erosion of imposed authority, of hierarchy, has prompted some of these scholars of "secondary orality" to speculate that, rather than being the higher stage of human development that our current narrative makes it to be, the "Gutenberg revolution" may in fact be proving to be a 500-year-long exception to how humans have always, and will again from now on, process information to create the "truths" they need and want. As has already been mentioned in Chapter Five, adherents of this line of thought speak of a "Gutenberg parenthesis" in human history, the left hand of which was laid down in the mid-fifteenth century and the right hand of which is now being closed by the internet, the cell phone, YouTube, Twitter, and the rest of it.[34] Once again, the "secondary oralists" argue, we will be in a world of "information tribes," groups bound together by beliefs, and the "facts" to prove them, which other tribes see as nonsense, conflicting as they do with their own beliefs and truths.

So what?

Nice talk, interesting idea … but how does this help me do my job *today*, asks the intelligence analyst, with complete justice. We may indeed be in the midst of an enormous information revolution, but – rather in the same way that the Catholic Church continued officially to reject the Gallilean universe until it quietly dropped its objections over the course of the eighteenth and nineteenth centuries[35] – large organizations must continue to function day-to-day according to their established assumptions and methods. For all that there is a general recognition that the information environment has changed, and that the analytic community must change with it, the press of daily business makes it an unimaginable luxury to have the time and resources to halt the current processes, rethink them, and start anew (the evocative phrase for such an attempt is "trying to remodel the plane in mid-flight"). Although the author of this book has views about how the analyst–policymaker relationship might profitably be changed,[36] it is not the purpose here to argue that point. Rather it seems best to close the volume with a few observations and suggestions about how to make better use of the fantastic volumes of information which we now can access.

- **Begin with a question:** Although this point has been made repeatedly, it should be made again, because a question offers the only means by which information can possibly be sorted. Learning to ask good questions is hard, and is even harder in an environment which makes it all but impossible for a young analyst to ask a policymaker why he or she wants a particular kind of information, what it is going to be used for, or to suggest better ways in which the question might be posed. As has been pointed out, most often the "intelligence question" is not even a question at all, but rather is a collection requirement. Even in those very unpromising circumstances, however, analysts should do the best they can to discern the question which might lie behind the collection requirement. Hints might be found in, for example, foreign policy discussions, public interviews given by the principles, or any changes in requirements that come in. Analysts might also assist the question iteration process by making explicit in their products the questions which they are answering, and then also show how different ways of posing the questions might yield different answers. Kahneman and Tversky showed that even something as simple as asking for conjunctive and disjunctive predictions about the same data set could elicit quite different results.

- **Know who else is interested in that information, and understand how they are sharing it:** Information has broken free of the channels ("medium," remember, means intermediary, the channel, the "thing-between") through which it once had to pass. The boundaries between what once were one-to-one communications and one-to-many (which for sake of simplicity might be called telephone, telegraph, and perhaps the individual letter, versus broadcasting media like radio, TV, and print) have now vanished. The one-to-many platforms now compete with one another so vigorously that the number of senders is always rising, and the size of the audiences they reach shrinks. The media that rely on large aggregate audiences to survive are dying, while what once may have seemed like a means of personal communication – the text of a blog, or a tweet sent on a cell phone – can now reach millions, becoming what Patrick O'Sullivan, of the communications department at Illinois State University, has dubbed "masspersonal" communication.[37] The source of information no longer determines the *value* of the information – stories that can prove to be important can break anywhere, while stories that powerful people or interests would like other people to regard as important can be ignored, no matter where they are placed.

The mutability of the information platforms can present a particular challenge to IC analysts, because the enterprise rules of the organizations where they work can prevent them from understanding the inventive ways in which people use devices, platforms, and web services. It is a particularly dangerous mistake to assume that others understand and use technology in the same way that we do – cases in point from the recent past might include the conviction that "access to the internet" is achievable only through desktop or laptop computers, without realizing that, for much of the world, the point of entry is the mobile device (since US cell-phone technology has lagged persistently behind that in Europe, Asia, and even Africa[38]); or the assumption that development of blogging or file-sharing cultures requires reliable internet access (thus making it easy to overlook places like Cuba and North Korea, which may lack internet access but are well computerized, thus making it possible for flourishing information-exchange environments to be sustained by the use of USB flash drives).[39]

- **Don't privilege particular kinds or sources of information:** In some regard this is another way of saying "try to answer a question" rather than "collect against requirements." Too much collection in the open source intelligence arena depends upon the status of source – which is fine, if the underlying intelligence question is "what are the official media saying?" However, as has been shown with Iran in 1979, the USSR in 1991, and, much more recently, Tunisia, Egypt, and Libya, the "authoritative state media" on which so much rote collection relies will never give notice of their own demise. Good open source intelligence will always keep the Lasswell formula in mind, but increasingly as the media environment mutates and evolves, the issues of greatest importance will be likely to lie not at the left end (who is sending?), but rather at the right end of the "flow" – what audiences are accessing what media for what purposes, and how are those media responding?

    In the intelligence and policymaking arenas this reminder has a particular sense as well – which is to be exceedingly wary of secrets and secrecy. Although the IC continues to hold tight to secrets as its major "value-added," the social constructs which surround secrecy are becoming demonstrably constrictive. Secrets are expensive to acquire and just as expensive to keep, making it easy for systems to over-invest in them without noticing the diminishing ROI they bring. Believing that information is more valuable simply because it was costly to obtain is an easy route to committing the kinds of mistakes that Robert Jervis argued were made in Iran, when efforts to get secret information completely overlooked the obvious changes that were occurring in plain sight. Secrecy can also make it harder to share information, thus causing the recurrent embarrassments of learning, after the fact, that various government agencies held parts of something, but no one could see it in its entirety, because secrecy rules made sharing impossible. This is not exclusive to the IC, of course – to cite again an example (from Chapter Seven), the defense and security firm Jane's discovered after 9/11 that its organization had "known" about the terrorist plot in advance (or at least most of its major parts), but had not "known that it knew." Morton Halperin identified the same phenomenon in the 1970s: "Information does not pass from the tentacle to the top of the organization instantaneously. Facts can be 'in the system' without being available to the head of the organization ... those who decide which information their boss shall see rarely see their bosses' problem."[40]

Secrecy also exposes governments to demonstrations of their own clumsiness, creating the kinds of contradictions that make hierarchical control look foolish. This is best demonstrated by the Wikileaks phenomenon – which, among other problems, created a situation in which the US government was trying to forbid its own employees, and even potential *future* employees,[41] from looking at information that was in the public domain, while at the same time also chastising places like China and Iran for trying to control the information their citizens access.[42] In addition to the fact that such contradictions create "bad optics," it also seems possible that one reason why IC analysts were slow to notice events unfolding in Tunisia was precisely the injunction against studying the leaked State Department cables, the contents of which are said to have been a major feeder for the anger in December 2010.[43]

- **Understand that information is a marketplace:** The present IC, like the policymaking community which it serves, was established at a time when information was relatively scarce, and moreover was, as was noted above, considered to be important only to the degree that it was "uplifting" or "educational." It has already been argued at length in Chapter Eight how the world in which the information "seller" was in command has vanished, replaced by one in which the information "buyer" rules. Open source analysts thus have to understand not just what "messagers" are saying, but also must be aware of what the competition for the attention of that particular target audience is doing, and what that means for how the message itself is being shaped. As the battle for attention intensifies, would-be message senders find themselves under ever-greater pressure to attract attention, which places profound pressures on them to balance the competing demands of the core message and what is required to get attention. Examples of this competition abound – even so "message-focused" an entity as Ayman Zawahiri, who claims to speak for God, found it necessary in 2008 to conduct an online "chat" with his audience, justifying and explaining himself (including rebutting accusations that he was merely a "media phenomenon").[44] Umair Haque, a blogger on the Harvard Business Review platform, has written of what he dubbed "gonzo marketing," or an attempt to gain attention that is so desperate that it turns toxic, getting the company notoriety, but also destroying whatever "credibility capital" it may have had.[45]

Indeed, this contest between institutional desires for top-down control and the exuberant "democracy" (or "vulgarity") of the cheap media seems likely to present ever greater challenges to institutions. As was discussed at the end of Chapter Nine, the US State Department has attempted to embrace the new media as enthusiastically as it can, but the combination of loss of message control (as when Assistant Secretary of State for Public Affairs P. J. Crowley was forced to resign for being too much a "genuine human voice" and not enough of an official spokesperson) and, perhaps even more importantly, the impossibility of observing in the new media rules and regulations which were laid down in a quite different media era, combine to make it difficult to compete successfully for audience attention. Indeed, it may be that the competition is impossible to sustain – although there has been no official explanation, and almost no publicity of the fact, the State Department's major "website to the world," www.america.gov, which was established with great fanfare under Deputy Secretary of State Karen Hughes in 2007, quietly went dark on 31 March 2011.

- **The story is everything:** As has been argued at several points in this book, data by themselves have very little meaning. It is only when they are embedded into narratives that they can be arranged against one another, acquiring (or losing) significance. The challenge facing any analyst (and indeed any policymaker) is to be sufficiently aware of the various narratives which he or she inhabits to be able also to understand that other narratives exist, what they are, and how they may weight phenomena differently, than do the ones within which one lives. The language here grows a bit tortured because the point is not whether a narrative is "true" or "better," but rather whether a story might have consequence.

    This is true not only of the societies and people whom we target – we also create stories which shape how we make our decisions. A good analyst will be alert to the metaphors which people are using, both among the target population, but also among those who use the intelligence which is being produced. Metaphors and similes are remarkably powerful entities, deeply shaping how people conceptualize the world about them. Morton Halperin has argued, for example, that a great deal of what drove US involvement ever deeper into Vietnam was "the impulse to avoid another Munich."[46] Similar arguments abound as to whether the US effort in Iraq in 2003 was "another D-Day" or "another Vietnam," or involvement in the former Yugoslavia in the late 1990s was "to avert another Rwanda" or running the risk of becoming "another Sudan." Such metaphors are important because, as behavioral psychologists continue to discover, humans are hard-wired to respond to perceived patterns (whether or not the patterns actually exist), with further actions made more likely by the trajectories suggested by the metaphor. Economist Deirdre McCloskey devoted an entire book to the various metaphors of how people talk about economics, arguing that metaphors could not be banished – speech is impossible without them – but rather that those who use them should be conscious of them *as metaphors*, because "metaphors evoke attitudes that are better kept in the open and under the control of reasoning."[47] A number of authors (George Lakoff, Drew Wessen, James Geary) have all argued in various ways that we use, and are persuaded by, various metaphors of orientation that can be exceedingly powerful, and also deeply misleading. Geary, for example, writes of the difference between "agent metaphors" like "the Dow climbed higher today" or "the economy is fighting off oil price shocks" and "object metaphors" like "the S&P plunged today" or "housing prices are in free fall." Agent metaphors, he argues, endow processes with living characteristics, prompting us to respond to them differently than we do to object metaphors, which we tend to understand as processes of nature with which there is no arguing or negotiating.[48]

Analysts must remember that not only do they have their own predominant metaphors, but so too do the people for whom they are writing. Although it is not always possible to do so, analysts should present their arguments in terms of the dominant metaphors of the context for which they work.

- **Don't be surprised by surprise:** Finally, neither analysts nor policymakers should be misled by the "sentinel" metaphor or the "dot-connecting" metaphor into believing that all bad things are foreseeable and preventable. Even if it were possible accurately to predict human behaviors (and no less a figure than George Tenet has reminded listeners at a conference that "Intelligence is always much better at counting heads than divining what is going on inside them"[49]), there are still unexpected physical events that can have profoundly disruptive effects. While this book was being composed there were at least two such events, the eruption of Iceland's Eyjafjallajökull volcano that disrupted travel all over Europe (and, it was argued, helped lead to the firing of US general Stanley McChrystal from his command post in Afghanistan[50]); and the series of massive earthquakes of Japan, which triggered a devastating tsunami that in turn caused catastrophic breakdowns, possibly melt-downs, at a whole string of nuclear reactors, which in turn nearly proved to be fatal for Japan's industry, because the half of the country originally serviced by Tokyo Electric company (roughly the west and the south) was based on a 50 Hz cycle standard used by the German-manufactured equipment purchased in the 1880s, while the part serviced by Osaka Electric Lamp company (the north and the east) had bought US equipment, which runs on a 60 Hz cycle, making it almost impossible for the western half of the island to compensate for the shutdown of the 11 generators on the eastern part.[51]

As those two events – themselves unexpected, and with consequences that were pretty much unpredictable even after the unexpected events had occurred – should remind us, the defensive posture inevitably fails, at least if success is defined as "no surprises." There is an instructive comparison here in regard to weather – author James Gleick points out it was not until the telegraph made it possible for people to be aware of events occurring simultaneously over a large area that it became possible to understand "weather" as an abstraction, a system which might be studied and its movements and possible future events predicted.[52] There are at least two points of comparison with the intelligence function which are worth drawing out here: the first is that, although weather forecasting has over the past 150 years or so become one of the most intensely-studied arenas of human endeavor, with huge computing resources and multi-billion-dollar research activities devoted to trying to make it better, forecasting still remains a science only of *potential*, and not of absolute prediction. The weather industry grows ever more adept at locating factors which *could* result in weather events – and yet the arrival of unpredicted blizzards[53] and predicted blizzards that never arrive[54] continue to make headlines every year.

The second point may be even more important however, which is that, no matter how good they are, weather predictions do nothing to prevent or forestall weather events. Weather continues to occur, as will events like tsunamis, earthquakes, volcanoes, and even cataclysmic asteroid impacts. The example of this last is instructive, if extreme. If an object as small as 50 yards in length were to strike Earth, it would release as much energy as 1,000 Hiroshima-sized bombs – more than enough to level a city. Although most scientists think that a strike of that size could occur as frequently as every 200 years, there is no political or administrative support for monitoring the skies for the possibility of such a strike, nor is there any agreement about what should be done if such a strike were ever to look imminent.[55] Events, in other words, will continue to occur – and most of them, whether predicted or not, are likely to be things which policymakers could do very little to prevent, no matter how much in advance they were warned (particularly since, as Sherman Kent suggested, the window for "timely long-range warning" in the intelligence analyst and policymaker communities lies somewhere between "this afternoon" and "next year"[56]).

Through a glass darkly...

Following the argument laid out above, about the power of heuristics, perhaps the best way to conclude this book is to return to Sherman Kent's simile, already noted in Chapter Six, that an intelligence organization should have the combined characteristics of "a large university faculty," "our greatest metropolitan newspapers," and an "organization engaged in the manufacture of a product."[57] The choice of comparisons is a useful one, for each of those forms of enterprise is now in profound trouble, and may indeed be facing, if not extinction, then a transformation so profound that what survives will be something else entirely, like the dinosaur that evolved to be a bird.

The collapse of the newspaper is easiest to defend. As has been widely chronicled, newspapers have been hemorrhaging money for at least a decade, as their advertising base moves elsewhere.[58] They have closed bureaus, reduced coverage, printed on smaller paper, and diversified into ever more unrelated fields – some of which have proven to be financially toxic, in addition to undermining the moral authority that "serious newspapers" used to claim.[59] Even more importantly, as has been argued above, the nature of what "news" is has changed dramatically, now to embrace celebrity "news," lifestyle "news," and other topics that would probably have been unimaginable in a "serious newspaper" of Kent's day.[60] The problems of industry are perhaps less clear-cut, as manufacturing of the sort that Kent would have recognized continues. However, the kinds of "product" that he probably had in mind have either moved their production overseas, have shut down entirely, or are in such deep trouble that it required US financial intervention to rescue them. Even education is changing – this includes not just the erosion of the core "liberal arts curriculum," as was discussed above, but has gone even farther, to the point that people are beginning seriously to question whether "higher education" has value at all,[61] or at least value sufficient to justify its enormous cost to the consumer.[62] Some have even begun to argue that online learning portals are making it possible for students to earn college-equivalent credentials without having to go through colleges at all.[63]

Clearly there is no one driver for all of this change, but the transformations of the information environment are surely a huge part of it, as linkages and activities that once were thought to be natural and inevitable increasingly prove to be contingent, accidents of the technology of the time. Newspapers, for example, were seen as the only "natural" way to deliver such disparate content as recipes, fashions, advertisements, entertainment news, editorials, dispatches from far-away places, and horoscopes – and each of those has now become "unbundled," wandering off to find its own audience, and its own channels for reaching them, leaving the institution of the newspaper tottering at the edge of extinction. Music too – once thought to be "owned" by the vinyl LP, the cassette, or the CD – suddenly is just a file, something that can be shared by millions, for nothing. The music industry fought back against this trend aggressively, but in the process destroyed itself – sales of recorded music have declined more than 50 percent in the past decade.[64] Text now too is unhooking itself from print, both with new texts, as authors increasingly bypass publishers to offer themselves directly to readers (whether through blogs or e-books), and with old ones, as Google and others digitize the books that already exist. The movie industry too has embarked on this struggle, battling both "content pirates"[65] and theater owners[66] as the industry attempts to hang onto the money and prestige that used to come with owning a medium.

One theme which seems common to all of this change is that information erodes form, which increasingly challenges organizations that define themselves by processes, requirements, and procedures, rather than by outcomes. As has already been noted, most of the legal structures that attempt to contain the information environment are built on analogies. Authors Hal Abelson, Ken Ledeen, and Harry Lewis have argued[67] that this approach not only creates inevitable conflicts, but further tends to make the attempts at control look clumsy (or worse). Much in the way that autos were first called "horseless carriages" or enterprises like Doctors Without Borders are called "non-governmental organizations," attempted legislation of the new information environment looks for what seems the closest analogy and then seeks to regulate it based on that similarity. The metaphors which attempt to track the technological fluidity of the new media to the more constrained media of the past are, in the view of Abelson and his co-authors, proving unusually paradoxical and misleading. Courts have had to decide, for example, whether internet providers are more like newstands, and therefore responsible for the content they carry, or like trucks, and therefore not responsible for the content which moves through their fiber.[68] Also at issue was whether the "community standards" measure of content offensive should apply at the point of origin, or anywhere the content could be accessed – one result of which was that French courts were able to require Yahoo to remove Nazi memorabilia offered for sale on US sites. An equally confounding problem is whether "anti-annoyance" rules enacted to protect people from unwanted harassing phone calls should also apply to the internet as a whole, because it is possible to make phone calls over the internet ... and so on. Scholar Zeynep Tufekci has dubbed this problem "the dictator's dilemma"[69] – try to shut off the internet, and you will not only fail, but you will cripple your own society; don't shut it off, and "counter societies" and censorship "work-arounds" will continue to flourish.

The challenge, however, is not just to dictators. Everyone agrees that the forces unleashed by cheap, easy, ubiquitous information are enormous, disruptive, and fundamentally unpredictable. Certainly it is far too early in the transformative process to make meaningful predictions about the changes that the information revolution may bring to the world of intelligence and policymaking. What does seem clear, however, is that the rigid, process-defined, "credentialing" structures of newspaper, university, and factory that Kent advanced to illustrate his vision of the intelligence community of (what to him was) the future are vanishing. It may be possible for a while yet to stave off that collapse through issuing orders and making rules – similar to what France tried to do, by giving all French citizens a free newspaper subscription on their eighteenth birthday[70] – but in the end it is going to be the organizations that change, and not the new ways that information moves. The genie will not go back in the bottle.

The challenge for organizations is going to be whether they face those challenges well, by re-inventing their original purposes in the context of the new conditions of information, or poorly, dragging out transformations that will come anyway, and damaging themselves in the process. One of the central texts of violent jihad, Abu Bakr Naji's *The Management of Savagery*,[71] argues that a fundamental goal of terror is to provoke governments into over-reacting, making disproportionate and futile responses to terror attacks, thus proving their own incompetence while also making life worse for those they claim to be protecting, and thus increasing sympathy and support for the jihadists. Writing from a totally different perspective, and with a completely different goal in mind, peace activist Gene Sharp, who recently emerged as one of the powerful influences on the shape of Egypt's ousting of the Mubarak family,[72] argued that one of the six factors that create political legitimacy are "skills and knowledge," thus suggesting that, once organizations are seen to be incapable of doing the things they claim they have taken power to do, their political legitimacy can vanish quite quickly.[73]

The challenge of information that is "fast, cheap, and out of control" is here to stay, and can only be prevented by returning one's society to some kind of pre-Gutenberg darkness (if indeed even that is possible). Just as with weather prediction, the important lesson for the intelligence function is that our ever-burgeoning supply of information can help us to build an ever-improving capacity to anticipate potentialities, to be ever more aware of events that *could* happen, and so makes it more likely that the policy-makers whom the analysts serve, and the publics whom those policymaker serve in their turn, can be better prepared to deal with the consequences of an event, when and if it does occur.

Notes

1 Michael Warner, "Wanted: A Definition of 'Intelligence'," *Studies in Intelligence*, vol. 46, no. 3, 2002, p. 21.

2 Charles Mangio and Bonnie Wilkinson, "Intelligence Analysis: Once Again," paper presented at the annual meeting of the ISA, 26 March 2008, accessed 13 April 2011, at: http://www.allacademic.com/meta/p253385_index.html

3 C. J. Bartlett and Calvin Green, "Clinical Prediction: Does One Sometimes Know Too Much?" *Journal of Counseling Psychology*, vol. 13, no. 3, 1966, pp. 267–70. As an indication of how strong faith was at the time in the soundness of social science, the two researchers remind readers that "knowledge of extraneous information responsible for prediction can act to contaminate the prediction." Proper predictions can only be made statistically as "a way of avoiding contamination by knowledge of too much information" (p. 269).

4 James G. March, *A Primer of Decision Making* (New York: Free Press, 1994), p. 25.

5 Ransom, p. 12.

6 See: https://www.cia.gov/about-cia/cia-vision-mission-values/index.html, accessed 6 March 2011.

7 Ransom, p. 57.

8 Kahn, "An Historical Theory of Intelligence," p. 89.

9 Thomas Fingar, speech given 21 August 2006, at: http://www.dni.gov/speeches/20060821_2_speech.pdf, accessed 13 April 2011.

10 Brzezinski, in *Watching the Bear*, p. 262.

11 Mark M. Lowenthal, "'Tribal Tongues': Intelligence Consumers, Intelligence Producers," in Loch Johnson and James J. Wirtz (eds), *Strategic Intelligence: Windows into a Secret World* (Los Angeles: Roxbury, 2004), p. 235.

12 Robert D. Blackwill and Jack Davis, "A Policymaker's Perspective on Intelligence Analysis," in Johnson and Wirtz, pp. 121, 124.

13 Paul D. Miller, "Lessons for Intelligence Support to Policymaking During Crises," *Studies in Intelligence*, vol. 54, no. 2, 2010, p. 7.

14 Barry Schwartz, *The Paradox of Choice* (New York: Ecco, 2003).

15 Siegried Streufert and Susan Streufert, "Stress and Information Search in Complex Decision Making: Effects of Load and Time Urgency," Technical Report No. 4, Contract No. N00014-80-C-0581, August 1981, original emphasis.

16 As quoted in "Déjà vu," *Lapham's Quarterly*, 25 August 2010, at: http://www.laphamsquarterly.org/deja_vu/2010/08/our-eyes-ache-with-reading.php.

17 Ann Blair, "Reading Strategies for Coping with Information Overload, ca.1550–1700," *Journal of the History of Ideas*, vol. 64, no. 1, 2003, p. 12.

18 Chip Heath and Dan Heath, *Made to Stick* (New York: Random House, 2008).

19 Schwartz cites a study which showed that when offered a choice among three jams, about 30 percent of those who stopped to look at the display bought; when there 24 jams set out, only 3 percent bought. Schwartz, *Paradox of Choice*, Kindle location 279–292 (Chapter "Let's Go Shopping").

20 Church Committee, p. 275.

21 Streufert and Streufert.

22 The "ur-texts" of this literature are the article by Daniel Kahneman and Amos Tversky, "Judgment under Uncertainty: Heuristics and Biases," *Science*, 27 September 1974, and the book they co-edited with Paul Slovic, *Judgement under Uncertainty: Heuristics and Biases* (New York: Cambridge University Press, 1982).

23 This word, now used to denote a perjorative heuristic, was repurposed by Walter Lippmann in his book *Public Opinion*. Prior to 1922, the word was used to mean the common phrases that typesetters frequently reused, and so did not take apart after each printing, in order to be able to drop them quickly into place when the phrase next appeared.

24 Kent, *Strategic Intelligence*, p. 117.

25 Both examples from *Watching the Bear*, pp. 254, 265.

26 Schwartz, *Paradox of Choice*.

27 Somewhat tangential to this argument, but worth noting here, is that Kent's formative years came at the very end of what might be called "the McGuffey period" of American life. The McGuffey series of readers, which specifically sought to teach reading through uplifting moral and patriotic tales, were used by "at least half" of the Americans who learned to read between "the Presidency of Martin Van Buren [and] that of Theodore Roosevelt." As a history of American thought written in 1927 put it, "In a country prone to change, McGuffey's had permanence for a strikingly long time." See Mark Sullivan, *Our Times: America Finding Herself* (New York and London: Scribners, 1927), pp. 20, 21.

28 Kent, *Strategic Intelligence*, pp. 4–5.

29 James Fallows, "Learning to Love the (Shallow, Divisive, Unreliable) New Media," *Atlantic*, April 2011, at: http://www.theatlantic.com/magazine/archive/2011/04/learning-to-love-the-shallow-divisive-unreliable-new-media/8415/, accessed 24 September 2011,

30 Morton Halperin, *Bureaucratic Politics and Foreign Policy* (Washington DC: Brookings Institute, 1974), p. 11.

31 Typically of the internet, a number of sites agree that these words were his, but none give the precise source of them.

32 See: http://www.the99.org, accessed 4 April 2011.

33 According to *The Guardian*, about a million copies of the comic books are sold every year, and themed amusement parks and animated movies are in the offing. See: http://www.guardian.co.uk/books/2009/jul/05/comic-collaboration-superheroes-dc-teshkeel, accessed 17 April 2011.

34 See for example: http://www.niemanlab.org/2010/04/the-gutenberg-parenthesis-thomas-pettitt-on-parallels-between-the-pre-print-era-and-our-own-internet-age/ and: http://campustechnology.com/Articles/2008/03/Web-20-Secondary-Orality-and-the-Gutenberg-Parenthesis.aspx?Page=1 and: http://web.mit.edu/comm-forum/mit5/papers/pettitt_plenary_gutenberg.pdf.

35 There are various stages to the Church's reversal of its condemnation, including dropping the ban on books not espousing geocentrism (1757), endorsement of the Copernican view of the solar system (1822), and the announcement that the condemnation of Galileo had been an error (1992).

36 Kerbel and Olcott, "Synthesizing with Clients, Not Analyzing for Customers."

37 Patrick O'Sullivan, "Masspersonal Communication: Rethinking the Mass-Interpersonal Divide," paper presented at the annual meeting of the International Communication Association, Sheraton, New York, at: http://www.allacademic.com/meta/p14277_index.html.

38 See for example Annette Hubschle, "Novel Uses of Mobile Phones, the Internet, and Social Media," at: http://www.the-african.org/blog/?p=519.

39 Newspaper accounts following the death of Osama bin Laden describe USB flash drives as a major way that bin Laden's network moved information around.

40 Halperin, p. 139.

41 See: http://www.foxnews.com/us/2010/12/04/columbia-u-students-warned-wikileaks/

42 Perhaps even worse, it was recently found that at least one government agency blocks websites that contain information about how to get around firewalls, even though the evasion tools were developed by the US government as a way to support "internet freedom" in China and Iran. See: http://www.ethanzuckerman.com/blog/2011/04/20/us-national-science-foundation-blocks-global-voices-advocacy-website/

43 See for example: http://www.dailymail.co.uk/news/article-1347336/First-Wikileaks-Revolution-Tunisia-descends-anarchy-president-flees.html.

44 The "Q&A" is described at: http://en.qantara.de/Free-Propaganda/8049c164/index.html, accessed 24 September 2011.

45 See: http://blogs.hbr.org/haque/2010/10/when_going_viral_is_not_engagement.html. Haque's example is to have a company's CEO and Chairman strip to their shorts, cover themselves with peanut butter, and then dance the Macarena, for posting on YouTube. One example of "bad attention choices" which has been much noted in the blogosphere is a "rap video" made by the senior management of Singapore's Media Development Authority – the country's combination media licensing and censorship body – to promote investment in the media sector. See: http://www.youtube.com/watch?v=nngYqmulLJI.

46 Halperin, p. 22.

47 Deirdre N. McCloskey, *The Rhetoric of Economics* (Madison, WI: University of Wisconsin Press, 1998), p. 46.

48 James Geary, *I is an Other: The Secret Life of Metaphor and How it Shapes the Way We See the World* (New York: HarperCollins, 2011).

49 *Watching the Bear*, p. 238.

50 See: http://abcnews.go.com/International/gen-stanley-mcchrystal-icelands-volcano/story?id=11016455 and: http://www.telegraph.co.uk/news/worldnews/northamerica/usa/7850705/McChrystals-firing-How-Icelands-Eyjafjallajokull-volcano-played-a-role.html, both accessed 19 April 2011.

51 See: http://www.itworld.com/business/140626/legacy-1800s-leaves-tokyo-facing-blackouts, accessed 19 April 2011.

52 Gleick, *The Information*, Kindle location 2616–2619 (chapter 5).

53 See: http://www.nydailynews.com/ny_local/galleries/boxing_day_blizzard_the_great_snowstorm_of_2010_rocks_new_yorkand_beyond/boxing_day_blizzard_the_great_snowstorm_of_2010_rocks_new_yorkand_beyond.html

54 See: http://www.recordonline.com/apps/pbcs.dll/article?AID=/20110402/NEWS/104020323

55 Tad Friend, "Vermin of the Sky," *The New Yorker*, 28 February 2011.

56 Davis, "Kent's Final Thoughts."

57 Kent, *Strategic Intelligence*, pp. 74–75.

58 Probably the best argument for this will be found in the Pew Center's Project for Excellence in Journalism, conducted annually since 2004. The most recent version is at http://stateofthemedia.org/.

59 In April 2011, for example, the *Washington Post* announced that 61 percent of its income comes from the Kaplan Educational division (now troubled because of its heavy reliance on students who take on unmanageable debt loads to access the company's services), versus 14 percent from the traditional news divisions. The company also was forced to sell its *Newsweek* magazine for $1 – less than the cost of a single issue. See: http://www.washingtonpost.com/todays_paper/Business/2011-04-10/G/1/14.0.1877296306_epaper.html

60 Although Kent is remembered as having a ribald sense of humor, it is hard to imagine what he would have made of this "product review" in a recent *New York Times*: http://www.nytimes.com/2011/04/21/fashion/21VIBRATORS. html?_r=1&scp=1&sq=vibrator&st=cse

61 For a discussion of a possible "education bubble" see: http://techcrunch.com/ 2011/04/10/peter-thiel-were-in-a-bubble-and-its-not-the-internet-its-higher-education/

62 See "Is a College Education Worth the Debt?", at: http://www.npr.org/ templates/story/story.php?storyId=112432364

63 See "Online Learning Portals: Customizing Colleges Right out of Higher Education?" at: http://chronicle.com/article/Online-Learning-Portals-/127694/ ?sid=at&utm_source=at&utm_medium=en

64 See: http://money.cnn.com/2010/02/02/news/companies/ napster_music_industry/

65 See: http://www.nytimes.com/2011/04/23/arts/television/doctor-who-us-premiere-will-not-be-delayed.html?scp=5&sq=Dr.%20WHo&st=cse

66 See: http://www.nytimes.com/2011/04/25/business/media/25vod. html?scp=6&sq=directv&st=cse

67 Abelson, *et al.*, *Blown to Bits*.

68 Abelson, *et al.*, *Blown to Bits*.

69 See: http://technosociology.org/?p=286, accessed 24 September 2011.

70 See: http://boingboing.net/2009/02/02/france-to-give-free.html

71 See: http://www.wcfia.harvard.edu/olin/images/Management%20of%20 Savagery%20-%2005-23-2006.pdf

72 See: http://www.nytimes.com/2011/02/14/world/middleeast/14egypt-tunisia-protests.html?ref=genesharp

73 Gene Sharp, *From Dictatorship to Democracy* (Boston, MA: Albert Einstein Institution, 2010), available at: http://www.aeinstein.org/organizations/org/ FDTD.pdf

Bibliography

Articles and reports

Ambinder, Marc, "Shutdown of Intelligence Community E-mail Network Sparks E-Rebellion," *The Atlantic*, 6 October 2009, at: http://www.theatlantic.com/politics/archive/2009/10/shutdown-of-intelligence-community-e-mail-network-sparks-e-rebellion/27790/.

Archetti, Christina, "Fighting Brand al-Qaida," paper for presentation at the UK Political Science Association annual meeting, April 2009, at: http://www.psa.ac.uk/journals/pdf/5/2009/Archetti.pdf, accessed 4 February 2011.

Auletta, Ken, "The New Pitch: Do Ads Still Work?" *The New Yorker*, 25 March 2005, at: http://www.newyorker.com/archive/2005/03/28/050328fa_fact.

Bain, Ben, "A-Space Set to Launch This Month," *Federal Computer Week*, 3 September 2008, at: http://fcw.com/Articles/2008/09/03/ASpace-set-to-launch-this-month.aspx.

—"FBI Creates Knowledge Wiki," *Federal Computer Week*, 26 September 2008, at: http://fcw.com/Articles/2008/09/26/FBI-creates-knowledge-wiki.aspx.

Bartlett, C. J., and Calvin Green, "Clinical Prediction: Does One Sometimes Know Too Much?" *Journal of Counseling Psychology*, vol. 13, no. 3, 1966, pp. 267–70.

Bates, Marcia, "The Design of Browsing and Berrypicking Techniques for the Online Search Interface," *Online Information Review*, vol. 13, no. 5, 1989, pp. 407–24.

Becker, Joseph, "Comparative Survey of Soviet and US Access to Published Information," *Studies in Intelligence*, vol. 1, no. 4, 1957, pp. 35–46.

Blair, Ann, "Reading Strategies for Coping with Information Overload, ca.1550–1700," *Journal of the History of Ideas*, vol. 64, no. 1, 2003, pp. 11–28.

Bogost, Ian, "The Rhetoric of Video Games," in Katie Salen (ed.), *The Ecology of Games: Connecting Youth, Games, and Learning*. Cambridge, MA: MIT Press, 2008, pp. 117–40.

Bohannan, Laura, "Shakespeare in the Bush," *Natural History*, August–September 1966, pp. 28–33.

Borel, Paul, "Automation for Information Control," *Studies in Intelligence*, vol. 11, no. 1, 1993, pp. 25–31.

Borkenau, Franz, "Getting at the Facts Behind the Soviet Façade," *Commentary*, April 1954, pp. 393–400.

Boynton, Robert, "North Korea's Digital Underground," *The Atlantic*,

April 2011, at: http://www.theatlantic.com/magazine/archive/2011/04/
north-korea-8217-s-digital-underground/8414/.

Calabresi, Massimo, "Wikipedia for Spies: The CIA Discovers Web 2.0," *Time*,
8 April 2009, at: http://www.time.com/time/nation/article/0,8599,1890084,00.
html.

Carver, Richard, "Broadcasting and Political Transition," in Richard Fardon
and Graham Furniss (eds), *African Broadcast Cultures: Radio in Transition*.
Oxford: James Currey, 2000, pp. 188–97.

Connable, Major Ben, "All Our Eggs in a Broken Basket," *Military Review*,
March–April 2009, pp. 57–64.

Davis, Jack, "Sherman Kent and the Profession of Intelligence Analysis," The
Sherman Kent Center for Intelligence Analysis, Occasional Papers: vol. 1, no. 5,
November 2002.

— "Sherman Kent's Final Thoughts on Analyst-Policymaker Relations," The
Sherman Kent Center for Intelligence Analysis Occasional Papers: vol. 2, no. 3,
2003, pp. 1–11.

Defense Science Board Task Force on Defense Intelligence, *Counterinsurgency
(COIN) Intelligence, Surveillance, and Reconnaissance (ISR) Operations*.
Washington DC, February 2011.

Doob, Leonard, "Goebbels' Principles of Propaganda," *The Public Opinion
Quarterly*, vol. 14, no. 3, autumn 1950, pp. 419–42.

Doostdar, Alireza, "The Vulgar Spirit of Blogging: On Language, Culture, and
Power in Persian Weblogestan," *American Anthropologist*, vol. 106, no. 4,
December 2004, pp. 651–62.

El-Hamamsy, Gazbeya, "Carving Up the Dish," *Business Today Egypt*, September
2005, at: https://www.zawya.com/.../sidZAWYA20050914100932.

Engerman, David, "Rethinking Cold War Universities: Some Recent Histories,"
Journal of Cold War Studies, vol. 5, no. 3, summer 2003, pp. 80–95.

Epstein, Edward Jay, "Have You Ever Tried to Sell a Diamond?" *The Atlantic*,
February 1982, at: http://www.theatlantic.com/magazine/archive/1982/02/
have-you-ever-tried-to-sell-a-diamond/4575/.

Epstein, Gady, "Golden Cow," *Forbes Asia Magazine*, 27 September 2010, at:
http://www.forbes.com/global/2010/0927/fab-50-10-china-mengniu-dairy-milk-
golden-cow.html.

Ewen, Stuart, "Reflections on Visual Persuasion," *New York Law School Law
Review*, vol. 43, 1999, pp. 811–20.

Fallows, James, "Learning to Love the New Media," *Atlantic*, April 2011, at:
http://www.theatlantic.com/magazine/archive/2011/04/learning-to-love-the-
shallow-divisive-unreliable-new-media/8415/.

Farrell, Stephen, and Tessa Lau, "Fringe Contacts: People-Tagging for the
Enterprise," IBM Research Report, RJ10384 (AO606-027), 20 June 2006.

Farrelly, M. C. *et al.*, "Youth Tobacco Prevention Mass Media Campaigns: Past,
Present, and Future Directions," BMJ Journals Online, at: http://www.ncbi.nlm.
nih.gov/pmc/articles/PMC1766092/pdf/v012p00i35.pdf, accessed 25 September
2011.

Flanagan, Ben, "Multi-screen Complex," *Media Week Middle East*, 17 May 2009.

Ford, Harold P., "The CIA and Double Demonology: Calling the Sino-Soviet
Split," *Studies in Intelligence*, vol. 42, no. 5, 1988–1989, pp. 57–71.

Friend, Tad, "Vermin of the Sky," *The New Yorker*, 28 February 2011, pp. 22–26.

Gerbner, George, and Larry Gors, "Living with Television: The Violence Profile," *Journal of Communication*, April 1976, pp. 172–94.

Gillespie, Thomas W., and John A. Agnew, "Finding Osama bin Laden: An Application of Biogeographic Theories and Satellite Imagery," *MIT International Review*, 17 February 2009, at: http://web.mit.edu/mitir/2009/online/finding-bin-laden.pdf.

Gladwell, Malcolm, "Open Secrets," *The New Yorker*, 8 January 2007, at: http://gladwell.com/pdf/opensecrets.pdf.

—"Small Change: Why the Revolution Will Not be Tweeted," *The New Yorker*, 4 October 2010, at: http://gladwell.com/2010/2010_10_04_a_twitter.html.

—"Does Egypt Need Twitter?" *The New Yorker*, 2 February 2011, at: http://www.newyorker.com/online/blogs/newsdesk/2011/02/does-egypt-need-twitter.html.

Gurri, Martin, Craig Denny and Aaron Harms, "Our Visual Persuasion Gap," *Parameters*, Spring 2010, pp. 101–109.

Heath, Robert, and Paul Feldwick, "Fifty Years of Using the Wrong Model of Advertising," *International Journal of Market Research*, vol. 50, no. 1, 2007, pp. 29–59.

Hilton, Denis, "Causality vs. Explanation: Objective Relations vs. Subjective Interests," *Interdisciplines*, Institute of Cognitive Sciences, University of Geneva, at: http://www.interdisciplines.org/medias/confs/archives/archive_6.pdf.

Hubschle, Annette, "Novel Uses of Mobile Phones, the Internet, and Social Media," at: http://www.the-african.org/blog/?p=519, accessed 11 August 2011.

Jackson, Joab, "Intellipedia Suffers Mid-Life Crisis," *Government Computer News*, 18 February 2009, at: http://gcn.com/Articles/2009/02/18/Intellipedia.aspx.

Kahn, David, "An Historical Theory of Intelligence," *Intelligence and National Security*, vol. 16, autumn 2001, pp. 79–92.

Kahneman Daniel, and Amos Tversky, "Judgment under Uncertainty: Heuristics and Biases," *Science*, 27 September 1974, pp. 1124–1131.

Katz, Elihu, "The Two-Step Flow of Communication: An Up-to-Date Report on an Hypothesis," *Public Opinion Quarterly*, vol. 21, no. 1, 1957, pp. 61–78.

Keller, Bill, "The Twitter Trap," *New York Times Magazine*, 18 May 2011, at: http://www.nytimes.com/2011/05/22/magazine/the-twitter-trap.html?_r=1.

Kelley, Captain Stephanie R., "Rumors in Iraq: A Guide to Winning Hearts and Minds," *Strategic Insights*, vol. 4, no. 2, February 2005, at: http://www.nps.edu/Academics/centers/ccc/publications/OnlineJournal/2005/Feb/kelleyfeb05.pdf

Kellow, C., and H. Steeves, "The Role of Radio in the Rwandan Genocide," *Journal of Communication*, vol. 48, no. 3, 1998, pp. 107–128.

Kelly, Patrick, "The Methodology of Ernst Bernheim and Legal History," at: http://www.scribd.com/doc/20021802/The-Methodology-of-Ernst-Bernheim-and-Legal-History-Patrick-Kelly, accessed 7 March 2011.

Kendall, Willmoore, "The Function of Intelligence: Review," *World Politics*, vol. 1, no. 4, July 1949, pp. 91–103.

Kent, Sherman, "A Crucial Estimate Relived," *Studies in Intelligence*, vol. 8, no. 2, 1964, pp. 111–19.

Kerbel, Josh, and Anthony Olcott, "Synthesizing with Clients, Not Analyzing for Customers," *Studies in Intelligence*, vol. 54, no. 4, 2010, pp. 11–27.

Kikuchi, Masaaki, "Open Source Conference Organized by the US Government," *IISIA Monthly Report*, October 2008, pp. 22–26.

Kimmage, Daniel, *The Al-Qaeda Media Nexus*. Radio Free Europe/Radio Liberty, 2008 at: http://docs.rferl.org/en-US/AQ_Media_Nexus.pdf, accessed 11 August 2011.

Kirkpatrick, Lyman, "Origin, Missions, and Structure of CIA," *Studies in Intelligence*, vol. 2, no. 1, 1958, pp. 1–5.

Kirmani, Mary, "RTLM: The Medium that Became a Tool for Mass Murder," in Allan Thompson (ed.), *The Media and the Rwanda Genocide*. Ann Arbor, MI and London: Pluto Press, 2007, pp. 110–24.

Knapp, Robert H., "A Psychology of Rumor," *Public Opinion Quarterly*, vol. 1, no. 8, 1944, pp. 22–37.

—OSS Secret Memo, "Criteria of a Successful Rumor" at: http://www.icdc.com/~paulwolf/oss/rumormanual2june1943.htm, accessed 26 September 2011.

Kraidy, Marwan, "Reality Television and Politics in the Arab World," *Transnational Broadcasting Studies*, vol. 1, no. 2, 2005, pp. 7–28.

—"Saudi Arabia, Lebanon and the Changing Arab Information Order," *International Journal of Communication*, vol. 1, 2007, pp. 139–56.

Lasswell, Harold D., "The Theory of Political Propaganda," *American Political Science Review*, vol. 21, no. 3, August 1927, pp. 627–31.

—"The Structure and Function of Communication in Society," in L. Bryson (ed.), *The Communication of Ideas*. New York: Harper & Row, 1948, pp. 37–52.

Lauw, Hady W., *et al.*, "Homophily in the Digital World: A LiveJournal Case Study," IEEE Internet Computing, vol. 14, no. 2, March/April 2010, pp. 15–23.

Leetaru, Kalev, "The Scope of FBIS and BBC Open Source Media Coverage, 1979–2008," *Studies in Intelligence*, vol. 54, no. 1, 2010, pp. 17–37.

Leigh, Robert D., "Politicians vs. Bureaucrats," *Harper's Magazine*, vol. 190, no. 1136, January 1945, pp. 97–105.

Liebowitz, Stan J., "The Elusive Symbiosis: The Impact of Radio on the Record Industry," *Review of Economic Research on Copyright Issues*, vol. 1, no. 1, 2004, pp. 93–118.

Macdonald, Neil, "Language Translation by Machine – A Report of the First Successful Trial," *Computers and Automation*, vol. 3, no. 2, February 1954, pp. 6–10.

Macey, Jonathan, "A Pox on Both Your Houses: Enron, Sarbanes-Oxley and the Debate Concerning the Relative Efficacy of Mandatory vs Enabling Rules," *Washington University Law Quarterly*, vol. 81, 2003, pp. 329–55.

MacFarquhar, Neil, "Fatwa Overload," *Foreign Policy*, 17 April 2009, at: http://www.foreignpolicy.com/articles/2009/04/16/fatwa_overload. May also be found in: MacFarquhar, Neil, *The Media Relations Department of Hizbollah Wishes You a Happy Birthday*. New York: Perseus Books, 2009, pp. 127–31.

Mandaville, Peter, "Reimagining Islam in Diaspora: The Politics of Mediated Community," *Gazette*, vol. 63(2–3), 2001, pp. 169–86.

Mangio, Charles, and Bonnie Wilkinson, "Intelligence Analysis: Once Again," paper presented at the annual meeting of the International Studies Association, 26 March 2008, at: http://www.scribd.com/doc/21602029/Intelligence-Analysis-Once-Again.

Masuda, Takahiko, and Richard Nisbett, "Attending Holistically versus

Analytically: Comparing the Context Sensitivity of Japanese and Americans," *Journal of Personality and Social Psychology*, vol. 81, no. 5, 2001, pp. 922–34.

McGonagle, John, "An Examination of the 'Classic' CI Model," *Journal of Competitive Intelligence and Management*, vol. 4, no. 2, 2007, pp. 71–86.

Mercado, Stephen C., "FBIS Against the Axis, 1941–1945," *Studies in Intelligence*, Fall–Winter 2001, pp. 33–43.

Miller, Paul D., "Lessons for Intelligence Support to Policymaking During Crises," *Studies in Intelligence*, vol. 54, no. 2, 2010, pp. 1–8.

Mirzoeff, Nicholas, "On Visuality," *Journal of Visual Culture*, vol. 5, no. 1, April 2006, pp. 53–79.

Mody, Meera, "Key Intelligence Topics (KITs) in Competitive Intelligence and Global Business," in David Blenkhorn and Craig Fleisher (eds), *Competitive Intelligence and Global Business*. New York: Praeger, 2005, pp. 17–31.

Moll, Yasmin, "Islamic Televangelism: Religion, Media and Visuality in Contemporary Egypt," *Arab Media & Society*, Issue 10, Spring 2010, at: http://www.arabmediasociety.com/?article=732.

Murphy, Cullen, "Watching the Russians," *Atlantic Monthly*, February 1983, pp. 33–51.

O'Day, Vicki, and Robin Jeffries, "Orienteering in an Information Landscape: How Information Seekers Get From Here to There," Hewlett-Packard Lab Reports, HPL-92-127 (R.1), September 1992.

Olcott, Anthony, "*Glasnost* and Soviet Culture," in Maurice Freidberg and Heyward Isham (eds), *Soviet Society under Gorbachev: Current Trends and the Prospects for Reform*. Armonk, NY: ME Sharpe, 1987, pp. 101–31.

—"The Challenges of Clashing IC Interests," *International Journal of Intelligence and Counterintelligence*, vol. 23, no. 4, 2010, pp. 623–35.

Osnos, Evan, "Angry Youth," *The New Yorker*, 28 July 2008, at: http://www.newyorker.com/reporting/2008/07/28/080728fa_fact_osnos.

O'Sullivan, Patrick, "Masspersonal Communication: Rethinking the Mass-Interpersonal Divide," paper presented at the annual meeting of the International Communication Association, Sheraton, New York, at: http://citation.allacademic.com//meta/p_mla_apa_research_citation/0/1/4/2/7/pages14277/p14277-1.php, accessed 26 September 2011.

Palmer, Carole L., and Cheryl Knott Malone, "Elaborate Isolation: Metastructures of Knowledge about Women," *The Information Society*, vol. 17, 2001, pp. 179–94.

Pettitt, Tom, "Containment and Articulation: Media, Cultural Production, and the Perception of the Material World," at: http://web.mit.edu/comm-forum/mit6/papers/Pettitt.pdf, accessed 7 December 2010.

Pinsky, Robert, "Start the Presses," *New York Times Book Review*, 13 August 2010, at: http://www.nytimes.com/2010/08/15/books/review/Pinsky-t.html?scp=9&sq=robert+pinsky&st=nyt.

Prescott, John, "The Evolution of Competitive Intelligence," *Journal of the Association of Proposal Management Professionals*, Spring 1999, pp. 37–52.

Purves, Dale, R. Beau Lotto, and Surajit Nund, "Why We See What We Do," *American Scientist Online*, at: http://www.colorado.edu/MCDB/MCDB3650/PurvesWhyWeSee.pdf, accessed 24 March 2011.

Random, R. A., "Intelligence as a Science," *Studies in Intelligence*, vol. 2, no. 2, 1958, pp. 75–79.

Rittel, Horst, and Melvin Webber, "Dilemmas in a General Theory of Planning," *Policy Sciences*, no. 4, 1973, pp. 155–69.

Ruggiero, Thomas E., "Uses and Gratifications Theory in the 21st Century," *Mass Communication and Society*, vol. 3, 2000, pp. 3–37.

Rush, Myron, "Esoteric Communication in Soviet Politics," *World Politics*, vol. 11, no. 4, July 1959, pp. 614–20.

Sakr, Naomi, "Fragmentation or Consolidation?: Factors in the *Oprah*-ization of Social Talk on Multi-channel Arab TV," in Graeme Turner and Jinna Tay (eds), *Television Studies After TV*. Oxford and New York: Routledge, 2009, pp. 168–78.

Schleifer, S. Abdallah, "Media Explosion in the Arab World: The Pan-Arab Satellite Broadcasters," *Transnational Broadcasting Studies (TBS)*, vol. 1, Fall 1998, at: http://www.tbsjournal.com/Archives/Fall98/Articles1/Pan-Arab_bcasters/pan-arab_bcasters.html.

Shainin, Jonathon, "The Ziggurat of Zealotry," *New York Times Magazine*, 10 December 2006, at: http://www.nytimes.com/2006/12/10/magazine/10section4.t-11.html?ex=1166590800&en=0ef1451c0d0e9cc5&ei=5070.

Shryock, Richard, "For an Eclectic Sovietology," *Studies in Intelligence*, vol. 8, no. 1, winter 1964, pp. 57–64.

Siforov, V. "Space Television Broadcast from Vladivostok to Moscow," *Current Digest of the Soviet Press*, 19 May 1965, p. 2.

Simon, Herbert, "Rational Choice and the Structure of the Environment," *Psychological Review*, vol. 63, no. 2, 1956, pp. 129–38.

Spink, A., *et al.*, "Overlap among Major Web Search Engines," *Proceedings of the Third International Conference on Information Technology: New Generations*, Washington DC, 2006, pp. 370–74.

Streufert, Siegried, and Susan Streufert, "Stress and Information Search in Complex Decision Making: Effects of Load and Time Urgency," Technical Report No. 4, Contract No. N00014-80-C-0581, August 1981.

Szabo, Gabor, and Bernardo Huberman, "Predicting the Popularity of Online Content," Social Science Research Network, at: http://papers.ssrn.com/sol3/papers.cfm?abstract_id=1295610, accessed 4 December 2010.

Teale, Edwin, "America Listens In," *Popular Science Monthly*, June 1941, pp. 74–77.

Thompson, Clive, "Is the Tipping Point Toast?" *Fast Company*, 1 February 2008, at: http://www.fastcompany.com/magazine/122/is-the-tipping-point-toast .html.

Warner, Michael, "Wanted: A Definition of 'Intelligence,'" *Studies in Intelligence*, vol. 46, no. 3, 2002, pp. 15–22.

Wheeler, David, "'Google Doesn't Laugh': Saving Witty Headlines in the Age of SEO," *The Atlantic*, May 2011, at: http://www.theatlantic.com/technology/archive/2011/05/google-doesnt-laugh-saving-witty-headlines-in-the-age-of-seo/238656/.

Williams, Martyn, "How Digital Technology Gets the News out of North Korea," at: http://www.itworld.com/personal-tech/125972/how-digital-technology-gets-news-out-north-korea, accessed 23 March 2011.

Books, dissertations, studies, and pamphlets

Abelson, Hal, *et al.*, *Blown to Bits*. Upper Saddle River, NJ: Addison-Wesley, 2008.

Abrahamson, Eric, and David H. Freedman, *A Perfect Mess*. New York: Little-Brown, 2008.

Alavi, Nasrin, *We Are Iran: The Persian Blogs*. Brooklyn, NY: Soft Skull Press, 2005.

Appadurai, Arjun, *Fear of Small Numbers*. Durham, NC: Duke University Press, 2006.

Arbel, David, and Ran Edelist, *Western Intelligence and the Collapse of the Soviet Union*. London and Portland, OR: Frank Cass, 2003.

Ariely, Dan, *Predictably Irrational*. New York: HarperCollins, 2008.

Arnas, Neyla (ed.), *Fighting Chance*. Washington DC: National Defense University Press, 2009.

Assessing the Impacts of Changes in the Information Techology R&D Ecosystem. Washington DC: National Academies Press, 2009.

Auletta, Ken, *Backstory: Inside the Business of News*. New York: Penguin, 2003.

Baker, Stephen, *The Numerati*. Boston: Houghton-Mifflin, 2008.

Bamford, James, *A Pretext for War*. New York: Anchor, 2005.

—*The Puzzle Palace*. New York: Penguin, 1982.

Barabasi, Albert-Laszlo, *Linked*. New York: Plume, 2003.

—*Bursts: The Hidden Pattern Behind Everything We Do*. New York: Dutton, 2010.

Beasley, Ron, and Marcel Danesi, *Persuasive Signs: The Semiotics of Advertising*. Berlin: Mouton de Gruyter, 2002.

Benkler, Yochai, *The Wealth of Networks*. New Haven, CT: Yale University Press, 2006.

Bernays, Edward, *Propaganda*. New York: H. Liveright Co., 1928.

Best, Richard A. Jr., and Alfred Cumming, *CRS Report for Congress: Open Source Intelligence (OSINT): Issues for Congress*, RL34270. Washington DCL GPO, 2007.

Bishop, Bill, *The Big Sort*. New York: Mariner, 2009.

Calishain, Tara, and Rael Dornfest, *Google Hacks: 100 Industrial Strength Tips and Tricks*. Santa Rosa, CA: O'Reilly Media, 2003.

Caplan, Bryan, *The Myth of the Rational Voter*. Princeton, NJ: Princeton University Press, 2007.

Carl, Walter J., *Measuring Word of Mouth*, vols. 1–4. Chicago: Word of Mouth Marketing Association, 2005–2008.

Carr, Nicholas, *The Big Switch: Rewiring the World, From Edison to Google*. New York: Norton, 2009.

—*The Shallows: What the Internet is Doing to Our Brains*. New York: Norton, 2010.

Chabris, Christopher, and Daniel Simons, *The Invisible Gorilla*. New York: Crown, 2010.

Chandler, Daniel, *Semiotics for Beginners*, at: http://www.aber.ac.uk/media/Documents/S4B/sem02.html, accessed 11 August 2011.

Church Committee Report, *Foreign and Military Intelligence: Book 1: Final Report of the Select Committee to Study Governmental Operations with Respect to Intelligence Activities, United States Senate*. Washington DC: GPO, 1976.

Clark, Robert M., *Intelligence Analysis: A Target-Centric Approach*. Washington DC: CQ Press, 2007.

Cohen, Bernard C., *The Press and Foreign Policy*. Princeton, NJ: Princeton University Press, 1963.

Commission on the Intelligence Capabilities of the United States Regarding Weapons of Mass Destruction (WMD Commission). Washington DC: GPO, 2005.

Committee on Scientific and Technical Communication, National Academy of Sciences, National Academy of Engineering, *Scientific and Technical Communication: A Pressing National Problem and Recommendations for its Solution*. Washington DC: National Academy of Sciences, 1969.

Congressional Reports: Joint Inquiry into Intelligence Community Activities Before and After the Terrorist Attacks of September 11, 2001, Part 1, 2002.

Cooper, Jeffrey R., *Curing Analytic Pathologies*. Washington DC: Center for the Study of Intelligence, 2005.

Creel, George, *How We Advertised America*. New York: Harper and Brothers, 1920.

Csikszentmihalyi, Mihaly, *Creativity*. New York: Harper, 1996.

Darling, Arthur, *The Central Intelligence Agency: An Instrument of Government, to 1950*. University Park, PA: Pennsylvania State University Press, 1990.

Darnton, Robert, *The Case for Books*. New York: Perseus, 2009.

Davenport, Thomas H., and John C. Beck, *The Attention Economy*. Cambridge, MA: Harvard Business School Press, 2001.

Davis, Mike, *Buda's Wagon: A Brief History of the Car Bomb*. New York: Verso, 2007.

de Borchgrave, Arnaud, Thomas Sanderson, and David Gordon, *The Power of Outreach: Leveraging Expertise on Threats in Southeast Asia*. CSIS Report, April 2009.

Deutscher, Guy, *Through the Looking Glass: Why the World Looks Different in Other Languages*. London: Arrow Books, 2011.

Diamond, Jared, *Collapse: How Societies Choose to Fail or Succeed*. New York: Viking Books, 2005.

Diamond, John, *The CIA and the Culture of Failure*. Stanford, CA: Stanford University Press, 2008.

Director of National Intelligence, *Vision 2015: A Globally Networked and Integrated Intelligence Enterprise*, http://dni.gov/Vision_2015.pdf, accessed 4 January 2011.

Dizard, Wilson P. Jr., *Inventing Public Diplomacy*. Boulder, CO: Lynne Rienner, 2004.

Douglas, Susan, *Listening In: Radio and the American Imagination*. New York: Random House, 2009.

Dover, Robert, and Michael Goodman (eds), *Spinning Intelligence: Why Intelligence Needs the Media, Why the Media Needs Intelligence*. New York: Columbia University Press, 2009.

Dreier, Thomas, *The Power of Print – and Men*. Brooklyn, NY: Mergenthaler Linotype Co., 1936.

Eisenstein, Elizabeth, *The Printing Press as an Agent of Change*, 2 vols. New York: Cambridge University Press, 1979.

—*The Printing Revolution in Early Modern Europe*. New York: Cambridge University Press, 2005.

Engerman, David C., *Know Your Enemy: The Rise and Fall of America's Soviet Experts*. New York: Oxford University Press, 2009.

Executive Summary, *Final Report of the National Commission on Terrorist Attacks upon the United States* (9/11 Commission Report). Washington DC: GPO, 2004.

Fischoff, Baruch, and Sarah Lichtenstein *et al.*, *Acceptable Risk*. New York: Cambridge University Press, 1981.

Fuld, Leonard, *The New Competitor Intelligence: The Complete Resource for Finding, Analyzing, and Using Information about Your Competitors*. New York: John Wiley & Sons, 1995.

—*The Secret Language of Competitive Intelligence*. New York: Crown, 2006.

Gardner, Daniel, *The Science of Fear*. New York: Plume, 2008.

Garfield, Bob, *The Chaos Scenario*. Nashville, TN: Stielstra Pubishing, 2009.

Gary, Brett, *Nervous Liberals*. New York: Columbia University Press, 1999.

Geary, James, *I is an Other: The Secret Life of Metaphor and How it Shapes the Way We See the World*. New York: HarperCollins, 2011.

Gentry, John A., *Lost Promise: How CIA Analysis Misserves the Nation*. Lanham, MD: University Press of America, 1993.

George, Alexander L., *The Scientific Status of Propaganda Analysis*. RAND Study P-616, 1954.

—*Propaganda Analysis*. Evanston, IL: Row, Peterson & Co., 1959.

George, Roger Z., and James B. Bruce (eds), *Analyzing Intelligence: Origins, Obstacles, and Innovations*. Washington DC: Georgetown University Press, 2008.

Gladwell, Malcolm, *Blink*. New York: Little, Brown, 2005.

Glander, Timothy, *Origins of Mass Communications Research during the American Cold War*. Mahwah, NJ: Lawrence Erlbaum Associates, 2000.

Glass, Lt Col. Robert, and Lt. Col. Phillip Davidson, *Intelligence is for Commanders*. Harrisburg, PA: Military Service Publishing, 1948.

Gleick, James, *The Information: A History, A Theory, A Flood*. New York: Pantheon, 2011.

Goldfarb, Charles B., *Cable and Satellite Television Network Tiering and à la Carte Options for Consumers: Issues for Congress*. Congressional Research Service. Washington DC: GPO, 2004.

Goldsmith, Jack, and Tim Wu, *Who Controls the Internet?* New York: Oxford University Press, 2006.

Goodman, Melvin A., *Failure of Intelligence: The Decline and Fall of the CIA*. Lanham, MD: Rowman Littlefield, 2008.

Graves, Harold N. Jr., *War on the Short Wave*. New York: Headline Books, Foreign Policy Association, 1941.

Haines, Gerald K., and Robert E. Leggett (ed.), *Watching the Bear: Essays on CIA's Analysis of the Soviet Union*. Washington DC: Center for the Study of Intelligence, 2001.

Hallin, Daniel, *The Uncensored War: The Media and the Vietnam War*. New York: Oxford University Press, 1986.

Halperin, Morton, *Bureaucratic Politics and Foreign Policy.* Washington DC: Brookings Institute, 1974.

Hampden-Turner, Charles M., and Fons Trompenaars, *Building Cross-Cultural Competence.* New Haven, CT: Yale University Press, 2000.

Harford, Tim, *The Undercover Economist.* New York: Random House, 2007.

—*The Logic of Life.* New York: Random House, 2008.

—*Adapt: Why Success Always Starts with Failure.* New York: Farrar Straus, Giroux, 2011.

Heath, Chip, and Dan Heath, *Made to Stick.* New York: Random House, 2008.

—*Switch.* New York: Random House, 2010.

Heil, Alan, *Voice of America: A History.* New York: Columbia University Press, 2003.

Heuer, Richards J. (ed.), *Quantitative Approaches to Political Intelligence: The CIA Experience.* Boulder, CO: Westview Press, 1978.

Hitz, Frederik, *Why Spy?* New York: Thomas Dunne, 2008.

Jervis, Robert, *Why Intelligence Fails.* Ithaca, NY and London: Cornell University Press, 2010.

Johnson, Jeannie L., Kerry M. Kartchner, and Jeffrey Arthur Larsen (eds), *Strategic Culture and Weapons of Mass Destruction: Culturally Based Insights into Comparative National Security Policymaking.* New York: Palgrave Macmillan, 2009.

Johnson, Loch, and James J. Wirtz (ed.), *Strategic Intelligence: Windows into a Secret World.* Los Angeles: Roxbury, 2004.

Johnson, Steven, *Everything Bad is Good for You.* New York: Riverhead, 2005.

Johnston, Rob, *Analytic Culture in the US Intelligence Community.* Washington DC: GPO, 2005.

Jones, Bryan, and Frank Baumgartner, *The Politics of Attention: How Government Prioritizes Problems.* Chicago, IL: University of Chicago Press, 2005.

Kahn, David, *The Reader of Gentlemen's Mail.* New Haven, CT: Yale University Press, 2004.

Kahneman, Daniel, Amos Tversky, and Paul Slovic, *Judgement under Uncertainty: Heuristics and Biases.* New York: Cambridge University Press, 1982.

Katz, Barry M., *Foreign Intelligence: Research and Analysis in the Office of Strategic Services 1942–1945.* Cambridge, MA: Harvard University Press, 1989.

Keefe, Patrick Radden, *Chatter.* New York: Random House, 2005.

Kelley, Captain Stephanie R., "Rumors in Iraq: A Guide to Winning Hearts and Minds," Naval Postgraduate School Thesis, 2004, at: http://www.au.af.mil/au/awc/awcgate/nps/kelley_sep04.pdf, accessed 11 August 2011.

Kelly, Kevin, *What Technology Wants.* New York: Penguin, 2010.

Kenneally, Christine, *The First Word: The Search for the Origins of Language.* New York: Penguin, 2007.

Kent, Sherman, *Writing History.* New York: F.S. Crofts & Co, 1941.

—*Strategic Intelligence for American World Policy.* Princeton, NJ: Princeton University Press, 1949.

Knee, Jonathan A., *et al.*, *The Curse of the Mogul: What's Wrong With the World's Leading Media Companies.* New York: Portfolio Press, 2009.

Lakoff, George, *The Political Mind.* New York: Viking, 2008.

Lanham, Richard, *The Economics of Attention*. Chicago, IL: University of Chicago Press, 2006.

Lanier, Jaron, *You Are Not a Gadget*. New York: Knopf, 2010.

Lazersfeld, Paul, and Elihu Katz, *Personal Influence: The Part Played by People in the Flow of Mass Communications*. Glencoe, IL: Free Press, 1955.

Le Bon, Gustave. *The Crowd: A Study of the Popular Mind*, electronic version at Electronic Text Center, University of Virginia Library, http://etext.virginia.edu/etcbin/toccer-new2?id=BonCrow.sgm&images=images/modeng&data=/texts/english/modeng/parsed&tag=public&part=all, accessed 10 March 2011.

Levine, Rick, and Christopher Locke, *et al.*, *ClueTrain Manifesto*. New York: Perseus, 2000.

Li, Charlene, and Josh Bernoff, *Groundswell: Winning in a World Transformed by Social Technologies*. Boston, MA: Harvard Business Press, 2008.

Lieberthal, Kenneth, *The US Intelligence Community and Foreign Policy: Getting Analysis Right*. Washington DC: Brookings Institution, 2009.

Linebarger, Paul, *Psychological Warfare*. Washington DC: Infantry Journal Press, 1948.

Lippmann, Walter, *The Political Scene*. New York: Henry Holt, 1919.

—*Liberty and the News*. New York: Harcourt, Brace, and Howe, 1920.

—*Public Opinion*. New York: Harcourt, Brace, and Co., 1922.

—*The Method of Freedom*. New York: Macmillan, 1934.

—*Drift and Mastery*. Englewood Cliffs, NJ: Prentice-Hall, 1961.

—*The Coming Tests with Russia*. Boston: Atlantic Monthly, 1961.

—*Early Writings*. New York: Liveright, 1970.

—*The Phantom Public*. New Brunswick, NJ: Transaction, 1993.

Lowenthal, Mark, *Intelligence: From Secrets to Policy*. Washington DC: CQ Press, 2003.

Mahbubani, Kishore, *Can Asians Think?* Singapore: Times Media Publishing, 1998.

Mandaville, Peter, *Global Political Islam*. New York: Routledge, 2007.

Manjoo, Farhad, *True Enough*. New York: Wiley, 2008.

March, James G., *A Primer of Decision Making*. New York: Free Press, 1994.

Marchand, Roland, *Advertising the American Dream*. Berkeley, CA: University of California Press, 1985.

McCloskey, Deirdre N., *The Rhetoric of Economics*. Madison, WI: University of Wisconsin Press, 1998.

McNair, Brian, *Glasnost, Perestroika, and the Soviet Media*. New York: Routledge, 1991.

Messaris, Paul, *Visual Persuasion: The Role of Images in Advertising*. London: Sage, 1997.

Milo, Paul, *Your Flying Car Awaits: Robot Butlers, Lunar Vacations, and Other Dead-Wrong Predictions of the Twentieth Century*. New York: HarperCollins, 2010.

Mlodinow, Leonard, *The Drunkard's Walk: How Randomness Rules Our Lives*. New York: Pantheon, 2008.

Monmonier, Mark, *Spying with Maps*. Chicago, IL: University of Chicago Press, 2002.

Moore, David, *Sensemaking: A Structure for an Intelligence Revolution*. Washington DC: NDIC Press, 2011.

Morozov, Evgeny, *The Net Delusion: The Dark Side of Internet Freedom*. New York: Public Affairs Books, 2011.

Myers, Brian, *The Cleanest Race: How North Koreans See Themselves and Why it Matters*. New York: Melville House, 2010.

Newcomb, Horace (ed.), *Encyclopedia of Television*. New York: Taylor and Francis, 2004.

Nisbett, Richard, *The Geography of Thought*. New York: Free Press, 2003.

Noam, Eli M., *Media Ownership and Concentration in America*. New York: Oxford University Press, 2009.

Ogle, Richard, *Smart World*. Boston, MA: Harvard Busines School Press, 2007.

Olcott, Anthony, *Russian Pulp: The Way of Russian Crime*. New York: Rowman Littlefield, 2003.

Ormerod, Paul, *Why Most Things Fail*. New York: Pantheon, 2005.

O'Toole, George J. A., *Honorable Treachery: A History of U.S. Intelligence, Espionage, and Covert Action from the American Revolution to the CIA*. New York: Atlantic Monthly Press, 1991.

Pariser, Eli, *The Filter Bubble: What the Internet is Hiding from You*. New York: Penguin Press, 2011.

Park, David, and Jefferson Pooley (eds), *The History of Media and Communication Research: Contested Memories*. New York: Peter Lang, 2008.

Pettee, George S., *The Future of American Secret Intelligence*. Washington DC: Infantry Journal Press, 1946.

—"Economic Intelligence," lecture to the Industrial College of the Armed Forces, 24 February 1950: https://digitalndulibrary.ndu.edu/cdm4/document. php?CISOROOT=/icafarchive&CISOPTR=17222&REC=20, accessed 31 May 2011.

Pettegree, Andrew, *The Reformation and the Culture of Persuasion*. New York: Columbia University Press, 2005.

—*The Book in the Renaissance*. New Haven, CT: Yale University Press, 2010.

Pink, Daniel H., *A Whole New Mind*. New York: Penguin, 2005.

—*Drive: The Surprising Truth about What Motivates Us*. New York: Penguin, 2009.

Pirolli, Peter, *Information Foraging Theory: Adaptive Interaction with Information*. New York: Oxford University Press, 2007.

Ponsonby, Arthur, *Falsehood in Wartime*. New York: Allen & Unwin, 1928.

Postman, Neil, *Amusing Ourselves to Death: Public Discourse in the Age of Show Business*. New York: Viking, 1985, reissued 2004.

Preparing for the 21st Century: An Appraisal of US Intelligence. Report of the Commission on the Roles and Capabilities of the US Intelligence Community (Aspin-Brown Report). Washington DC: Government Printing Office, 1996.

Quiggin, Thomas, *Seeing the Invisible: National Security Intelligence in an Uncertain Age*. Singapore: World Scientific, 2007.

Ransom, Harry Howe, *Central Intelligence and National Security*. Cambridge, MA: Harvard University Press, 1959.

Rheingold, Howard, *Smart Mobs*. New York: Perseus, 2002.

Richards, Julian, *The Art and Science of Intelligence Analysis*. Oxford: Oxford University Press, 2010.

Robinson, Gordon, *The Rest of Arab Television*. Report by the USC Center on Public Diplomacy. Los Angeles: USC, 2005.

Roop, Joseph E. *Foreign Broadcast Information Service: History Part I: 1941–1947*. CIA internal document, April 1969: https://www.cia.gov/library/center-for-the-study-of-intelligence/csi-publications/books-and-monographs/foreign-broadcast-information-service/index.html, accessed 13 July 2010.

Rush, Myron, *The Rise of Khrushchev*. Washington DC: Public Affairs Press, 1958.

Rushkoff, Douglas, *Life Inc.: How the World Became a Corporation and How to Take It Back*. New York: Random House, 2009.

Russell, Richard, *Sharpening Strategic Intelligence*. New York: Cambridge University Press, 2007.

Saunders, Kimberly, *Open Source Information – A True Collection Discipline*. Master of Arts in War Studies dissertation, Royal Military College of Canada, 2000.

Schmitt, Major Daniel, *Cultural Terrain—Mapping Out the Future*. Master of Operational Studies dissertation, School of Advanced Warfighting, Marine Corps University, 2007.

Schneier, Bruce, *Secrets and Lies: Digital Security in a Networked World*. New York: Wiley, 2000.

Schwartz, Barry, *The Paradox of Choice*. New York: Ecco, 2003.

Scott, James C., *Seeing Like a State*. New Haven, CT: Yale University Press, 1998.

Seife, Charles, *Decoding the Universe*. New York: Penguin, 2006.

Sharp, Gene, *From Dictatorship to Democracy*. Boston, MA: Albert Einstein Institution, 2010.

Sherman, Chris, and Gary Price, *The Invisible Web*. Medford, NJ: Information Today Inc., 2001.

Shibutani, Tamotsu, *Improvised News: A Sociological Study of Rumor*. Indianapolis, IN: Bobbs-Merrill Co., 1966.

Shirky, Clay, *Here Comes Everybody*. New York: Penguin, 2008.

—*Cognitive Surplus*. New York: Penguin, 2010.

Shorrock, Tim, *Spies for Hire*. New York: Simon and Schuster, 2008.

Shrader, Charles R., *History of Operations Research in the United States Army*, vol. 2. Washington DC: Government Printing Office, 2008.

Smith, Anthony (ed.), *Newspapers and Democracy: International Essays on a Changing Medium*. Cambridge, MA: MIT Press, 1980.

Smith, Christian, *Moral Believing Animals: Human Personhood and Culture*. Oxford and New York: Oxford University Press, 2003.

Soley, Lawrence C., *Radio Warfare: OSS and CIA Subversive Propaganda*. New York: Praeger, 1989.

Solomon, Norman, *War Made Easy*. New York: Wiley, 2005.

Srebreny-Mohammadi, Annabelle and Ali Mohammadi, *Small Media, Big Revolution: Communication, Culture, and the Iranian Revolution*. Minneapolis, MN: University of Minnesota Press, 1994.

Standage, Tom, *The Victorian Internet*. New York: Walker & Co., 1998.

Starr, Paul, *The Creation of the Media*. New York: Basic Books, 2004.

Steele, Robert David, *The New Craft of Intelligence: Personal, Public, and Political*. Oakton, VA: OSS International Press, 2002.

Sullivan, Mark, *Our Times: America Finding Herself*. New York and London: Scribners, 1927.

Taleb, Nassim Nicholas, *Fooled by Randomness*. New York: Random House, 2005.

—*The Black Swan*. New York: Random House, 2007.

Tapscott, Don, and Anthony D. Williams, *Wikinomics: How Mass Collaboration Changes Everything*. New York: Penguin, 2006.

Tekir, Selma, *An Implementation Model for Open Sources Evaluation*. Master of Science dissertation, Izmir Institute of Technology, Izmir, Turkey, 2004.

Tetlock, Phillip, *Expert Political Judgment: How Good Is It?* Princeton, NJ: Princeton University Press, 2005.

Thomas, Timothy L., *Cyber Silhouettes: Shadows over Information Operations*. Fort Leavenworth, KS: Foreign Military Studies Office, 2005.

Thompson, Nicholas, *The Hawk and the Dove: Paul Nitze, George Kennan, and the History of the Cold War*. New York: Henry Holt, 2009.

Treverton, Gregory, *Approaches to 'Outreach' for Intelligence*. Center for Asymmetric Threat Studies Report, December 2008.

—*Intelligence for an Age of Terror*. Cambridge: Cambridge University Press, 2009.

—, and Bryan Gabbard, *Assessing the Tradecraft of Intelligence Analysis*. Rand Technical Report, 2008.

Troy, Thomas F., *Donovan and the CIA*. Frederick, MD: Aletheia Books, 1981.

Turner, Stansfield, *Burn Before Reading*. New York: Hyperion, 2005.

US Department of State, *Foreign Relations of the United States: 1945–1950: Emergence of the Intelligence Establishment*, introduction, at: http://webdoc. sub.gwdg.de/ebook/p/2005/dep_of_state/www.state.gov/www/about_state/ history/intel/intro.html, accessed 25 July 2010.

Vanderbilt, Tom, *Traffic*. New York: Knopf, 2008.

Vasiliyev, V. N., *et al.*, *Sekrety Sekretnykh Sluzhb SShA* [Secrets of the Secret Services of the USA]. Moscow: Izd. Politcheskoy Literatury, 1973.

Vinten-Johansen, Peter, *et al.*, *Cholera, Chloroform, and the Science of Medicine: A Life of John Snow*. Oxford: Oxford University Press, 2003.

Wallace, Robert, and H. Keith Melton, *Spycraft*. New York: Plume, 2009.

Watts, Duncan, *Small Worlds*. Princeton, NJ: Princeton University Press, 1999.

—*Six Degrees: The Science of a Connected Age*. New York: Norton, 2003.

—*Everything Is Obvious: Once You Know the Answer*. New York: Crown, 2011.

Weimann, Gabriel, *Terror on the Internet*. Washington DC: USIP, 2006.

Weinberger, David, *Everything is Miscellaneous*. New York: Times Books, 2007.

Westen, Drew, *The Political Brain*. Cambridge, MA: Perseus Books, 2007.

Willford, Hugh, *The Mighty Wurlitzer: How the CIA Played America*. Cambridge, MA: Harvard University Press, 2008.

Wills, Garry, *Bomb Power: The Modern Presidency and the National Security State*. New York: Penguin, 2010.

Winks, Robin, *Cloak and Gown*. New Haven, CT: Yale University Press, 1996.

Wise, Lindsay, "'Words From the Heart': New Forms of Islamic Preaching in Egypt," Master of Philosophy dissertation, St. Antony's College, Oxford University, Trinity Term 2003.

Wolf, Maryanne, *Proust and the Squid*. New York: HarperCollins, 2007.

Wu, Tim, *The Master Switch: The Rise and Fall of Information Empires*. New York: Knopf, 2010.

Zagoria, Donald S., *The Sino-Soviet Conflict: 1959–1961*. Princeton, NJ: Princeton University Press, 1962.

Zegart, Amy B., *Flawed by Design: The Evolution of the CIA, JCS, and NSC*. Stanford, CA: Stanford University Press, 1999.

Zittrain, Jonathan, *The Future of the Internet—and How to Stop It*. New Haven, CT: Yale University Press, 2008.

INDEX